# The War against Authority

## Other Books by Nicholas N. Kittrie

*The Mentally Disabled and the Law*

*The Right to Be Different: Deviance and Enforced Therapy*

*The Comparative Law of Israel and the Middle East*
(editor)

*Crescent and Star: Arab and Israeli Perspectives on the Middle East Conflict*
(editor, with Y. Alexander)

*Medicine, Law, and Public Policy*
(editor, with H. Hirsh and G. Wegner)

*Legality, Morality, and Ethics in Criminal Justice*
(editor, with J. Susman)

*Sanctions, Sentencing, and Corrections*
(editor, with E. Zenoff)

*The Uncertain Future: Gorbachev's Eastern Bloc*
(editor, with I. Volgyes)

*The Tree of Liberty:*
*A Documentary History of Rebellion and Political Crime in America*
(editor, with E. Wedlock, Jr.)

# THE WAR AGAINST

# AUTHORITY

*From the Crisis of Legitimacy*

*to a New Social Contract*

# NICHOLAS N. KITTRIE

THE JOHNS HOPKINS UNIVERSITY PRESS

Baltimore / London

© 1995 The Johns Hopkins University Press
All rights reserved. Published 1995
Printed in the United States of America on acid-free paper
04 03 02 01 00 99 98 97 96 95
5 4 3 2 1

The Johns Hopkins University Press
2715 North Charles Street
Baltimore, Maryland 21218-4319
The Johns Hopkins Press Ltd., London

ISBN 0-8018-5050-9

Library of Congress Cataloging-in-Publication Data will be found
at the end of this book.

A catalog record for this book is available from the British Library.

For the Memory of

My Father, Samuel Eli,

and in Tribute to

My Mother, Perla Pnina,

Who Sought and Found

Their Promised Land

Woe to him that claims obedience when it is not due;
Woe to him that refuses it when it is.

—Thomas Carlyle

# Contents

PART FOUR

## From the Crisis of Authority to the Restoration of Legitimacy

# *Preface*

In considering the insanity of power, we may look at it in two ways, the madness of the tyrant in abusing it and the madness of the people in submitting to it.

—W. W. Ireland, *The Blot upon the Brain*

The real slavery of Israel in Egypt was that they had learned to endure it.

—Rabbi Hanokh of Alexander, in Victor Gollanz, *Man and God*

As the twentieth century draws to a close, undeclared yet unceasing civil and communal wars rage around the globe. The battlegrounds are widespread—Bosnia and the countries of the former Soviet Union, Kashmir and Sri Lanka, Rwanda and South Africa, Mexico and Colombia. The struggles also go on at the gates of America's embattled abortion clinics, in our own urban ghettos, and even in our suburban neighborhoods and homes.

The raging civil battles are between those who proclaim their individual or communal rights to greater autonomy (whether political, ethnic, religious, cultural, or economic) and those who profess to speak for the state or for other established institutions of authority. Broadly underlying these specific conflicts is, moreover, a cresting current challenging the legitimacy of practically all existing institutions of governance, be they the nation-state, the church, or the family.

This growing challenge to authority—whether in the name of autonomy, justice, equality, historical entitlement, scriptural commands, or some other conviction, ideology, or claim—is evident everywhere. Yet to date it has failed to receive adequate scrutiny and analysis from scholars and leaders of religion and morality, psychology and sociology, criminology and law, or politics and military science. Governments, as well as the news media and the public, have been similarly unable to formulate coherent, responsible, morally consistent, and effective responses to the turmoil posed by those challenging power and authority.

The voids in scholarly knowledge and in public policy-development and application are due in the first place to the many and conflicting roles played by those who contest political power. The cadres of political dissidents and rebels—who emerge on the stages of politics and law as either heroes or villains, conspirators or prisoners, asylum seekers or extradition resisters—may in fact consist of reformers and reactionaries, domestic dissenters and international warriors, freedom fighters and terrorists. The absence of a clear understanding of the political rebel or resister may stem, next, from the conflicting perspectives from which governments, scholars, the media, and public opinion view and judge political activists and their endeavors. Such contradictory appellations as *terrorists, traitors, criminals, political prisoners, prisoners of conscience, insurgents, guerrillas, resisters,* and *freedom fighters* testify to the loose and indiscriminate criteria applied to those fighting for political change. This confusion often serves well the ideological proclivities of those doing the labeling, for as Humpty Dumpty points out in *Alice in Wonderland,* "A word means just what I choose it to mean."

The absence of adequate scholarly and governmental attention, especially in the United States, to the problems posed by the growth of rebellion and political criminality, accompanied by the general diminution of the legitimacy of authority, may be attributed, finally, to the smug and fanciful notion that politically related violence and disorder are primarily a problem for the newer, less stable, and more ethnically and ideologically fragmented countries of Africa, Asia, and Latin America. It is not surprising, therefore, that texts in the areas of criminological, social, or behavioral sciences, governmental documents and statistics, usually do not refer to or discuss such concepts or categories as "political legitimacy," "political offenses," and "political criminals." Not until 1979 did *Webster's New Collegiate Dictionary* provide for the first time an entry for *political criminal.*

Given this historical background, the author's and reader's threshold task, then, is to purge their personal and professional perspectives of partisan biases. At the onset, one is invited to shed the distorting labels imposed by historical and sectarian visions of political dissidence and rebellion and to join in an unusually rich, multidisciplinary, and impressionistic investigation into the perpetual struggle between authority and autonomy, which has now erupted in epidemic proportions.

The research for this book was begun a decade and a half ago in an effort to explore and document the unheralded role of dissidence and rebellion in America's historical quest for political and civil justice. We sought also, concurrently, to assess the prospects for political tranquility and order in the unfolding third century of the United States' existence. The evidence of that initial examination of dissidence and rebellion in America's domestic politics and law was contained in our book, co-edited with Eldon D. Wedlock Jr., *The Tree of Liberty: A Documentary History of Rebellion and Political Crime in America* (Baltimore: Johns Hopkins University Press, 1986).

But the contemporary increase in political dissent and resistance world-wide could not be ignored. Hence the call for and the eventual emergence of this volume. Undertaking this new pursuit, we realized that the global struggle against authority—represented not only by individual protest but also by collective protest under such noms de guerre as *civil wars, uprisings, revolutions,* and *insurgencies*—is a problem that transcends national concerns. It became apparent, moreover, that the treatment of the modern struggle against authority necessitated vigorous excursions into foreign and international history, politics, and law. The complexity of the topic, therefore, required inquiries beyond law and history (the author's primary disciplines), and extensive incursions into such diverse fields as political theory, sociology, psychology, and philosophy.

This new work's twin objectives have been to review the long history and to map the wide-ranging territories of political resistance and rebellion, a complex of phenomena with overlapping borderlands combining politics, crime, and warfare. But our effort, however comprehensive, could not address all questions raised by the disparate forms of political dissidence and disorder. In this first and thoroughly multidisciplinary study of the subject, we have been satisfied to explore some of the more crucial issues relating to the war against authority, hoping to stimulate further work, by fellow scholars and analysts, on the other important questions posed by the growing crisis of legitimacy in modern society.

The study commences with the Prologue's brief and critical examination of legitimacy and the historical efforts to justify political power. Part One continues with an attempt to construct a sociopsychological profile of the political rebel—a rebel engaging in political dissidence and protest in the pursuit of autonomy or in some other professedly "noble" objective. Part One proceeds, next, to review the exercise of authority as well as the abuse of governmental power and to determine the factors that give rise to political discontent and violence. Part One's dual portrayals of the primary protagonists (those exercising governmental power and those defying it) are followed by Part Two's explorations of the historical roles played by rebels, dissidents, and political offenders in the economic, social, and political development of the United States. Part Three similarly records the historical and contemporary struggle between the possessors of political authority and its defiers in other Western as well as non-Western countries and societies. Finally, the

Epilogue seeks to forecast the roles of rebels, dissidents, and other political offenders, who often describe themselves as pursuers of "higher" values and law in a less-than-perfectly-just and well-ordered world. It concludes with an exploration of remedies for the possible restoration and reconstruction of political legitimacy.

The primary focus of this endeavor, then, is civil or domestic strife (as distinguished from international warfare) and its symbiotic relationship to the erosion of state power and authority. The decline of political authority, as reflected by the escalation of civil wars, ethnic conflicts, revolutions, terrorism, and other forms of political protest, is scrutinized here through a variety of multidisciplinary perspectives. Both the history and the casts of characters involved in the war against authority are carefully considered. The volume thus examines and attempts to unify a variety of interrelated topics: the dialectic of the never-ceasing struggle between the rebel and authority, the nature of abuse of power as a ruler's resort, the history of rebellion both domestic and international, and the etiology of conflict in contemporary society. The task is brought to a conclusion, finally, by the consideration of political reforms that are responsive to human diversity and pluralism, such as decentralization of authority and accountability of power.

In no way must this book be viewed, however, as an apologia for those who resort to extralegal and often violent means in order to secure self-proclaimed, or even universally agreed upon, objectives. As much as one must skeptically view self-serving propaganda by oppressive regimes, all too inclined to label their political opponents as *criminals, traitors,* and *terrorists,* one must also reject the opposite argument by political zealots that all means are just for the attainment of their "noble" political goals.

Evaluating the claims of both those in authority and their antagonists, one must remain mindful that political violence and disorder are double-edged swords, as capable of serving oppression and tyranny as they are of advancing the causes of liberty and justice. Moreover, political extremism on the part of those in authority, as well as those defying it, can and often will deteriorate into mindless, indiscriminate, and pathological violence and terror. To counter such extremes, this volume begins exploring theoretical as well as practical standards for the guidance of both those resisting authority and those entrusted with its enforcement.

The task at hand is most pressing. During much of the earlier years of this century the campaign against colonialism and for self-determination loomed as a lodestar on the agenda of the world community. But much of that struggle for self-rule and autonomy has given way in recent times to domestic battles for political, social, and economic justice. The new universal call for liberation, not only from foreign rule but also from domestic despots and injustices, makes an evaluation of the policies of America and its allies regarding intranational political unrest and rebellion particularly timely.

How should this country, and other states that profess democratic aspirations, respond to individuals and communities that, finding themselves subjected to genocide and oppression within their own boundaries, resort to unlawful means in their struggles for political, social, and economic human rights? What weight should the democratic nations continue to place on their traditional commitment to the primacy of national sovereignty, especially when this doctrine collides with the mandates of a growing international system of human rights? As the gap widens between rich and poor communities, between economically endowed and economically hopeless peoples, how should nations committed to orderly politics or reform respond to the growing worldwide violence wrought by alleged modern-day William Tells and Robin Hoods?

# Acknowledgments

I am grateful to the many organizations and individuals without whose assistance this volume could not have been commenced, carried on, and concluded. The National Endowment for the Humanities in 1973 provided the assistance for the initiation of this work, permitting the author unencumbered time to plan his research during a visiting professorship at the London School of Economics. The National Institute of Justice of the United States Department of Justice next granted the author a visiting fellowship in 1980, allowing him to compile much of the data and complete an early draft of this manuscript. For over a decade, research for this volume was carried out both in the United States and abroad—in Egypt, Germany, Guatemala, Hungary, Israel, Italy, Ivory Coast, Japan, Korea, Kenya, Lebanon, the Philippines, Poland, El Salvador, Thailand, Togo, the former Soviet Union, and the United Kingdom.

The work has benefited from the assistance and counsel of many students, colleagues, and friends, including Christina Cerna, H. H. A. Cooper, the late Franco Ferracuti, Matthew Lippman, Stephen Schafer, Judith Weintraub, James Boyle, Robert K. Goldman, James May, and Burton Wechsler. Former Deans Thomas Buergenthal and Claudio Grossman and presiding Dean Elliott Milstein of the American University Law School generously supported the various stages of this undertaking. My sons Orde F. and Zachary McN. Kittrie have been responsible for some editing and editorial restructuring, and my daughter, Norda Nicole, has helped with the selection of graphics. Beth Levenson participated in the earlier editorial work. Professor Eldon D. Wedlock, of the University of South Carolina, successfully undertook the task of revising several earlier drafts of this manuscript as well as contributing significantly to its subsequent versions. Alan M. Fisher, Brad Flecke, Anthi Jones, Anne-Marie Kagy, Robert K. Morrow, and Philip Mueller participated in the research, drafting, and editorial updating of the product, and David Trieloff played an important role in various stages of editing and rewriting. To John Nahajzer the author wishes to convey special thanks for his loyal and thorough contributions both substantive and organizational. Particularly significant was his role in updating the discussion of natural law and legitimacy, and the preparation of the notes and index. Mark Williams was responsible for the final composition of the index.

Grateful acknowledgment is due to several members of the staff at the United States National Institute of Justice, particularly Winifred Reed and Patrick Langan. To Dr. Eugene Miknowski I owe much gratitude for helping maintain my physical and mental health during the excruciating birth pangs of this volume. Finally, one could barely enumerate the services of Georgette J. Sobel, without whose tactical support neither the research nor the finished document could have been successfully achieved. The responsibility for typing the final draft of this manuscript was discharged patiently, cheerfully, and effectively by Martin Ernst, Robert J. Kelso, Katharine Lukianoff, Kriselda V. P. Valderrama, Linda Clark, Ana Granados, Bernard Stokes, Donna Bradley, Elma Gates, Michelle Chapman, and Sharon Huie.

*The War against Authority*

# Prologue:
# The Search for Legitimacy

The rich man in his castle,
the poor man at his gate,
God made them, high or lowly,
and order'd their estate.

    —Cecil Frances Alexander, *All Things Bright and Beautiful*

Governments are instituted among Men, deriving their just Powers from the Consent of the Governed.

    —United States Declaration of Independence, 1776

The Court's power lies in its legitimacy, a product of substance and perception that shows itself in the people's acceptance of the judiciary as fit to determine what the Nation's law means and to declare its demands.

    —*Planned Parenthood* v. *Casey* (United States Supreme Court, 1992)

## WE AND THEY

Most pundits of the increasingly precarious worldwide balance between order and chaos seem to be on the wrong trail. While sundry scholars and agencies (including the United States State Department and congressional committees on foreign affairs and relations) keep speculating about where the next decade's or era's international arenas of conflict are likely to be, it is highly probable that the greatest contemporary and forthcoming world crises will be domestic. The escalating global disorder seems to derive from internal, rather than international, confrontations.

Today, more countries than ever before—north and south, east and west—are being torn asunder by internal conflicts and communal violence. More than one-quarter of all independent states, some 50 out of more than 180 worldwide,[1] are involved in wrenching and divisive domestic contests:

between citizens and citizens, between one community and another, and between communities and their governments.

While usually the result of long-festering political, religious, ethnic, or economic grievances, these conflicts are often provoked by new complaints or aspirations. Those mounting the barricades in this struggle usually invoke such universal slogans as "liberty," "equality," "self-determination," or "justice." But many are urged on by different or narrower orthodoxies: historical justice, divine rights, tribalism, ethnicism, racism, religious fundamentalism, totalitarianism, Marxism-Maoism, or some other brand of absolutism. Whatever the rationale claimed by the protagonists, the real common denominator of the struggle is the continuing conflict between those who possess and exercise political power and those who oppose it.

Rudyard Kipling, colonialism's poet laureate, wryly observed at the conclusion of the last century that "All the people like us are We. And everyone else is They."[2] Throughout history the primeval struggle between "We" and "They" has raged between indigenous populations and later arrivals, kings and their subjects, empires and their vanquished, the free and the enslaved, masters and servants, the well-endowed and the disenfranchised, majorities and minorities, oppressors and the oppressed, the imposers of duties and the claimers of rights. And despite the growth in this century of national self-determination and individual human rights, the historical struggle has not ceased.

Currently the United Nations Security Council spends most of its time not on international conflicts but on internal conflicts and civil wars, reports political writer Stephen S. Rosenfeld.[3] Internal strife, whether sparked by single-minded lone crusaders or by the uneasiness of restless masses, whether spontaneously erupting or carefully planned, whether expressed through peaceful dissent and civil disobedience or through indiscriminate violence and terror, has thoroughly contaminated contemporary politics worldwide. Political commentator Pranay Gupte attributes this epidemic of domestic unrest to an overall decline in the cohesive power of the modern state. Not only the young postcolonial countries of Asia, Africa, and the Americas but also many long-established states, in Europe and elsewhere, are "confronted with the depressing reality that in countries that are multiethnic and multicultural, the most riveting issues" and loyalties "are often and increasingly communal and tribal, not national."[4]

It would seem that those who oppose the power of the state and of the other traditional institutions of authority are winning. The modern nation-state, long believed to be the cornerstone of political cohesion, order, stability, and freedom, today finds itself increasingly beleaguered by the emergence of new centrifugal forces and the resurgence of sectarianism. Pulitzer Prize–winning reporter Thomas L. Friedman recently emphasized that "becoming increasingly common are challenges to the sovereignty and sanctity of nation-states from within—from ethnic, tribal and religious groups dissatisfied with the shape or content of their nations and ready to use any sort of violence to bring about change."[5] So prevalent has intranational, as opposed to international, dissidence become that some commentators have provocatively inquired whether we must "say goodbye to the nation-state."[6]

Most recent commentators on this modern centrifugal phenomenon have bemoaned what they describe as a return to tribalism, sectarianism, and other archaic forms of human organization. Few have offered meaningful explanations. It is our thesis that the escalating fragmentation is the result of growing pluralism (simply put, communal diversity) within what used to be more homogeneous and conformist entities. Recent economic and social developments, including immigration trends, have even acted to expand this pluralistic reality. Pluralistic forces and zeal are being unleashed, furthermore, by the growing assertiveness of subnational minorities or groups, be they the Tamil in Sri Lanka, Native Americans in the United States, Quebeçois in Canada, women in Saudi Arabia, the fundamentalist Moslem Brotherhood in Egypt, or reform-minded students in China.

Growing pluralistic awareness and assertiveness are not only a belated and spiraling reaction to the promises of self-determination advanced by the United States at the end of World War I. Neither are they merely a response to the "rights" movements that have typified post–World War II America (from the rights of children to the rights of the handicapped, from the rights of gays and lesbians to the rights of fetuses). Pluralistic awareness and confrontations are being further fanned worldwide by a vigorous contemporary media. Yet for good or for bad, expanding pluralistic realities are with us, and they exert increasing pressures upon existing power structures and public order.

A brief preliminary commentary on the concept of the pluralistic society is in order, both to fix the definition of the term firmly in the reader's mind and to forestall possible misunderstandings of this overused and often little-comprehended word. *Pluralism*, when used generally in the context of this work, simply refers to any federation, state, nation, unit, or community that is made up of diverse populations. Diversity may be racial, ethnic, linguistic, religious, sexual, or the result of any other of the myriad human characteristics or identities that might account for divisiveness and for distinct and conflicting loyalties. Recognizing the reality of pluralism does not necessarily indicate a preference for, or a tolerance of, these differences. On the contrary, as the subsequent text reveals, many of the most pluralistic states and communities are those that have had the greatest difficulty in establishing and maintaining the legitimacy of their authority.

Yet pluralism is the norm in almost all human communities throughout today's world. Tribal differences in African states, Sunnis and Shiites in Islam, Catholics and Protestants in Christendom, the ethnic rivalries in the southern rim of the former Soviet Union, and the mixture of African American, white, Hispanic, Asian, and other groups in the American city—all these are pluralist societies. Not all of them have handled pluralism well or with aplomb.

## THE DECLINE OF THE OLD ORDER

Even among the most ancient and primitive of clans, tribes, and other human congregations, those in authority sought to justify themselves by something more mysterious and transcendental than the mere de facto possession and exercise of power. In many early societies the brute power, intimidation, and fear supporting the structure of authority were reinforced not only by various rituals and symbols (i.e., crowns, scepters, totems, and taboos) but also by an underlying system of beliefs and mores. Priestly anointments, reliance on the supporting role of the shaman, claims to abnormal or divine descent, the invocation of heroic ancestors and common traditions, and the articulation of divine commandments (e.g., "Love thy Lord" and "Love thy father and mother") played important roles in shoring up the foundations, as well as extending the longevity, of ancient institutions of authority.

To lead the notoriously rebellious tribes of Israel, Moses paraded the Ark of the Covenant, invoked the authority of his priestly brother, Aaron, and relied on his own ability to offer signs and perform miracles. This striving for a less mortal and more enduring source of legitimacy, which permeates modern political dynamics, was identified by Italian political philosopher Gaetano Mosca in his concept of the "political formula." Mosca's theory refers to the ruling class's advancing of a metaphysical or ideological formula that justifies their possession of power as the logical and necessary consequence of the beliefs of the people over whom the power is exercised.[7] "Among ancient peoples the political formula not only rested upon religion but was wholly identified with it. Their god was preeminently a national god. He was the special protector of the territory and the people. He was the fulcrum of its political organization."[8]

In the palaces, temples, and marketplaces of antiquity, the legitimacy of authority was eventually enveloped in a variety of political formulas ranging from those denominated as the divine right of kings to such other legitimating theories as the patrimonial and aristocratic (requiring descent from a ruling "line"), or the scriptural (claiming ordination by some "revealed" source of truth). These claims of divinely established or otherwise tradition-derived legitimacy have persisted throughout much of human history. As late as 1955, the newly drafted constitution for a proposed modern Ethiopia proclaimed:

The Imperial dignity shall remain perpetually attached to the line of Haile Selassie I, whose line descends without interruption from the dynasty of Menelik I, son of the Queen of Ethiopia, the Queen of Sheba, and King Solomon of Jerusalem. . . . By virtue of His Imperial Blood, as well as by the anointing which He has received, the person of the Emperor is sacred, His Dignity inviolable and His Power indisputable.[9]

Admittedly, the assertion of the divine right of Ethiopia's emperors seems somewhat anachronistic so late in human history. By the second half of the twentieth century, efforts to legitimate authority have generally abandoned the divine claim and have sought to rely on other, more up to date, yet similarly mysterious and inflexible, formulas. The first of these revolves around the doctrine of the sovereign state (usually referred to as the *nation-state*)[10] as the sole representative of the nation or people and thereby the lone wielder of the instruments of power—the police and army. The second formula was founded on the inviolable force of the "social contract" as an expression of the people's "general will."

It is to Niccolò Machiavelli (1469–1527) that the doctrines of the state and of national sovereignty owe a great debt of gratitude for his having served, during the Italian Renaissance, as their early proponent. A Florentine, like Dante before him, Machiavelli rejected his predecessor's devotion to universalism and to the unifying mission of the Roman Empire and Church. Instead, he preached Italy's liberation from foreign occupation and called for its political unity. In *The Prince*, Machiavelli not only introduced the concept of the state into political literature but visualized a new state, one in which national power became an end in itself and in which all means to that end were justified. About this consuming task he did not equivocate: "Where it is an absolute question of the welfare of our country, we must admit of no considerations of justice or injustice, of mercy or cruelty, of praise or ignominy, but putting all else aside [we] must adopt whatever course will save . . . [our country's] existence."[11]

The doctrine of the social contract (often accompanied by the theory of the general will) was to emerge next as an additional legitimating principle for state power. The notion of the contract, like the earlier doctrine of the state, has ancient origins but was amplified by several well-known writers at the time of the newly dawned Age of Enlightenment.[12] Three members of that Enlightenment, John Hobbes, John Locke, and particularly Jean-Jacques Rousseau, share the primary credit for grafting the legitimacy of government to the implied contract (or compact) of the populace. The term *social contract* was viewed as a figurative expression, although sometimes, as demonstrated by the Mayflower Compact (1620), the populace indeed entered into an explicit agreement,[13] giving greater credence to the conclusion that the general will is binding upon all members of a society, be they in agreement with it or not. The force of the social contract as an expression of the general will and as supporting majority rule was strongly argued by John Locke: "And thus every man, by consenting with others to make one body politic under one government, puts himself under an obligation to every one of that society to submit to the determination of the majority, and to be concluded by it. . . . For where the majority cannot conclude the rest, there they cannot act as one body, and consequently will be immediately dissolved again."[14]

Throughout the march of history, each of these original doctrines, relied upon for the legitimation of political authority, has been subjected to excruciating challenges. The dawn of the Age of Reason found the earliest magical formulations of authority dramatically eroded. The divine right of kings, closely affiliated with the earlier preternatural formulations of authority, came under nearly fatal attack during the Age of Revolutions, and now it no longer possesses a formidable standing in either politics or law. Even when not extinct but functioning as a symbol of authority (such as in the contemporary United Kingdom), monarchy finds that its older claim to divine ordination has been greatly diminished by the less-than-divine conduct of many contemporary royal claimants. Patrimonial and aristocratic doctrines, although still in practice throughout the world, have similarly lost much of their glamor in both the scholarly and popular markets.

Two hundred years after the blossoming of the doctrines of nationalism and of national sovereignty, the nation-state (a political entity supposedly consisting of a nation) similarly finds itself subjected to many challengers and protected by fewer and fewer true believers. The most vocal post-Machiavellian support for the nation-state came from the emerging national movements of the eighteenth and nineteenth centuries—whether Greek, Italian, or German. The Pan-Greek, Pan-Italian, and Pan-German nationalists urged not only the expulsion of foreign rulers but also the ingathering of each nation within a greater homeland. The nation-state was thus to be a dramatic departure from the classic, territorially defined, Greek city-states and the similarly fractious principalities of the Middle Ages. It was also to contrast with such multinational and multireligious entities as the Holy Roman or the Hapsburg empires.

Modern reality discloses, however, that most states are not the homogeneous nation-states called for by eighteenth- and nineteenth-century visionaries. They are, instead, pluralistic admixtures made up of diverse (both cooperating and conflicting) tribal, ethnic, racial, religious, and linguistic communities. For many of the subnational groups or communities that make up these composite contemporary states, neither needs of group security nor communal strivings for identity, security, nondiscrimination and prosperity are acknowledged to be adequately served by the existing systems of power-sharing. New and drastic internal redistributions of power and authority might offer acceptable solutions for some of these troubled multinational or otherwise pluralistic states. In many instances, however, nothing short of a total dismantlement of the compounded states offers a realistic resolution (e.g., Czechoslovakia and Yugoslavia).[15]

The social compact doctrine (incorporating by implication a reliance on majoritarian rule) has likewise been besieged by those who challenge the binding power of one generation's social compact upon succeeding generations. Radical questioning of the legitimating function of the social contract (and its political embodiment, the constitution) over time and over new populations emerged as early as a century and a half ago. Lysander Spooner, an American lawyer from Massachusetts, set out the claim in his 1870 treatise, *No Treason*, that the constitution as then existing was unconstitutional. Wrote Spooner:

> The Constitution has no inherent authority or obligation. It has no authority or obligation at all, unless as a contract between man and man [woman and woman]. And it does not so much as even purport to be a contract between persons now existing. It purports, at most, to be only a contract between persons living eighty years ago. . . . Those persons, if any, who did give their consent formally, are all dead now. . . . And the Constitution, so far as it was their contract, died with them. They had no natural power or right to make it obligatory upon their children. . . . That is to say, the instrument does not purport to be an agreement between anybody [except] "the people" then existing. . . . [Indeed] the language neither expresses nor implies that they had any intention or desire, nor that they imagined that they had any right or power, to bind their "posterity" to live under it. . . . It only says, in effect, that their hopes and motives in adopting it were that it might prove useful to their posterity, as . . . [it was] to themselves.[16]

A similar argument is currently reverberating in the United States and throughout the world. It suggests that the legitimacy of power and authority cannot simply be attributed to a one-time compact, constituent assembly, constitution, referendum, or election. Addressing the question of emerging aspirations and needs, French philosopher Michel Foucault pointed out how newly heard voices, which initially were marginalized and suppressed in the historical drive for a social compact and order, now act to destabilize claims of legitimacy in contemporary society.[17] The insurrection of the subjugated voices, according to Foucault, not only destabilizes the legitimacy of the state but further demonstrates the fragility of the foundations and premises underlying many of our other societal institutions (including church, school, and family).

For a social contract, or constitution, to persist, to survive and to thrive, it must rely on the people's continuing support, now and in the future. It must rely on an intergenerational acknowledgment of its ongoing legitimacy. It must rely on a continuing popular subscription to its tenets. That is a most difficult task because communities and states are either unwilling or incapable of expeditiously modifying the terms of their power-sharing systems to accommodate the new aspirations and needs of emerging groups and generations.

To be accepted as representing the people's general will, today's social compact, or constitution, must therefore reflect the growing changes of society. Political space must be granted or made by the modern compact to accommodate the long-suppressed, marginalized voices in society, which have gained in recent years legitimacy and power. A constitution must allow for these voices to be heard. The old monological, univocal social compact must be made to accommodate the constantly changing new realities of a pluralistic society. The parties to the social compact have indeed changed and will change again in the future. A new, responsible, and polyvocal world order must be constructed to permit pluralistic societies to function.

The challengers of the social compact, who are indeed the focus of this work, question both the legitimacy and the morality of majoritarian principles and majority decisions. They argue that abuse of power is as likely under republicanism as under an oligarchy or monocracy, and that the tyranny of the majority is no more tolerable than that of other tyrannies. The questioning of the traditional symbiosis between the doctrine of the social compact and the principle of majoritarian rule did not originate recently with populist presidential candidate Ross Perot. Thomas Jefferson, probably the most democratic of America's Founding Fathers, spoke frequently of the dangers of "elective despotism," pointing out that "one hundred and seventy-three despots would surely be as oppressive as one."[18] Writing in 1894, when women and Native Americans were denied the franchise, Matthias N. Forney complained, "What does majority representation mean? It means that the majority shall have everything and the minority nothing."[19] An even broader hypothesis was advanced by Simon Sterne: "The process of creating a majority demoralizes most of those who compose it; it demoralizes them in this sense, that it excludes the action of their higher moral attributes, and brings into operation their lower motives."[20]

Forney and Sterne merely followed in the footsteps of Leonard Courtney, who two decades earlier had pointed out:

> You cannot trust any exclusive party to act with justice to those who are wholly in their power, and whose cause cannot be pleaded before them. If the minority have not someone to speak up for their feelings and desires, the majority will act with injustice towards them; and it is not so much from any set purpose to be unjust as from the natural incapacity of men to understand the . . . [sufferings] of their neighbors. . . . As the old proverb says, "No one knows how the shoe pinches except him who wears it."[21]

Thus, while majoritarianism has often been advanced as a defensible formula for relatively homogeneous societies (in which a system of safeguards for the protection of minorities is believed to suffice as a countervailing force), contemporary countries with pluralistic compositions must search for more effective systems of power-sharing in order to balance existing diversities and conciliate competing intrastate interests. Simple majoritarianism has proven inadequate in complex societies, for which more complex and decentralized systems of governance must be discovered. Absent such systemic reforms, majoritarianism fails as a reliable principle for maintaining public confidence in the legitimacy of power.

It is evident from these observations that the erosion of the historic pillars upon which the legitimacy of authority has traditionally been based (divine rights, nationalism, the social contract, and majoritarianism) has greatly weakened both the ideological and institutional edifices of public order during the second half, and particularly the final quarter, of the twentieth century. Increasingly, therefore, internal conflicts and violence have become the rule rather than the exception in the domestic affairs (political, religious, and familial) of states and lesser communities.

CENTER STAGE:
PROTEST, INSURGENCY, AND POLITICAL CRIME

"Conflict . . . is a theme that has occupied the thinking of man more than any other, save only God and love," claimed Anatol Rapoport, a historian and conflict resolution expert.[22] The Bible supplies a never-ending record of conflicts between divine power and the forces of the profane, between the "chosen people" and the heathens, between roaming shepherds and tillers of the land, between brother and brother (Cain and Abel, Joseph and his brethren), between father and son (David and Absalom), between the ruling Egyptians and the enslaved descendants of Jacob, between the triumphant tribes of Israel and earlier Canaanite and Philistine settlers, between King Saul (the Lord's first anointed), and his successor David, between the House of David in Jerusalem and the secessionist Kingdom of Jeroboam in Shechem, between the kingdoms of Judah and Israel and the invading armies of Assyria and Babylon, between the Maccabees and their Greek overlords, between Jerusalem's Essene purists and the opposing Sadducee priests, between the money lenders in the Temple and the reforming Jesus, and, finally, between the Jews and the conquering Romans.

The Greek, Roman, Islamic, Teutonic, Nordic, and Asian literatures are likewise replete with sagas of conflict, strife, warfare, and conquest. Whether between competing brothers, fathers and sons, husbands and wives, or between neighboring clans, tribes, hostile faiths, and economic classes, conflict appears to

be the core of ancient history and literature.[23] The Middle Ages similarly reflected not only a general explosion of local and sectarian hostilities but also conflicts
produced by major population shifts (from the prairies of Asia and the sands of
North Africa to Europe) and religious campaigns (Christian crusades against the
Muslim occupiers of the holy lands and Muslim expansions in Asia and Africa).

In the modern era, the discovery and conquest of the New World, the acquisition and dismantling of empires, the building of new nation-states, and
competition between emerging national interests became the dominant forces
fueling the never-ceasing political cauldron. The Napoleonic Wars, the Franco-
Prussian War, the Balkan Wars, two world wars, and dozens of lesser
conflagrations supply ample evidence of the global dimensions of modern political conflict and violence.

The post–World War II era, however, has demonstrated a new and domestic direction in political tensions and disorder world wide. This direction
must be distinguished from the earlier and predominantly international
dimensions of political conflict. British philosopher Sir Isaiah Berlin attributes the new rage of domestic violence to the severe suppression of ethnic,
racial, and other group instincts in the recent past: "[A] wounded *Volksgeist*, so
to speak, is like a bent twig, forced down so severely that when released, it
lashes back with fury."[24] Sir Isaiah adds that "sooner or later, the backlash
comes with irrepressible force. People tire of being spat upon, ordered about
by a superior nation, a superior class, or a superior anyone. Sooner or later,
they ask the . . . questions: 'Why do we have to obey them?' 'What right have
they . . . ?' 'What about us?' 'Why can't we . . . ?' "[25]

The escalating recent destabilization of public order, in America and world
wide, may be attributed, in addition, to two other developments in the second
half of the twentieth century. The first of these developments is doctrinal-ideo-
logical and the second geo-political. The aging post–World War I doctrine of
self-determination (reinvigorated by the 1948 United Nations' Universal
Declaration of Human Rights) gave birth in the second half of the twentieth
century, in the United States as well as throughout the world, to a vigorous new
progeny: an explosion of rights doctrines, movements, and militancy. Fetuses,
minors, women, sexual orientationists, minorities, foreign workers, would-be
immigrants, HIV-infected persons, indigenous peoples, and nations without
states—whether acting *pro se* or through spokespeople—have all stood up to
demand their rights. The "marginalized voices," which Foucault recognizes,
have spoken out for recognition and legitimacy within the monological and univocal modern nation-state.

Increasingly alerted to issues of powerlessness and discrimination, these
interest groups have all sought empowerment by rallying under the new and
powerful flags of "rights." Admittedly, the demands of unprivileged and
unrepresented communities for power-sharing and justice have been gener-

ally meritorious, and the rights movement has succeeded in correcting many egregious evils.[26] However, the predominant and growing emphasis on a terminology and jurisprudence of rights, without countervailing attention to duties and responsibilities, has greatly destabilized contemporary institutions and has undercut the overall legitimacy of prevailing authority.[27]

This doctrinal challenge to traditional institutions of authority has been accompanied, in the past decade, by the weakening and eventual collapse of both fundamental Marxist dogmas (including principles such as the dictatorship of the proletariat and one-party rule) and the Communist totalitarian superstructure itself. The Marxist doctrine, like most early claims to legitimacy, was based upon having one "true" and "correct" method or system of government. The communist state model was thus a monological system of governance that allowed no political space for the "other" in society. With Marxism reflecting the will of the people in a single, unifying voice, no room was allowed for special groups, outsiders, or marginalized voices. Marxism's collapse supplies additional testimony to the dangers and vulnerability associated with monological systems of governance.

With the dismantling of the Soviet Union and the overthrow of the Communist Party, a vacuum of legitimacy has been created not only in the six nations of the Eastern Bloc and the three liberated states of the Baltic Sea but also within the emerging and sovereign Soviet Union's successor states. Within each of these newly liberated or created sovereign entities, the vacuum of legitimacy waits to be filled. In the interim, political order is in decline.

To this mounting destabilization of authority in Eastern Europe should be added the geopolitical side-effects of the virtual ending of the Cold War. The original East-West conflict often "froze" developments and prevented changes in volatile or sensitive regions and countries of the world. Among the states sheltered by this imposed status quo one might count Cuba, the two Germanies, former Czechoslovakia, and former Yugoslavia. Neither one of the superpowers was willing to tolerate a power vacuum in these borderlands of the Cold War. Yet, the end of the seventy-year ideological war between communism and capitalism exposed these and other artificially protected states to the contemporary crisis of legitimacy.[28] Among the noted results of the ideological thaw are the unification of Germany, the genocidal Yugoslav civil war, and the benign Czechoslovak divorce after four generations of binational existence. The status of Cuba still remains "under wraps."

Having observed the decline of the traditional doctrines that have served to legitimate authority in the Western World since the Enlightenment, and being cognizant of the newly created ideological vacuums in the former Soviet camp, one must next address the status of political legitimacy in what is generally described as the Third World. We need first reiterate that the

Western-type nation-state, based on an assumed social contract of the citizenry, is hardly a universal fixture. Many new states consist of lands and populations arbitrarily put together by former colonial masters—"states" without national identities. Many other states cannot lay claim to nationhood because they combine tribes, castes, sects, clans, and peoples forcibly brought together by military might or religious militancy. In many of these arbitrarily gerrymandered entities—where a unified national authority has never been legitimized—one cannot observe conditions that parallel the unraveling of the nation-state in the older and mostly Western countries of the world.

Throughout many parts of the world it is often substate organizations, such as extended families, villages, tribes, guilds, and brotherhoods, that are the source of the people's security and satisfaction. "Confidence in the 'small' organization and distrust of the apparatus of the state continue to mark life in [these] modern non-Western states," wrote Professor Adda Bozeman in 1971. Her observations still hold at the end of the century, when factionalism and intrigue, coups d'état, assassinations, revolutions, and rebellions testifying to the alienation from "national" governments by so many people.[29]

The unprecedented 1991 alignment of twenty-three United Nations members against Iraq's attempted conquest of Kuwait—an alliance expressing the international community's respect for the security of boundaries between sovereign nations—supplied an occasion for many commentators to raise troublesome questions about comparisons between domestic and international conflicts and warfare. Thomas L. Friedman quoted an official of the American Council on Foreign Relations to the effect that the Gulf War is the war of the past. India, Ethiopia, Yugoslavia, and the breakup of the Soviet Union are the wave of the future.[30] Friedman elaborated further on this theme:

> It is not the Gulf War, but events that have taken place since, that really characterize the dominant trend and challenge in the post-cold war world—the Kurdish drive to split off from Iraq, the assassination of Mr. Gandhi by opponents amid ethnic strife in India, the takeover of Ethiopia by secessionist rebels from Eritrea and others seeking to replace Ethiopia's traditional tribal elite. Indeed, it is the same from Yugoslavia to Quebec and from the Soviet Union to South Africa: the predominant threat to stability [is] within nations and not between them.[31]

### THE NEW CONSENT OF THE GOVERNED

Any commitment to building fortifications against the escalating war against authority must commence with urgent and thorough attention to the identification of new principles and processes for enhancing governmental legitimacy. Innovative principles and processes of governance—which recognize the globe's growing pluralistic realities and which are based on greater tolerance for diversity, incorporate new forms of federalism and consociationism, and enhance local autonomy and communal empowerment—are essential if states are to avoid the divisiveness and turmoil that are increasingly in evidence today.

It is in this light that we must view and assess the growing worldwide confrontation between the forces of religious-political fundamentalistm and the forces of pluralistic democracy. The first camp (in places like America's Amish communities, the Vatican, Iran, Algeria, or Israel's Mea Shearim) admittedly proclaims and adheres to the absolute primacy of some never-changing scriptural or ideological truth, be it Christian, Islamic, or Jewish law.[32] The second camp (however diverse and disparate) places its reliance on a democratically derived and constantly modifiable social compact. The deepening conflict between these two dramatically opposite approaches to the formulation and structuring of political legitimacy is now threatening to replace the earlier Cold War as a major axis of global conflict. Because of this troublesome potential, it is doubly urgent that the concept of political legitimacy and its diverse and often conflicting formulations be reexamined.

It is increasingly apparent, moreover, that just as international standards regarding the conduct of war and peace were formulated for the taming of international conflicts, a new need now exists for the drawing of standards applicable to domestic threats to world tranquility. The need for appropriate doctrines and standards is becoming particularly critical, as was recently pointed out by Harvard University's Stanley Hoffman: "There is very little in our repertoire of ideas that helps us to cope with such internal disorders. Each time statesmen have opened this Pandora's box of what goes on inside states, they have closed it in horror."[33]

What hides within this Pandora's box? To answer that question we must take a dangerous leap from the safety of the past and the present to the uncertainties of the future: to project conflict potentials, in the United States and abroad, during the remaining years of this millennium and in the early decades of the twenty-first century. More and more often the conflicts to come are likely to be *within* and *between* clans, tribes, economic classes, and ethnic communities. They might be, furthermore, between such groups or communities and nation-states. They might consist, as well, of other miscellaneous ideological, political, social, and economic contests between claimants of authority and pleaders of autonomy, between abusers of power and their resisters.

In one's attempt to peek into the future, to ascertain prospects for domestic tranquility under a proposed New World Order, one could probably do no better than to lend a careful ear to the conclusions drawn by Sir Isaiah Berlin from his life experiences:

On this score, let me make a prophecy for the twenty-first century. Aldous Huxley's *Brave New World*—a less dramatic but in a way more insidious prospect than Orwell's *1984*—could perhaps be established, in part as an irresistible response to the endless ethnic violence and nationalist rivalry at the turn of the millennium. Under this system everyone would be clothed and fed. All would live under one roof, following one single pattern of existence.

But sooner or later somebody will rebel, somebody will cry for room. Not only will people revolt against totalitarianism, but against an all-embracing, well-meaning, benign system as well.

If there is anything I'm certain about, after living for so long, it is that people must sooner or later rebel against uniformity and attempts at global solutions of any sort.

Sir Isaiah concludes by retelling an ancient story about a ruler who decided to banish one of his wives, ordering her sealed up, with her son, in a barrel set afloat at sea. The son, after some time, unable to tolerate the confinement, insisted that he longed to stretch out. Fearful of the exercise, the mother warned him that in the process of stretching he would push out the barrel's bottom, and both would drown. Several days later, however, the son could no longer withstand being so cramped. "So be it," he proclaimed, "I must stretch out, just once, come what may." The moral of the story, says Sir Isaiah, is: "He got his moment of freedom, and perished."

Indeed, the autonomy for which men and women so instinctively and persistently yearn often extinguishes or infringes on the rights of others. Often it also extinguishes the rights or lives of the yearners. Such is the intricate and eternal dichotomy between the maintenance of authority and the strivings for autonomy.

*Part One*

# THE CONTEST BETWEEN "AUTONOMY" AND "AUTHORITY"

Thou shalt not revile the gods, nor curse the ruler of thy people.
    —Exodus 22:28

That the King can do no wrong, is a necessary and fundamental principle of the English constitution.
    —Sir William Blackstone, *Commentaries on the Law of England*

The struggle between Liberty and Authority is the most conspicuous feature in . . . history.
    —John Stuart Mill, *On Liberty*

# CHAPTER ONE

# Firebrands:
# Contenders for Change

I can't breathe. There is a rioting mob inside me. . . . I am the Revolution.

> —Marat, in Peter Weiss, *The Persecution and Assassination of Jean-Paul Marat*

I rebel—therefore we exist.

> —Albert Camus, *The Rebel*

A most insidious form of fear is that which masquerades as common sense or even wisdom, condemning as foolish, reckless, insignificant or futile the small daily acts of courage which help to preserve man's self-respect and inherent human dignity.

> —Aung San Suu Kyi, Burmese dissident and 1991 recipient of the Sakharov Prize for Freedom of Thought, *Bangkok Post*, July 13, 1991

## PROMETHEUS—THE DEIFICATION OF REBELS

History is rife with accounts of persons, in antiquity as well as in modernity, who stood up to challenge existing power and authority, religious, political, social, or economic. From the biblical Israelites who bitterly denounced Moses and his Sinai-derived commandments ("Whence did you get your authority . . . to lift yourself up above the congregation . . . making yourself a prince")[1] to present-day challengers and breakers of idols, the rebel and resister to authority has constituted an intriguing and usually controversial figure.

Most rebels, particularly if unsuccessful in their autonomous pursuits, are relegated to ignominy by those who defeat them. Yet a few manage, in victory or even in defeat, to ascend to the lofty status of demigods and are accorded the laurels and rewards of heroes and patriots, often posthumously.

The contender for autonomy, drawn from a primal archetype, is both creator and destroyer of authority and culture, a manifestation of Shiva in universal garb. Like Prometheus, the rebel endows us with "fire," the indispensable element of civilization, stolen from the Gods on Mount Olympus. Biblical Adam and Eve brought mankind the forbidden fruits of the tree of knowledge: self-awareness and the ability to discern right from wrong. Rollo May, a noted American psychoanalyst, enumerates Socrates, Jesus, Buddha, and Krishna among the other culture-creating heroes, arguing that throughout history, the rebel has been a positive force, a mover and shaker—the *primum mobile* of our society.[2] May suggests that, like Orestes in Greek mythology, the rebel is a symbol of man's assumption of responsibility for his life. This responsibility, he writes, is "the life-blood of culture, the very root of civilization"(pp.220, 223).

The fate of the rebel often includes martyrdom. In particular, the idealistic, creative rebel (the one with a "vision of [a better] life or society"[p.221]) almost inevitably becomes a victim of the forces of authority. Prometheus, for his gift to men, was chained to Mount Caucasus for eternity, as vultures tore at his entrails. Adam and Eve were cast out of Eden, to eat their bread by the sweat of their brow, an angel with a flaming sword posted to bar their return. Socrates was given his hemlock, and Jesus met his fate at Golgotha. More recently, John Brown was hanged as a traitor by the forces of "law and order."

Modern rebels and political offenders often meet similarly tragic ends, though not always at official hands. Mahatma Ghandi's and Martin Luther King's reform campaigns were interrupted by criminal assassins' bullets. These deaths became martyrdoms as well—attributed to society's resistance to change. Thus martyrdom frequently becomes the prerequisite for entry into the annals of history. Rollo May notes the "startling regularity through history with which society martyrs the rebel in one generation and worships him in the next. . . . The list is as endless as it is rich"(p.4).

While recognizing the rebel's function as a creative hero, we must also recognize his or her role as a destroyer. History's most reviled rebel, the archangel Lucifer, was expelled from Heaven for his disobedience of God's commandments. "Better to reign in Hell," he proclaimed, even though this meant spending eternity immovably frozen in a sea of polluted ice, chewing forever on the world's most distasteful sinners.[3] History is replete with these destructive rebels—aggressors, insatiable power seekers, tyrants, and megalomaniacs who abuse authority and pursue, and often tragically obtain, power as an end in itself. For these self-centered and "pseudoconvictional" rebels (the Nebuchadnezzars, Neros, Genghis Khans, Hitlers, and Stalins, as well as for the lesser-known victimizers, avengers, and aberrant butchers) destruction becomes more important than creation.[4] Contemporary culture all too often glamorizes this sort of destructive or negative rebel. Among our most successful popular culture idols are those who express their contempt for the "establishment" and its values—from America's James Dean, the "rebel without a cause," and numerous heavy metal and rap music groups, to Ulricke Meinhof, founding mother of Germany's Baader-Meinhof terrorist gang.

The quest for mere change, if unaccompanied by a definite and responsible plan for creating something new, can be futile and destructive; imagine Prometheus without his fire, Adam and Eve without the self-knowledge they gained at such terrible cost. Worse yet, the aim of many rebels is self-interest, to "simply substitute one kind of government for another, the second no better than the first . . . [making] the individual citizen, who has to endure the inevitable anarchy between the two, worse off than ever before."[5]

When rebellion is an end in itself, when the ascension to power becomes a self-contained objective, the darker side of the rebel prevails. The act of rebellion then tends to become an infliction of nihilistic terror—designed to revenge, to destroy, to disrupt, to frighten, to cow, to shock, and to disgust, rather than to create or to renew.

But regardless of his message or mission, creative or destructive, the rebel often encapsulates the people's eternal strivings for change, a desire to sweep out the old. This is why, whether he be creative or destructive, popular culture often endows the rebel with superhuman proportions. The rebel is portrayed as a man or woman who transcends the rules, who proceeds despite the inhibitions of the law, who achieves against all odds, who comes from a unique mold reserved for the demigods.

The rebel's image as a figure somehow larger than life has tended to make us insensitive to him or her as the recipient of worldly rewards or punishments. The deification, and sometimes demonization, of the rebel makes it possible for us to view this defier of authority as a rarity, incapable of being properly understood or judged by legal tribunals and common social institutions. Law and public policy can safely disclaim the need to take particular account of such men and women of destiny, who act beyond the law. History, they assume, will make the final judgment anyway. Indeed, only time can winnow the creative rebel from the destroyer, the good from the evil.

But does not this superhuman myth bear scrutiny? Are rebels really created in a unique mold? Or are they ordinary people who find themselves in extraordinary situations? If the latter, then should we not pay more attention to what separates the worthy rebel from the unworthy? Should our public policy and law not respond in some fashion to the rebel's common humanity? And should we not do this in advance of history's final judgment?

Instead of coming to grips with these questions, our institutions of justice continue indiscriminately to pursue and punish all rebels for their offending words, deeds, or very being. Like the Gods on Olympus, we do not deign to

consider the mitigating circumstances of the rebel's grievances, hopes, and motives. By casting our rebels into the pit, we choose to uphold law and order at the expense of truth and change.

As either creator or destroyer, the rebel poses unique problems for society, morality, and law. The rebel's desire for new institutions, new society, and new thought inevitably presents a threat to existing institutions, society, and thought, which many may believe are unimprovable, or at least sufficiently good. Those who ostensibly seek new and positive goals, moreover, are sometimes merely making excuses for their own selfish, nihilistic, or psychopathological missions.

Perpetuating the undifferentiated image of the defier of authority as a unique and uncommon actor does not assist us in dealing with the worldly problems posed by political dissidence and rebellion. It does not help us determine when the political rebel should be considered a beneficent bringer of civilization and change, or when a destructive and selfish force. Society and its institutions must look for a different way to approach these thorny questions, as means of checking the destructive side of the rebel without stifling the forces of progress, renewal, and change that might move him or her. Our first step would be to consider the potential for rebellion, which may be found in us all, by looking at the makeup, life forces, and experiences of political resisters and rebels whom we know.

The role of the rebel is evidently more complex than one might suppose at first glance. The rebel is a dominant force both produced by and contributing to the growing crisis of legitimacy. Waving the banner of "autonomy" in the war against authority, the rebel can serve as either a delegitimating destroyer of the old or a noble and progressive legitimator of the new, or as both, depending upon historical and societal contexts or circumstances and his or her perceived objectives.

As the age-old struggle between autonomy and authority continues to be expressed through ongoing cycles of legitimation and delegitimation, the rebel must maintain center stage. The introduction and acceptance of a legitimating formula (what, as we previously noted, Mosca calls a "political formula")[6] necessarily produces, in its own time, the antithesis, the delegitimating response. Michel Foucault thus carefully pointed out how the creation of artificial legitimating formulas brings about their counter, or opposite, formulations, and thus their own seeds of destruction.[7] The rebel, therefore, must continue to exist as long as the quest for legitimacy and for political formulas goes on, serving as an indispensable actor in the dialectic between autonomy and authority. Being a mover and shaker, whether in furthering societal cohesion or in tearing society apart at its seams, the rebel's central role in the struggle for legitimacy must not be ignored or misunderstood.

## SEARCHING FOR COMMON THREADS

"What made an elite [of] prosperous and conservative members of the Establishment . . . turn against their king and start a revolution?" asked historian Richard B. Morris in *Seven Who Shaped Our Destiny: The Founding Fathers as Revolutionaries*.[8] After vividly exploring the backgrounds and exploits of Benjamin Franklin, George Washington, John Adams, Thomas Jefferson, John Jay, James Madison, and Alexander Hamilton, Morris set out to identify common features among this diverse group of American political heroes.

The Founding Fathers were all men of principle, dedicated to public service and convinced of the rightness and necessity of their cause. They were bound by a commitment to American independence and by a belief in the superiority of republicanism over monarchism.

On the more personal level, these "revolutionaries" all suffered some disappointment in their professional aspirations. Complex individuals, talented and ambitious, all seven underwent identity crises at various stages of their lives. Morris found other common denominators. Overall, most did not appear to have had fully satisfying marriages. Despite their heritage of wealth and security, each man had encountered circumstances in which he felt the need to prove himself. In the process, each developed an enthusiasm for controversy. Most significantly, their activities and associations brought them into contact with others who also had grievances against the Crown.[9]

It would be difficult, and scientifically faulty, to draw significant conclusions from so small yet so diverse a group as the Founding Fathers. Even more futile would be the search for a commonality in personality, background, and motivation between America's earliest rebels and political offenders and those who followed them, here and abroad. Nevertheless some quests for common strands have been carried out, with the hope of casting new and useful light on the persons and environments that give rise to political criminality and rebellion. Several older, as well as contemporary, findings deserve our attention.

### CLASS AND STATUS

Various aspects of the social, psychological, and moral makeup of the rebel have been examined by both classical and modern writers. Political dissidents and offenders represent the powerless, argued William Adriaan Bonger, a Dutch lawyer and criminologist, who published his famous volume *Criminality and Economic Conditions* at the conclusion of the nineteenth century.[10] Bonger identified the powerless with an economically "oppressed class," and defined the rebel, or political criminal, as one who struggles against "the political power of the ruling class."[11] Pursuing a Marxist perspective, Bonger sought to understand political crime and rebellion in terms of economic determinism. He suggested that political crime naturally emerges whenever economic and social developments lag behind or run ahead of political developments.[12] He viewed the oppressed class, due to its limited power, as unable to change the status quo by peaceful and legal means. Where this imbalance in social power continued, there would always be the "danger that one of those oppressed will kill the autocrat, either to better the situation or to take revenge for what he and his have suffered."[13] Statistical data demonstrates, however, that while political offenders might often be acting on behalf of underprivileged and powerless classes, they have not necessarily risen from that background. Interesting evidence is contained in an analysis of some 2,564 individuals charged with illegal revolutionary activities in czarist Russia during the period of 1873 to 1879. Members of the ruling or upper classes constituted a majority of these offenders, though otherwise they came from diverse backgrounds: aristocrats (28.2%); clergy (16.6%); military (13.4%); peasants (13.4%); urban workers (13.4%); merchants (4.2%); and intelligentsia (3.3%).[14] A related study of the vocational and professional backgrounds of some 1,703 Russian political offenders sentenced during the 1870s supplied a similar breakdown: university students (17.3%); urban workers (16%); high school students (9.7%); teachers (7–8%); peasants (3.7%); and military (2.8%).[15] Since Marxism invariably views class background and political revolution as closely allied, Marxists have sought comfort in the myth that the Russian Revolution had a primarily proletarian background. Nevertheless, other historiographers have pointed to three distinct groupings and stages in the Russian Revolutionary movement—aristocratic, intellectual, and proletarian—based on the class background of the leaders of each stage. It is therefore quite accurate to conclude that the Russian Revolution, rather than fitting into a neat Marxist categorization of "proletarians" rising against an "overclass," was essentially "an intelligentsia revolution."[16]

The overwhelming evidence supports the conclusion that the educated sons and daughters of the privileged classes have been the ones to hold leadership positions in the ranks of political dissidence not only in czarist Russia but also elsewhere. Studies of recently apprehended terrorists in Italy confirm that a great number of these offenders came from well-to-do family backgrounds.[17] Likewise, the Colombian M-19 terrorists (who seized the Embassy of the Dominican Republic in Bogotá in February 1980 and held fourteen ambassadors as hostages) also consisted "mostly of [the] alienated sons and daughters of prominent families."[18]

But studies that identify political offenders today with either rich or poor backgrounds ignore the mounting data supporting the conclusion that the most militant political activists come from the middle class. Social psychologists Schmidt and Leiden are among the few to argue that the ambitious middle class is the greatest source of young rebels eager for opportunity and success. The upper class, they submit, is too satisfied to rebel, and the lower lacks the necessary skills.[19]

Still, former assessments of the roles of class and status in the formation of the political offender remain inconclusive. The diverse memberships of America's civil rights, anti-Vietnam, environmental protection, and abortion rights movements in the past two decades, as well as of the recent popular upheaval and mass rebellions in Eastern Europe and the former Soviet Union, might lead one to the conclusion that socioeconomic class is not a factor central to political activism.

Karl and Dwight Armstrong, charged with the 1970 fatal bombing of the Army Mathematics Research Center at the University of Wisconsin, came from a close-knit, liberal, middle-class family background.[20] Their father, on his own since age sixteen, advanced from being a chauffeur to becoming a buyer for a manufacturing company. Proud of his skills and self-reliance, the elder Armstrong felt that his own outspoken contempt for the Vietnam War had probably influenced his sons. The mother responded to her family with utmost pride and passion. "There never would have been a bombing," she said, "if people my age had done something, instead of letting our children do it." Both parents regarded the young researcher who had been killed in the explosion, his widow, and three children as "victims of the violence Vietnam bred in people at home."

As if relying on the Armstrongs as prototypes, political writer J. Kirkpatrick Sale claims the following common elements among the families of youths active in America's Vietnam protest movement: (a) a comfortable and professional middle-class background, (b) two employed parents, (c) an evident sense of social consciousness, and (d) dinner table discussions that are likely to be liberal. That milieu, suggested Sale, is "almost predictable for contemporary activists."[21]

It is apparent, however, that these "common denominators" are far from universal when one examines more critically the backgrounds of other political offenders here and abroad. The not atypical background of America's Diana Oughton, who abandoned her conservative and authoritarian Republican family for life as a Weatherman revolutionary,[22] gives credence to the assertion by criminologists Clinnard and Quinney that "such characteristics as age, sex, ethnicity, and social class do not differentiate political offenders as a whole from the population in general."[23] Participants in recent protests against abortion clinics, for example, fall decidedly outside Sale's categories. Even a cursory review of their economic and social backgrounds reveals the absence of a permissive or liberal family milieu. On the contrary, most of these radicals claim adherence to fundamental creeds and authoritarian value systems.

Perhaps class and status play a merely incidental role in creating the political resister. Activist leadership often comes not from any particular socioeconomic "class" but from more informal clusters of individuals who find their personal paths for advancement blocked by a common obstacle. More than a decade ago African American leader Bayard Rustin, regarding the American civil rights movement, observed that "it is not the *lumpen-proletariat*, the Negro working classes, the Negro working poor, who are proclaiming: 'We want Negro principals, we want Negro supervisors, we want Negro teachers in our schools.' It is the educated Negroes . . . being blocked from moving up, [they] become not only interested in Negro children, but in getting those teaching jobs, supervisory jobs and principal jobs for [their] own economic interest."[24]

Many political activists find a disparity among their backgrounds, their educational accomplishments, and their existing social status. Sociologists have coined the term *status incongruence* to describe situations in which a person's socioeconomic achievement level is inconsistent with what he or she expects because of education, or such other factors as family, ethnic, or class background.

Status incongruence arises when cultural and economic decline befall those in the established and well-heeled classes. It can also occur when the education and cultural emergence of members of the lower socioeconomic strata are unaccompanied by adequate opportunities for professional and economic enhancement. A recent survey of Italian political militants has revealed that "the 'open university' policy of Italian universities in recent years has produced an abundance of unemployable and often underqualified terrorists. These universities continue to provide a source of recruits and support for the terrorists."[25]

It may be the case that status incongruence can produce social and economic restlessness and agitation, conditions favorable for gestating political activists. However, more specific generalizations about political offenders cannot be made on the basis of data derived from such communities as different as the Founding Fathers, Russian revolutionaries, European terrorists, and contemporary American civil disobedients. We might be better advised to seek commonality among more homogeneous categories of activists, for the insurgent or guerrilla is likely to differ drastically from the political activist who refuses military service, as is the one who engages in a lonely dissent from the one who joins in collective protest. Likewise, rebels who are committed to violent and militant action may not necessarily resemble those who scrupulously adhere to peaceful means.

Status incongruence might account for much of the general turmoil among the world's youth, religious and ethnic militants, the restless urban dwellers, and other categories of rebels and resisters, specific manifestations of political activism by members of those groups might indeed reflect the actors' social and educational levels, to their environments, and to the societal norms that surround them. Rather than seeking a comprehensive profile for all or most political offenders, it may indeed be more productive to discern common characteristics within particular groups of political extremists: presidential assassins; skyjackers; participants in racial, ethnic, and religious unrest; and the sometimes-distinguished, sometimes-infamous ranks of female offenders.

## PRESIDENTIAL ASSASSINS AND ASSAILANTS

After studying the profiles of American presidential assassins, the National Commission on the Causes and Prevention of Violence concluded in 1969 that "neither socioeconomic class nor employment seems to establish a common thread."[26] The raw data revealed, however, that, of a group of seven assassins, two came from well-to-do middle-class families, another from a family that owned a bar and a tenement, and the rest from craftsman or skilled worker backgrounds. One striking common element was the fact that all these presidential assassins had lost their employment, because of physical disability or some other circumstances, within one to three years prior to the assassination efforts. For every member of this troubled group, their major lawful avenue for economic livelihood and social advancement— work—had thus been blocked (pp.62–67).

Scrutinizing the individual histories of these presidential assassins, sociologist Doris Y. Wilkinson reported to the Commission that every one presented an instance of status incongruence—an expectation/achievement gap. Although members of the Commission continued to press for a more definite causal connection between that observation and political violence, they concluded that "the question of why the psychic distress derived from status incongruence became politicized in the form of a deadly attack upon a high political officeholder remains unanswered" (p.66).

Another characteristic shared by many of America's assailants of presidents was their relatively recent foreign roots, a possibly contributing factor to a sense of status incongruence. The first attempt against the life of a United States president took place in 1835 when Richard Lawrence shot Andrew Jackson. The would-be assassin, a native Englishman, had moved to Washington with his parents when he was twelve years old. John N. Schrank, who in 1921 shot Theodore Roosevelt in another unsuccessful assassination attempt, was born in Bavaria, having emigrated to the United States when he was thirteen. Guisseppe Zangara, who attempted to assassinate Franklin D. Roosevelt in 1933, was born in Italy, emigrating to the United States at the age of twenty-three. Leon F. Czolgosz, born only a few months after his parents emigrated to the United States from Poland, assassinated William McKinley in 1901. Similarly, the parents of John Wilkes Booth, who assassinated Lincoln in 1865, came to America from England after Booth's mother had become pregnant with her first child. Sirhan Sirhan, the assassin of presidential candidate Robert F. Kennedy, was a native of Jordan. Only Charles J. Guiteau, the 1881 assassin of James A. Garfield, and Lee Harvey Oswald, John F. Kennedy's assassin, were native-born Americans (pp.49–61), as were Lynette "Squeaky" Fromme and John Hinkley, the assailants of Presidents Gerald Ford and Ronald Reagan.

Status incongruence and foreign birth undeniably loom large in the portraits of past presidential assailants. So striking had the historical evidence been that after the assassination of presidential candidate Robert Kennedy, the National Commission on the Causes and Prevention of Violence noted that a profile of potential presidential assassins should describe the prospective offender as "short and slight of build, foreign born, and from a broken family"(p.66).

How does this typical presidential assailant in America relate to the principal actors of this volume: those taking militant roles in the conflict between "authority" and "autonomy" and precipitating the crisis of political legitimacy? One might conclude that unlike regicides, and unlike violence against figures and symbols of political authority elsewhere, American presidential assaults are carried out by pseudopolitical activists, who merely vent in their violence personal anger, dissatisfactions, grievances, hatreds, and dysfunctions.[27] Other observers might argue, however, that despite the missing causal connections, the American assailant attributes an ultimate figure of authority with responsibility for the ills and dissatisfaction resulting from other confrontations he or she has had with lesser institutions of authority. Either way, the very moment the assassin strikes out against the symbol or figurehead of authority, the leader and the legitimacy of government is called into question, whether the assassin was motivated by political concerns or by an emotional or psychological disturbance.

It is thus evident that one must be careful not to insist on ascribing the behavior of the rebel to a single cause, as this might result in misinterpretation of the character of the war against authority and the complex relationship between authority and autonomy. The friction between the rebel or political offender and the enforcer of authority is not always directly related to political factors, as the following sections will further demonstrate. The identity of the instigator as well as the triggering reasons for the eruption of the war is often mysterious and difficult to ascertain. What is important to note, however, is the great diversity in human motivations and interactions, the very amorphous constitution of the rebel community. Such awareness might constitute the best safeguard against simplistic and premature answers to the complex questions posed by the war against authority.

### PIRATES IN THE SKY

In the late 1960s, David G. Hubbard, a Texas psychiatrist, conducted extensive psychiatric interviews with fifty-two confirmed American and Canadian skyjackers, out of about one hundred and sixty held in custody at the time.[28] The results were compared with similar interviews with a nearly equal number of Black Panthers and members of the French-Canadian Front for the Liberation of Quebec. Hubbard's conclusions take issue with previous attempts to divide hijackers into such diverse groups as "emotionally disturbed," "fleeing felons," or "political activists." Such classifications, Hubbard asserts, are spurious. Since there are millions of emotionally disturbed persons in each country, why do only a handful elect to participate in hijacking or related violence? Since there are thousands of fleeing felons, why do only a very few commit air piracy? Since many millions are committed to political change and activism all over the world, why do only a small number use terrorist tactics? The "real question," according to Hubbard, is "what do these tiny handfuls of men have in common?"[29]

It is this commonality that the Hubbard studies have sought to identify. Hubbard's research claims that hijacking offenders share great psychological similarities with one another regardless of their national, racial, or cultural backgrounds. Skyjackers raised overseas (in Scotland, Guatemala, and Cuba) shared much with those raised in North America (in Savannah, Georgia; Seattle, Washington; or Ottawa, Canada). The picture was not affected by the offenders being black, white, or Hispanic.

Several unexpected similarities existed in the backgrounds of Hubbard's interviewees. Many grew up in violent families with chronically alcoholic fathers. Typically, mothers were religious zealots. Hubbard debunks the popular concept of the skyjacker as a strong, tough, left-wing idealist who is fleeing persecution. Those interviewed turned out to be timid, sexually inadequate, and generally ineffectual. They resembled the would-be skyjackers portrayed in the film *Dog Day Afternoon*, who resorted to skyjacking at a time of total personal unraveling as a decisive act of redemption. Each of the skyjackers interviewed, asserted Dr. Hubbard, had a "better, more tolerable body image and self-image *after* the crime than he had before."[30]

Hubbard's findings, he claims, contributed to the designing of a profile of potential skyjackers. Utilized in the antiskyjacking campaign developed jointly by the U.S. government and the airlines, the profile was given considerable credit for reducing the number of offenses against U.S. aircraft from the annual high of forty in 1969 to a mere four in 1976, and thirteen in 1979.[31]

ETHNIC AND RELIGIOUS MINORITIES

The prominence of ethnic and religious minorities within the leadership of revolutionary and insurgency movements also highlights the possible role of status incongruence in political activism. Several of the most noted leaders of the Russian Revolution were members of the country's minorities. Leon Trotsky was of Jewish extraction, and Joseph Stalin was a non-Russian ethnic from the mountainous hinterland of Georgia. At the turn of the last century, Vyacheslav Constantinovich von Plehve, the man who shaped czarist Russia's antirevolutionary and counter-terrorist policies by directing the Oprichnina, the czarist secret police,[32] recognized the unique social and ethnic background of the country's political activists. Inspecting a prison for political detainees, he commented: "I view all political offenders as ambitious aspirants seeking status—is it not true that each of them had dreamt of becoming a representative in Parliament?"[33] Von Plehve considered the wide community of expelled and dropped-out university students as a particularly rich pool for revolutionary recruitment.

In response to a Jewish delegation's complaint about government inaction during the 1903 anti-Jewish pogroms, von Plehve, then serving as Minister of the Interior, sought the delegates' assistance in curtailing the growing political activism within the Jewish intelligentsia. "Much is said about Jewish cowardice, but this is not true. The Jews are the most courageous people. In Western Russia, 90 percent of the revolutionaries are Jewish and, in all of Russia, they constitute 40 percent," von Plehve affirmed.[34]

To this day a disproportionate number of the former Soviet Union's human rights activists and political dissenters continue to be members of ethnic, cultural, or religious minorities. A recent example is Anatoly Shcharansky, a Russian Jew, who was shuttled from one Soviet penal institution to another and was eventually released from political exile through an international exchange of prisoners. He stands as a standard-bearer for millions of Jewish and other minority political dissenters and protesters in the former Soviet Union.[35]

In other countries, as well, the avant-garde of political militancy often contains a disproportionate number of minority populations. This phenomenon is reflected in the divergent militias of Lebanon, the cadres of Maoist Shining Path terrorists in Peru, the Tamils of Sri Lanka, and the Miskito Indians in Nicaragua. While status incongruence could partially account for these disparities in the rebel communities, it is possible also that the values, belief systems, and oppressive experiences of these ethnic and religious minorities might form the basis for these communities' objections to the institutional authority. At times, these minority activists rise only in response to specific campaigns of governmental oppression against their communities. Often, however, the activists do not speak exclusively for their narrow constituencies but lead broad national campaigns for reform or revolution.

### JAEL AND HER SISTERS: FEMALE ACTIVISTS

In biblical accounts, Jael, the wife of Heber the Israelite, "smote a nail" into the temples of Sisera, the captain of an oppressive enemy who sought refuge in her tent.[36] Judith, the Apocryphal heroine, likewise slew the Assyrian conqueror Holofernes in order to prevent the destruction of her native Jerusalem.[37]

Other exceptional women are known from later historical accounts, including world-famous leaders such as Jeanne d'Arc and Marat's lone assassin, Charlotte Corday. But the political isolation of women in Eastern cultures and their diminished public place throughout most of Western history have generally obscured whatever roles they have had in the arenas of political activism and crime. Indeed, it was the diffident treatment afforded American women by their male colleagues in the mid-nineteenth-century abolitionist movement that subsequently gave rise to widespread feminist political activism—the suffragist movement itself. Later, at the end of the nineteenth century, the anarchist movement also brought the female role in political militancy into sharper focus.

Sergei Nachaeyeff, the master strategist of anarchism, discussing, in his essay "Revolutionary Catechism,"[38] the revolutionary's relationship with various elements of society, found it especially important to concentrate upon the role of women, whom he divided into three categories. The first, those who were "frivolous, thoughtless, and vapid," he compared with men of privilege and found them, like the men, fit only for exploitation. In the second category were those who were "ardent, gifted and devoted," who had not achieved the "passionless and austere" dedication required of revolutionaries. These women he compared with those men who, even if doctrinally and ideologically committed, were mostly idle word-spillers rather than activists. This group he perceived as being capable of supplying potential supporters, but not useful fighting troops. "Finally," said Nachaeyeff, "there are the women who are completely on our side. . . . We should regard these women as the most valuable of our treasures; without their help it would be impossible to succeed."[39]

Recent history has recorded the dramatic increase of female roles in public life. In America, as elsewhere, early images of thousands upon thousands of unidentified women struggling in the fields or in the rank-and-file of trade unionism gave way to portraits of such diverse militant activists as Emma Goldman, Ethel Rosenberg, and Angela Davis taking their place in the front lines of political rebellion. By 1978, criminologist Freda Adler, in *Sisters in Crime*, wrote:

> Another area in which young women have begun to express their aptitude for assertive behavior is political protest. In the storm of dissent which swept across the country in the late sixties, the adolescent female was an enthusiastic participant in the demonstrations and the coequal cell-mate in the jailings. Initially, during the early sixties, the movements were planned, led, and executed by males while females performed their traditional functions as office workers, coffee makers, and overseers of routine chores. But by the end of the decade, a by now familiar transformation had occurred.[40]

American women played unreluctant roles in the leadership of the most radical student, antiwar, and political revolutionary cadres of the 1960s and 1970s. Their role in pro-choice and pro-life movements of the 1980s and 1990s was even more dominant. Diana Oughton and Kathylin Wilkerson were prominent in the hierarchy of the militant Students for Democratic Action. Throughout the world, criminologist H. H. A. Cooper noted, the female protester and terrorist was no longer content "just to praise the Lord and pass the ammunition."[41] Cooper further discerned "a cold rage" about some of these women militants, which even the most extreme and alienated of their male colleagues seemed incapable of emulating.

The women members of West Germany's Baader-Meinhof Gang testify to this type of total commitment. In a West German study, out of a sample of forty major terrorists, twenty-four were female and sixteen were male. This disproportionality, a 60 percent female rate among terrorists, appears in striking contrast with a 7 percent female rate in robbery and a 20 percent female share in other crimes of violence.[42]

Women have also played an increasingly important role in nonviolent political activity. In the Soviet Union, Natalia Gorbanevskaya helped organize the *samizdat*, the underground press, in the late 1960s. Dr. Yelena Bonner, a Soviet pediatrician, was instrumental in establishing the unauthorized Helsinki Watch Group, a citizen organization monitoring Soviet departures from the human rights provisions of the Helsinki Accord. (Bonner became better known when she later married Nobel Peace Prize winner Dr. Andrei Sakharov, another Russian human rights activist.) In Britain, women have played similar leading roles in civil disobedience, including the campaign against the installation of United States cruise missiles. Women from many segments of British society participated in protest gatherings at nuclear weapons facilities, most notably at Greenham Commons, where they established permanent encampments on the perimeter of the base and persisted despite periodic evictions by the police. Many have gone to jail for setting up human roadblocks and breaching base security—both as a means of protest and to demonstrate the vulnerability of the missile sites to other, less-responsible interlopers.[43]

The norm today for women in the United States is to take the same risks as men do, whether in opposition to nuclear armaments and abortion clinics or in aid of Central American refugees through the new Underground Railroad of the sanctuary movement. While no statistics reflecting female participation in these political resistance movements are available, the sexes have been treated equally by the courts—with a federal judge in Arizona typically allocating similar sentences to women and men for smuggling illegal aliens into the country.[44]

Though significant numbers in particular subclasses of political offenders, such as presidential assassins and skyjackers, might fall into narrowly defined socioeconomic, religious, or gender categories, observations of other and broader classes of political activism belie such categorizations. Political offenders are not only represented by both sexes but also emerge from widely diverse class, family, ethnic, and social backgrounds. At the same time they are apparently inspired and driven by an equally diverse variety of causes and beliefs.

Political dissidents, the evidence suggests, can be outsiders in a given society—for example, women or ethnic and religious minorities—or they can be insiders—coming from the predominant ranks of gender, race, class, or faith. Though status incongruence may serve as a valuable common denominator for many of these actors, it would be difficult if not impossible to explain through it such diverse phenomena as the activist middle-class Greenham women in England, the militant zeal of India's poor Muslim—and Hindu—masses, the broad spectrum of participants in America's civil disobedience movements, the numerous aristocrats among the leaders of the French Revolution, or the significant role of the intelligentsia in czarist Russia's November Revolution. This diversity leads to the conclusion that a profile of the political offender cannot be accurately painted without giving equal attention to the individual psychological factors and group dynamics that produce individual and collective outbreaks of political criminality and rebellion.

## VARIATIONS ON A PSYCHOLOGICAL THEME

Criminologist Stephen Schafer, writing in 1974, claimed that "the state of mind of the offender and his emotional balance" have perhaps been the most challenging questions for those trying to understand political crime.[45] Nearly a century earlier, the father of scientific criminology, Cesare Lombroso, ambitiously set out to divide all offenders into three major classes: the born criminals, the insane, and the criminaloids.[46] The born criminals were those who exhibited atavistic physical characteristics and possessed a deficient moral sense. The criminality of the insane offenders was attributed to physiological or mental defects, thus relieving the actors of personal responsibility. Finally, the criminaloids were those with weak natures, "who are candidates for good or evil according to circumstances."[47] Within the criminaloid class Lombroso included the category of "criminals by passion," encompassing, for example, brothers who murder their sister's rapist, the unmarried mother who strangles her illegitimate infant, and the husband who kills an unfaithful wife. But Lombroso recognized that the passion of the criminaloids was not always personal. "Some times," he noted, "the [passionate] motive is a patriotic one."[48]

Lombroso sought to further identify members of each criminal class by physiognomy, describing criminals of passion as handsome, with lofty foreheads and serene and gentle expressions. Criminals of passion were also endowed, according to him, with acute sensitivity and characterized by a high degree of excitability and exaggerated reflex action. Psychologically, criminals of passion possessed an excessive amount of those qualities that are considered desirable in "good and holy persons—love, honor, noble ambitions, patriotism. . . . The motive [of the passion criminal] is always adequate, frequently noble, and sometimes sublime"(p.119). Although Lombroso's physiognomic methods of classification were naive, in addition to being racially and culturally parochial, many of his other theses regarding the political offender have withstood the test of time.

Lombroso recognized that just as not all criminals of passion were patriotically or politically—rather than personally—motivated, not all political offenders were impelled solely by passion. He saw the ranks of political criminality as diverse:

[It] recruited from all ranks and conditions—men of genius, intellectual spirits who are the first to realize the defects of the old system and to conceive a new one, synthesizing the needs and aspirations of the people; lunatics, enthusiastic propagandists of the new ideas, which they spread with all the impetuous ardor characteristic of unbalanced minds; criminals, the natural enemies of order, who flock to the standard of revolt and bring to it their special gifts, audacity and contempt of death. These latter types accomplish the work of destruction which inevitably accompanies every revolution: they are the faithful and unerring arm ready to carry out the ideas that others conceive but lack the courage to execute.

Finally, there are the saints, the men who live solely for high purposes and to whom the revolution is a veritable apostolate. . . . They are consumed by a passion for altruism and self-immolation, and experience a strange delight in martyrdom for their ideals (pp.297–98).

Although viewing passion as a prominent feature of the political offender, Lombroso recognized that political unrest and insurrection attracted also the passionless and opportunistic. At the opposite end of the spectrum, he acknowledged that "passion" could explode into insanity, and that those with unbalanced minds were often accorded the opportunity to play important roles in the revolutionary camp.

During the final stages of his career, Lombroso focused more specifically on political and revolutionary offenders[49] and upon anarchists in particular.[50] He became inclined to accord even greater weight to the role of those with atavistic and abnormal psychological makeups, stressing the important place of common criminals in revolutionary movements. "The crimes of anarchists tend to mingle with ordinary crimes when certain dreamers attempt to reach their goal by any means possible—theft, or the murder of a few, often innocent, persons. It is easy to realize, therefore, why, with a few exceptions, anarchists are recruited from among ordinary criminals, lunatics, and insane criminals."

For all their sophisticated research and elaborate diagnostic techniques, modern psychiatry, psychology, and criminology have done little to advance the understanding of political dissidents beyond Lombroso's intuitive groupings. The distinctions between the genuinely political offender and the common criminal (or, on the other hand, the mentally abnormal activist) continue, by and large, to be subjective and biased by cultural and political proclivities. The marked tendency to label all that is different and unorthodox as either *crime* or *insanity* thus continues unchallenged.

Professor Robert K. Merton led another, more contemporary attempt to vanquish this bias and to distinguish the political offender from both the common and the mentally ill criminal.[51] In an effort to chart the whole panorama of dissident behavior, Merton first distinguished between "aberrant" and "nonconforming" conduct. He described aberrant conduct (which he attributed to both common and mentally ill offenders) as a pathological form of behavior. Secretive, selfish, and antisocial qualities usually typify aberrant conduct. Nonconforming behavior, on the other hand, is entirely another matter. The nonconforming offender often announces his dissent publicly rather than seeking to hide his deviance. Also, he directly challenges the legitimacy of the norms and laws he violates. This is in sharp contrast to the common criminal, who usually acknowledges the legitimacy of the laws he breaks. Finally, and perhaps most importantly, the nonconforming offender claims to depart from prevailing social norms for communal rather than for selfish reasons. He or she asserts adherence to a higher morality, one that surpasses existing social values.

Merton classifies the politically motivated offender under this "nonconforming" label. Political dissidence, unlike aberrant or pathological criminality, he concludes, "is not a private dereliction but a thrust toward a new morality or a promise of restoring a morality held to have been thrust aside in social practice."[52]

Merton's "Typology of Modes of Individual Adaptation" further charts the distinctions between the law-abiding citizen, the common criminal, the mentally ill deviant, and the ideologically motivated (or rebellious) offender.[53] In Table 1 we present, in a somewhat modified manner, Merton's summation of the reactions of various categories of actors—conformists, criminals, the mentally ill, and rebels—first to society's "goals" and then to the institutional avenues (or "means") it authorizes for the attainment of these goals.

### TABLE 1
### RESPONSES TO SOCIETAL GOALS AND MEANS

| Categories of Response | Modes of Response to Societal Goals | Modes of Response to Institutionalized Means |
|---|---|---|
| Noncriminal ("Conformity")* | Acceptance | Acceptance |
| Criminal ("Innovation")* | Acceptance | Rejection |
| Mentally ill ("Retreatism")* | Rejection | Rejection |
| Political Criminal ("Rebellion")* | Rejection and Substitution with New Goals | Rejection and Substitution with New Means |

*Adaptation*

Merton suggests that the law-abider, or "conformist," accepts both social goals and institutional means. The common criminal, on the other hand, generally accepts the shared cultural values and goals of society but rejects and resists the institutional means. These common offenders, whom Merton designates "innovators," have assimilated the majority's cultural goals (including "success" and "economic wealth") without equally internalizing the societal norms governing the means for attaining these goals (such as "education" and "work"). The third category, the mentally ill offender, or Merton's "retreatist," shirks from or is unable to cope with either the cultural goals or the institutionalized means of society.

The political criminal (Merton's "rebel") falls into an entirely different category. He or she rejects the goals of the dominant culture, substituting reformist or revolutionary ideals. At the same time, the rebel also rejects the means endorsed by society, advancing new and non-institutional means for the pursuit and propagation of the new ideals.

Though Merton does distinguish the political criminal's motivations and outlook from those of other offenders, he does not specify the dynamics of the political offender's evolution. This is our next task: to consider the distinct stages in a man's or woman's process of becoming a protestor, dissident, and rebel.

## THE DYNAMICS OF RADICALIZATION

### THE SENSE OF DIFFERENCE

The rebelliousness of the political offender is often coupled with a perceived sense of moral superiority over people and powers with which he or she contends. This perception often flows from the offender's view of the existing order as corrupt and unworthy of obedience and his or her claimed commitment to a calling higher than the prevailing authority.

The leaders of the American Revolution rejected British law because they perceived it to be the product of an oppressive and illegitimate parliamentary process. Similarly, the leaders of the Confederacy left the Union, claiming it had betrayed the covenant of the Constitution. Abolitionists defied the law because of the moral repugnancy of slavery and because of their religious and social commitment to the brotherhood of man. In this country and abroad, draft resisters and pacifists either rejected the morality of particular conflicts or of war per se, proclaiming the moral superiority of the dissident over the conformist. The rebel's superior posture toward existing authority and law, as we will see later, is not only derived from personal convictions and experiences but also often supported by religious, philosophical, and jurisprudential doctrines that elevate morality above the prevailing law.

Yet how does one's zeal to remedy injustice, real or imagined, turn into political protest, crime, or rebellion? A sense of uniqueness appears to have marked many political activists during their youth. Describing one of his heroines, J. Anthony Lukas writes in *Don't Shoot—We Are Your Children!*: "Sue was gripped with a sense of her own specialness. . . . The other children [did not] make much out of this specialness. . . . But Sue felt it intensely."[54] In some instances, this "sense of difference" is related to the early development of a young person's social and political awareness. This uniqueness, specialness, or difference may be expressed as an alienation from one's family, peers, or the community.

SDS leader Diana Oughton rejected the privileged position enjoyed by her family in their hometown. The other children in school would teasingly refer to her as "Miss Moneybags." When she was six, she reportedly inquired of her nanny, "Ruthie, why do we have to be rich?"[55] She frequently expressed her wish to be like the "ordinary people." Kathylin Wilkerson, a central figure in the Weatherman organization, similarly reported, "I've been a radical most of my life. I was young during the Korean War; for 6 or 7, I was highly conscious of the A-bomb. Gradually I became alienated from the suburban middle-class lifestyle and the values it offered."[56]

The sense of uniqueness might be generated by an awareness of a "higher calling" rather than by worldly exposure. *Religious fundamentalism* is a term often applied to individuals or groups professing to follow this "higher calling." In their quest to obey higher commands, fundamentalists view as illegitimate the laws proclaimed by human beings.[57] Indeed, the secular state or government may appear irrelevant, or at best secondary, in light of what the fundamentalist believes to be overriding religious values and laws. To some Islamic faithful in the former Soviet Union, or in present-day Iran or Arab Middle-East, Marxist-Leninist ideologies, modern nationalism, or even Western democratic values and principles are in direct conflict with the implementation of a Nation of Islam.[58]

"I have only one choice—my ministry in response to God," wrote David Dellinger. "If the government puts me in jail for following that ministry, that is its choice, not mine."[59] Jim Corbett, a Sanctuary worker convicted and sent to prison, believed that "if you really think that God is calling you to serve the needs of refugees then you must meet their most apparent need, which is to avoid capture, inevitable torture and death."[60] Father J. Guadelupe Carney, an American Jesuit priest who joined a guerrilla troop shortly before his murder at the hands of the Honduran Army in 1983, likewise summarized his calling: "To be a Christian is to be a revolutionary."[61]

The political offender often describes his or her sense of uniqueness in terms of individual morality. Personal integrity and "honor" are key expressions in the dictionary of the political offender. "To be a man, with honor, means to say no to the ugly gnawing creature that is the U.S. foreign policy," wrote draft resister James Taylor Rowland.[62] Activists have also fondly quoted Che Guevara: "This type of fight gives us the opportunity of becoming the human species, and it also permits us to graduate as men."[63]

Much of the political offender's strength is derived from the steadfast belief in his or her own moral purity. Dietrich Bonhoeffer describes the "responsible man" who speaks and acts out against injustices when others remain silent. "Who stands his ground? Only the man whose ultimate criterion is not in his reason, his principles, his conscience, his freedom or his virtue, but who is ready to sacrifice all these things when he is called to . . . action in faith and in exclusive allegiance to God."[64]

The political offender's response to a higher calling manifests itself not only in his or her self-image but also with interaction in the world. The radical activist, believing that he or she adheres to a superior and distinct value system that rejects established societal goals and methods, decides to affect the establishment from the outside, not the inside. Daniel Ellsberg writes about his decision, while working with AID officials in Vietnam, to challenge the system and to seek an end to war:

> The AID man there . . . said: "Don't do this Dan. You're just the sort of man we want here for this kind of advice. We need you, the government needs you, and you can do good work in this relationship. . . . This gives you access, it gives you a chance to say what you think to the officials. . . . Don't cut yourself off. Don't cut your throat." I had to say to him "I'm not cutting my throat." I said, "life exists outside the executive branch. You know, there is nourishment. You can sustain life out there."[65]

The political offender therefore accepts, and at times welcomes, the personal sacrifices required by his or her cause. Martyrdom is indeed more than a professional risk: it is a reward. Karl Armstrong, bomber of the Wisconsin University Mathematics Center, explained his mission: "I was born on the day they hung the Nazis at Nuremberg. . . . The only real resolution I ever made in my whole life was that I would be prepared to give up my life so that wouldn't happen here in America."[66]

While rejecting existing social values, political offenders appear to possess an acute sense of personal responsibility toward others and toward what they consider to be their flawed society. "I intend to devote all my time to the peace movement," proclaimed one unidentified young activist.[67] He continued, "I will not run to Canada. This is my country and I love it dearly. Because of this love I cannot stand by and watch people kill people in the name of freedom." As the commitment to social betterment assumes all-consuming proportions, the would-be offender's personal identity becomes merged in the public mission. "For the first time," reports another of Kenneth Keniston's young activists, "I really began to feel a part of the Movement. . . . I began to be able to trace my own roots in terms of being able to feel actually *of* it, not only in it."[68]

A similar vision of the interrelationship between the individual and his or her public mission was offered by Sam Melville, a leader in the prisoners' revolt at Attica. In his search for self-respect and dignity, Melville eventually concluded that his identity was merged with the struggle for social justice. "I don't think you can have inner peace," he wrote, "without outer peace, too. . . . There is not individual change without social change."[69] Melville, the man who persuaded Jane Alpert to bomb a federal office building, died in the Attica riots of September 1971.

## THE SEMINAL EVENT

The transition from alienation and disaffection to radicalism and rebellion is often brought about by a seminal event that triggers or intensifies the rebel's process of politicization. At times it is a dramatic event that shocks or deeply affects the potential activist. Witnessing the self-immolation of a sixteen-year-old boy in front of the Syracuse cathedral, in protest against the Vietnam War, was the seminal event in Daniel Berrigan's career as a political offender. Berrigan later visited the boy as he lay dying in the hospital. There Berrigan "smelled, for the first time . . . the odor of burning flesh."[70] When the boy later died, Berrigan felt that the tragic sacrifice had not been in vain. The youth's death had "brought something to birth" in him. He had been transformed. He would carry on the boy's fight.

In other cases, the ignition is supplied by normal events that most individuals would view as quite ordinary. Diana Oughton was shocked by what she observed during her travels in Guatemala. It was there that she began to "see for the first time that the rich are afraid of the poor, and that the poor hate and envy the rich."[71] Dr. Benjamin Spock's sudden realization that "the whole *world* was in peril" because of the global nuclear threat, spurred him to join the peace movement.[72] Karl Armstrong believed that the tragic events at Kent State initiated his radicalization. He was shaken by the killing of students, which he said "meant that the U.S. Government had declared war on the students. . . . It was then that I made the decision to destroy AMRC [the Army Mathematics Research Center at the University of Wisconsin]."[73]

One woman's account typifies the mind-set of hundreds of others who in the recent past fought pitched battles of civil disobedience at the Greenham Commons nuclear weapons facility in Britain:

> When I was about seven and a half months pregnant, I watched *Horizon*, about the 'Protect and Survive' plans. We in Wales would not be hit directly, and it became very plain to me that I would have to sit and watch my children die. Children are much more susceptible to radiation than adults, and I would have to watch them die in agony and then die myself. Suddenly it became obvious to me that I had to do something for my children.[74]

The seminal event has more than symbolic significance. The single event becomes a lens through which the activist reexamines the entire society. In the case of some revolutionaries and terrorists, the distaste for, and opposition to, one aspect of society may thereby become extended to other social and political institutions. The gap between ideals and reality becomes intolerable. At that stage the revolutionary is no longer willing to be satisfied with partial or reasoned reform; instead he requires a total restructuring of society. "Suddenly, for all of us," reported Daniel Berrigan, "the American scene was no longer a good scene. It was, in fact, an immoral scene. . . . Ours was a scene that moral men could not continue to approve if they were to deserve the name of men."[75]

While a seminal event may help explain the triggering of outrage in hitherto naive or trusting people, how is one to understand the deeper, more gradual process that transforms the politically sophisticated moderate into a firebrand? Here too the seminal event plays a role. We have seen previously how the process of radicalization feeds on an initial self-perception of uniqueness, a belief in moral purity, and a sense of personal responsibility. This self-image is not unique to political offenders, but it is shared by many politically orthodox reformers. Thus, the frustrations of experience often result in the erosion of the orthodox reformer's faith in the system within which he or she works. When basic precepts of law and order lose their sanctity, either through experience or education, the seminal event will supply the catalyst for breaking with the past, impelling the future political offender into action.

For the founder of the radical environmental group Earth First!, the political erosion grew slowly out of long personal experience in the field of conventional Washington politics. Dave Foreman, former chief lobbyist for the well-respected Wilderness Society, describes his experience:

> Time and time again, we'd come out of those meetings having made all the concessions, rather than having gained any. We bent over backward to be reasonable and credible and politically pragmatic. And by contrasting that timid stance with the emotional, hard-line, no-compromise approach taken by the mining, timber, and livestock industries . . . in their lobbying efforts, it wasn't hard to figure out why they were winning and we were getting only the crumbs. . . . Our group would operate outside the political system and make it known that we had fundamental differences with the worldviews of the political/industrial establishment.[76]

## THE INDIVIDUAL AND THE COLLECTIVE

Having withdrawn from a corrupt society and political system, and having made a new commitment to establishing a better moral order, few political offenders seek an individual apotheosis. Instead, at this stage the rebel often seeks others who share common visions. Not surprisingly, the rebel often finds them looking for him or her as well. Perhaps by joining others in a common cause and by taking the collective efforts to the public stage, the political offender affirms self-worth and belies the prospect that his or her alienation from society will be viewed as the outcome of a personal flaw.

For many political offenders, the hearing of a "call" and a clear vision of the future are not sufficient to lead them to radical action. Despite their rejection of the larger society, the dissenter still longs to belong and seeks membership in movements or causes to overcome or avoid social isolation. The involvement in a collective organization or conspiracy often supplies the potential activist with a gratifying opportunity to conform to the norms of a group, albeit an illegal or socially rejected one, and to be perceived by others as a contributing member of a cadre with a positive agenda. Eventually the "follower" may assume a more active role.

SDS activist Jane Alpert, for example, fell in love with a young man who was on the fringe of the radical left in the 1960s. When the young man became involved with two fugitive French Canadian separatists, Alpert, fearing she would be excluded, plunged into his cause by bombing first one federal building and later others. In retrospect, she reported, "the threat of being left out, especially at a time when Sam was drifting away from me, was enough to make up my mind."[77]

Interestingly, even those that practice the paradigm lone-wolf political offense—presidential assassination—have been described by the National Commission on the Causes and Prevention of Violence as people who tried earlier to identify with some cause or ideologically based movement. But these assassins, despite their noted efforts, seem unable to participate with others in an orderly pursuit of a cause.[78] Booth identified strongly with the Southern cause but was unable to stay in uniform. Guiteau tried unsuccessfully to become a member of the Oneida religious community. Czolgosz was a disillusioned Roman Catholic. Moreover, virtually all the assassins in these studies denied their own responsibility for their life failures. Most suffered from a high degree of self-loathing, resulting in an escape to fantasy. Anxious to purge themselves of this loathing, and incapable of sustained work toward a long-range goal, the assassins developed the compulsion for one tremendous burst of frenzied activity that would "accomplish something of great worth."

Often, the opportunity to join with others in a common enterprise that includes dissent, disobedience, violence, or rebellion is critical to the incipient political criminal's radicalization. Exposure to hard-core radicals (as in a prison or military setting) or to other favorable environmental factors (such as those supplied by religious and academic enclosures) can be an important step in the process.

In the 1960s academic institutions provided a fertile hothouse for the growth of the anti-Vietnam protest movement. Religious congregations have supplied a similarly supportive environment for sanctuary workers and for Central American peace protestors since the 1980s. Churches and their members have been so closely interconnected with political activism that an Oakland County sheriff's deputy noted to a reporter, "Now if we want to know when there's a crime wave of civil disobedience coming, we consult the [churches'] liturgical calendar."[79] Religious retreats also gave rise to Witness for Peace, a grassroots effort to keep United States armed forces out of Nicaragua. One participant in a meeting called in late 1983 at the Kirkbridge Retreat Center in northeastern Pennsylvania, for the purpose of Bible study and prayer—and for political action—reported the following:

> We . . . together drew up a statement pledging ourselves to a plan of action in the event of a United States invasion of Nicaragua. That "contingency plan" was subsequently presented to each of our constituencies in the churches and sent to every member of Congress, to the Departments of State and Defense, to the CIA, and to the president, informing them of our intentions should they undertake direct military action against Nicaragua.[80]

The religious activists, in their Pledge of Resistance, called for peaceful occupation of the field offices of all United States senators and representatives until they voted to end American intervention in Nicaragua. A year later, in December 1984, the civil disobedience pledge was expanded to include the occupation of "pre-designated U.S. federal facilities, including federal buildings, military installations, offices of the Central Intelligence Agency, the State Department, and other appropriate places."[81] By January 1986 more than seventy thousand people had signed the pledge, thus constituting one of the largest publicized organizations of potential political offenders in American history.

Not all associations of prospective political offenders operate in the open. Some are decidedly unwilling to submit either their tenets of belief or their membership lists to open scrutiny. The right-wing organization Posse Comitatus has sought an unusual level of secrecy, making pursuit and investigation by the authorities a difficult matter. It is reported that

> indeed, the Posse has no discernable leader, and only the vaguest structure. Michael Beach, a retired machinist from Portland, Oregon, is thought to have founded the Posse in 1969. Yet there is no evidence that he ever exerted or tried to exert much control over the group. The Posse has no national headquarters, no executive board, no letterhead. In two years of investigating the

radical right, I have never come across a Posse Comitatus booth at a convention or even a central mailing address for the group. There are loosely organized state branches in Oregon, California, Wisconsin, and Missouri, but the Posse consists mostly of local bands among friends and acquaintances. A typical Posse meeting involves eight or ten men sitting around a kitchen table, complaining of injustice and planning to exercise rights that, by law, they don't have. Recruitment is entirely by word of mouth and personal contact.[82]

Some of these political action associations, structured or loose, overt or covert, formed at universities, churches, or kitchen tables, provide a support structure for rebellious activism. The activist's sense of special destiny and of separation from the conformist society now becomes reinforced by a new camaraderie and organizational affirmation. As with a feedback loop, a bonding by common goal and deed intensifies the identity of the offender as different and special. One friend of the Berrigan brothers wrote about their exclusive "club," consisting only of those who had ventured out into danger in the name of a cause: "You can't criticize the Berrigans this year. They look down on anyone who hasn't risked as much as they have. They'll barely break bread with you if you haven't burned your draft card. Talk about ghettos! That ghetto of martyrs is the most exclusive club of all."[83]

Clinard and Quinney point out that the political offender often seeks, furthermore, to enhance his or her sense of self-worth by soliciting strong sympathy and even support from "the people."[84] In any society, there may be a wide segment of the population ready to respond in the way the political criminal hopes. Segments of society that do not share majority values or that are excluded from political power may welcome and even celebrate political dissent and disobedience.

In the United States, the historic "peace churches" (the Church of the Brethren, the Society of Friends, and the Mennonites) have provided community support to war resisters during World War II, the Korean War, and the Vietnam conflict. Similarly, the African American community has offered at least psychological support to the rebels and rioters of the incendiary 1960s. The Southern rebels in the American Civil War relied not only on community support but also on the state-like apparatus of the Confederacy. Many subsequent and contemporary insurgents—whether in South Africa, Vietnam, Quebec, Afghanistan, Ireland, Nicaragua, or Israel's West Bank—have been successful in representing not only individual but also communal dissension from the ruling regime. Thus, the political activist may find gratification in believing him- or herself a representative of a wider political collective, much as the soldier in uniform is confident he or she speaks for the nation or country.

## INSANITY AND THE POLITICAL OFFENDER

Since public opinion, as well as modern psychology, might view the political offender's behavior as egocentric, monomaniacal, or megalomaniacal—though history may later view it as altruistic, patriotic, and farsighted—it is not surprising that the political offender's mental health is often put to the test by society and by those in authority. Often, there is considerable room for doubt.

### A STUDY IN IDEALISM AND DISILLUSION

In June 1976, Charles A. Tuller, a white 52-year-old former high official in the federal government, went on trial in Houston, Texas.[85] With his sons Jonathan, age twenty-one, and Bryce, twenty-two, Tuller was charged with hijacking an Eastern Airlines plane from Houston to Havana, Cuba. During the hijacking an airline ticket agent had been killed by the hijackers. Before that the three defendants, then residing in Alexandria, Virginia, had killed a bank manager and a policeman while unsuccessfully trying to rob a bank in Crystal City, Virginia.

At the trial, Dr. Duard Bok, a Houston psychiatrist, described Charles Tuller as "partly mentally ill," suffering from a delusion that he was being persecuted by the authorities for activities that were personally and professionally correct. Tuller perceived the government in general and the Justice Department, his recent employer, in particular, as corrupt and dishonest. He also believed it was morally correct for individuals to resort to violence in order to achieve justice. "If he had not been mentally ill and delusional, he would not have committed the acts he did," Dr. Bok testified.

Tuller's former wife described her husband as "highly intelligent" but subject to violent outbursts. She testified that Tuller, a civil rights worker, had became obsessed with the plight of the minority groups he was trying to help and "totally lost his professional detachment."

"I feel that what I did, I did with honor, and with the intention of making my country a more humane place," said Charles Tuller after his arrest.[86] *Washington Post* reporter Eugene L. Meyer, interviewing him at the Arlington County Jail, described Tuller as balding, with a gentle-looking face and wire-rimmed glasses. "I have broken the laws of this country, and therefore I am a criminal," Tuller added. "I have no argument with this, and no doubts about it. But I think that a higher law must consider a man's motivations, his principles, his aims and goals."

A native of Toledo, Ohio, Tuller graduated from the New School for Social Research in New York City, and worked as a Wall Street broker and later as an operator of a small business. Becoming engrossed in the civil rights movement in the early 1960s, he served as vice-chairman of the Newark, New Jersey, branch of the Congress on Racial Equality and was an employee of Newark's Business and Industrial Coordinating Council, which sought jobs for unemployed African Americans. The businessman-turned-reformer had then served as a troubleshooter for the Community Relations Service of the U.S. Department of Justice and concluded his career working with the Office of Minority Business Enterprise (OMBE) at the Commerce Department.

"Over these years," Tuller reported, "I began to realize there were basic things wrong, that we were treating symptoms not causes." In the late 1960s he became convinced that "direct action" by a young, revolutionary avant garde was required, since "the idea of a loyal opposition in this country was overall quite ineffectual." In early 1971, Tuller, his sons, and a couple of other young men decided to form an action group. They set out to equip themselves doctrinally and militarily so they "could eventually break with our government or what is called law, and try to do something about reconstructing a new system." Although Tuller claimed that the group's physical conditioning and familiarity with the use of arms was purely defensive, and that their intent was merely to "talk with local people and find indigenous leaders to engage in radical politics of change," their revolutionary strategy took a violent turn when he realized that the group lacked the funds to carry out its plans.

By October 1972, the Tullers found themselves in the lobby of the Crystal City Bank, guns blazing, in the middle of a shootout. Bank Manager Harry J. Candee refused to surrender his keys and Israel P. Gonzalez, a police officer making his rounds, surprised the impoverished revolutionaries in the midst of their holdup attempt. After killing the bank manager and Officer Gonzalez, the robbers fled to Houston, where the elder Tuller knew of a surgeon who could help the injured members of the gang. Since the surgeon was out of town for the weekend, the group decided, apparently on the spur of the moment, to hijack a plane to Cuba.

After shooting a ticket agent at the Houston airport and successfully landing in Havana, the group was dismayed to find that their "idealistic views about Cuba" were quickly shattered by personal experiences. They found a Cuba dominated by Russians and by a caste system, with most of the population having little opportunity to "become part of the decision-making mechanism." Living on small stipends provided by the Castro government, they did not go to work, however, "because that was the first step to being Cubanized."

At the first opportunity, and with funds provided by the Cuban government, Tuller and his sons left for Nassau and from there went to Miami, passing undetected through United States Customs. Although they had hoped to pick up their revolutionary mission where they had left off, there was still the problem of a depleted treasury. The family's next "fund raiser" took place in a K-Mart in Fayetteville, North Carolina. This robbery attempt, too, was foiled and resulted in the capture of Bryce, the oldest Tuller son, by store employees.

On July 7, 1973, the remaining family members decided that they were "not going to leave Bryce behind . . . that's just the kind of family we are." They turned themselves in to the F.B.I. Summarizing the events of the previous three years, Charles A. Tuller concluded, "All I can say is we were three or four people who tried, and the fact that we weren't seemingly very successful I don't think at all [detracts] from the idea that people have got to dedicate themselves in some meaningful way to stopping this [national] suicide we're involved with."

Charles A. Tuller was first tried in Arlington, Virginia, for the murders of the bank manager and the police officer. He was found competent to stand trial, as well as sane and criminally responsible for his deeds. Upon conviction he was sentenced to a minimum of thirty years in prison. Later, in Houston, Tuller was also tried in federal court for air piracy in connection with the hijacking. Once more the court determined that he was sane and accountable for his crimes.

While the courts concluded that Tuller was sane under the law, the family's escapades leave a lingering suspicion that Tuller and his sons did not have a firm grasp on reality or on their place in it. There is little doubt that their activities were politically motivated: they sincerely believed that they were operating on a higher moral plane than the government officials whom they blamed for the callous treatment of society's ills. Nevertheless, even by the most lenient appraisal, their plots and deeds might be considered sufficiently bizarre to raise doubts about the judicial conclusion of "sanity."

## INSANITY OR SERVICE TO HIGHER MORALITY?

Whatever might be said about the Tuller family, delusion and insanity do lie in the background of some rebels and political offenders. In 1918, criminologist Maurice Parmalee concluded that mental illness or disorder, of one type or another, was prevalent among most political offenders.[87] After dividing political offenders into three categories—the pathological, the emotional, and the rational—Parmalee observed that those who fit in the "rational" category were by far the least numerous.[88] The predominant category, he concluded, was the emotional one. Those within this category he viewed as "sympathetic" persons who responded compassionately to human misfortunes and who set out to ameliorate them. "Pathological" political offenders included those who were psychologically inclined to acts of violence against individuals of authority or of prominence, with whom they had little or no personal contact.

The image of the political criminal as mentally abnormal has been reiterated by other criminologists and psychiatrists. In 1969, the National Commission on the Causes and Prevention of Violence, which looked into the roots of political assassination in America, noted that most, if not all, assassins and assailants had experienced a disruption of normal family or parent-child relationships. Of the men, all were reported to be loners, having had difficulty making friends of either sex, and particularly in establishing lasting relationships with women. On this and other evidence, some of the Commission's experts suggested that "all those who have assassinated or attempted to assassinate Presidents of the United States . . . have been mentally disturbed persons who did not kill to advance any rational political plan."[89] One of the Commission's consultants, Dr. Lawrence Z. Freedman of the University of Chicago, strongly argued that the typical offenders against United States presidents were "mentally disturbed persons" and that with one possible exception, "there have been no [genuine] *political* assassination attempts directed at the President of the United States."[90] Excepting from his analysis the Puerto Rican nationalists' attack upon President Truman, Freedman concluded that all other attacks were "products of mental illness with no direct political content"(p.2). Another consulting psychiatrist went so far as to diagnose the assassins' mental illness as constituting "schizophrenia, in most instances a paranoid type"(p.62).

Despite the Violence Commission's subsequent conclusion that a diagnosis of mental illness alone did not explain why certain disturbed persons sought to become assassins (rather than undertake different types of criminal, antisocial, or bizarre behavior) (pp.63–64), other social and behavioral scientists have nevertheless seen the Commission's conclusion as a psychiatric or psychoanalytic overindulgence. Criminologist Stephen Schafer, for instance, criticized the report for speaking "in orthodox Freudian terms, hinting at the offenders' unconscious need to commit political crimes."[91] Indeed, the Commission consultant's willingness to offer "paranoid schizophrenia" as the specific mental malady of presidential assailants whiffs suspiciously of a snap diagnosis. One wonders how diagnosticians personally unacquainted with their subjects could so precisely define their ailment.

## THE UTILITY OF INSANITY

Clearly, the question of the political offender's mental health has a direct bearing on such pragmatic issues as his competence to stand trial, the likely success of a plea of insanity, and the suitable sanctions to be imposed on him or her. But the label of "insanity" has other uses as well. First, it cloaks the seemingly inexplicable violence with a scientific patina and conceals an insidious questioning of the validity of the actor's cause. A mentally aberrant offender, characterized as out of touch with reality, may taint the cause for which he or she stands and fights. To the political offender, who undertakes the offending deed in hope of eventual popular support, a court's finding of, or even the plea of, insanity is an ignominious defeat.

Thus the political offender tends to vehemently resist the insanity defense. When Charlotte Corday was tried for the assassination of French revolutionary leader Jean-Paul Marat and her advocate pleaded her insane, she complained that the defense was unworthy of her.[92] The Marquis de Sade, allegedly, was confined to a mental institution rather than to a prison, in order to lessen his standing and to remove his "obscene" plays and novels from the French intellectual community. American abolitionist John Brown, after his conviction for the Harper's Ferry raid, strenuously resisted the urging of some of his sympathizers to enter a plea of insanity. Callazo, the Puerto Rican who attempted to assassinate President Truman, refused to allow his lawyers to plead insanity, despite the psychiatric claim that his goal and plan of action showed little grasp of reality.[93] And Sirhan Sirhan similarly rejected the double-edged effects of the insanity defense. Only poet Ezra Pound, to avoid a public trial for treason (for making radio broadcasts on behalf of fascist Italy in World War II) was persuaded to accept the alternative of confinement to a mental institution.

Moreover, a previous study by this author of the treatment of the mentally ill, alcoholics, drug addicts, and "sexual psychopaths" in the United States clearly demonstrated that the resort to therapeutic or psychiatric labels and measures for dealing with various classes of social deviants, including political offenders, has not been without substantial peril.[94] Unwittingly, the therapeutic and assertedly nonpunitive approach can be turned into an oppressive tool in the hands of functionaries who discover that under the guise of "therapy" the state may mete out greater sanctions than those available under the penal process. Despite the therapeutic label's promise of humanitarian protections, most societies have seen to it that a high price, in terms of liberty as well as of status, is exacted for the questionable benefits of being considered "insane."

The fallacy, cruelty, and human rights abuses inherent in attributing the political offenders' deeds to mental disorder are now widely known. For nearly half a century, the Soviet Union relied on special mental clinics for the detention and reorientation of political, religious, and ideological opponents.[95] Responding to charges that mentally sound opponents of the regime were being suppressed in insane asylums, the Soviet Union's official daily, *Izvestia*, assured its readers in 1972 that the Soviet institutions contained only those "who have committed socially dangerous acts in a state of derangement."[96] These "socially dangerous" and "deranged" acts included such activities as membership in the Seventh Day Adventist Church and adherence to its dietary rules, as Birute Poskene, a Lithuanian mother who lost custody of her children and was confined to a mental hospital, was to discover.[97]

No wonder, therefore, that even when faced with death, incarceration, or other punishment, political offenders have resisted the mental illness label. Despite the apparent benefits of a finding of insanity (exemption from criminal responsibility and punishment), political offenders would, as a rule, rather be labeled criminal than ill. The record of the former Soviet Union's abuses demonstrates to future generations that the designation of rational political offenders as insane not only overlooks the true underlying causes of their behavior and risks unnecessary overreaction to the dangers they pose but also unduly diminishes their role and status in the estimation of existing and future societies.

## HONOR FOR THE UNDESERVING:
## THE RUSH TO BE POLITICAL

Exploring social and psychological factors in the making of the political dissident, we should not underestimate the role of the media in identifying the discontented and, frequently, in lending undue substance and credibility to their claims. In any political struggle the contending parties themselves can always be counted upon to appeal to popular myths and support either by lauding the altruism (or proclaiming the viciousness) of the rebels, or, on the other hand, proclaiming the legitimacy (or decrying the wickedness) of those in authority. These claims are almost always countered by a barrage of opposite propaganda from the other camp. A major strength of the mass media is its ability to reach out to inform and empower the discontented by bringing an end to their ignorance and isolation. Not many years ago, such isolation was common. In 1937 George Orwell observed that "talking once with a miner I asked him when the housing shortage first became acute in his district; he answered 'When we were told about it,' meaning that till recently people's standards were so low that they took almost any degree of overcrowding for granted."[98] Coleman was one of the first to point to the vital role of the mass media in the development or expansion of communal conflicts: "Whether the local newspaper creates an issue through editorial activity or sensationalist reporting, or whether it merely seeks out and reports events which create an issue, it is true that many controversies are born when community members unsuspectingly open their newspaper one morning. Similarly, in times of disaster or crisis, the mass media become of crucial importance."[99]

Contemporary mass media technologies far exceed the opportunities offered by earlier eras' marketplace rumors or angry citizens' gatherings for the fanning of popular discontent. By 1937 the power of a newsreel showing Chicago police firing point-blank into a crowd of labor pickets, killing nine, riveted the attention of congressional investigators.[100] The civil rights movement of the 1960s was greatly aided by news footage of police using cattle prods, dogs, and clubs against peaceful marchers in Birmingham and Selma, Alabama. Bringing the horrors of the Vietnam War into the living rooms of America each night is accredited with accelerating and deepening opposition to that war. Some insist that global communications through television and facsimile machine are responsible for the success of the "velvet revolution" in Eastern Europe and the brief success of the democracy movement in the People's Republic of China. The 1991 anti-Gorbachev coup attempt in the Soviet Union, likewise, was foiled in part by the ability of its opponents to keep open the lines of communication to and from the rest of the world.

The speed with which news can reach around the world and the inability of governments to control communications in and out of their countries means that those seeking sympathy and support have a greater chance of success than ever before. While much communication competes for print space and air time, there is nothing like a massacre, an assassination, the bombing of an aircraft, or the razing of houses to rivet the attention of millions. Ted Koppel, host of ABC's *Nightline*, would agree that "without television, terrorism becomes rather like the philosopher's hypothetical tree falling in the forest: no one hears it fall and therefore it has no reason for being. And television, without terrorism, while not deprived of all interesting things in the world, is nonetheless deprived of one of the most interesting."[101]

Rapid and ubiquitous communications mean that the processes that may escalate disquietude into rebellion will be accelerated. It is no wonder that political dissidents actively seek the media stages of the world, often by creating what has come to be called a "media event"—a demonstration or other activity that has no other purpose than to obtain mass attention for the political platform of the activists.

The media, for its part, has duly and eagerly reported the adventures and misadventures of challengers to authority. Episodes of political, racial, social, and economic unrest, graduating into violent assaults and terrorism against persons and property, have received widespread coverage in the printed press, radio, and television, as have the perpetrators' political grievances and agendas. Together with this coverage often comes an unwarranted aggrandizement of the activists, contributing to the heroic myth of political crime and rebellion.

As the strains and stresses in American society came into full bloom in the late 1960s and early 1970s, virtually every social problem was translated into radical political terminology. Claims of racial, economic, and social deprivations all came to be expressed as political issues. With the growth of the feminist and gay rights movements, sexual relations assumed new political dimensions. In addition, the rights of Native Americans, prisoners, students, the handicapped, children, and senior citizens were all cast more as political than as racial, cultural, socioeconomic, religious, medical, or historical problems. America's political activists were not reluctant to adopt the rhetoric and style (if not always the violence) of insurgent groups and guerrilla movements around the world—challenging America's police, courts, prisons, and universities, as well as the defense establishment and its "military-industrial complex." As these claims were seriously considered by the media, ever-larger numbers of common offenders asserted political motives for their deeds, seemingly in an effort to rationalize the stigmas of their common crimes.

Skyjackers, who revived the long-dormant practices of piracy (carried out in earlier days for personal greed and adventure), transmuted these ancient crimes to aircraft seizure in the name of political protest. These new pirates of the air sought applause and asylum for their acts. Some modern freelance espionage agents shed their dark and old-fashioned identities as adventurers and entrepreneurs to emerge as activists for global peace, disarmament, or similar noble ends. Like America's Ethel and Julius Rosenberg, convicted of sharing the atom bomb secrets with the Soviets, or like England's Kim Philby, a high-placed spy who ultimately sought refuge in Moscow, they proclaimed themselves "political offenders" dedicated to higher causes rather than traitors who served foreign powers for money or thrills.

Whole classes of conventional offenders pressed their claim to be political prisoners on the theory that their offenses were rooted in, and attributable to, a socially, economically, racially, or politically exploitative system. Describing themselves as political prisoners, the inmates of the Attica, New York, penitentiary in 1972 sought release and mass transportation to a politically sympathetic country of asylum. Samuel Melville, later killed in the Attica uprising, wrote in his prison newspaper, *Iced Pig*:

> Of primary importance is t[he] coming awareness of ourselves as *political prisoners*. No matter how heinous t[he] "crime" u have been convicted of, u are a political prisoner just as much as Angela [Davis]. *Every act has a cause and effect.* T[he] cause of your "crime" is that u found yourself in a society that offered no prospects for a life of fulfillment and sharing with your brothers and sisters. A society where u were taught to compete and beat t[he] guy next to u

because if u didn't, he'd beat u. A society whose every facet and angle is thoroughly controlled by t[he] Pig-dogs of t[he] corporation giants of Amerika.[102]

Even perpetrators of the most base offenses, motivated by personal pathology and urges for bestial gratification, often received undeserved and uncritical media attention when they portrayed their crimes as a function of some new "political" insight. Eldridge Cleaver, later Minister of Information of the Black Panther Party, advanced the proposition that interracial rape should be viewed as a political protest when carried out by a male of a deprived class or race against a female of the oppressing society. In his letters from prison, Cleaver asserted:

> I became a rapist. To refine my technique and *modus operandi*, I started out practicing on black girls . . . and when I considered myself smooth enough I crossed the tracks and sought out white prey. I did this consciously, deliberately, willfully, methodically . . . rape was an insurrectionary act. It delighted me that I was defying and trampling upon the white man's laws, upon his system of values, and I was defiling his women.[103]

Leaders of the anti–Vietnam War movement, like Father Philip Berrigan, himself imprisoned for destroying United States selective service records, gave support to the claims of common criminals to political status: "So we had that common bond with them; in a very wide sense, almost everybody there was a political prisoner. And almost all of them had the firm conviction of confronting the system, using the best means at hand."[104] The then United States Ambassador to the United Nations, Andrew Young, indeed conceded at a New York press conference that a large number of the country's prison inmates were "political prisoners," and the media faithfully gave additional credence to this claim.

Even such pathological misfits as Charles Manson and his followers (the "Family"), who were charged with some of the most atrocious and gratuitous murders in California history, found the media listening when they cast their deeds as revolutionary acts designed to bring down a "corrupt" system. Manson asserted that his "family's" killings would help trigger a racial war— prophesied by a lyric from the Beatles' hit "Helter Skelter." After "helter-skelter," the war in which African Americans would be exterminated and whites militarily exhausted, Manson and his disciples were to emerge from hiding and ascend to political supremacy.[105]

The image of Charles Manson as a political revolutionary was given considerable credence in the Yippie and leftist fringe literature of the time. Political militant Bernadine Dohrn told a convention of the Students for a Democratic Society that "the Weathermen dig Charles Manson." A San Francisco underground paper, *Tuesday's Child*, which described itself as the

Voice of the Yippies, named Manson "Man of the Year." And after visiting Manson in jail, political activist Jerry Rubin, of Chicago Seven Trial fame, proclaimed, "I fell in love with Charlie Manson the first time I saw his cherub face and sparkling eyes on TV."[106] More important than the beliefs of Dohrn, Rubin, and the Yippies, their attractions to Manson were widely broadcast by the mass media to a less-than-comprehending public.

The culmination of the era's dance between self-styled revolutionaries and a sensationalism-prone media came in the spring of 1974.[107] After kidnapping Patricia Hearst, daughter of *San Francisco Examiner* publishing magnate William Randolph Hearst, a group identifying themselves as the Symbionese Liberation Army failed to demand ransom for their captive. Instead, they commenced a publicity campaign, filing their taped "communiqués" with various radio stations and other media outlets. The published "objectives" of the SLA were a potpourri ranging from the destruction of capitalism and corporate institutions to the opening of prisons, from the abolition of marriage to the humane and loving care of the aged and the young. Ultimately they demanded that Mr. Hearst provide free food to welfare recipients, government pensioners, disabled veterans, and released convicts. In mid-April, the SLA, together with Ms. Hearst, robbed a bank at gunpoint, and several people were wounded. In a communiqué from Ms. Hearst, newly converted to the revolution and now calling herself "Tania, a soldier in the people's army," the SLA defended the robbery as necessary to support the revolutionary cause, noting that "the difference between a criminal act and a revolutionary act is shown by what the money is used for." A month later, the SLA, never numbering more than ten, was virtually extinguished by the death of six members in a shootout with Los Angeles police, telecast live.

Despite her claims to have been sexually assaulted and coerced into ostensible cooperation with the SLA, Ms. Hearst was later convicted and sentenced to seven years for her part in the bank robbery. She served twenty-two months before President Carter commuted her sentence. Two months later she married her former bodyguard and slipped back into privileged seclusion.

The appeal of a claimed political justification for such offenses is illustrated by the lengthy conversations between author Robert B. Kaiser and the imprisoned Sirhan Sirhan, the Jordanian assassin of presidential candidate Robert F. Kennedy. In the interview Kaiser probed into Sirhan's motives for the shooting of Kennedy. "Well, with [John F.] Kennedy, I loved him," Sirhan responded, "and to me, President Kennedy was infallible. He was a man, you know, I loved him! And I thought Kennedy, Bob, would do the same, you know, do the same. But, hell, he fucked up."[108] Sirhan was referring to Robert F. Kennedy's alleged "betrayal," his failure to stand up for the Palestinian cause.

Throughout the continuing interview, Sirhan frequently and vigorously objected to Kaiser's personal line of inquiry. Particularly when pressed to detail his own youthful disappointment by his father's desertion of the family, a fact suggested by some psychologists as the underlying cause for Sirhan's preoccupation with Robert Kennedy's "betrayal," Sirhan reiterated, "They're all trying to dig into my family background. That had no effect on my actions. . . . Had I killed my wife, had I killed my brother . . . [I could] understand their trying to delve into my background. But, you see, this was political."

Once more, when Kaiser sought to explore Sirhan's relations with a young woman, Sirhan retorted, "Don't talk about women to me." Taken aback, the interviewer asked the reason for Sirhan's objection. "This is political," said Sirhan. "This is politically motivated," he started to giggle nervously. "This is heh heh, political, heh heh, politically motivated."[109]

In his exploratory book, *The Political Crime: The Problem of Morality and Crime*, criminologist Stephen Schafer identifies a category of political activists and dissidents he designates "pseudoconvictional."[110] This group, observes Schafer, consists mostly of common criminals who posture themselves as acting out of altruistic convictions. Unlike most common criminals, the pseudos' goals need not necessarily be personal gain of a material sort. Instead, they might be motivated by the thrill of adventure: living beyond and outside the law and sharing in popular fame and adulation. Their claims of political motive, however strenuously asserted, are thus mere excuses.

Pseudoconvictional criminals can be found not only among those struggling against authority but also in the ranks of those serving political authority. Many despots, tyrants, and dictators throughout history have abused authority and exploited society not for some political and public objectives but for their own pathological gratification. Similarly, many individuals and groups who proclaim political causes to justify their resistance and rebellion against authority are merely pseudoconvictional offenders. How then are the genuine political dissidents to be distinguished from the pseudos?

### ACCENT ON THE POSITIVE

While those in authority usually seek to discredit the political rebel and offender by pointing to his dysfunctions, pathologies, or disingenuousness, other social observers and behavioral scientists see the rebel in a more favorable light. Criminologist Stephen Schafer voiced fundamental objections to the characterization of politically motivated offenders as psychiatrically unbalanced. Instead, he viewed political offenders as those who had escaped the stifling conformity imposed by society. Rejecting psychiatric labeling, Schafer relied instead on what might be described as "learning theory" to explain the apparent specialness of the political offender:

> To think of political criminals in terms of "abnormality" or some kind of mental derangement appears reasonable only to those who forget the pluralistic nature of morality and the inadequacies of the socialization process. . . . In the false assumption that all members of the society are well socialized and thus can and do understand the "command" of morality, the sovereign cannot believe that anybody with a sane mind would rebel against his moral tenets. . . . But those who do not accept these moral principles (*because* their socialization to this morality has been inadequate), and therefore do not feel happy with the morality that guides their society, are not necessarily mentally sick. . . .
>
> The political criminal sees no reason for believing that man's true happiness and perfection depend on understanding the place the sovereign assigned to him in this globe. He does not suffer any kind of mental disorder; he is just an inadequately socialized explorer of a vision—a vision that would not emerge if he were adequately socialized.[111]

While Schafer's inherently favorable portrayal of the political rebel attributed his specialness to "inadequate" socialization, Harvard social psychologist Lawrence Kohlberg viewed the rebel's uniqueness as a product of special and favorable developmental factors. Seeking an explanation for the rebel's escape from conformity, Kohlberg elucidated what he perceived as man's or woman's common "stages of moral development," clustering around three distinct levels—the preconventional, the conventional, and the postconventional.[112] At the preconventional level, a person responds to existing rules of right and wrong by considering them in terms of hedonistic consequences (punishment and reward). At the conventional level, one's maintaining the standards of his or her nation, peer group, or family is perceived as valuable and desirable in its own right. Right behavior at this stage consists of doing one's "duty," of maintaining law and order for their own sake.

Finally, Kohlberg argued that while all humans go through the same sequence of stages, only a chosen few reach the postconventional level. Among the latter he lists Martin Luther King Jr. and Mahatma Gandhi. At this highest level, one is motivated by sensitivity and concern for others, and by a commitment to a universal and higher law.[113] These chosen few observe moral values and principles that have validity and application without regard to the authority of the nation or group to which they belong. "At heart, these are universal principles of justice, . . . of . . . equality, of human rights, and of respect for the dignity of human beings."[114] Stirred by this noble image of the postconventional political rebel, Kohlberg was not only seeking greater understanding of the process of moral development that leads to this higher stage but also entertaining futuristic hopes to create or nurture more such righteous individuals to serve as humanity's eternal guardians against abusers of power.

It is evident, however, that despite the urge to either discredit or enno-
ble the political offender, both common intuition and scholarly literature
strongly suggest that the potential for rebellion exists in all. This conclusion is supported by American historical experience. It was also suggested
in the early part of this century by Maurice Parmalee's three categories of
political offenders.[115] Parmalee found the so-called "rational" political offenders the least prevalent. He believed that those with highly developed reason-
ing capacities—as contrasted with those possessing sympathetic and com-
passionate personalities—were unlikely to resort to violence as a means of
social reform except in instances of last resort.[116] But Parmalee maintained
throughout that any person might become a political offender for reasons of
individual or collective belief or of conviction under particularly stressful
circumstances.

A more recent public opinion poll conducted in Florida confirmed Parmalee's observation by disclosing that 58 percent of those interviewed professed
their willingness to violate state laws that conflicted with strongly held religious or moral convictions.[117] The large numbers and diverse types of people
who have been involved in political activism throughout the world's and this
nation's history, and the wide range of offenses with which they have been
charged, confirm that neither theories of psychological or social pathology nor
doctrines of socialization and moral development (much like the theory of status congruence discussed earlier) can alone explain the widely disparate
phenomena of human determination, courage, and sacrifice in standing up
against authority. That not all political offenders are moved by a single force
or combination of forces must readily be admitted. What is important is the
inescapable conclusion that nearly any man or woman might venture out to
resist abuse of power when individual and communal pressures become
unbearable. There is no universally held value or common denominator
among those who struggle against authority. In this fight ordinary people
pushed too far join ranks with the embittered, the alienated, the criminal, and
the insane. Anyone can become a political offender, a combatant in the war
against authority—regardless of status, class, race, gender, religion, or ethnicity. Indeed, it may be said that rebellion is the one nearly universal constant of
the human condition, the one experience that most of us have shared at one
time or another, in response to different manifestations of abuse of power.

The human capacity, indeed propensity, for rebellion works to erode
power and authority at every level of society: international, national, local, and
familial. Foundations of power and legitimacy crumble under the unceasing
attack of political strife and rebellion. Each time a fragment is removed from
the foundation of legitimacy by a rebellious individual or faction in pursuit of
greater autonomy, the stability of the foundation is endangered, increasing
the possibility that the entire structure could collapse.

The rebel and his or her makeup are thus crucial to the balance of forces needed for the maintenance of political legitimacy. We now understand at least half of the zero-net-gain equation that reflects the historical contest between authority and autonomy. Moving on from our study of the main actors in the camp of autonomy, we must now proceed to examine the forces of authority.

# CHAPTER TWO

# Abuse of Power:
# The Roots of Rebellion

The sword comes upon the world on account of the delay of justice and the perversion of justice.

— Judah Hanassi, *In Ethics of the Fathers*

The fanaticism of the political offender is frequently matched only by the fanaticism of the government agent.

— Modified from Francis A. Allen, *The Crime of Politics*

[Revolutions are the] sudden rotations in human affairs . . . permitted by Providence, to remind mankind of their natural equality, to check the pride of wealth, to restrain the insolence of rank and family distinctions, which too frequently oppress the various classes in society.

— Mercy Otis Warren, "History of the Rise, Progress, and Termination of the American Revolution" (1805), in Virginius Dabney, *The Patriots: The American Revolution—Generation of Genius*

## THE DEMONIZATION OF AUTHORITY

In the previous chapter, we examined the rebel's stirring of the simmering sociopolitical cauldron and described the rebel's Promethean task as a bearer of progress. This portrayal, of course, casts "authority"—the rebel's eternal antagonist—in a most unflattering light. Whenever the rebel stands for reform and progress, the existing authorities (political, religious, social, or economic) are left to stand for the less-glamourous cause, regressive resistance to change. But as we know from the lessons of history, not all resistance to change need be viewed as either stifling or evil.

In the first place, not all, and not even most, exercises of authority are tyrannical or malevolent. In many countries, communities, and smaller political groups, a strong case can be made that both the holders of the reins of power and the institutions of governance are sensitive to the public good and give the people an appropriate choice in what happens to them. In these situations, where an honest attempt is made by those in power to accommodate evolving needs and demands within an existing framework, the government's resistance to unorthodox means of change can be viewed as mere steadfastness in the preservation of liberty, justice, and peace. Such steadfastness (often labeled "conservatism") is not to be condemned.

Nevertheless, those representing authority and its institutions are invariably demonized by those calling for change. Aspiring and triumphant rebels usually paint those who have gone before them in shades of ungodliness, evil, and corruption. The rebels' legitimacy, support for their cause, and their potential success are indeed dependent upon the people's acceptance of the demonic portrayal of those they seek to overturn.

The demonization of authority is well illustrated as far back as the biblical accounts of the Hebrews' struggle against Pharaonic exploitation and enslavement. So persistent was Pharaoh in his tyrannical abuse of the Israelites that ten plagues had to be brought upon the land of Egypt before its ruler would let the children of Israel go.[1] Regardless of the accuracy of the historical details of this story, it is evident that without a corrupt and evil Pharaoh there could be no just Exodus, no eventual triumph for an oppressed people, and no Passover or Easter.

It is at the feet of another demonized authority—a corrupt, self-serving and indigenous Sadducee priesthood cooperating with an alien Roman occupying army—that Christianity lays the crucifixion of Jesus and the promise of his glorious return. The subsequent heroism of many early Christians is likewise celebrated for the martyrs' resistance to "pagan and degenerate" rites that perpetuated a corrupt Roman social and political culture.[2]

In time, after the Christians themselves had solidified their power in Rome, they in turn were portrayed as emissaries of evil by a new group of challengers—first the mendicant friars and later the leaders of the Protestant Reformation. Professing revulsion at the decadence and corruption of the papacy and its hierarchy, the reformers rose to undo the grip of the See of Rome, portrayed by them as the lair of the Anti-Christ.

Many of the immigrants to the New World similarly echoed a condemnation of the Old World and its abusive institutions of authority: political (royalty and nobility) or religious (Catholic and Protestant). Claiming to flee a morally decaying and doomed Babylon, these professed possessors of the true reforming spirit went on, of course, to commit their own excesses of power in the new Eden founded by them. Resorting to new inquisitions, genocide for indigenous people, and enslavement for those imported, these immigrants in turn became themselves the target of demonization by new generations of rebels.

Throughout history, the demonizers have often and much too rapidly stepped into the shoes of those whom they previously demonized. The French Revolution of the late eighteenth century is recorded as an uprising against privileged, insensitive, and tyrannical authority. Yet the reign of terror imposed by France's revolutionaries exceeded the abuses of Louis XVI and the evils of his Bastille. The American Civil War, popularly depicted as a struggle for the liberation of African Americans from the inhumanity of slave labor, was followed by political powerlessness and continuing social degradations for a new subject class of "freemen." Similarly, the 1917 Russian Revolution, portrayed as a workers' and peasants' uprising against a thoroughly abusive autocracy, quickly created its own and even more terrifying reign of terror.

The process of demonization has not ceased in modern times. In fact, the growing availability of mass media has accelerated the process (often accomplished through the spread of "disinformation") and made it a major part of any revolutionary's agenda. Revolutionaries and counterrevolutionaries increasingly describe each other in stark, polarizing rhetoric. To enhance their own legitimacy, domestic dissidents, as well as external enemies, describe their adversaries as tools of "Evil Empires," as practitioners of racism, or as purveyors of other intolerable doctrines or creeds. Conflicts over power, status, land, and other resources are invariably portrayed as struggles by "liberators" against "enemies of the people." Whether accurately or not, those in authority are frequently depicted as "communists," "fascists," "racists," "tyrants," or "sexists." Even personal power struggles, devoid of ideological content, are characterized by their partisans as "campaigns of justice" and "wars of liberation."

At times, demonization can indeed serve as a useful tool for humanity's mobilization (e.g., by placing Naziism and racism beyond the human pale). The United Nations designation of apartheid as a crime against humanity thus fortified the world resolve against racism and enhanced the struggle for social and economic justice in South Africa. However, demonization can also be used for the character assassination of political opponents, as was the case of the United Nations declaration, only recently overturned, equating Zionism with racism.

We warned the reader, in the previous chapter, against the temptation to view all rebels as positive and heroic figures. Neither the proclaimed objectives nor the tools resorted to by many self-described "reformers," "liberators," and "messiahs" merit their inclusion in the ranks of those truly struggling for justice and brotherhood. As much as we must be on guard against the indiscriminate deification of those resisting and defying political power, we must equally be prepared to dispel similar efforts to demonize all those exercising legitimate leadership in the execution of responsible authority.

Neither Germany's post–World War I Weimar Republic nor Czechoslovakia's pre–World War II republican regime justified the demonic portrayals resorted to by their Nazi adversaries in an effort to legitimate their own aggression. In many contemporary countries and societies, one would be equally hard put to describe the forces of authority as less deserving, less lawful, and less just than those who have set out to challenge the established order. Quite often, those rebelling against existing authority are motivated not by the quest of just causes but by aggressive drives and brute ambition, propelled by an insatiable appetite for personal or clannish glory and power. Especially in the face of the spreading challenge to prevailing authority by ideological extremists, religious fundamentalists, and other political, ethnic, and cultural fanatics, a more thorough study and objective assessment of the government's uses of power and the legitimacy of its authority are very much required.

## THE OTHER FACE OF JANUS: DESPOTISM, TYRANNY, AND DICTATORSHIP

Janus, the dual-faced Roman deity, reflects well the symbiosis between authority and its challengers, between the wielders of power and those pressing for autonomy. While one face of Janus stands for authority, the other reflects its defiers. It is impossible, therefore, to understand the making of the political offender, or to assess his or her place in the eternal struggle between those in possession of power and those aspiring to it, without giving due attention to both the legitimacy and the debasement of authority, to governmental order and its abuses of power.

In his portrayal of man, the state, and legitimate order, contemporary French political philosopher Michel Foucault pointed to the "double" or "shadow" that he believed constantly pursued and mirrored truth and legitimacy.[3] A century earlier, anarchist philosopher Mikhail Bakunin claimed that "all who acquire power are fatally induced to abuse it."[4] Lord Acton, member of the nineteenth-century British Establishment, paraphrased Bakunin when he reiterated their shared fear of political power: "Power tends to corrupt and absolute power corrupts absolutely."[5] Leonard Boudin, an American civil liberties lawyer, reiterated recently that "all governments abuse power. Every one of them."[6]

From the beginning of human history, mankind has chronicled despots whose selfish will and caprice dictated the affairs of state without regard to the people's well-being. The biblical prophets railed against unrighteous kings and evil empires—not merely in adjacent Canaan and in distant Egypt, Assyria, and Babylonia, but also in their homelands of Judea and Israel. Warning the tribes of Israel against the hazards of monarchy, the prophet Samuel explained:

This will be the manner of the King that shall reign over you: he will take your sons, and appoint them . . . to be his horsemen; and some shall run before his chariots.

And he will . . . set them to plough his ground, and to reap his harvest, and to make his instruments of war. . . .

And he will take your daughters to be . . . cooks, and to be bakers.

And he will take your fields, and your vineyards, and your oliveyards, even the best of them, and give them to his servants.

And he will take the tenth of your seed . . . [and the tenth of your sheep.]

And he will take your menservants, and your maidservants, and your goodliest young men, and put them to his work . . . and ye shall be his servants.[7]

The literature of classical Greece and Rome similarly documents and usually denounces the rule of tyrants and dictators. Aristotle points to some of the underlying evils of tyranny:

That tyranny has all the vices both of democracy and oligarchy is evident. As of oligarchy so of tyranny, the end is wealth (for by wealth only can the tyrant maintain either his guard or his luxury). Both mistrust the people, and therefore deprive them of their arms. Both agree too in injuring the people and driving them out of the city and dispersing them. From democracy tyrants have borrowed the art of making war upon the notables and destroying them secretly or openly, or of exiling them because they are rivals and stand in the way of their power.[8]

Abuse of power has been practiced by such ancient tyrants as Croesus of Lydia, Polycrates of Samos, Periander of Corinth, and Pisistratus of Megara (in Greece, Asia Minor, and Sicily) some twenty-six hundred years ago,[9] and by later Roman dictators such as Sulla, Nero, and Caligula in the first century.[10] From the murders, exploitations, and treacheries of Italy's Alfonso of Aragon, Rome's Cola Di Rienzo, and Pope Alexander VI's son Cesare Borgia (Machiavellian princes of the late Middle Ages and the Renaissance)[11] to the totalitarian and authoritarian despots and juntas of modern Europe, Africa, Asia, and Latin America, abuse of power, aimed at opponents and innocents alike, has been a fixture of political life in almost every era and in almost all parts of the globe.[12]

George Hallgarten, who studied despotism from its ancient origins to its contemporary manifestations, relies heavily on Aristotle in pointing out the recurring similarities in all abusive regimes, be they labeled tyrannies, dictatorships, or despotisms. The vicious struggles of tyrants and dictators to gain and maintain power necessarily forces them to extreme measures. To retain his authority, the tyrant must put to death any natural leaders and be constantly on his guard against anything likely to inspire courage, self-confidence, and independence among his subjects. He must prohibit education and gatherings that do not serve his causes. He must recruit spies to uncover real or imagined plots against him. The special art of the tyrant is to set citizens against citizens, the populace against the notables, and the rich and powerful against each other. He needs to keep the people impoverished and busy, so that no energy is left in them for conspiracy or rebellion. He tends to build edifices, intended not merely to glorify himself, but also to give the people employment in order to keep them occupied. The tyrant, Hallgarten points out further, also needs constantly to make war, so that his subjects will continue looking to him for leadership in crisis. The tyrant, finally, dislikes and often destroys anybody who possesses high qualities or is independent in mind or means, viewing that person as a potential enemy of authority. The "tyrant always wants to shine alone in his glory."[13]

Revolutionary France, with its guillotines and witch hunts, introduced a new terminology to describe the inevitable excesses of tyranny—the *reign of terror*. Ever since, the term has been applied to governmental use of oppression and violence for political purposes. In more recent decades the term *state-terrorism* has taken over as the preferred description for the indiscriminate violence unleashed by those in authority against perceived enemies —domestic or foreign.

## MODERN REPRESSION, GENOCIDE, AND OTHER ABUSES OF POWER

Some historians maintain that the Ottoman Empire's calculated policy of murder and forced deportations against the Armenian Christian minority from Turkey's eastern provinces during World War I constituted the first ethnic genocide of the twentieth century. Henry Morgenthau, the United States ambassador to Turkey at the time, described the events as "the murder of a nation."[14] As many as one million Armenians are claimed to have perished at the hands of the Turks. The Armenians' alleged siding with the Russian enemy in the World War supplied an initial excuse for the anti-Armenian sentiments and persecution. Goaded into rebellion by the Turks' brutality and misgovernment, the Armenians revolted, which served as further justification for a massive military campaign against the men, women, and children of the Armenian villages. The oppression and murder wrought on the suspect population was extraordinary. "Of the one and a half million Armenians who had lived in Anatolia before World War I, only about seventy thousand remained in the Turkish Republic in 1923. . . . A people who had lived in eastern Anatolia since before recorded history were simply gone."[15]

Only twenty years later, German Naziism, during its twelve years in power, made the Turks' campaign seem almost banal. The Nazi holocaust, bringing death and immeasurable suffering to scores of millions of inno-cent men, women, and children collectively designated as enemies of the Third Reich, is unparalleled in scope and cold-bloodedness.[16] So-called protective custody camps were established to carry out a campaign of mass exploitation, abuse, and murder. Political opponents and other "enemies" were subjected to forced labor, medical experimentation, and, ultimately, extermination within the Reich's expanding boundaries. In keeping with traditional Germanic exactitude, the Nazi administrators kept a thorough account of their prisoners and of their fates. Although the number of pris-oners reportedly never exceeded 714,211 at any given time, "millions went through the camps, and the overwhelming majority met their death."[17]

Soviet Stalinism, which preceded the Nazi brutalities, created its own grim roster of more than 20 million Russian citizens who died in the regime's labor camps, forced collectivization programs, mass executions, and deliber-ately caused famines.[18] As if echoing Aristotle's description of despotism, Robert H. McNeal, in his *Stalin: Man and Ruler*, writes:

> If Stalin was mad, he possessed the genius of projecting his own reality into large numbers of normal people. They were ready, for the most part, to believe that large numbers of their erstwhile comrades were traitors. They were ready to denounce, to turn away from the incriminated and even from their spouses and children. . . . The atmosphere of devotion to the leader and alienation from suspect "comrades" led to the atomization of members of the Soviet life. Normal human relationships, within a certain level of soci-ety, dissolved.[19]

The modern era seems only to have increased the efficiency of tyrannical abuse. The latest four decades have witnessed new forms of abuse of power, reigns of terror, and genocide in many and diverse parts of the world. "Genocides and other kinds of large-scale political murder more often than not happen in distant lands, away from the TV cameras, to globally unim-portant peoples whose suffering is quickly forgotten in the vagaries of international politics," wrote American human rights activist David Hawk in 1982.[20] In the 1970s and 1980s, in the remote Cuchumatn highlands of Guatemala, the native Mayan populations of the Ixil country, suspected of sympathy toward the rebelling forces of the Guerrilla Army of the Poor (EGP), were subjected to extremely brutal counterinsurgency measures by government forces. In the early 1980s Amnesty International reported wide-spread abuses of the rural Indian population, including the indiscriminate killing of pregnant women and children, and the rape and the torture and live burial of suspects. In one year alone some twenty-six hundred people were killed in at least 112 separate incidents of torture and mass execution.[21] One observer described the events as "genocide being carried out in the Indian regions" and another concluded that "Indians are systematically being destroyed as a group."[22]

The testimony of the survivors, given under oath to American interviewers, is shocking in its brutal similarity to the earlier campaigns of genocide by the Ottomans and Nazis:

> On August 29, [1982,] we interviewed (x) in Rancho Tejas. She told us that she is thirty years old, and a citizen of Guatemala. She said that she is pregnant, and the mother of three children who are the ages of twelve years, four years and one year. She further stated that on or about May 6, 1982, she left her village . . . in the Department of Huehuetenango, because Government troops burned it and killed many of its residents. She described that incident to us as follows:
>
> At 6:00 A.M. on May 6, 1982, about one hundred soldiers whom she could identify by their camouflage suits and pistols, arrived on foot in her village and surrounded it. Villagers then were robbed of their clothes and money, and their houses were burned. Many were hacked, beaten, and shot to death. She alone saw soldiers kill fifteen people, as she stood twenty-five meters away. She was raped. Her husband and brothers were killed inside their house. Shortly after this, she fled to Mexico.[23]

Reviewing demographic tables for the Indian populations of the Cuchumatn highlands in the years between 1984 and 1987, one researcher concluded that he could not account for some fifty thousand "missing" persons.[24]

In the Middle East, nearly 20 million Kurdish people (who come from Aryan stock, adhere to the Muslim religion, and inhabit an area roughly equal in size to that of France that is divided between the former Soviet Union, Turkey, Iran, Iraq, and Syria) have been subjected to similar persecution and ethnocide since the conclusion of World War I. Promises of a Kurdish homeland seemed near when, on August 10, 1920, the Treaty of Sèvres bound the defeated Turkish government to grant "local autonomy" to the Kurds. Article 64 of the treaty made it possible, furthermore, for the Kurds to petition the League of Nations for independence and, upon that body's approval, to establish an independent Kurdish state.[25] But these hopes were dashed by the Turkish nationalists, under Mustafa Kemal Ataturk, who succeeded to the Ottoman Empire in 1923.

Ever since, the divided people of Kurdistan have been in a constant state of political ferment. They have also been oppressed, warred upon, and collectively massacred by the military forces of several of the new states that now hold sway over the land that the Kurds have inhabited since prehistoric times. In Iraq some three hundred fifty thousand Kurdish villagers have been displaced and deported due to the government's plan to "Arabize" strategic regions, including the area around the Kirkuk oil field.[26] Turkey's estimated 8 to 10 million Kurds are not even recognized as an official minority, a status granted to such smaller Turkish communities as Armenians and Greeks. For decades, the Turkish parliament has banned books and newspapers in the Kurdish language.[27] In adjacent Syria the authorities refuse to give many of the nearly one million Kurds full citizenship, and in Iran, the fundamentalist Shiite regime views the Kurds and their more secular version of Islam with suspicion and constant apprehension. Again and again, the Kurdish people take to the mountains, "awaiting word from their leaders, wondering if they will be able to return to their homes safely, or whether they face yet another chapter in a long history of betrayal."[28]

The record of governmental abuse in the second half of the twentieth century must also include the extraordinary Cambodian brutalities in the period between 1975 and 1979. David Hawk, former executive director of Amnesty International in the United States, reported:

> From the middle of 1975 to the end of 1978, between one million and three million Cambodians, out of a population of about seven million, died at the hands of Pol Pot's Khmer Rouge. Former government employees, army personnel, and "intellectuals" were executed in the hundreds of thousands. Others were killed by disease, exhaustion, and malnutrition during forced urban evacuations, migrations, and compulsory labor. Families were broken apart and communal living established; men and women were compelled to marry partners selected by the state. Education and religious practices were proscribed.[29]

More particularly, those in authority in Cambodia during this era reportedly caused the death of as many as forty thousand members of the Cham community, a non-Khmer Islamic minority group, in the Kompong Cham province. According to one writer, "over one-third" of the Cham minority perished at the hands of the Pol Pot regime.[30] Nor were Buddhist monasteries and monks spared. Even though Buddhism had been the country's established state religion before 1975, once the Khmer Rouge came to power, Buddhist temples, statues, and books were systematically desecrated, worship and meditation were prohibited, and Pali and Sanskrit, the languages of Buddhist scriptures, were outlawed. Of a total of 2,680 known Buddhist monks in one region's eight monasteries, only 70 survived this holocaust.[31]

Based on reports of Amnesty International, the International Commission of Jurists, and several concerned governments, a United Nations Human Rights Subcommittee concluded that the Cambodian situation was "the most serious that occurred anywhere in the world since Naziism" and "was nothing less than autogenocide."[32] What happened in Pol Pot's Cambodia was not merely a gross violation of internationally recognized human rights, "it was something more akin to Stalin's Russia or Hitler's Germany."[33] Traveling to Cambodia after the ouster of the Pol Pot regime, Hawk described the systematic machinery set up for carrying out the national genocide. Cambodia, he emphasizes, was not "without its bureaucracy of torture and death, its Asian equivalent of Auschwitz . . . where Khmer Rouge officials kept meticulous records of their murders."[34]

In the last decade of the twentieth century, the end of tyranny, abuse of power, reigns of terror, and genocide by those in authority—and sometimes by those resisting it—is still not in sight. In 1989, the leaders of Iran's fundamentalist Islamic revolution, while reputedly seeking international recognition for their "increasing moderation," executed more than one thousand political opponents in a period of a mere six months. The victims of the purge included socialists, suspect members of the clergy, women, and random representatives of the Kurdish minority.[35] Three years later, Yugoslavia was dismembered in a resort to violence against civilians by the military and civilians alike. More than twenty thousand civilians died in the Bosnia-Herzegovina campaign alone, and more than three million people were turned into refugees. Concentration camps, torture, and mass executions were utilized by the warring parties, in the name of "ethnic cleansing."[36]

In Somalia, similarly, all semblance of legitimate governmental order collapsed when the country's competing tribal warlords, vying for power, not only waged war against each other but also mounted a campaign of terror against the country's starving civilians. Only direct humanitarian military intervention by the community of nations brought an end to the widespread abuse of power.

But subtler forms of oppression by those in authority also abound. Three decades ago, in his classic work *Political Justice*, social philosopher Otto Kircheimer enumerated the panoply of other, less-violent governmental abuses, including the suppression of speech, religion, rights of association, assembly, elections, and travel.[37] Kircheimer's work continues as a comprehensive inventory of oppressive ends and unlawful means used by government in the pursuit, consolidation, and preservation of its power. More recent accounts of governmental illegality and violence are contained in Patricia Hewett's *The Abuse of Power: Civil Liberties in the United Kingdom* and in the Aspen Institute's *State Crimes*.[38] For the latest update on governmental misconduct, against the very populations with whose well-being they are charged, the reader is referred to the volumes of Amnesty International,[39] the Lawyers' Committee on Human Rights, the Helsinki Watch committees, and the reports of numerous other human rights monitoring organizations.

Comparable political injustices have often taken place in the United States.[40] The partial ethnocide of Native Americans, the brutal oppression of

African Americans, the disenfranchisement and subjugation of women, the harassment, exclusion, and deportation of political radicals, and the World War II uprooting of Japanese Americans are described in greater detail in later chapters.

The Watergate and the Iran-Contra affairs offer recent illustrations of the attraction of extralegal means to those in power. Not surprisingly, therefore, within the last decade—as the Western democracies, the Third World, and the newly liberated Eastern European nations have been attempting to construct a jurisprudence for the definition and curtailment of governmental terror, injustice, and illegality—*abuse of power* has been coined as a new term of art within the literature of the United Nations.[41]

By definition, reigns of terror and abuse of power are imposed by those in authority. But violence and illegality, as previously seen, owe no partisan or political allegiances. Like the two-faced Janus, abuse can look in both directions for victims. Though the regime can impose a reign of terror, its opponents can mount a siege of terrorism. From the biblical Maccabees to the partisans in Nazi-occupied Europe, from the antifundamentalists' resistance in Islamic Iran to Ceaucescu's executioners in Rumania, individuals and groups have frequently offered violent retaliation to their abusers and tormentors.

When those in power use illegal means to achieve their ends or politicize the institutions of government, and when they use justice to serve their goals, their victims might turn to such unlawful forms of resistance as treason, sedition, civil disobedience, mass demonstrations, strikes, and armed rebellion. In these cases, one might say political offenders are frequently those who set out to right an oppressive regime's "unrightable wrongs." They might be the antibodies combatting infections in the political system.

## FROM ABUSE OF POWER TO RESISTANCE

Having seen before that the political offender's claim to legitimacy, and thereby to public support and possible victory, rests in great part upon his or her securing an unworthy and evil adversary, one might expect resistance and rebellion to thrive most where evil governance and oppression are greatest. But cumulative data does not confirm this initial hunch about rebellion always or usually constituting a response to abuse of power, nor, furthermore, does it confirm the likelihood of rebellion's occurrence at times and places where abuse of power reaches its apex. Anatol Rapoport, in *The Origins of Violence: Approaches to the Study of Conflict*, explores the psychological as well as other underpinnings of rebellion and violence, pointing to evolutionary, sociobiological, behavioral, strategic, and systematic causations.[42] Kenneth

Moyer has emphasized the difference between emotional aggression or resistance and instrumental rebellion.[43] The evidence often suggests, moreover, that popular perceptions of oppression, which give rise to unrest and resistance, do not necessarily coincide with actual realities of oppression. With these preliminary warnings in mind, we must set out to determine the relationships between abusive governance and political discontent and rebellion. When might an exercise of power foster popular disquiet and opposition? Which preconditions and precipitating events are likely to give rise to an individual's or people's resistance? And what continuing conditions, if unalleviated by those in authority, will turn an initial grievance into popular resistance and a successful rebellion?

In a somewhat impressionistic study of rebellion and insurrection, British author Brian Crozier concludes that "frustration is the one element common to all rebels, whatever their aims, political ideas, or social backgrounds."[44] Having so identified frustration as the raw material of rebellion, Crozier further differentiates between its two distinct classes: the purely personal or psychological frustration, which those in authority have no or little power to relieve, and frustration derived from sociopolitical conditions, which government can more readily remedy.

To illustrate the sociopolitical and remediable grievances, Crozier focuses on Belkacem Krim, leader of the native anti-French rebellion in Tunisia. Crozier quotes Krim, typifying the frustration produced by alien authority, in a rare 1958 press interview: "Wherever I turned, there was injustice. There were always differences between us, the Moslem inferiors and the superior Europeans."[45] The perceived injustices imposed by the colonial "power" upon Krim and other indigenous leaders produced a lingering frustration that went unrelieved for many decades.

If psychological and sociopolitical frustrations are the primary instigators of rebellion, Crozier points to the political authority's continued misgovernance and its denial of relief as aggravating factors. Shortcomings in governmental response he divides into two kinds: sins of omission (the failure to regard early warnings and take remedial social or political action) and sins of commission (responses that aggravate rather than improve a frustrating situation).[46] Like John Locke long before him, Crozier sees the failure of those in power (be they kings or legislatures) to observe warning signals and to respond in a timely and appropriate manner as a major source of revolution.[47] Crozier dwells on the faulty sense of timing by those in authority as a critical factor. "The date is all," he insists. "In the year of rebellion no solution is politically possible (that, indeed, is why there is a rebellion); but earlier it might have been."[48]

Other, both earlier and later, studies of the etiology of rebellion have shared many of Crozier's observations, yet sought to bring greater specificity to both the initial causation and the escalating stages of protest and resistance. Having studied the great English revolution of the seventeenth century, James Harrington came to the conclusion that economic causes predominate over the previously noted political, social, and psychological forces. Accordingly, he advanced the well-known thesis that dissatisfaction turns into revolution when the distribution of political authority is incongruent with the distribution of economic power within a society.[49]

Equally important is the growing recognition that social, economic, and political deprivations are not the sole cause of rebellion against authority. After analyzing military rebellions from ancient times to modern days, T. H. Wintringham concluded that "the puzzle becomes not why did the mutiny occur, but why did men, for years or generations, endure the torments against which in the end they revolted."[50] If deprivations alone suffice, the doubters insist, why was it that African American slaves or India's outcasts did not take up arms during centuries of oppression? It is clearly not mere injustice but the expectation of change—if unsatisfied (as de Tocqueville insisted)—that must be given credit for the revolutionary explosion.

There have been many other modern students of rebellion and political crime. Some, like Crane Brinton, in his famous *Anatomy of Revolution*, sought to find the answers to causation by comparing different cultures and their revolutionary patterns.[51] James Rosenau sought to divide all civil strife into three major or ideal types: personal wars, structural wars, and authority wars.[52] Harry Ekstein, in *Internal War*, engaged in the classification and definition of basic categories of internal conflict and war as a preliminary step to the articulation of a comprehensive theory.[53] In his classification he utilized the term *internal war* to denote the genus that includes such "species" as political revolution, social revolution, civil war, revolt, rebellion, uprising, guerrilla warfare, mutiny, riots, coups d'état, terrorism, and insurrection.[54] Seeking to construct a model of how internal wars begin, Ekstein differentiated between preconditional situations (circumstances that make it possible for precipitating events to bring about political violence) and the precipitants themselves (those events that actually start the war). Concentrating upon preconditions, he divided them into intellectual situations (such as the existence in a society of unrealizable values or myths), social factors (the inflexibility of elites in absorbing newcomers or disruptions brought about by great social mobility), and, finally, political factors (bad government, oppressive government, and the estrangement of rulers from those they rule).[55]

Most modern students of the struggle against authority begin with Aristotle. From Aristotle's *Politics* comes the reminder that protest and rebellion are derived from society's failure to realize equality—which Aristotle views as the foundation of justice. Distilling Aristotle's observations, James C. Davies writes that "the [masses] of society, when [they] revolt . . . , do . . .

so because . . . [they] see the leading, ruling . . . [class] getting too many goods and too much honor; the . . . [ruling class, whether distinguished by ancestry, wealth, or ability], when it revolts, does so from fear that it will lose the share of goods and honor which it has come to expect as its right."[56]

A Hebraic source, the Talmud, supports Aristotle's claim that it is the absence of justice that leads to popular discontent and violence. Judah Hanassi, a second-century Jewish sage, observed that "the sword comes upon the world on account of the delay of justice and the perversion of justice."[57]

With time, the study of conditions and forces productive of public discontent, and, eventually, of eruption into disorder, acquired greater refinement. The earlier emphasis upon the denial of equality and justice was coupled with a growing awareness of a new social concept—that of rising expectations. This factor added particular insight to the understanding of discontent and its evolution. "For a hundred and forty years the French people had played no part on the political stage and this had led to a general belief that they could never figure there," pointed out Alexis de Tocqueville in his masterful search for the roots of the French Revolution.[58] Yet during the very century and a half to which he alluded, the values of the French people had constantly changed—becoming increasingly egalitarian—and neither the country's social or political institutions had kept up with, or responded to, the new expectations.

It was through the revolution that the people's rising and unsatisfied expectations were finally expressed. Eric Hoffer, more recently, summarized in similar manner the relationship between revolution and the changes that bring it about: "We are usually told that revolutions are set in motion to realize radical changes. Actually, it is drastic change that sets the stage for revolution. . . . Where things have not changed at all, there is the least likelihood of revolution."[59]

A particularly dynamic and economically oriented approach to the understanding of unrest and disorder was offered by Marx and Engels. Their 1848 *Communist Manifesto*, preceding de Tocqueville's more politically and socially weighted 1856 tome on the roots of the French Revolution, placed them together with him among the leading theorists of revolution. Sharing Aristotle's focus on equality, Marx and Engels saw class differences as the major cause of inequality and concluded that "the history of all hitherto existing society is the history of class struggles."[60] As long as classes persist, the two argued, the struggle must continue. Since modern bourgeois society, "[which] has sprouted from the ruins of feudal society, has not done away with class antagonism," the preordained struggle remains unavoidable. Also predetermined, in their opinion, is the revolutionary timetable imposed by history. Marx and Engels' conviction was that the modern epoch streamlined and sharpened class antagonisms by increasingly splitting society into two great and hostile camps (the bourgeoisie and the proletariat). They argued that it is the intensity of this cleavage that determines the time of the revolutionary reckoning. The more developed and advanced industry becomes, the nearer the "decisive hour" for the ultimate class struggle.[61] Only the coming of a classless society can end the conflict.

The Marxist understanding of the psychological or relativistic causes for a people's sense of deprivation and frustration is particularly useful to our understanding of revolution. Frustration, Marx and Engels pointed out, must be viewed as derived not from an objective measurement of deprivation but from one's subjective and comparative sense of well-being and socioeconomic standing: "Our desires and pleasures spring from society; we measure them, therefore, by society and not by the objects which serve for their satisfaction. Because they are of a social nature, they are of a relative nature."[62]

Supplementing these classical predecessors, later students of political conflict and violence have relied on new sociological and psychological tools of analysis to chart the course of rebellious behavior. Particularly in America, the decades of the 1960s and 1970s saw a dramatic effort to produce comprehensive and multidisciplinary theories regarding political unrest and violence. One formula, advanced by James C. Davies in "Toward a Theory of Revolution,"[63] still continues as a widely accepted thesis of group and individual rebellion.

Paying tribute to both Marx and de Tocqueville for their initial contributions, Davies quotes from the latter with approval:

> Revolutions are not always brought about by a gradual decline from bad to worse. Nations that have endured patiently and almost unconsciously the most overwhelming oppression often burst into rebellion against the yoke the moment it begins to grow lighter. The regime which is destroyed by a revolution is almost always an improvement on its immediate predecessor. . . . Evils which are patiently endured when they seem inevitable become intolerable when an idea of escape from them is suggested.[64]

Relying on de Tocqueville for a point of departure, Davies proceeds to advance his own theory of protest and revolution. Resistance to authority is most likely to surface when socioeconomic or other gratifications, which accompany rising expectations, are followed by a sudden curtailment of gratifications while expectations continue to rise. In his own words, the "widening gap of individual dissatisfactions," which causes "economic or social dislocation . . . makes the affected individual generally tense, generally frustrated," and more willing to join the cause of rebellion.[65] To elucidate his theory

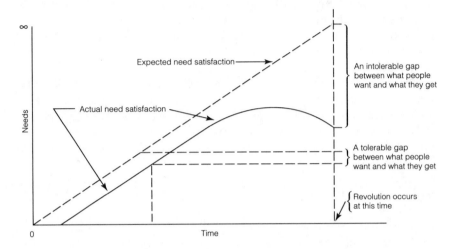

*Rebellion, according to Davies, takes place when an "intolerable gap is created between what people want and what they get."*

Davies offers his well-known graph on need satisfaction and the revolutionary process.[66]

A more complex and multivariate theory of the evolution of rebellion was introduced by Ted Gurr in his *Why Men Rebel.*[67] Gurr focuses on political violence, encompassing within the term all collective militancy (guerilla wars, rebellions, coups d'état, and riots) against prevailing political authority. Less-violent forms of protest and resistance—as well as those consisting of individual rather than mass conduct—were not encompassed in his work.

Reviewing former studies of political disorder, Gurr concludes that countries experiencing extensive manifestations of one type of political unrest are likely also to be afflicted by other kinds of political disorder, yet are "neither more or [sic] less likely to be engaged in foreign conflict."[68] Much like Crozier before him, Gurr sees the genesis of political discontent in frustration.[69] He postulates that from one's sense of perceived deprivation a frustration-anger-aggression syndrome develops. The deprivation—the discrepancy between what people believe they are rightfully entitled to and what they are given an opportunity to attain—may relate to one or more of the well-known categories of needs suggested in the previous work of A. H. Maslow: those

that pertain to welfare, to power, or to interpersonal relations.[70]

In the welfare category Gurr includes the economic and physical needs for well-being. In the power category he includes needs for communal and individual security, order, and role definition. In the interpersonal category he lists needs of self-esteem, respect, and status. Gurr argues that most populations feel their deprivation most intensely with regard to the welfare/economic category, less with respect to the power/security needs, and least with regard to self-esteem/status expectations. Concluding that deprivation-induced discontent supplies the spur to rebellion, Gurr points out that the greater the frustration, the greater the quantity of aggression that will be directed against the existing power that is the source of frustration.

Several subtheories are propounded by Gurr regarding the dynamics that govern the conversion of frustration into aggression and rebellion. He notes that when men live close to the economic subsistence level, almost any marginal economic decline can precipitate an outburst of aggression. He next observes that groups that experience consistent increases in well-being develop expectations about continued improvements and are particularly quick to anger when these fail to materialize. Finally, he postulates that a highly competent leadership is necessary for the creation, direction, and maintenance of a successful mass rebellion.

Another attempt to chart the escalation from political discontent to rebellion was undertaken by James C. Coleman in *Community Conflict*.[71] Coleman, like other students of conflict, points to three primary sources of frustration and discontent: clashing economic interests, contests over political power and authority, and conflicting "cultural values or beliefs"(p.6). Reviewing the historical records of political resistance and rebellion, Coleman reiterates that the "most striking fact about the development and growth of community controversies is the similarity they exhibit despite diverse underlying sources and different kinds of precipitating incidents"(p.9).

Coleman points out that while usually commencing with a specific and single grievance, controversies often expand to include wider issues. Unresolved disagreements then turn into violence and disorder. He illustrates this dynamic evolution of conflict through a tabular progression (p.11):

| (1) Initial single issue | (2) Disrupts equilibrium of community relations | (3) Allows previously suppressed issues against opponent to appear | (4) More and more of opponent's beliefs enter into the disagreement | (5) The opponent appears totally bad | (6) Charges against opponent as a person | (7) Dispute becomes independent of initial disagreement |
|---|---|---|---|---|---|---|

Coleman further points to the growing communal polarization produced by the escalating controversy. New affinities rise and flourish within each clashing camp, and old affiliations wither away between persons and organizations on opposing sides. With time new communal structures, formal and informal, come into being within the rebelling community, and new leaders emerge to lead the discontented.

## AUTHORITY AND ITS DISCONTENTS

The frequency of resort to political disorder is further dependent, in Gurr's view, upon identifiable social and cultural variables. These include such factors as a given society's historical and cultural record of militancy and aggression, the success of past political violence in alleviating deprivations, the perceived legitimacy of the existing political system, and the efficacy of the government's responses to impending political disorder.

Persistent differences exist among societies with regard to the styles and incidence of political unrest and violence. "Within most complex societies," Gurr asserts, "some groups, and some regions manifest types of violence different from, and magnitudes of violence greater than, those of other groups and regions."[72]

Picturesque portrayals of diverse styles of political violence have been supplied by several scholars. Edwards, in *The Natural History of Revolution*, specifies some cultural variations:

> Ancient Jewish mobs always stoned their victims to death, Alexandrian mobs nearly always threw theirs from the tops of high buildings . . . Medieval mobs regularly decapitated those they killed. Except in unusual circumstances American mobs use the noose. A Belfast mob could no more be brought to lynch negroes than a Chicago mob could be brought to lynch Catholics.[73]

Societies not only tend to develop their own particular styles of political unrest but also become habituated to violent means as tools of social change. Gurr argues that the more successful a populace has been in alleviating past deprivations through rebellion, the greater the likelihood that discontented citizens will resort to violence in order to compel change or attention to still-unresolved needs.[74] Accordingly, while political violence is episodic in the history of most political communities, it has become chronic in some.

The legitimacy of a prevailing authority is often another critical element in fostering rebellion. A complex term, *legitimacy* encapsulates the citizens' feelings, attitudes, and trust toward their rulers and political institutions. In new as well as in older nations, political, religious, and cultural traditions help determine the populace's sociopsychological commitment to authority and to the persons who hold the reins of power. "In new nations . . . the legitimacy or lack of legitimacy of a national leader like Nasser, Ayub Khan, or Nyerere may be far more consequential in people's attitudes . . . than . . . [the people's] feelings about the propriety of the state and its institutions," Gurr argues.[75] He points to low levels of legitimacy or allegiance as sources of political instability and unrest in new nations in particular.

The less vested a regime's legitimacy is, the greater the likelihood that unorthodox political means will be successfully used to produce its fall. Describing legitimate authority as the capacity of government to maintain confidence in the power system, Hannah Arendt writes that "no revolution ever succeeded, few revolutions ever started, so long as the authority of the body politic was indeed intact."[76] In countries and under regimes with many historical institutions that confer legitimacy, resistance and rebellion are less likely. "Legitimate power is the grand prize because it makes it possible to reconcile the losers to their disadvantaged position," claims William Gamson.[77]

The character and speed of the response by those in authority to complaints of deprivation and to manifestations of resistance is another critical factor in the outcome of confrontations between the forces of authority and their challengers. "The most fundamental human responses [sic] to the use of force is counterforce," Gurr points out.[78] The justification for counterforce is that it deters, but Gurr repeats the oft-cited warning that particularly severe sanctions are often counterproductive. Disproportionate sanctions tend to escalate the conflict, inviting greater numbers of dissidents to resort to force. "Force empowers its own adversaries. It raises up its own opposition. It engenders its own destruction."[79] Nonetheless, Lasswell and Kaplan have argued that the extent of a regime's control over the instruments of violence and the degree of the military's loyalty to an existing authority are fundamental determinants of a regime's stability and ability to overcome opposition.[80]

Gurr and others reaffirm the axiom that making nonviolent means available for the alleviation of perceived deprivations is the best countermeasure to violence, because "only men who are enraged" are likely to prefer the risks of violence to effective nonviolent alternatives for satisfying their expectations.[81] But the traditional assumption that discontent has its roots primarily in economic and material causes is considered to be no longer accurate. "Men aspire to many other conditions of life than physical well-being, not the least of which are security, status, a sense of community, and the right to manage their own affairs."[82]

It is at this point that political, social, and economic explanations of the conflict between authority and autonomy begin to mesh with psychological and psychoanalytical hypotheses. Psychoanalysis, in particular, advances the thesis of an *oedipal* archetype—the young rebelling against the paternal sexual authority—and of rebellion as a primeval life force. Freud writes, in *Civilization and Its Discontents*, that in the "primitive family one essential feature of civilization is still lacking. The arbitrary will of its head, the father, was unrestricted."[83] It is against this unrestricted authority that the son and his brothers rebel. "From a psychoanalytical standpoint all authority is the father," pointed out Harold Lasswell in his *Psychopathology and Politics*.[84] The rebelling Oedipus kills his father, and Freud notes that the "human sense of guilt goes back to the killing of the primal father. . . . His sons hated him, but they loved him, too. After their hatred had been satisfied by their act of aggression, their love came to the fore in their remorse for the deed."[85] Freud concludes on a more general note that "the urge for freedom, therefore, is directed against particular forms and demands of civilization or against civilization altogether. . . . A good part of the struggles of mankind centre round the single task of finding an expedient accommodation . . . between [the] claim of the individual and the cultural claims of the group."[86]

There is a wealth of insight and understanding in the writings of many others on the causes of political violence and disorder in ancient, as well as in modern, societies. In his *Theory of Collective Behavior*, Neil Smelser addresses "discontent" (what others defined as "frustration" or "perceived deprivation") and concludes that a well-designed system of governance must incorporate ways of alleviating underlying causes of discontent and of directing its expressions into orderly channels.[87] William A. Gamson seeks to determine the impact of "political trust," paralleling Gurr's concept of "legitimacy,"[88] upon the conduct of the discontented.[89] Political trust, Gamson argues, forms a reservoir of good will that helps individuals accept or tolerate government policies and actions that they oppose or see as damaging to their interests. The existence of a great reservoir of such trust is likely to make compromises easier—the discontented being more accepting of the attitude that "honest men may disagree and one cannot expect to win every time" (p.51).

When the reservoir of political trust is limited, and when abusive government action is seen as part of a continuing pattern, perceived deprivation begins to mount. Public trust eventually becomes alienation from authority when those in power are "regarded as incompetent and stupid in achieving collective goals and [as] being biased against . . . [particular groups] in handling conflicts of interest" (p.56).

As alienation intensifies, those in power might seek to stem the tide of protest and rebellion by (a) isolating potential activists, (b) applying sanctions against them, or (c) persuading them to return to orthodox means of political change and to take part in political solutions (co-option). Isolation and sanctioning of offenders often lead to further and more permanent breaches between those in authority and those rebelling against it. Neither is co-option easily attained, for compromises are regarded as risky by both sides. Since co-option requires a new mixing or distribution of political power, those in authority fear that the newcomers might dominate the mix, while those invited to join fear that the old elite will continue its dominance (p.137). Only if the apprehension of both groups is overcome can discontent result in peaceful compromise and reform.

Regarding resort to political compromise, one must note in conclusion that few students of political rebellion and resistance have addressed the forces and fears that militate against the structuring of an appropriate and just balance of power between those who rule and those who are being ruled. By and large, most commentators fail to consider one of the main factors that retards power-sharing by those in authority: the belief that authority and power are not, and in fact can not be, endless and flexible commodities. Can the head, or father, in Freud's primitive family, give up his unrestricted power and remain the "head"? Can an ethnic group, nation, or state give up its sovereignty and remain autonomous? "Politics is often regarded simply as a struggle over scarce [commodities]" is how William C. Mitchell characterized this dilemma.[90]

Few historical or modern studies point to the need for an authority or regime to be extraordinarily evil before it will have to face political resistance or rebellion. Abuse of power, tyranny, and reigns of terror are not prerequisites for political dissent or violence. Many studies of individual or communal political conflicts point to the presence of lesser and relatively common ingredients of dissatisfaction—some possibly being preterrational—that may suffice for combustion.[91] Generally, however, common preconditions and precipitants of rebellion are the following:

- the existence of individuals, communities, or groups of the population perceiving a grievance or deprivation—economic, social, political, cultural, or ideological;
- the lack of appropriate mechanisms for addressing and alleviating the grievance, resulting in growing frustration and in the growth of a conflict over a particular issue into a deeper dispute;
- a perceived sense of the rulers' neglect or even bias, eroding the aggrieved individual's or community's "political trust" in the existing authority;
- the error or inefficacy of the responses by those in authority;
- the presence of militant, and sometimes uncritical, media attention, as well as of broader community sympathy for the aggrieved group, thus broadening the dispute and creating new alliances of interests; and
- the availability of external or international public opinion, material support, and leadership, for the discontented forces.

These ingredients for rebellion's prosperity are not in themselves the stuff of legends. They are not peculiar to unduly oppressive or tyrannical regimes. They are pedestrian and commonplace in every family, clan, tribe, city, county, nation, or state in the world. A great rebellion can have its beginning in a small discontent, a slight, a slur, an injustice gone unremedied. While it is true that full-scale civil disobedience, rebellion, or civil war might require a great abundance of these ingredients, that does not belie the fact that the potential for turning people into political activists, resisters, and rebels is omnipresent. The potential is realized more often than is admitted or is necessary, frequently challenging the myth that wars against authority are limited to contests between shining heroes and dark knights, between worthy rebels and wicked rulers.

We set out to assess, in this chapter, the other half of the equation of the legitimacy of power supplied by existing systems of authority. We hope we have given some initial clues to the reasons behind opposition to and war against authority—both tyrannical and merely commonplace, historical and contemporary. Because the common dissident plays as important a role in political strife as the rebel touted a legend, it is important not to underestimate the role played by either one in the decline of authority faced by societal institutions, be they the state, the church, or the family. Each repression and abuse of power, however high or low, plays a role in the weakening of authority. Similarly, smaller political institutions and subdivisions, not merely the state, play a role in maintaining the equation of the legitimacy of power. Understanding the roles and functions that these smaller vestibules of power play in our political world will, it is hoped, lead us to realize the critical need for more responsible, accountable systems of governance and, indeed, ways of life.

## Part Two

# DEFIANCE AND ENFORCEMENT OF AUTHORITY IN AMERICA

## "A Land Heaven Smiled Upon"

Even God cannot change the past.
—Agathon (447–401 B.C.), attributed by Aristotle,
*The Nichomachean Ethics*

It has been said that although God cannot alter the past, historians can.
—Samuel Butler (1835–1902), *Erewhon*

CHAPTER THREE

# A Rebellious Nation: Seeds of Discontent

Almighty God, we make our earnest prayer that Thou wilt . . . incline the heart of the citizens to cultivate a spirit of subordination and obedience to government.

—George Washington, *Prayer after Inauguration*

If there be any among us who wish to dissolve this Union or to change its republican form, let them stand undisturbed as monuments to the safety with which error of opinion may be tolerated where reason is left free to combat it.

—Thomas Jefferson, *First Inaugural Address*

### PAINTING A NATIONAL PORTRAIT: APPROACHES TO THE STRUGGLE BETWEEN AUTHORITY AND AUTONOMY

The brinkmanship of the lone crusader, the daring exploits of small bands of political dissidents, the accounts of rebel armies who courageously take on the overwhelming power of the state—these have always fascinated Americans. It might even be said that the history of disobedience, of political offenses and offenders, and the parallel account of the government's exercise and defense of authority, is the history of America.

In Part One, we set out to introduce the reader to the antagonists of *The War against Authority*. "The Firebrands," in Chapter 1, described the making and the pursuits of the proponents of rebellion and political resistance, both in the United States and elsewhere. In Chapter 2, which explored "Abuse of Power," we endeavored to uncover the roots of rebellion in the unjust exercise of power by those in authority, once more looking at the domestic and international arenas.

In the next three chapters, subsumed within this Part Two, we will review the dramatic historical conflicts between the massive forces that have defended, and the lesser bands of those who have defied, existing political power in America, from colonial times to the present. These chapters reflect, as well, the constant destabilization and reconstruction of authority and legitimacy occurring within the struggle for power throughout American history. Our historical examination is critical, however, not only for understanding the former roles of rebels and those holding the reins of power in American society but also to be better able to gauge the marshaling of the forces of authority and autonomy today and in the future. America's unique and perhaps leading role in creating, through conflict, a well-ordered pluralistic society needs to be examined and better understood as a means for learning to respond more justly and effectively to challenges to authority and internal conflicts that so plague our world, and American society as well, today.

The legend of America's success in molding a pluralistic society has been told and retold in numerous variations. Most accounts have sought out and dwelled on harmonizing elements and influences. Few have viewed the initial hardships or the continuing internal conflicts as more than temporary digressions and roadblocks on the path toward national unity. Yet, one may advance the thesis that America's unique success and its peculiar sensitivity to questions of justice and equality stem from the stresses of its historical adversity and political strife.

The heroes and battles of the War of Independence have stimulated an unmatched body of historical literature. Similarly, the actors and campaigns of the second major episode of political crime in the nation's existence—the Civil War—have been recorded in greater detail than the people and events that form any other episode in America's history. But not only the sagas of the Founding Fathers and of the leaders of the Union and the Confederacy have been enshrined by history. The lives and exploits of other actors in America's political struggle—John Peter Zenger, John Brown, Susan B. Anthony, Eugene V. Debs, and Martin Luther King Jr.—have also sprouted innumerable celebrations, monuments, and biographical treatments. Even the more controversial activities of Aaron Burr, John Wilkes Booth, Ezra Pound, Ethel and Julius Rosenberg, Alger Hiss, Lee Harvey Oswald, Eldridge Cleaver, and John W. Hinckley Jr. have been the subjects of inexhaustible curiosity, investigation, and sometimes sympathy.

Moreover, the spotlight has been directed beyond the leading personalities in America's political rebellions and resistance. The various types, classes, and subcategories of political protest and warfare have been similarly scrutinized. Hardly a class of political dissidence—be it treason, sedition, assassination, rioting, draft evasion, labor militance, civil disobedience, or membership in outlawed parties—has escaped research and analysis. Finally, the defenses voiced by the defiers and the sanctions applied by those in authority (legislatures, the executive, the police, and the courts) against the wide spectrum of American political offenders have been similarly assessed in considerable detail.

For the most part, however, former accounts have focused on single phases or narrow manifestations of political crime, often dealing exclusively with offenders, offenses, or governmental responses. There have been few attempts at recording and analyzing political resistance and criminality in a comprehensive manner, at offering an understanding of the intricate interactions between political authority and political offenders, between political offenses and the forces of law and order in America.

Richard B. Morris carried out a monumental task in exploring the roots of this country's rebelliousness by concentrating on the histories and personalities of the *Seven Who Shaped Our Destiny: The Founding Fathers as Revolutionaries.*[1] Kenneth Keniston, similarly, produced an excellent study of *Young Radicals.*[2] Nathaniel Weyl, on the other hand, concentrated on a comprehensive chronology of political opposition in *Treason: The Story of Disloyalty and Betrayal in American History.*[3] James Willard Hurst, taking yet a different approach, chose, in *The Law of Treason in the United States*, to dwell on governmental responses by studying the developments in the law of treason during the early stages of the nation's history.[4] Most others tended to similarly confine their perspectives, each supplying only a chapter of the total story.

What complicates the task of presenting a comprehensive and balanced overview of political protest and resistance in America is not merely the inadequacy of official data-keeping on political crime (in contrast with the richness of the historical record) but also the added difficulty in selecting an appropriate focus. Should attention be given to obscure dissidents, or need the focus always remain on prominent personalities who spring forth during critical periods in the country's existence? Should one de-emphasize leaders and focus upon militant movements and organizations (including the Industrial Workers of the World, the Ku Klux Klan, the Communist Party, and the Black Panthers) which have risen throughout this nation's history? How much play should be given to specific and often erratic outbursts of mass disorder and violence (such as the lynch mobs of the post–Civil War South and the urban riots of the late 1960s)? And what of the many legislative enactments and criminal justice measures that have sought to respond to the perceived and real threats posed by political dissidence and disorder?

Confronted by these choices, we concluded that an emphasis on the life stories of noted political offenders is likely to sacrifice an understanding of political crime's broader socioeconomic underpinnings to a mythology of personalities. A focus upon political movements might tend, on the other hand, to overlook significant personal elements in the success or failure of resistance and dissent. Emphasizing mass violence and disorder will tend to stress communal strife over individual protest, while a focus upon law enforcement practices may tend to favor pragmatic and, at times, overzealous reaction over an understanding of the maladies.

Our objective, therefore, is the pursuit of a composite, multifaceted product. We will define major categories of political resistance and dissidence, and their characteristics. We will record the lives and deeds of both renowned and lesser-known political offenders. We will describe and assess both public and legal responses to unorthodox political actors and the defiance of authority. Our intention, therefore, is to cast a broad light on the times, the causes, the protagonists, and the dynamics of political dissent and rebellion, as well as upon the sanctions levied against those engaging in, or suspected of, resistance to the forces of authority. An examination of these intricate interactions will also operate to shed light on the efforts of America and its societal institutions for the attainment and maintenance of political legitimacy. This examination should further demonstrate the effect upon American society—its psyche, attitudes, and views of government—of the rebel's struggle for and against authority.

Our account—recording the changing symbiosis between socioeconomic factors, political forces, offenders, offenses, and legal systems—must therefore reflect a great degree of flexibility in emphasis. In some periods, portrayals of individual political offenders will loom largest. In other eras, accounts of the prevailing sociopolitical climate and of mass protest and resistance will receive greatest attention. For still other times, the story might dwell on governmental perspectives and measures for the defense of authority.

We hope these methodological notes will provide some organizing principles for what is to follow: a broad-ranging and chronologically ordered account of American protest, dissidence, resistance, and rebellion—collective and individual, violent and pacific, righteous and iniquitous. As this account unfolds, one increasingly realizes that neither Washington's prayer for citizens' obedience to government nor Jefferson's invocation of tolerance towards dissenters ever came to fruition in this country's political reality.

## ENGLISH AND COLONIAL FOUNDATIONS

"Divinity doth hedge a King," asserted Claudius, King of Denmark and Hamlet's uncle, in response to threats against his royal personage.[5] In Europe during the Middle Ages, the alleged divine rights of rulers were further reinforced by the doctrines and practices of feudalism, which considered an inferior's betrayal of the fealty due his lord to be the gravest of all mortal offenses.

The true implications of these dogmas were reflected in the harsh punishments meted out against traitors well into the modern age. In England, from the War of the Roses until the nineteenth century, the standard penalty for treason consisted of drawing and quartering:

> The traitor was drawn [head down] by a horse over rough ground to the gibbet. This was often mitigated . . . [by] allowing a hurdle to be placed under the condemned man, in part for mercy, and in part to insure the hangman a living body for torment. The prisoner was then hanged until nearly dead, cut down and disemboweled, with a partial burning sometimes . . . preceding the final beheading. . . . [The execution] was followed by quartering the traitors' parts and their display for the edification of the populace.[6]

Only English convicts of illustrious rank and character were fortunate enough to avoid the full measure of these cruel and degrading penalties. Mercifully beheaded, their heads nevertheless continued to be displayed on London Bridge, while their quarters were hung at the four city gates. When Sir Thomas More, the author of *Utopia,* was executed, his head was left hanging on the bridge for several months. It was his daughter Margaret who finally bought it from the authorities when it was "about to be thrown into the Thames to make room for others."[7]

With the scope of treason under the English common law being vague and elastic, those charged with the defense of authority were constantly labeling lesser forms of political protest and opposition as treason. During the reign of Charles II (1660–1685), when apprentices rioted in London and burned the city's infamous bawdy houses, they were convicted of treason "for encompassing the death of the King."[8] With social and economic reforms presumed to be the Crown's prerogative, efforts by the common masses to affect changes were often considered an invasion of the king's sovereignty. So widely was the law of treason stretched by the king's agents, that Parliament complained that "no man knew how he ought to behave himself, to do, speak, or say, for doubt of such pains of treason."[9]

Admittedly, Parliament had succeeded much earlier, by taking advantage of the Crown's financial overextensions (caused by the king's support of foreign wars, expensive courtesans, and court pageantry) during the reign of Edward III (1327–1377), in effecting a substantial reform of the treason laws. To prevent abuses, the reform-minded law 25 of Edward III (1352) defined *treason* in precise terms:

> When a man does encompass or imagine the death of our Lord the King, or our Lady his Queen or their eldest son and heir; or if a man doth violate the

King's companion, or the King's eldest daughter unmarried, or the wife of the King's eldest son and heir; or if a man do levy war against our Lord the King in his realm, or be adherent to the King's enemies in his realm, giving them aid and comfort in the realm or elsewhere, and therefore be probably attained of open deed.[10]

But the limiting words of this reform measure were soon ignored, misinterpreted, and again unduly broadened by England's courts. Still, from it the American Founding Fathers eventually borrowed the principal ideas and quaint phrases for their own constitutional definition of *treason* in America's constitution.

Other severe challenges confronted the first English settlers on these shores even before their landing. When in December of 1606 three small ships—the *Susan Constant*, the *Godspeed*, and the *Discovery*—sailed down the Thames River on their way to settle the distant colony of Virginia, storms prevented them from promptly leaving the English Channel. Numbering approximately one hundred five men, not including the crews of the three ships, the Virginia settlers later made several stops in the Canaries and in the islands of the West Indies, further delaying their arrival in the New World and diminishing their stores of supplies.

But from their very first day of arrival in the spring of 1607, the new settlers, in addition to battling the physical and economic hardships of colonizing a wilderness (for which these gentlemen-adventurers were ill-prepared), became embroiled in political strife. Natives attacked an exploring party of the empire builders even before the party had selected a place for their permanent colony. Within the first year, George Kendall, one of the seven councilors initially put in charge of the colony by King James's authority, was charged, convicted, and shot for conspiring against the colony. In 1622, the struggling colony was almost obliterated during a mass Indian uprising in which more than three hundred fifty white settlers of all ages and both sexes perished (blacks were left unharmed).

By 1635 long-brewing controversies between the settlers and their council and the Crown-appointed governor, Sir John Harvey, erupted into open revolt. Critics and leaders of the opposition were arrested on the governor's orders and were held to be tried under martial law. In the ensuing confrontation with the council, the governor charged a councilor with treason against the king. The council summoned forty musketeers previously planted around the chamber into action, and the conflict did not subside until Governor Harvey departed in haste for England. This was possibly the first coup d'état in the new colonies. Indeed, not until after the suppression of the 1676 popular rebellion commanded by Nathaniel Bacon, an aristocratic Cambridge-educated member of the council who led opposition to another royal governor, did Virginia achieve a temporary political respite.[11]

Although the English colonists of the seventeenth century brought with them the institutions of English law and custom, the remoteness and isolation of the colonies initially made any continuing guidance from the mother country very difficult. English lawbooks did not become available in America until the late 1600s.[12] The major legal sources for the colonists were contained in the royal charters and proprietary grants and in the individuals sent over to rule the colonies. Thus the colonies imported the English common law, which recognized the crime of treason and conferred on the colonial proprietors and governors general authority to exercise criminal and martial law for the suppression of treason and rebellion.[13] Local authorities, however, frequently created supplementary laws and fashioned their own idiosyncratic interpretations of common law.

In the colonies, as in England, attempts to modify public policies through mass protest were at times interpreted as a "constructive" levying of war against the sovereign. The inclusion of political criticism and civil unrest under the definition of *treason* unduly broadened the scope of the crime. When in the 1680s a number of Virginians attempted to control tobacco prices by destroying young plants, Governor Culpeper forced their prosecution for treason,[14] even before the colonial legislature could define such destruction of tobacco plants and storage facilities as "treasonous."[15] In New York, one Nicholas Bayard was likewise prosecuted in 1702 under a law that made any act of opposition to the government treason.[16] Fortunately for Bayard, who had circulated petitions critical of the colonial government, his treason trial resulted in an acquittal of the charge of "levying war."

Despite the English heritage of the colonies, not all settlers agreed with England's legal principles or with their application. Many colonists sought to create radically different forms of government on this continent. Some hoped to establish a theocracy. The New Haven Colony demonstrated its religious commitments in relying upon the Bible as authority for its criminal laws. The 1656 Laws of New Haven cited both Numbers and Samuel (Num. 16, 2 Sam. 18, and 2 Sam. 20) in support of the community's treason provisions.[17]

Colonial treason laws frequently reflected local realities and concerns. A Maryland Act for Treasons, considered at the 1638 session of the General Assembly, defined as treasonous such conduct as the joining, adhering, or confederating "with any Indians."[18] A similar concern with issues of communal security was manifested in the Massachusetts Bay Act of August 31, 1706, which outlawed "all traiterous [sic] correspondence with the French king, or his subjects, or the Indian enemy or rebels, and supplying them with warlike or other stores."[19]

Of special significance in colonial history were the distinct social and legal standards applicable to freemen, women, slaves, indentured servants, and Indians. Each of these groups possessed particular and distinct rights and obligations, departures from which often constituted criminality—even treason. Many of the restraints and penalties were imposed not for prohibited activities but as a consequence of racial, socioeconomic, or sexual status. A woman, for example, could be charged with petit treason for offending her husband-master.[20] Completely barred from participation in political life, women also suffered other disabilities with regard to family and testamentary law. Yet, other societal functions of women remained unaffected.

In the early colonial period, slaves and indentured servants were almost indistinguishable and were subject to similar rules and restraints. But as the African population increased, the law began to distinguish between the two. While indentured servitude continued as a racially blind contractual obligation for a limited term, slavery became an exclusively racial and innate status, usually continuing for life and through generations.[21] Regulated strictly were not only the slave's relationship with his or her master but also the whole range of social relationships between slaves and freemen, as well as a host of activities within the slave community proper, including matters of commercial, conjugal, and religious intercourse.

For the indigenous peoples (perceived and legally designated as independent nations) the colonial law reserved a fiction of freedom. But political and economic realities accorded Native Americans few, if any, of the rights enjoyed by the colonists.

Status alone—determined by membership in racial, gender, political, or economic groups—thus sufficed to render a majority of the colonial people subject to special restraints, the violation of which was criminally and otherwise punishable. Slaves were punished for attending school, women for attempting to cast their ballot, and Indians for refusing to relinquish their ancestral preserves.

Attempts by colonists themselves to exercise greater religious and press freedom frequently resulted in political prosecutions, trials, and harsh punishments. Among the noteworthy colonial examples of political repression were the 1660 trial and execution of Quaker Mary Dyer for venturing forth to preach her dissident Quaker gospel in the Massachusetts Bay stronghold of puritanism,[22] and the 1735 New York trial of John Peter Zenger for seditious libel against colonial governor William Cosby.[23]

A particularly bloody event of that era was Bacon's Rebellion in Virginia. In 1676 Nathaniel Bacon rose in armed resistance against the policies of the corrupt William Berkeley, the colonial governor. Bacon's resistance was labeled treason, though his acts were directed not against the colonial authority but against the frontier Indians (who were attacked by Bacon's men after Berkeley had refused to protect the Virginians' settlements). Following their defeat, Bacon's followers were subjected to extremely harsh penalties. Subsequently removing Berkeley from office, Charles II lamented the governor's lack of leniency: "That old fool has hanged more men in that naked country than I have done for the murder of my father."[24]

By the eighteenth century, as they were entering adolescence, the American colonies began to rely strongly on the strictures of the English statute of Edward III as a means of restraining the insidious reach of the crime of treason. Before that the brutal punishments accompanying treason in England never seemed able to cross the Atlantic. Colonial trial judges did relish reading aloud the barbarous English formulas that called for drawing and quartering, often embellishing their descriptions with style and whim. However, the colonial court usually commuted the sentence to death by hanging.[25] This policy of restraint may account for the lack of public outcry against the law of treason at the time of the American Revolution.

Still, the eighteenth century brought fiercer winds of change both to the New World and to the Old. The onset of modern industry and the rise of the nation-state had hastened the demise of feudalism. Even before the American colonies began their trek toward independence, rebellious voices began suggesting that representative and secular government should displace hereditary and divine authority. Nevertheless, the deep connections between sacrilege, feudal fealty, and treason failed to fade away quickly. Under new labels, severe penalties continued to be preserved for offenses that threatened the "sovereign" (the designated symbol of authority) or "sovereignty" (the institutions of government). While new philosophies advancing the notion of government by "social contract" supplied justification for popular rebellion against evil rulers and rules, treason continued to be universally despised. To paraphrase Dryden, even when treason was considered necessary, the traitor continued to be hated.[26]

### THE REVOLUTIONARY ERA: TRAITORS OR WARRIORS?

Three centuries ago, English essayist Sir John Harrington recognized the critical role of outcome in the assessment of treason:

Treason doth never prosper—what's the reason?
If it doth prosper none dare call it treason.[27]

American historian Nathaniel Weyl similarly concluded that failed rebellion was punished as treason, whereas treason that succeeded was honored as patriotic revolution.[28] Not surprisingly, therefore, the anti-English agitation and unrest that erupted in the colonies during the years leading up to the

American Revolution were viewed by Americans as just in the struggle for the basic rights previously accorded to all Englishmen. At the same time, the colonial pursuit of greater autonomy was seen as treasonous by those in authority in the mother country.[29]

At that hour in history, the English had at their command a formidable array of measures for maintaining public order. In England, riots, resistance to law, criticism of the king and his government, and other forms of physical, or even verbal, protest had been punished as treason. Yet in the colonies, an explosion of incendiary writings, civil disobedience, boycotts, and even military engagements initially failed to bring forth formal English charges of treason and criminality—despite frequent rhetorical references to treason in Parliament and the English press.[30]

The colonial resistance to the 1764 Sugar and 1765 Stamp Acts was one spur to English cries of "treason." Opposition to the Sugar Act, which levied new taxes on imports of non-English sugar and banned all imports of rum, finally led to a boycott of British goods.[31] The protest gained momentum through publicly circulated letters and newspaper articles. The assertion that taxes were being levied on the colonies without colonial representation in Parliament was first heard at this time. Opposition to the Stamp Act—designed to raise money for colonial defense through the imposition of revenue stamps on legal, commercial, and other printed matter—was similarly expressed in pamphlets and local newspapers. British officials referred to these writings as "scandalous and treasonable." General Thomas Gage, the English commander, reported that he was disturbed "to see the Public Papers crammed with treason."[32]

Colonial turbulence grew as the first shipment of stamps arrived in New York. The second shipment, two months later, was burned before it could be unloaded. The English quickly asked the New York Council to suppress all "treasonable" writings and to provide a police force to maintain order. Neither of these measures was undertaken by the colonists. Indeed, before the Stamp Act went into effect, every stamp agent in the colonies had been badgered into resigning, or promising not to execute, his commission.[33] Widespread rioting by the Sons of Liberty took place in Boston, Philadelphia, Newport, and Charleston, as well as in New York. No further English effort was made to enforce the Stamp Act, and both it and the Sugar Act were later repealed.

Two distinct British policies were discernible in response to the American unrest. The first assumed that the colonial resistance was the product of a few incendiary leaders, and that if these troublemakers could be silenced—or made an example of—the unrest would cease. The second policy saw the problems as community-wide and relied on collective sanctions for their suppression. The latter policy called for isolating certain political or geographic areas, considered to be in a state of rebellion, and for imposing coercive measures against these particular enclaves.[34] Often, the two distinct policies overlapped.

The British effort to root out ringleaders was first manifested in response to the colonial resistance to the 1767 Townsend Acts, named after the English Chancellor of the Exchequer. The Acts imposed new duties on consumer goods and provided that customs commissioners were to receive their pay from the collected funds. In the collection of duties, commissioners were also authorized to seek assistance from various colonial officials and the courts.

The colonists condemned the Acts and responded by forming a strong nonimportation movement.[35] The colonial boycott had its desired effects. Parliament, under pressure from English merchants, repealed all the duties except the one on tea; this temporarily satisfied the colonists, and the boycott was abandoned.

In 1768 the agitations and riots led to an investigation by high officials of the British government into the feasibility of conducting treason trials in the colonies. Suspicious of the sympathy that local juries were likely to display toward American defendants, the English sought means to bring those accused of treason to trial in England. The legal mechanics were found in an obscure statute, passed in the reign of Henry VIII, providing for transportation of overseas traitors for trial in England.[36]

Many in the British camp speculated that a dramatic trial, followed by the execution of some of the colonial resistance leaders, would serve to deter the undecided and to pacify America. Yet some of the king's own law officers argued that the colonial actions of the time had not amounted to treason under the statute of Edward III.[37] A stalemate ensued. The desirability of an English trial for selected colonists continued to be debated in Parliament and between the king's counselors. Even Parliament's passage of the Bedford Resolution, urging the king to make examples of the discontented leaders, did not result in the initiation of treason prosecutions.[38]

Britain's policies toward the colonies continued to be ill-defined until the East India Tea Act of 1773, which eventually brought about the most famous outbreak of opposition. The Act placed a new duty on tea but compensated for it by allowing the direct shipment of tea from India to America without previous routing through England.[39] With direct shipment, even after the duty was applied, the Indian tea was less expensive for the colonists than tea previously available through either English imports or smugglers. Some of the objections to the new tax were thus raised by local merchants who had stocks of smuggled tea from Holland, which they did not want undersold.

Once more the principle of "no taxation without representation" was voiced, and more vigorously. Resistance was strongest in Rhode Island,

Philadelphia, New York, and, of course, Boston. Following heated public debates, a boycott was declared, and finally the tea, which was still on ships in the harbor of Boston, was dumped into the sea by the Sons of Liberty.[40]

The English responded with collective sanctions, the second of the policies offered for the suppression of American unrest. Determining the city of Boston to be in a state of rebellion, Parliament, in 1774, passed a series of acts (known in the colonies as the Coercive or Intolerable Acts) to punish the entire city. The Acts closed the port of Boston, provided that an official indicted in Massachusetts for a capital offense occurring while enforcing English law could be tried in England, dissolved the elected council, and installed a new council appointed by the king. The Acts also declared it treason for inhabitants to assemble or to form associations for the purpose of considering grievances.[41]

A new Quartering Act was imposed as well, specifying that British troops could be housed, without permission, in buildings belonging to the colonists. The contemporaneous passing in Parliament of the Quebec Act, strengthening and expanding a territory viewed by the colonists as a potential competitor, appeared as yet another threat to the colonies' security, especially since the Act recognized the binding effect on the American continent of French laws (including nonjury trials).[42]

Beyond the imposition of collective sanctions, the English officials tried once more to bring selected individuals to trial. Samuel Adams, John Hancock, the entire Boston Committee of Correspondence, the selectmen of the city, the town clerk, and members of the House of Representatives were named as possible traitors, subject to arrest and prosecution in England. But the Privy Council in London failed to take the necessary action to implement prosecution.[43]

The strict procedural requirements of the English treason law, requiring two witnesses to every overt act charged, worked to the Americans' advantage. To the English law officers, it seemed that the requisite witnesses from the colonies could never be assembled, and therefore the charges could not be proved by the required evidence. In the face of such legal uncertainty, final orders were never given for the transportation of colonial suspects for trial in England.

Strong opposition to the Coercive Acts was voiced by the First Continental Congress (assembled in 1774 with representatives from all colonies except Georgia). The famous Suffolk Resolves denounced British policy and declared a full boycott on all commerce with Great Britain and the British West Indies.[44] More significantly, the Resolves authorized the colonies to raise their own army. These actions led to new and even stronger British considerations of treason trials for colonial leaders, but again with no apparent results.

Learning of the Suffolk Resolves, the Crown sent a "secret letter" to England's colonial commander, General Gage, which many historians believe instructed him to go into the countryside around Boston to seize arms and to arrest patriot leaders.[45] Whatever his intentions were in going to Lexington and Concord, the result was a British humiliation and the first skirmish between Americans and British, the so-called "shot heard round the world."

A new English plan to destroy the resistance was promulgated during the winter of 1774–75. A general pardon was proposed for all political activists (except the leaders) who would surrender and take an oath of allegiance to England. The hope was that this would leave most leaders, especially Samuel Adams and John Hancock, standing alone and vulnerable. The proposed general pardon was accompanied, nevertheless, by a declaration of martial law.[46]

When these measures failed, the policy aimed against individual political leaders was again discarded, and a new and broader program of general sanctions was instituted. Parliament declared the existence of a general state of rebellion, severed all trade with the colonies, commanded military and civilian officers to bring traitors to justice, and asked the aid of England's population for the trial of those, in the mother country, carrying on any "traitorous correspondence" with the American rebels.[47]

The capture of Colonel Ethan Allen in the fall of 1775 provided a turning point in the hitherto uncertain English policy regarding the treatment of rebellious colonists. Allen, leader of the Green Mountain Boys, gained renown for his unauthorized takeover of British Fort Ticonderoga in May 1775. When captured by the British, Allen was advised that he would be dealt with as a traitor. Taken to England for trial, he claimed to be a prisoner of war. The American leaders, including George Washington, communicated to General Gage and the other English officials that if Allen were treated as a traitor, there would be retaliation against British prisoners held in the colonies. After lengthy deliberations and bitter disagreements, the British Cabinet reached the precedent-making decision to treat Allen as a prisoner of war. With a writ of habeas corpus for his release being successfully sought at about the same time, in less than three weeks Allen was on a ship bound for New York.[48]

Under the new English policy, colonial dissidents were to be confined with no entitlement to bail and with no right to habeas corpus. Trials were not to be held, however, without Privy Council consent. The point of no return had been reached. From then on, especially after the Declaration of Independence on July 4, 1776, the colonists were in fact no longer to be considered traitors but rather as belligerents protected by the laws of war. The compromise retained serious risks. It implied that the prisoners would be released if America's war of independence was successful, but if America failed in its mission, the dissidents could still be destined for the traitors' gallows at England's Tyburn.[49]

## FROM REVOLUTION TO CONSTITUTION

The question of allegiance was one of the most traumatic of the revolutionary period. In the years immediately preceding and following the Declaration of Independence, the colonial population was confronted with new political entities claiming entitlement to the allegiances formerly owed to England and the king. One could not insist on being politically passive or neutral in the face of these developments. Citizens found themselves suspected of disloyalty and labeled "traitors" for failure to renounce their former allegiance to the Crown in favor of governments that had yet to be officially formed. There remained only a short period during which a person could elect where his loyalty lay. This was the time between the Declaration of Independence and the passage of treason laws by the respective states.[50] After that there existed no place or time for doubts. The states would refuse to protect the liberty or property of those who shunned the risks of choice in the hope of identifying with the eventual victor. These were, as Thomas Paine said, "the times that tried men's souls."

The country's new state governments were inclined to avoid the legal issue of loyalty as long as possible—the question seeming too controversial and ambiguous to be immediately faced. Even in the new Continental Congress, where patriot leaders assembled, a majority professed their loyalty to George III until late in the summer of 1776. Since the states showed a reluctance to deal with this sensitive issue, the new American standards pertaining to loyalty and treason were abdicated from the states to the new federal authorities.

The federal standards grew out of the experience of the Continental Army, which could not long ignore the problem. As early as June 30, 1775, the Continental Congress passed legislation establishing the Articles of War for the Continental Army, thereby authorizing punishment, short of the death penalty, for mutiny and sedition against the newly created country. The Articles also made criminal the act of harboring the enemy or providing him with supplies. These offenses constituted the military equivalents of traditional treason: levying war against the sovereign or adhering to the enemy and giving him aid and comfort. Because a new loyalty was pledged, and old allegiances dissolved, through military service, those who joined the Continental Army became in effect the first colonists to owe allegiance to the new country.

The original Articles of War soon proved to be inadequate. The treason of Benjamin Church, chief surgeon of the Continental Army, who had acted as an informer for British General Gage, demonstrated the need for stricter standards. When Church's offenses came to light, the military punishment of cashiering, authorized by the Continental Articles of War, was considered insufficient.[51] Stricter penalties were not available under state law because Massachusetts, where the offense allegedly occurred, was still an English possession, and treason under its laws consisted of betrayal of the king. How could Church then be accused of actions hostile to the confederacy or the state when his activities were taken on behalf of the king? To overcome the deficiencies in state laws, Congress stiffened the national laws of war, authorizing the death penalty for Continental soldiers who remained loyal to George III.[52]

Sentiment against loyalists ran high during the winter of 1775–76, but the governments of the thirteen colonies still refused to act with regard to civilian, as contrasted with military, treason. The control of disaffected civilians fell by default to the army, with George Washington recognizing that he had to act despite the absence of specific congressional authorization. As the army began to administer loyalty oaths to suspected Tories in Rhode Island, and to disarm and arrest others in New York, the civilian governments felt the need to assert their supremacy against the threat of military dominance. Even some in the military objected to such intervention in civilian matters, and General Charles Lee argued that "there can be no liberty where the military is not subordinate to the civil power in everything not immediately connected with their operations."[53]

By January of 1776 Congress had passed the Tory Act, which allowed the disarming of those not committed to the cause of independence, providing also that the more dangerous Tories be taken into custody. After June 1776 the American law of treason began to develop ever more rapidly. Early in that month a large ring of counterfeiters, using bogus money to recruit pro-British troops in New York, was discovered. There was talk of a plot, involving Thomas Hickey, one of Washington's personal guards, to assassinate George Washington. Hickey was convicted by a court martial for sedition, mutiny, and holding a "treacherous correspondence" with the enemy. The following day he became the first person to suffer death under the American law of treason.[54] His execution signaled that a new government, demanding new allegiances, had come into being.

After the mayor of New York City was implicated in the Hickey plot, the Continental Congress adopted the Congressional Resolves of June 24, 1776. The Resolves, a de facto declaration of independence, were the first public act to openly defy the king of England and to name him as the enemy. Becoming the ultimate basis of every treason statute and prosecution during the Revolution, the Resolves relied on the familiar words of the treason statute of Edward III:

That all persons abiding within any of the United Colonies, and deriving protection from the laws of the same, owe allegiance to the said laws. . . .

That all persons owing allegiance to any of the United Colonies . . . who shall levy war against any of the said colonies . . . or be adherent to the king of Great Britain, or others the enemies of the said colonies . . . giving to him or them aid and comfort, are guilty of treason against such colony.

That it be recommended to the legislatures of the several United Colonies, to pass laws for punishing, in such manner as to them shall seem fit, such persons before described.[55]

Under pressure from Congress the states began to pass their own treason laws. Within six months of the Declaration of Independence, six states had laws on their books defining treason.[56] The other states followed suit shortly afterward. State legislatures used three basic models for defining treasonous conduct.[57] The first, continuing the English practice of subsuming all prohibited political activities under the term *treason*, incorporated the language of Edward III, as well as the English common law, into existing state law.[58]

The second formula specified the particular acts that would constitute "levying of war" or "adherence to the enemy," adding to, limiting, or otherwise changing the common law's interpretation of these phrases. Pennsylvania's statute, for example, included under high treason attempts to erect an independent government within any territory of the Commonwealth.[59] The New York statute included, as did several other laws, the crime of sedition within the definition of treason:

That if any . . . Citizen or Subject of this State, or of any of the United States of America . . . shall maliciously, advisedly and directly, by preaching, teaching, speaking, writing, or printing, declare or maintain, that the King of Great Britain hath, or of Right ought to have, any Authority . . . in or over this State, or the Inhabitants thereof . . . he shall be adjudged guilty . . . and shall suffer the Pains and Penalties prescribed by Law in Cases of Felony without Benefit of Clergy.[60]

The third approach consisted of passing a narrowly defined treason statute accompanied by ancillary laws defining political offenses that were lesser than treason. The Maryland Act of December 3, 1777, thus made it an offense for any inhabitant of the state to go on board any vessel of war or transport belonging to the enemy, to enter any city in enemy possession, or otherwise to receive any protection from the enemy. The prescribed penalty was a fine not to exceed "ten pounds for every hundred pounds of property belonging to such person within the state." The court was permitted further to order the offender "whipped not exceeding thirty-nine lashes."[61]

The new ancillary offenses, including many so-called anti-Tory provisions, were considered "inferior in malignity to treason" but still acts "injurious to the Independence of America."[62] Some prohibited acknowledging the sovereignty of the king; others made it illegal to persuade citizens to abandon their colonial allegiance, discourage them from enlisting in the American forces, or incite them to disorders. A few specifically prohibited speaking or writing against the new state governments, spreading discouraging rumors, or even drinking to the king's health.[63]

These lesser political offenses were usually punished by fines, imprisonment, deportation, or involuntary military service. The new offenses were useful in controlling the remaining pockets of "Toryism" in states such as Maryland, where pro-British populations and economic interests were strong. Uniquely revealing of the new campaign against disloyalty was the 1777 Maryland Act to "Punish Certain Crimes and Misdemeanors, and Prevent the Growth of Toryism." Maryland's new law prohibited citizens, under penalty of banishment for life or of five years' imprisonment, from maintaining that the king or Parliament had any authority over the United States. Oaths of allegiance were imposed on all voters. Citizens adjudged guilty of treason against the state were to be put to death without benefit of clergy, and their estates were to be forfeited to the state.

Maryland's 1777 law was replete with controversial practices that were to resurface in later periods of political stress in America: the prohibition of seditious speech; the imposition of loyalty oaths; the requirement that citizens report all those suspected of treason to the authorities; the restriction of travel; the detention without trial of "dangerous" persons; and the suspension of habeas corpus—the legal writ that had traditionally protected individuals from unlawful imprisonment.

To gain perspective on the American experience during this critical period in the nation's history, one must rely primarily upon the evidence derived from the newly minted laws. The era's record of judicial opinions and decided cases is scarce.[64]

An initial examination of the statutes might lead one to believe that treason prosecutions were widespread and the penalties severe, that there was frequent use of special loyalty tribunals and military commissions, and that bias and prejudice prevailed. But the reported trials, however few, lead to a contrary conclusion. The great majority of cases were tried under traditional procedures before regularly constituted, nonmilitary courts. The less-formal trials authorized by some states did not materialize, because there was reluctance to depart from established legal practices. Even the military, forced by wartime circumstances to handle some treason cases, was reluctant to do so. Significantly, a group of officers in New York urged civil supremacy by contending that "State prisoners should and ought to be tryed [sic] by a Court of this State where they should have all the priviledges [sic] of the Law, as Freemen. . . . we fear whilst we are strugling [sic] for the Sacred Name of Liberty we are establishing the fatal Tendency to Despotism."[65]

Many of those committed to the new liberties for which the revolution was fought were eager to protect the rights of their opponents not only by making the definition of treason precise but also by maintaining procedural proprieties. Practically all of the treason laws enacted at the time required the testimony of two credible witnesses and incorporated the other protective procedures contained in the English act of Edward III. Only two states retained the common law's harshness in automatically condemning an accused who refused to plead and chose to stand mute. Most states left to the jury the disposition of those not pleading. Those found incapable of pleading due to insanity were imprisoned until they had recovered, and for all others failing to plead, a plea of not guilty was entered. The English practice of *peine fort et dure*, which consisted of piling iron weights on the naked body of a mute accused until he pleaded or died, was never used in this country.[66]

Few vestiges of the cruel English law survived. The ancient institutions of corruption of blood, outlawry, and confiscation were among those that did. Corruption of blood, which prevented the convicted person from inheriting or passing any property through his blood line, was uncommon in America, and three states imposed outright bans against it.[67] Outlawry was resorted to when judicial proceedings against an individual could not be carried out, usually because of the suspect's escape. The accused in such an instance was proclaimed an outlaw and subject to punishment without further trial. Confiscation was the most widespread penalty, imposed on those convicted of treason as well as on untried absentee property owners suspected of loyalist affiliations.

The new statutes were generally aimed at individuals who sought foreign refuge during the Revolutionary War, and ordered them to return to take a loyalty oath or to stand trial to clear themselves. Those failing to return were considered to have gone over to the enemy, and their property was forfeited. The laws, in addition, also made limited use of banishment for those who had withdrawn to enemy-controlled territory or who had refused to swear allegiance to the newly independent colonies.[68]

These severe enactments were only sporadically enforced. Revolutionary America's record of enforcement of treason and lesser political offenses reflected the reluctance of the citizenry and the leadership to resort to drastic nonconciliatory measures. The states displayed more and more caution as the process moved from lawmaking toward actual execution of an alleged offender. Although the provisions of the law were draconian and arrests were relatively common, grand jury indictments were few. Judges and juries exhibited great restraint in deciding treason cases, and convictions were rare. Pardons, finally, prevented most executions from being carried out.[69]

Virginia may well have illustrated the country's mood. The state underwent considerable turmoil during the Revolutionary War. After four years of war, with a steady drain of men, money, and supplies, the Militia Act of 1780–81 was too much for many Virginians to bear. Antidraft riots erupted, which resulted in forty-one people being arrested by the militia for treason. On the day of the trial, sorrowful families gathered to pay their final respects to their loved ones, who expected to be hanged shortly. But the budding tragedy ended on a farcical note when the special commissioners appointed to try the case never arrived. Instead, a pardon was sent for all except John Claypoole and the other leaders. Soon they too were freed. Despite the considerable Tory threat and the several convictions for treason that were handed down, no one was hanged in Virginia for treason throughout the Revolutionary War.[70]

Pennsylvania offers another insight into the nation's response to treason and traitors. The end of the British occupation of Philadelphia and the American reentry in 1778 led to a number of criminal prosecutions. On returning to the City of Brotherly Love, the new authorities enacted a confiscation law that included bills of attainder for thirteen named individuals.[71] The list of marked persons then grew to 450.

The Philadelphia prosecutions that followed were the most important treason trials of the period. Although by resolution of Congress, civilians had been made liable to military trial for acts of treason, the accused were nevertheless brought before civil courts. The grand jury of the September 1778 assize considered forty-five bills of indictment, and twenty-three cases were set for trial. Of these cases, all ended in acquittals except two: those of Abraham Carlisle and John Roberts.

The two had entered the service of the enemy when the British had occupied the city. Carlisle had served as a gatekeeper, while Roberts had gotten more closely involved with the occupiers, recruiting men and furnishing supplies to them. The trials of Roberts and Carlisle, according to contemporary accounts, were moderate and fair.[72] The accused had excellent counsel, including James Wilson, who was later to play an important role in writing the United States Constitution's definition of treason. Both defendants were sentenced to hang. By the time the trials were concluded, Roberts and Carlisle had become objects of pity. Despite the public clamor for pardons, the pleas were in vain. Fearing that a pardon would encourage others to contemplate treason in the future, those in authority imposed upon Roberts and Carlisle the ultimate penalty.

## TREASON AFTER THE CONSTITUTION

During the postrevolutionary period, the country continued to be governed by the 1781 Articles of Confederation, which had created a loose grouping of strong, independent-minded states and delegated little power and responsibility to a weak and poor central government. After the independence of the United States was recognized by the 1783 Treaty of Paris, the nation's governmental formula was increasingly deemed to be inadequate. It became apparent that thirteen new and separate states could not overcome the domestic problems produced by a postwar economic depression, accompanied by high taxes and unsound local currencies. Neither did the loose federation possess sufficient clout to be effectively heard in the political and economic arenas of the world.

The growing crisis was reflected as well in two serious manifestations of political rebellion. The first was an attempt by the territory of Vermont to gain total independence. Under the leadership of Ethan Allen, the Green Mountain Boys sought to make the virtually unpopulated wilderness of Vermont wholly separate from the United States. Allen even offered to "do everything in [his] power to render this state a British province"[73] if Great Britain would guarantee Vermont's secession. Writing to Congress in March of 1781 he declared, "I am resolutely determined to defend the independence of Vermont as against the Congress of the United States, and rather than fail will retire with the hardy Green Mountain Boys into the desolate caverns of the mountains and wage war against human nature at large."[74] But as Vermont's population grew, the plan faded and in 1791 Vermont was admitted to the Union as the fourteenth state. No action was taken by the national authorities against the autonomy-minded Vermonters.

A far more serious national disruption occurred in the years 1786–87. While there existed at the time, as Washington put it, "the combustibles of revolt in almost every state," only in Massachusetts did they catch fire.[75] A short prosperity that followed the 1783 peace gave way to serious financial difficulties, particularly among the middle and lower classes. Mortgages were foreclosed, farms were seized and sold for failure to pay taxes, and debtor's prisons were beginning to overflow. The problems of high taxes and mounting debts, combined with declining farm prices and the new Massachusetts legislative demand that all debts be paid in rare specie (i.e., hard money), led to the uprising known as Shays' Rebellion.

Many of those most affected by the economic depression were, like Captain Daniel Shays, veterans of the Revolution who had never received their army compensation because of Congress's inability to collect revenues from the states. Shays and the other insurgents were inland farmers who had to pay as much as one-third of their income in taxes. Because of necessity, Shays was even forced to sell a commemorative sword presented to him, during the Revolution, by the Marquis de Lafayette.

Agrarian activism had long been a familiar phenomenon in Massachusetts. Following a pattern set more than a decade earlier in response to the English Coercive Acts, mobs led by Captain Shays closed the courts to prevent what were considered unjust foreclosures and judgments for debts.

Ironically, former firebrand Samuel Adams, now a member of the state council, proposed to hang those who employed the very tactics he himself had used in 1774.[76] Although the goal of the rebellion was tax relief and a settlement of grievances, the Massachusetts legislature and executive declared the rebellion to be treason.[77] After several brief encounters with the state militia, national troops not being available, the rebellion was crushed in early 1787. Shays escaped to Vermont, but fourteen of his followers were captured and sentenced to death. All participants in the locally popular uprising were pardoned, however, in 1788.

The rebellion shocked the newly established American republic. There was in evidence considerable public sympathy for Shays because many of the problems resulting in his revolt had prevailed throughout the country and were not restricted to rural populations. While most political leaders were disturbed that the national Congress was unable to act in support of Massachusetts, others were appalled that a rebellion had been attempted in the first place. Some believed that the incident may have frightened the monied classes into more readily accepting the new federal Constitution and its promise of centralized power.

Few public figures, however, took Shays' Rebellion as philosophically as did Jefferson. Professing that he liked "a little rebellion now and then," Jefferson wrote, "God forbid we should every twenty years be without such a rebellion."[78] The drafter of the Declaration of Independence considered the spirit of resistance to government so valuable that he believed it was better that the people voice their protest even when wrong than have the spark of rebellion lost entirely. Jefferson's views notwithstanding, new methods were soon being sought for strengthening the national government in order to prevent similar disruptions from occurring in the future.

In 1787 a convention was called at Philadelphia by Congress, purportedly "for the sole and express purpose of revising the Articles of Confederation."[79] The assemblage of fifty-five delegates who attended was probably the most august ever to gather on this continent. Twenty-six of the delegates were college graduates,[80] and nearly three-fourths had sat in the Continental Congress. Eight had signed the Declaration of Independence, and twenty-one had fought in the Revolution. When Jefferson, then in Paris, read the names of the participants, he proclaimed the meeting "an assembly of demi-gods."[81]

When the Committee of Detail, led by James Wilson and Edmund Randolph, drafted the treason clause in August of 1787 and reported it to the Convention, the foundation was set for a restrictive approach to this ancient crime. The definition of treason, according to the draft, was not to be in the hands of Congress, as some had suggested, but was to be specifically included in the Constitution.[82] Congress was given only the power to fix penalties. Madison noted that the "Framers left neither the courts nor Congress any method for creating [the] constructive treasons which terrorized the people of former years."[83] The intent to create a restrictive definition of the crime was further demonstrated in the debate of the Committee of the Whole on August 20, 1787.[84] Gouverneur Morris, a delegate from Pennsylvania, urged that it was "essential to the preservation of liberty to define precisely and exclusively what shall constitute the crime of treason."[85] Some Federalists subsequently argued that even in the absence of a bill of rights, the rights of individuals against governmental abuse would be adequately protected through this narrow *treason* definition.[86]

The Founding Fathers' deep concern that under the guise of punishing treason the government might curb political activity and dissent resulted in treason becoming the only crime to be defined by the Constitution. The constitutional language contains both a substantive definition of *treason* and the procedural requirement of a confession or testimony by two witnesses to the same overt act. These limitations were considered necessary because, as Benjamin Franklin said, "prosecutions for treason were generally virulent, and perjury too easily made use of against innocence."[87] Although the Constitution delegated to Congress the power to set the punishment for the offense, it abolished some of the penalties previously used. Borrowing from the English law of treason, the new Constitution's Article III, section 3, declared:

> Treason against the United States, shall consist only in levying War against them, or in adhering to their Enemies, giving them Aid and Comfort. No Person shall be convicted of Treason unless on the testimony of two Witnesses to the same overt Act, or on Confession in open Court.
>
> The Congress shall have Power to declare the Punishment of Treason, but no attainder of Treason shall work Corruption of Blood, or Forfeiture except during the life of the Person attainted.

Those who had themselves engaged in treason under the former English law now had an opportunity to formulate their own standards for this most feared of all crimes. The new constitutional language was more precise than that employed by the English law that they had broken. From an offense against the British monarch, his person and his institutions, treason in America evolved into a crime against the new sovereign—the nation. Less punitive than its predecessor, the new law was also more restrictive and far more difficult to apply, in order to "take out of the hands of tyrannical kings, and of weak and wicked ministers, that deadly weapon, which constructive treason had furnished them with."[88] The design was to prevent the previous abuses, which, according to Jefferson, had "drawn the blood of the best and honestest men in the kingdom."[89]

It was the constitutional draftsmen's clear intent to prevent treason from ever again becoming a dreaded weapon in the hands of those in authority, used to crush unorthodox causes or reform-minded citizens. But while the new law of treason could no longer be readily expanded to suppress mere unorthodoxy or dissent, other laws were soon to be enacted for the purpose of controlling or silencing broad varieties of political opponents, protesters, and resisters—those whom we usually designate "political offenders."

## FROM THE WHISKEY REBELLION
## TO THE ALIEN AND SEDITION ACTS

The first test of treason under the new Constitution came with the Whiskey Rebellion. Farmers, who had played a central role in Daniel Shays' 1786 Massachusetts rebellion and in an earlier 1784 effort to set up the secessionist state of Franklin in western North Carolina, constituted at the time the nation's most volatile population. The Whiskey Rebellion, an armed attempt by western Pennsylvania farmers in the 1790s to test the federal government's new taxing powers, thus became the most dangerous threat to the newly established federation.[90]

In 1791, as part of the Assumption Plan proposed by Secretary of the Treasury Hamilton, a federal excise tax was placed on all distilled goods. The tax was designed to restore confidence in federal finances by permitting the repayment of debts owed to veterans of the Continental Army. The new tax hit the six counties of western Pennsylvania hardest. Claiming to receive no benefits from the distant federal government, the frontier farmers challenged its right to tax them. In addition to the broader political complaints, the Pennsylvania farmers raised specific economic objections to the tax. Western Pennsylvania, isolated by the rugged Allegheny Mountains, was predominantly a grain-producing region. Without other cash crops, the population relied on barter, primarily whiskey, as the means of exchange. In distilled form, the grain was easier to transport, less likely to spoil, and more marketable. The federal tax on distilled goods hit the region's economy severely. Western Pennsylvania contained about one-quarter of the nation's alcohol stills at the time. The newly imposed tax was to average about $1.50 per family per year, but in a region where the average annual cash income was a mere $25.00, the impact was considered unbearable.

Jefferson, leader of the Anti-Federalists, as the Democratic-Republican opposition party was called, warned that the whiskey tax was unwise because it would commit "the authority of government in parts where resistance is most probable and coercion least practicable." Some believed that Hamilton, who supported the tax, realized the danger but deliberately provoked the confrontation as a means of demonstrating the emerging power of federal authority.

At first, resistance consisted of failure to register stills. John Holcroft, using the pseudonym Tom the Tinker, emerged as leader of the opposition, claiming that he would "mend" the stills of farmers who voluntarily registered to pay the tax. These "repairs" were to be made with crowbars, torches, and buckshots. Serious violence indeed erupted in July 1794 when federal agents began to issue processes against unregistered still owners, requiring them to appear before the nearest federal court, in distant Philadelphia. On July 15, United States Marshall David Lenox served process on farmer William Miller, and word got around. Rumors spread that Lenox was staying at the Bower Hill estate of John Neville, the aristocratic head of the Federalist Party in western Pennsylvania. A mob gathered, and a delegation of 500 armed men went to search for Lenox. The estate was looted and burned in the process.

David Bradford stepped forward to lead the insurrection. Recently immigrated from Maryland and serving as deputy state's attorney in Pennsylvania, he was aware of the uprising's implications of treason. Concerned that the government might isolate and prosecute those who had led the Bower Hill action, he believed that the only protection was in broadening the insurrection to include in it as many participants as possible, making it unlikely that the government would apply the treason law. Bradford decided upon open rebellion and a march on Pittsburgh to seize the federal arsenal located there. Five thousand men eventually marched with great enthusiasm into Pittsburgh, which surrendered without much struggle.

The ultimate objectives of the marchers were, however, vague. There were suggestions of rejoining the British, of allying with the Spanish, or of forming a new state called Western Pennsylvania. Many rebels, satiated with liquor and success, soon returned quietly to their farms and families. The Federalist administration, however, reacted with alarm to the events. Hamilton advised Washington to crush the rebellion with a show of imposing force. A call was issued for a 13,000-man militia from Pennsylvania, New Jersey, Virginia, and Maryland. Hamilton, it appears, wanted the opportunity to use force in putting down the rebellion, and he so advised

Rufus King, his friend and associate, during the march on western Pennsylvania.[91] James Madison believed that Hamilton sought military force both to strengthen the Federalist Party and to establish the need for a standing army. Although the rebellion was put down with considerable brutality, all its leaders either escaped, were ignored, or were pardoned. Bradford himself fled to Nachez in the Spanish Territory, and when eventually pardoned, in 1799, he refused to leave his plantation and return to the United States.

Only two persons were eventually indicted for treason, but neither had played a significant role in the insurrection. One, a Pennsylvania Dutchman by the name of Weigel, was generally considered to be insane; the other was a simple-minded man named Mitchell. They were tried in Philadelphia before Judge Paterson, who found the rebellion to be "levying war," thus constituting treason.[92]

Convicted and sentenced to be hanged, Weigel and Mitchell—described as a madman and a moron[93]—were the first to be sentenced as traitors under the new Constitution. In time President Washington pardoned them both, and they returned home.

The Whiskey Rebellion was not, however, the last challenge to the new national authority. The governing Federalists were facing new domestic and international tensions. In the summer of 1798, the United States, under President John Adams, was being drawn toward the European crisis produced in the aftermath of the French Revolution. America's flirtation with revolutionary France had come to a sad ending. American representatives in Paris were being badly treated by French Foreign Minister Charles Maurice de Talleyrand-Perigord. American boats were left to rot in French harbors, and their cargoes were confiscated. American prestige and national honor were at stake. While the United States administration was preparing to recruit an army and repel a potential enemy invasion, privateering and naval engagements against the French had already commenced. By escalating the military crisis, the Federalists were hoping to reverse their probable defeat in the upcoming 1800 elections.

With time, the Federalist regime became increasingly uncomfortable with the growing opposition and the independent press criticism of its policies. The government's renewed search for tools to control public dissent recalled Rufus King's suggestion at the Constitutional Convention some eleven years earlier that the debate on defining treason narrowly might turn out to be a tempest in a teapot, since "the legislators might punish capitally under other names than Treason."[94]

In the face of the growing emergency, Alien and Sedition Acts were approved in the summer of 1798 by narrow Federalist majorities in Congress. The Alien Law[95] authorized the president to deport any foreigners whom he considered dangerous or whom he "suspected" of "treasonable" or secret machinations against the government. The law vested in the chief executive the power to order aliens out of the country without setting up any criteria—other than the president's judgment—and without due process of law. The Sedition Law[96] was even more questionable. It provided for the punishment of any person who wrote or said anything "false, scandalous and malicious" against the government, the president, or the Congress with "intent to defame" them, or to "bring them . . . into disrepute; or to excite . . . the hatred of the good people of the United States, or to stir up sedition within the United States." The Federalists had originally proposed the death penalty for violations of this law, but the final language called for imprisonment for not more than two years and a fine not to exceed $2,000.

The Alien Law was designed mostly against Irish patriots who had found asylum in the United States. The Federalist leaders viewed these men as undesirable "fugitives from the justice of Great Britain." Under the Sedition Act, diverse political enemies of John Adams's administration were imprisoned, a great number of opposition editors were indicted, and freedom of speech and the press were greatly curtailed.

A proposal on the floor of the House of Representatives to resume negotiations with France was denounced as sedition, and a New York representative was warned by a Federalist member of Congress that he had been guilty of sedition in opposing the Alien Bill. Penalties for those subsequently convicted of violations included a four-month prison sentence against Congressman Matthew Lyon, Republican of Vermont, who published a letter stating that Congress should commit President Adams to the madhouse. A jail sentence of eighteen months and a fine of $400 were imposed on a Dedham, Massachusetts, resident who erected a liberty pole with the inscription: "No Stamp Act, no Sedition, no Alien bills, no Land Tax; downfall to the Tyrants of America, peace and retirement to the President."[97]

Under America's new Sedition Law—as contrasted with the common law of seditious libel—the truth of an allegedly damaging statement constituted a sufficient defense. But rabidly partisan judges convicted opposition speakers who disagreed with the Federalist policy regardless of the truthfulness of their statements.

Both the Alien and Sedition Laws were defended by George Washington as necessary weapons against subversive efforts to poison "the minds of our people . . . in order to alienate their affections from the government of their choice."[98] Jefferson, on the other hand, declared the Sedition Act to be unconstitutional. He objected to it because in his view it exceeded the limited congressional power to "punish treason, counterfeiting the securities and current coin of the United States, piracies and felonies committed on the high seas, and offenses against the law of nations, and no other crimes, whatsoever."[99]

The Alien and Sedition Laws have been generally viewed as a final effort by the Federalists to consolidate their power. This was the first time that the power of Congress was exercised to punish dissent and putative disloyalty that failed to come within the strict bounds of treason. Historian Nathaniel Weyl, in his thorough study of the era, concluded that "between 1798 and 1800, a remorseless manhunt for traitors' [sic] and seditionist' [sic] swept over the country. Under the guise of saving the nation in a desperate emergency, a miniature Reign of Terror was created. . . . With few exceptions, the men victimized by the Alien and Sedition Acts were guilty of no disloyalty."[100]

Under Jefferson's and Madison's leadership, the state legislatures of Kentucky and Virginia—after hinting at secession—declared these draconian laws unconstitutional and refused to enforce them. John Marshall also opposed the Sedition Law and disregarded party discipline in order to vote for its repeal in 1800. When popular opposition swept the Jeffersonians into power in 1800, the Sedition Act had already expired and President Jefferson promptly pardoned all those convicted under it.

The early problems confronted by the founders of this country might serve us well in our comprehension of the war against authority in this country and abroad. The delegitimation of British colonial power and the tentative nature of authority in the newly independent early American states parallels the experience of many of the newly emerging states after the Second World War and the conclusion of the Cold War. Although ultimately successful in achieving widespread legitimacy in the eyes of its citizenry, the early American government was often perceived to be unjust or even despotic. The fact that sometimes severe sanctions had to be taken to secure the preservation of authority demonstrates how many birth pangs this emerging and pluralistic society had to endure in its struggle to attain and maintain legitimacy. From these early experiences, we must distill the steadying, as well as the disruptive, factors employed by the American founders and determine their role in forestalling the crises of the following generations.

# Sharing in the Benefits of the Promised Land

Even in savage bosoms, there are longings, yearnings, strivings, for the good they comprehend not.
—Henry Wadsworth Longfellow, *Hiawatha*

God is angry with the wicked every day.
—Psalms 7:11

## DIVIDING THE SPOILS OF LIBERTY

Much of America's political energy from the turn of the nineteenth century to the eruption of the Civil War was spent on consolidating the nation and protecting the country against a new threat of rebellion, arising from the long-suffering and neglected, and on efforts to control or tame populations: African Americans, Native Americans, workers, immigrants, and women. Despite earlier American articulations of the people's right to autonomy, resistance, and revolution, the prevailing view had shifted toward disavowing political activism except by conventional means. With scholarly and popular opinion reiterating the notion of a government subject to the will of the people, the ballot box increasingly came to be viewed as the only legitimate tool for curbing oppression and instituting change. More and more the nation was ready to deny the legitimacy of recourse to such unorthodox political means as civil disobedience, strikes, protest, resistance, and rebellion. Yet in most states the circle of political power was small, with slaves, Indians, women, and nonpropertied laborers being totally excluded from the ruling process. Under the United States Constitution, state electoral restrictions limited access to the federal ballot as well.

Speaking to the 1821 New York Constitutional Convention, James Kent, president of the state's court of chancery and one of the country's leading legal scholars, felt compelled to warn against expansion of the franchise. "By the report before us," he cried, "we propose to annihilate, at one stroke, all [previous] property distinctions and bow before the idol of universal suffrage. That extreme democratic principle . . . has been regarded with terror, by the wise men of every age, because in every . . . republic, ancient and modern, in which it has been tried, it has terminated disastrously, and has been productive of corruption, injustice, violence, and tyranny."[1]

Yet there was a growing popular expectation that the laws and practices that oppressed large segments of the population could be remedied through an enlargement of the democratic political process. America's newly settled frontier, now stretching outward to the Mississippi River, became an important factor in the expansion of democratic expectations. The new states increasingly grew and exported not only corn and tobacco but also liberal, populist doctrines, including the abolition of slavery and the reform of property qualifications for suffrage. But impatient and provoked by perceived injustices, the disenfranchised continued to respond with unlawful forms of protest and violence. Correspondingly, government and its allies in authority went on resorting to criminal and martial law to suppress those who resisted their assigned roles in America's promised land.

## AFRICAN AMERICANS AND NATIVE AMERICANS

The containment and regulation of African Americans and Native Americans formed a major concern of the time. The 1820 census showed a total American population of 9,638,453. The African American population, of which nearly 90 percent was enslaved, amounted to 1,771,656 of the total. Violence by masters against slaves was a common occurrence in America. Slave revolts, on the other hand, were relatively infrequent. Nevertheless, they were harshly suppressed. In 1712, when some New York City African Americans and Native Americans planned a revolt and attacked their masters, the governor sent out troops to end the uprising. Eighteen slaves were put to death after trial, some by hanging and others by torture and fire.[2]

A century later, in 1831, more than one hundred fifty whites and blacks were killed during Nat Turner's Virginia slave rebellion and the manhunt that followed. Twenty rebels, including Turner, their leader and an African American preacher, were executed after a brief trial. The reaction of the South to this violent political outburst was extraordinary. A general slave revolt was the secret fear of every master, and the rage reflected by the insurrection terrified many. Turner's interrogator, a certain T. R. Gray, described him somewhat melodramatically as "a gloomy fanatic . . . revolving in the recesses of [whose] own dark, bewildered and overwrought mind [were] schemes of indiscriminate massacre . . . schemes . . . executed as far as his fiendish band proceeded in their desolating march."[3] Prior to his conviction Nat Turner offered a confession of sorts. Believing in the righteousness of his course, he made no attempt to exculpate himself but frankly acknowledged his full participation in the uprising. Turner's captors attempted to make him renounce his acts, asking him, "Do you find yourself mistaken now?" Turner responded without hesitation, "Was not Christ crucified?" Despite the deaths of several innocent people during the insurrection, Turner remained steadfast in his belief that the rebellion and his actions were morally justified.[4]

The fear of slave revolts, as well as the growing militancy of the abolitionist movement, produced stringent regulations not only of slaves but also of all others suspected of being unsympathetic toward the existing social and political order. Free African Americans, in particular, were viewed as uniquely dangerous on account of their greater degree of education and mobility.[5]

An 1820 South Carolina statute required that during any foreign ship's stay in state ports its free African American seamen be imprisoned ashore.[6] Virginia laws prohibited the education of African Americans,[7] and in 1853, Mrs. Margaret Douglas was sentenced to a year in prison for teaching free African American children to read.[8] Legal attitudes in the North often were not much more charitable. New York's 1846 constitution retained a property qualification for black voters that had been abolished for whites,[9] and in 1850, the Massachusetts Supreme Judicial Court upheld racial segregation in Boston public schools.[10] Criminal laws were extensively utilized throughout the South, and even the North, to suppress abolitionist and reformist sentiments and publications.

The Native Americans, particularly in the Southeast, faced similarly brutal treatment at the hands of the state and federal governments. In the Revolutionary War, the powerful tribes of the southern Appalachian Mountains had fought with the British, believing that the rights guaranteed to them under King George would be abrogated by the Americans who had continued to press westward. The Cherokee Nation, refusing to recognize the end of hostilities brought about by the 1783 Treaty of Paris, insisted upon a separate treaty of peace with the United States to preserve their ancient rights. The result was the 1785 Treaty of Hopewell,[11] which confirmed the treaty process as the method of political interaction between Native Americans and the newly sovereign United States. This treaty was not, however, the first treaty between Indians and the United States. There existed an earlier mutual defense treaty, with the Delawares, against the British. Article VI of that treaty suggested that future negotiations would consider the establishment of a new state, consisting of the Delawares and other tribes friendly to the United States, with representation in Congress.[12]

Despite the treaties, old tensions between settlers and Native Americans were further exacerbated by state claims to sovereignty over the Western

Territory, extending from the Appalachians to the Mississippi, which was ceded to the United States by England. Eventually, these claims were settled between the United States and the respective states. But Georgia, then a narrow strip of land along the Savannah River and looking to expand westward into rich forests and farmlands, had extracted a promise from the United States to remove, as soon as reasonably practical, all Native Americans from its newly claimed territory.

The Cherokees, the major Indian nation affected by this agreement to which they were not a party, saw no good reason to leave their fertile ancestral homeland. They began, instead, to adopt many of the trappings of Western civilization, establishing permanent settlements, erecting churches, and building schools. After twenty-five years with no progress toward the removal of the Cherokees, and urged on by the recent discovery of gold in the Indian Territory, Georgia unilaterally proclaimed an extension of its state sovereignty over the area. When the Cherokees appealed for protection to the United States, President John Quincy Adams was quick to quash Georgia's expansionism. The next year, however, Andrew Jackson of Tennessee, a veteran of the Creek War, was inaugurated as president.

In his first message to Congress, Jackson addressed the United States' "Indian problem." He reiterated the paternalistic claim that the welfare of Native Americans required that they be physically isolated from the influence of the whites. He proposed, and Congress soon passed, legislation authorizing negotiations and funding for the removal of the Five Civilized Tribes (Cherokee, Creek, Crow, Choctaw, and Seminole) to a territory west of the Mississippi. There they were to be allowed to order their society according to their own laws and customs. Alternatively, Native Americans could choose to remain East, but they would be required to submit to the jurisdiction and laws of the states or territories in which they resided.

As the resettlement process dragged on, Georgia took the initiative, once again asserting jurisdiction over the Cherokee lands. This time, the Cherokees appealed to the courts, and in the landmark opinion of *Cherokee Nation v. Georgia*, the Supreme Court held that the federal courts did not have the authority to hear cases brought by Native American tribes. The Indian Nations were neither individuals nor American or foreign states, and under the Constitution, only these entities could bring suit.[13] Described by Chief Justice Marshall as "domestic dependent sovereignties," the Native American nations were "in a state of pupilage" to the United States.[14]

Shortly thereafter, President Jackson withdrew federal protection from the Cherokees. The Treaty of New Echota (1835)[15] was "negotiated," and the Trail of Tears began—the forced march, under military escort, of virtually the entire Cherokee Nation to the Indian Territory (occupying what are now the states of Arkansas and Oklahoma). Twenty-five thousand Native

Americans are estimated to have perished during the 1830s in the forced migrations of the Five Civilized Tribes. The process was not totally peaceful. Remaining in their strongholds in the Gulf Coast swamps of Florida and Alabama, the Seminoles, under Chief Osceola, joined with escaped African American slaves in resisting the new federal policies most vigorously. They engaged the United States in a costly seven-year guerrilla war.[16]

The troublesome facts regarding the treatment of African Americans and Native Americans have been much discussed. What have been lacking are the more subtle conclusions that flow from these chapters in America's national history. Although the law treated African Americans somewhat differently than Native Americans, it regulated them for similar reasons. Both groups constituted identifiable populations who were not viewed as capable of integration and whose allegiance to the dominant authority and social order was deemed suspect. No place, therefore, was to be accorded to these communities in the nation's political power structure.

African Americans were necessary to the economic prosperity of the South, and their continued presence in the region was essential. To prevent African Americans from realizing, or taking advantage of, their important socioeconomic role in Southern society, the design of those in authority was to criminalize African American attempts at education, organization, and other means leading to emancipation.

Native Americans, by contrast, were more economically independent and were well organized into coherent societies that concededly owed no allegiance to the federal government or to the states. Furthermore, within their tribal lands they were theoretically immune from economic, social, and political control and oppression by white society. The direction the United States government's Native American policy took, therefore, was to totally banish this entire expendable suspect population whose social and political order could not be accommodated within the manifest destiny of the United States.

## WORKERS AND WOMEN

Sprinkled throughout this era were several other developments that hinted at different future conflicts between authority and liberty in the decades to follow. Struggles for workers' and women's rights were first recorded during this time. In an 1834 letter to the Workingmen, a radical political party of Massachusetts, historian George Bancroft wrote, "The Feud between the capitalist and laborer, the House of Have and the House of Want, is as old as the social union and can never be entirely quilted."[17] Toward the middle of the nineteenth century, European immigrants—especially on the eastern seaboard—combined with American craftsmen to create a laboring class striving for fair wages and humane working conditions. The efforts to organize workers, to achieve collective power and bargaining strength, frequently triggered prosecutions on charges of criminal conspiracy. The 1836 New York trial of twenty journeymen tailors resulted in their conviction on the grounds that the labor organizations they belonged to were "a conspiracy and injurious to trade."[18]

It was this period that witnessed also, in July of 1846, the first Women's Rights Convention held in Seneca Falls, New York. The convention's concluding declaration, modeled after the Declaration of Independence and relying on a doctrine of "natural rights" to justify the full emancipation of women, was described by freed slave and political reformer Frederick Douglass as "the basis of a grand movement for attaining the civil, social, political, and religious rights of women."[19] The document, which justified disobedience to unjust man-made laws, furnished the foundation for the protests and civil disobedience activities of suffragist Susan B. Anthony and the modern feminist movement that was to follow. For the time being, however, women continued to be prosecuted and convicted for attempting to cast their ballots "without the lawful right to vote"[20] and for militantly protesting their lack of franchise.[21] It was not until nearly three-quarters of a century later that the National Suffrage Amendment was passed at the urging of ailing President Woodrow Wilson.

Once again, long-simmering resentments were rising to the surface. Increasingly rebellion by various groups in society was shaking the foundations of the traditional political and social control.

### ANNEXATION AND SECESSION

The decades leading to the Civil War, sometimes described as an age of "consolidation and schism," also reflected several other strands of the continuing conflict between political authority and autonomy. On June 20, 1835, American colonists in the Mexican territory of Texas, who were led by William B. Travis, seized the Mexican garrison of Fort Anahuac at the mouth of the Trinity River. Three months later the first major battle of the Texas Revolution took place between the American settlers and the Mexican cavalry. A Mexican army of some six thousand men under General Santa Anna crossed into Texas in early 1836, and the war of secession escalated. On March 1, 1836, the Texas Declaration of Independence was promulgated, citing the natural rights of Texans, and declaring the dissolution of the old "social compact" between Texas and the other members of the Mexican confederacy.[22]

Though the Texas secession from the Mexican nation was received with general approval north of the border, other efforts by Americans to establish their own autonomous existence in the barren and remote West met with cries of treason. Founded by Joseph Smith, the prophet of the Latter Day Saints, the Mormon Church and its members encountered savage persecution wherever they went. Hounded out of Missouri in 1838, Joseph Smith founded the all-Mormon city of Nauvoo on the Mississippi River in Illinois. By 1840, Nauvoo was more populous than Chicago. The murder of Joseph Smith by a hostile mob and the destruction of Nauvoo elevated Brigham Young to leadership and resulted in the Mormon move west. In their proposed State of Deseret—which would have contained present-day Utah, Nevada, half of California and Arizona, and parts of Oregon, Idaho, Wyoming, Colorado, and New Mexico—the Mormons sought to maintain cultural and religious purity as well as political hegemony.

After assuming the presidency in 1850, Millard Fillmore named Brigham Young as territorial governor of Utah. But tensions mounted between Mormons and non-Mormons (labeled Gentiles) in the new territory. Soon Brigham Young and his followers were charged by their opponents with establishing a virtual dictatorship in the Utah Territory, with instituting discrimination against non-Mormons, and with fostering disloyalty toward the federal government. This threat to central authority could not be permitted to continue. In June of 1857, President Buchanan dispatched an expeditionary force of twenty-six hundred men from Fort Leavenworth to Utah, to install non-Mormon officials in positions of authority in the territory.

In response, Brigham Young ordered his forces in mid-September to "forbid all armed forces of every description from coming into this territory under any pretense whatever."[23] He further instructed his followers to put the torch to all structures in the path of the marching federal force. Historian Nathaniel Weyl summarized the confrontation: "The founders of Mormonism in Utah were unquestionably guilty of treason against the United States. They levied an army, declared martial law in [the] Utah Territory, prepared to repel an American expeditionary force, raided its supply depots, attempted to starve its enemy in the desert, and carried out the first scorched earth program in American history."[24]

In 1858 President Buchanan issued a calming proclamation in an effort to stop what he considered "the first rebellion which has existed in our territories." Although Young had planned to burn down Salt Lake City and retreat into the southern wilderness, the spirit of compromise finally prevailed. Alfred Cumming, the newly appointed territorial governor, counseled negotiations, and in return for Young's recognition of his ultimate authority, President Buchanan issued a general amnesty to the rebels of the "Utah War." The decisive yet conciliatory role played by Washington thus brought an end to Mormon separatism. Another clash between those seeking autonomy and the guardians of the nation-state had come to an end.

## THE CIVIL WAR:
## SOUTHERN TREASON OR NORTHERN AGGRESSION?

The war against authority was to take many forms in the period known as the Civil War. Slaves fought against masters; masters sought to maintain their privileges. States claimed the right to autonomy against centralized political authority, and Northern industrialists, seeking economic as well as political integration, clashed with Southern landowners favoring economic separatism.

Even before the outbreak of the war between the states, the existence and operations of the "abolitionist movement created the most acute strain on freedom of expression in the pre-Civil War era."[25] Although understandably sensitive to growing antislavery sympathies, the South nevertheless tolerated a reasonable degree of free discussion prior to 1830. Eventually, however, every Southern state (with the exception of Kentucky) passed laws limiting abolitionist speech and press. In 1837 an Alabama court held that any person "who shall proclaim to our slaves the doctrine of universal emancipation" would be subject to criminal prosecution. In 1849 the Virginia Code imposed imprisonment of up to one year, and a fine of up to $500, on any person who in speech or writing "maintains that owners have no right of property in slaves." Louisiana, even less tolerant, prescribed penalties ranging from twenty-one years' imprisonment to death for speech "having a tendency to promote discontent among free colored people, or insubordination among slaves."[26]

The rising tide of discontent was fostered by other aspects of the conflict between authority and autonomy. The slavery issue only crystallized the growing economic, social, ideological, and political conflicts between two largely independent regions. The North had a relatively free population of twenty-two million. In the South there were nine million people, more than one-third of them slaves.[27] The commercial North had begun moving toward an industrial society in which machines were eventually to replace individual labor as the crucial component in manufacturing processes. The agrarian South, for the time being, continued to stand for the plantation economy, where cheap labor—and particularly slavery—remained an essential ingredient of production. There were, accordingly, pronounced social differences between the immigration-enriched community of skilled craftsmen and tradesmen, who constituted the broad power base of the more urban Northeast, and the entrenched elites that controlled the class-stratified rural Southern society. Ideologically, also, the North represented a more diverse, progressive, and confident outlook than the more homogeneous, tradition-bound, and parochially nationalistic South. "The fundamental and passionate ideal for which the South stood and fell was the ideal of an agrarian society," said historian Frank L. Owsley.[28] Yet it was "states' rights," the issue of decentralization of government versus centralization, that became the ostensible rallying cry of the conflict.

The decade of the 1840s witnessed the virtual doubling of the United States' territory. Texas was annexed, the Oregon lands were secured from England, California was taken over, and the Southwestern Territories were wrested from Mexico by war. A major issue posed as a result of these acquisitions of the federal government was whether they would be open or closed to the slave system of labor: whether they would become part of the South's decentralized feudalism or the North's modern industrialism. Northern abolitionists, led by William H. Seward, demanded that Congress, through its "constitutional power," ban slavery from the new territories, insisting further that a "higher law than our Constitution" made human bondage illegal.

Efforts were made by President Zachary Taylor and by his successor, Millard Fillmore, to end the controversy through the Compromise of 1850— which undertook to maintain a carefully designed balance in the newly acquired areas.[29] But despite the hopes of the moderates, more militant regional activists were not satisfied with the outcome. Southern activists, including John C. Calhoun and Jefferson Davis, feared that the compromise would permanently reduce the slave-based South to a beleaguered enclave. To overcome this imbalance, Cuba and Nicaragua were eyed by Southern adventurers, called "filibusters," for colonization, annexation, and eventual incorporation into the Union as slave states.

The mid-1850s saw Kansas become the battleground of the rival forces. The Northerners were armed with "Beecher's Bibles," the Sharps rifles that were popularly named after the New Haven minister who described them as having a greater moral force than the Holy Scriptures. But the Southerners, counting on the strength of slavery supporters in Missouri, launched the first attacks of a fourth-month civil war that cost the lives of some two hundred persons. Three years before his ultimate raid of the federal arsenal at Harper's Ferry, abolitionist John Brown took an active part in this conflict. The raid on Harper's Ferry, intended as a first step in a broader plan to arm the slaves and lead them in a triumphant freedom march through the South, ended in Brown's capture. He was tried and executed for treason under the laws of Virginia[30]—a state to which he owed no allegiance and against which he could accordingly commit no treason.

These events presaged the Civil War, the greatest political and human ordeal in the relatively short history of the American republic. The military emergency faced by President Lincoln resulted in a series of stringent measures carried out under the executive power of the presidency. These actions, taken in the weeks between the April 12, 1861, firing on Fort Sumter and the special session of Congress convened on July 4, 1861, included a directive that the Post Office be closed to "treasonable correspondence" and an order suspending the writ of habeas corpus. The suspension of habeas corpus "caused persons who were represented to . . . [the president] as being or about to [be] engage[d] in disloyal and treasonable practices to be arrested by special civil as well as military agencies and detained in military custody when necessary to prevent them or deter others from such practices."[31] It has been estimated that pursuant to this presidential authority some thirty-eight thousand executive arrests were authorized during the Civil War. The actual but incomplete records of the War Department showed over thirteen thousand detentions.

Lincoln's imposition of martial law, closely intertwined with his suspension of habeas corpus, was based on two fundamental and far-reaching considerations. The first was Lincoln's belief that his principal task during the national emergency was to *prevent* people from engaging in dissidence and political crimes, rather than to punish them for offenses they had already committed. The political crisis, in his view, required confining people "not so much for what has been done, as for what probably would be done."[32] Since the traditional peacetime legal process failed to grant such preventive powers to those in authority, martial law was required. The second consideration was Lincoln's lack of faith in the efficacy of the jury process, especially during the rebellion. "Again, a jury frequently had at least one member more ready to hang the panel than to hang the traitor," he is reported to have said.[33] Resort to special military tribunals and to their more informal procedures, free of jury and other constitutional requirements, was deemed necessary.

Lincoln's suspension of the right of habeas corpus was undertaken pursuant to the constitutional language providing that "the privilege of the writ of habeas corpus shall not be suspended, unless when in cases of rebellion or invasion the public safety may require it."[34] But Chief Justice Taney of the United States Supreme Court (sitting in the circuit court in Baltimore in 1861) decided soon after the suspension that since the suspension clause was in the article of the Constitution detailing congressional authority, the president lacked the power to exercise this drastic measure without congressional authorization.[35] Both Lincoln and the military simply ignored this decision. In a subsequent message to Congress, Lincoln argued:

> It was decided that we have a case of rebellion, and that the public safety does require the qualified suspension of the privilege of the writ. . . . Now it is insisted that Congress and not the executive, is vested with this power. But the Constitution itself is silent as to which or who is to exercise the power; and as the provision was plainly made for a dangerous emergency, it cannot be believed the framers of this instrument intended that in every case the danger should run its course until Congress could be called together, the very assembling of which might be prevented as was intended in this case, by the rebellion.[36]

Not until March 3, 1863, some two years after the fact, did Congress ratify Lincoln's executive suspension of habeas corpus. Only after the war ended did the Supreme Court of the United States review more authoritatively some of the related constitutional issues involved in Lincoln's actions. In 1866 the Court held that the writ of habeas corpus could not be suspended and that a military commission could not try a citizen so long as the civil system of justice continued functioning and the courts remained open. Said the Court in *Ex parte Milligan:* "Martial law cannot arise from a *threatened* invasion. The necessity must be actual and present; the invasion real, such as effectually closes the courts and deposes the civil administration."[37]

Of possibly even greater public and legal concern at the time was the status of those serving the Confederate cause. Were they exercising a lawful right of secession or did their conduct constitute treason? Senator Lyman Trumbell was emphatic on the rebels' punishment as traitors: "When the rebellion is put down . . . it is to be put down by driving into exile, or killing upon the battlefield or hanging upon the gallows."[38] To the Southern leaders, however, the villain was the North—unlawfully using force of arms to deprive Southern states of their constitutionally protected rights. Those serving the cause of the South thus claimed to be assuming the hallowed mantle of the revolutionary Founding Fathers, claiming to battle for freedom and autonomy while holding in chains millions of oppressed slaves.

Congress's response was the passage of the Conspiracies Act providing punishment for those plotting "to overthrow the Government of the United States or levy war against them."[39] The Act was passed by the House over the opposition voiced by a minority that feared that the constitutional safeguards regarding treason prosecutions would be nullified if Congress created new crimes "kindred to treason" that required less evidence to prove.

The United States Supreme Court was eventually to endorse the doctrine that the Confederates were guilty of treason.[40] Under the treason statute of 1790, capital punishment was the sole sanction for convicted offenders. Yet under prevailing thinking it seemed that death should be reserved for the chief leaders only, while milder penalties should suffice for lesser participants. The Treason Act of 1862 was therefore promulgated to provide an option of either capital punishment or, at the discretion of the court, imprisonment of not less than five years and a fine not smaller than $10,000.

Yet another weapon in the arsenal against disloyalty was the newly created crime of "insurrection." The penalty for this was the liberation of the offender's slaves.[41]

Prosecutions for treason and related violations commenced early in the Civil War. Toward the end of 1865, there were more than nineteen hundred indictments for treason on the dockets of Eastern Tennessee alone. Maryland's authorities believed that every man who left the state to enroll in the Confederate forces should be convicted as a traitor, and a list of 4,000 names was submitted to a grand jury for indictment. But this great mass of treason indictments never resulted in trials. The Union's apparent strategy was to intimidate and deter prospective rebels by bringing indictments— while rarely proceeding beyond that stage.

Since several million men were technically traitors and any prosecution was likely to produce reprisals against Union prisoners, the United States government tacitly accorded the Southern forces the status of belligerents.[42] Captives were subsequently treated as prisoners of war rather than as traitors or criminals. When the war and its furor were over, not a single person was hanged for betraying his loyalty to this country during the war.

Even Jefferson Davis, arrested in May of 1865 and indicted for treason a year later, was not brought to trial for three years.[43] Davis was charged with leading the rebellion against the United States, but the prosecution continued to plead that it lacked the necessary evidence. Finally, in 1868, R. H. Dana, one of the government's attorneys, wrote a letter proposing that the prosecution be dropped. Dana thought that there was little legal precedent to be set by a prosecution since the Supreme Court had already held the Confederate rebellion to be treason, and hanging Jefferson Davis four years after Appomattox would serve no useful purpose. Moreover, it was questionable whether a Southern jury would convict Davis, and an acquittal would harm the perception that the cause of union was a righteous one. The letter was forwarded to President Johnson. The president apparently agreed with Dana's counsel because, on Christmas Day 1868, a general pardon was issued to all participants in the rebellion.

The efforts of those in authority to control subject groups within American society did not end with the granting of pardons to those who had served the military cause of the Confederacy. The post–Civil War period, like the revolutionary era, also saw the extensive use of loyalty oaths as a prerequisite for voting, for holding public office or public employment, or for engaging in certain occupations. The Supreme Court of the United States ruled one such oath unconstitutional in the case of a Roman Catholic priest convicted for teaching and preaching without having complied with the oath requirements of the state of Missouri. The particular oath, challenged in *Cummings v. Missouri*,[44] embraced more than thirty distinct tests or affirmations. The oath taker was required not only to confirm that he had not participated in "armed hostility to the United States" but also to assert that he had not manifested a sympathy toward those engaged in the rebellion or ever indicated, in any manner, his disaffection with the government of the United States.

In *Cummings* and in the later case of *Ex parte Garland*,[45] involving the requirement of a loyalty oath for the practice of law, these oaths, which penal-

ized specially selected classes of people for behavior that had not been outlawed when engaged in, were declared contrary to the constitutional
prohibition against bills of attainder and ex post facto laws.[46] Nevertheless,
despite this unfavorable judicial response to the imposition of oaths,
America's executive branch, in the twentieth century, would again turn to
loyalty oaths in its war against political opponents.

### FROM POLITICAL SECESSION TO CLASS WARFARE

From the ashes of the Civil War, a tired but hopeful President Lincoln
planned to build a new and more perfect union. Conciliation and
Reconstruction were the official policy, as evidenced by the 1863 presidential
proclamation restoring suffrage to all Southern voters willing to take the prescribed oath of loyalty to the United States. Only the leaders of the
Confederacy were excepted from this privilege. As soon as 10 percent of the
voters in any state, including African American males, had taken the oath,
they could form their own government and be entitled to recognition by the
president of the United States. Unfortunately, hopes for an early reconciliation died with Lincoln, the victim of an unrepentant Confederate. Years of
occupation by the United States Army followed, reflecting an ongoing
national struggle between those who favored quick reunion and cooperation
with the newly "freed" Southern states and the Radical Republicans in
Congress, who sought political vindication and revenge through reconstruction of the South.

While several provisions of the reconstruction plan were "a bitter pill for
the former Confederates,"[47] one after another of the Southern states yielded
to its dictates. But the control of Southern governments by blacks and
by those whites who had not been disenfranchised for supporting the
Confederate cause was relatively brief. Through open as well as covert
actions, the old Southern forces of "white supremacy" soon reasserted their
grip on political power. A campaign of fear kept African Americans away from
the polls, while the Ku Klux Klan and other secret societies mounted a reign
of terror, running "carpetbaggers" and "scalawags" out of the region.[48]

The emancipation of African Americans through the Civil War, and the
enactment of the Thirteenth Amendment and the Civil Rights Acts of 1866
and the 1870s, formally removed the old restrictions on the political and civic
activities of African Americans. However, new restrictions arose with the end
of Reconstruction. New "Jim Crow" laws reinstituted many of the old controls over African Americans, while the United States Supreme Court, by
limiting the scope of the Fourteenth Amendment's power to override state
authority,[49] remained unwilling to ensure that African Americans could participate in the political process. Moreover, the white political power struc-

ture enforced these restrictions through ostensibly private terrorist organizations, such as the Ku Klux Klan and the Knights of the White Camelia. The ascendent ideology of white supremacy not only argued for the inherent mental and genetic inferiority of African Americans, but also taught that social and political participation by African Americans posed a threat to civilization itself.

In preventing African Americans from asserting themselves, the legal system attempted to criminalize the status of "blackness." The process of criminalization was collective rather than individual. The crime *was* being African American, and one did not need a trial (except in marginal circumstances) to establish the suspect's overt threat to the desired political and social order. The Supreme Court was eventually to approve this legislative campaign of oppression through the formula of "separate but equal."[50]

A similar policy of segregation was applied to Native Americans through the so-called peace policy. With the closing of the frontier, geographical relocation was replaced by the reservation system, which coupled federal subsistence support for the reservation Indians with the ruthless use of military power against those who attempted to escape the reservation boundaries. Under this "peace policy," the new Bureau of Indian Affairs cynically structured its allocation of supplies to support plentifully the stronger and more warlike tribes, while leaving the weaker ones to languish in malnutrition and poverty.[51] The practice served as an expedient measure to lull the more dangerous Native American peoples into lassitude, diminish their battle skills, and reduce them to permanent dependence.

The more militant face of the peace policy produced such notable United States Army feats of arms as the Sand Creek Massacre, the thirteen-hundred-mile fighting retreat of Chief Joseph's Nez Perce, the war with the Chiracowa Apaches under Geronimo, and the ending of the Ghost Dance Uprising with the massacre at Wounded Knee. The military stance was distilled in the observation attributed to Civil War hero General Philip Sheridan: "The only good Indian is a dead Indian." Celebrated United States Army victories often pitted cavalry against women, children, and old men. With a few exceptions, such as Sitting Bull's victory over Custer's Seventh Cavalry at the Little Big Horn, the defeated Native Americans were poorly equipped and badly outnumbered.

Despite the violence and depravity of the peace policy, it nevertheless acknowledged the sovereignty of Native Americans by continuing the treaty-making process between the United States and the Indian nations. Neither had Congress as yet acted to regulate the conduct of individual Indians in their tribal or social relations within their territories. Native Americans supposedly continued to function outside the domestic political power of the United States.

Soon, however, new voices—some humanitarian, some rapacious—condemned the peace policy as a sham and a failure. What was required, it was argued, was to assimilate the Native American people into the population of the United States.[52] The "assimilationist" policy was not an entirely new development. As early as 1717, Connecticut had legislated an "Act for the More Effectual Well Ordering of the Indians," providing for the establishment of Indian "villages, after the English manner," and apportioning parcels of land to Indian families to be handed down from father to children in order "to encourage them to apply themselves to husbandry."[53] The potential impact of the new federal policy was not lost upon the Native Americans, who objected to it strenuously.

The central feature of the newly proposed solution to the "Indian problem" was to divide up tribal lands among individual Indians. The tribes objected, contending that, under the old treaty process, this allocation could not be accomplished without their assent. But when the Supreme Court ruled, in a remotely related case, that Congress had the authority to punish Indian conduct against Indians on Indian territory,[54] the remaining constitutional barriers to the congressional allocation of Indian territory to individuals seemed to be swept away. The path was thus opened for congressional and executive actions designed to undermine the authority and structure of the Native American communities. Laws and regulations were adopted to suppress Native American religious practices and the teaching of Native American languages in the reservation schools. While not as militant as the previous peace policy, the assimilationist measures were just as degrading, hypocritical, and ethnocidal.

During this same period, the country's treatment of other emerging groups demanding autonomy was equally reprehensible. The demands of immigrants for social justice were met with violence and repression. From Ireland, Germany, Russia, Poland, and Italy, increasing numbers had fled Europe's political unrest and economic depression to seek freedom and opportunity in the New World. Out of a total United States population of some ninety-two million in 1910, one-third were either foreign-born or first-generation Americans. Concurrently, the country's expansion westward and the tremendous growth in industry, mining, and transportation depended on a new working class with yet uncertain powers and rights.

Even before the Civil War, the northeastern United States witnessed increased anti-immigrant hostility, manifesting itself in both ethnic and religious bigotry. From time to time violence would erupt against recent immigrant communities. The American Nativism movement burned convents and staged anti-Catholic riots.[55] The Protestant Crusade eventually led to the more politically oriented, clandestine Know Nothing movement. As the nineteenth century wore on, each region of the country targeted its hostilities on different immigrant groups. Anti-Chinese agitation was prominent in California and the West. Italian immigrants were the victims of mobs in New Orleans. In the East, Irish and Italian immigrants (as well as other arrivals from the poorer, and predominantly Catholic, countries of central, eastern, and southern Europe) found themselves in conflict with business owners, foremen, and skilled workers of older American stock. Immigrants also had to face such newly formed and bigoted organizations as the American Protective Association.[56] A newly reconstituted American Party campaigned politically on anti-alien sentiment. And in 1882, after a formal finding that continued Chinese immigration threatened the public welfare, Congress passed the Chinese Exclusion Act, which not only barred further Chinese immigration but prohibited all Chinese natives from acquiring United States citizenship.[57] This was the first of many restraints on the full acquisition of citizenship for Asians.

These ethnic conflicts often contributed to labor tensions. Historian Richard M. Brown[58] observed that labor strife was often, in essence, immigrant or ethnic conflict, with old-stock Americans on one side and unskilled immigrants on the other. But what started out primarily as an ethnic confrontation grew to become a more general economic or class conflict. Although a rudimentary labor force—sailors, longshoremen, and other workers of the maritime industry—existed in the port cities of colonial America, it was not until after the Civil War (with the blossoming of the industrial revolution and the speedy growth of local manufacturers) that a strong labor movement got underway. The instruments of the new class conflict were largely formed during the first decades after the Civil War: the Knights of Labor, the American Federation of Labor, the American Railway Union, the Western Federation of Miners, and the Industrial Workers of the World (IWW). Through these organizations, the strike became a major tool for organizing workers and for improving working conditions. Frequently violence broke out along with the strike.[59]

The first national emergency in industrial labor relations was reported in 1873 in connection with railroad workers strikes. President Hayes concluded at the time that he had the authority to declare martial law and dispatch the army to control the conflict.[60] Another noted incident of labor-connected violence was the great railroad strike of 1877, which triggered a major military response in Pittsburgh and in several other cities.

The Molly Maguires, a secret organization of Irish miners, reached the peak of their war of assassination and mayhem against their employers in the coal fields of eastern Pennsylvania at the same time. Next came the 1886 Haymarket Square Riot in Chicago, where eight police officers intent on dispersing a meeting of labor sympathizers were killed by a bomb explosion. The history of that period also includes the Homestead Strike by steelworkers, who took over a town in southwestern Pennsylvania in 1892, and the unrest at the Coeur d'Alene, Idaho, silver mines the same year.

Given the climate of growing socioeconomic hardships, it is surprising that the campaigns of labor were not laced with more violence. In 1893 the United States had three million unemployed workers and more than six hundred bank failures. After years of bustling economic growth, rampant speculation in the stock market, and overextended industrial production, corporate profits fell rapidly, and wages dropped drastically. Labor, acknowledging the depressed economic conditions, submitted to management's stringent measures. The economy showed some improvement the following year, but it failed to make a substantial recovery. Restless, labor again responded with an explosion of strikes and other disturbances. In 1894 the nation was confronted with the Pullman strike, or "Debs' Rebellion," in which George Mortimer Pullman and the railroads were pitted against labor leader Eugene Victor Debs and the American Railway Union.

The strike paralyzed transportation from Chicago to the Pacific Coast, and railroad operators beseeched President Grover Cleveland to intervene. He did, sending 2,000 troops to keep the trains moving. The power of the United States was enlisted further in aid of management, which sought and obtained injunctions under the Sherman Antitrust Act to restrain Debs and his union from their activities. When Debs defied the injunctions, which he viewed as being favorable to management, the court cited him for criminal contempt and ordered him punished by six months in jail.[61]

Debs sought a writ of habeas corpus from the United States Supreme Court to review the lawfulness of his imprisonment for participation in the railroad strike. The plea fell on deaf ears. Despite the fact that no specific law of the United States was defied, the court concluded that the government's interest in the movement of the mails was sufficient cause to issue the injunction against the strike and to uphold Debs's imprisonment for criminal contempt in violating it. Of particular note is the court's reiteration of the doctrine that all social wrongs must be addressed through the traditional political process. Mr. Justice Brewer spoke for the Supreme Court: "A most earnest and eloquent appeal was made to us in eulogy of the heroic spirit of those who threw up their employment, and gave up their means of earning a livelihood . . . in sympathy for and to assist others whom they believed to be wronged. . . . [However,] under this government of and by the people the means of redress of all wrongs are through the courts and at the ballot-box, and . . . no wrong, real or fancied, carries with it legal warrant to invite as a means of redress the cooperation of a mob, with its accompanying acts of violence."[62]

Despite the relief offered by the ballot box, labor-connected strands of violence continued well into the beginning of the twentieth century. The labor-management troubles in Colorado's mines took the form of a "Thirty

Years' War," which lasted from 1884 to 1914. The war climaxed in the coal miners' strike against the Colorado Fuel & Iron Co. in 1913–14. Eighteen persons were killed during the first five weeks of the strike. The strike ended with the burning of the striking miners' tent city—which took the lives of two mothers and eleven children and resulted in ten days of vengeful and unrestrained warfare by the mourning miners. Smaller in proportion, but of similar impact, was the 1910 dynamiting of the Los Angeles Times Building by the labor-connected McNamara brothers. It was only appropriate that this cross-century period of violence become labeled as the American "era of labor relations through dynamite."

Much like Daniel Shays' agrarian uprising in Massachusetts, the Whiskey Rebellion in Pennsylvania, and John Brown's militancy in Kansas and Virginia, the struggle of labor for justice, including many violent manifestations, has been endowed over the years with myths of public adulation. "The Ballad of Joe Hill," a leader in labor's struggle for independence and change, continues to this day as an inspiring call for justice and social reform:

> I dreamed I saw Joe Hill last night,
> Alive as you or me.
> "But Joe," I says, "you're 10 years dead—"
> "I never died," said he."[63]

Historian Richard M. Brown summarizes the historical record of the American Labor Movement: "Most would agree that by raising the health and living standard of the working man the American labor movement has been a significant factor in advancing the social well-being of the nation. But the labor movement reveals the same mixture of glorious ends with inglorious means—violence—that has characterized the agrarian [reform] movement."[64]

While generally viewed as quests for social and economic justice—including such objectives as increased wages, shorter work hours, improved working conditions, and the right to organize—the exploits of the labor movement can equally be viewed as a struggle for a greater political role. The pursuit of increased political power appears, in retrospect, as central to the aims and successes of both emerging groups—immigrants and workers. But the traditional histories of the period tended to view the struggle almost exclusively in ethnic, religious, or economic terms. The very size of the workers' communities frequently meant that local police and courts could not adequately cope with labor-connected crises. Although American labor conflicts did not engender disorders and violence of dimensions justifying resort to widespread military control, similar, though less drastic, measures were often used. Only the engagement of the federal military succeeded in ending what was described as the "anarchy and unrestrained class warfare" of the mining conflict in southern Colorado. State militias were required in other parts of the country, from time to time, to cope with increasing instances of labor, ethnic, racial, urban, and other forms of mass unrest. This use of state and federal military forces produced an extensive body of state and federal laws and administrative regulations specifying and limiting the conditions for intervention by state and national militias in local law enforcement.[65]

Public concern over the economic and political activism of immigrants and workers was amplified by the fact that there was much class turmoil in Europe, and leaders of European radicalism frequently sought refuge in America. The anarchist movement was especially feared. In 1876 at an anarchist congress held in Berne, Switzerland, the principle of "propaganda by the deed" (referring to violence and terror) was promulgated and given wide attention. The principle was based on the premise that peaceful efforts were inadequate to rouse the masses and to achieve reforms for the working class. To many anarchist sympathizers the doctrine meant a call for insurrectionary tactics and terrorism, directed not merely against government but also against politically and economically prominent individuals and institutions.

At times the economic pursuits of both immigrants and workers coincided with the objectives of these more ideologically radical and militant political movements. Several of the anarchist leaders in America were immigrant, and many anarchist adherents were active in the labor movement. It was never discovered, for example, who had thrown the bomb responsible for the death of the eight police officers in Chicago's 1886 Haymarket Square riots. But eight anarchists were tried and convicted for murder on the ground that their speeches and writings had been responsible for the killing.[66] Louis Lugg, the only Haymarket defendant to resist arrest, committed suicide in his cell the night before his execution with a hidden dynamite cap. His closing speech before the court terrified middle America and helped precipitate a violent public reaction against anarchism:

> I declare again, frankly and openly, that I am in favor of using force. . . . You laugh! Perhaps you think 'you'll throw no more bombs,' but let me assure you that I die happy on the gallows so confident am I that the hundreds and thousands to whom I have spoken will remember my words; and when you shall have hanged us they, mark my words, they will do the bomb-throwing! In this hope do I say to you: 'I despise you, I despise your order, I despise your force-propped authority.' HANG ME FOR IT![67]

Of the convicted defendants, four were hanged, one committed suicide, and the others were pardoned by Governor Altgeld after three years' imprisonment. The assassination of President McKinley by an anarchist sympathizer only increased the popular revulsion against the "foreign doctrines" of anarchism.

In response, states began to pass vague and restrictive statutes aimed at suppressing "criminal anarchy." New York's 1902 law, basically a state anti-sedition measure, made it an offense to advocate, advise, or teach, by word or writing, "the doctrine that organized government should be overthrown by force or violence, or by assassination of the executive head or of any of the executive officials of government, or by any unlawful means."[68] The law also made it a felony to join any organization that taught or advocated anarchist doctrines. But the New York and other state laws did not deter the more radical worker groups from continuing to preach and advocate doctrines of class struggle and antistate warfare. The IWW, known derisively as "Wobblies," indeed increased its belligerent struggle against the new curtailment of the right of free speech. In many locations violent clashes erupted between the Wobblies and local police and municipal authorities. Reaching their peak in 1909, these free-speech campaigns continued practically until the outbreak of the First World War.[69]

The conflict between radical labor and the forces of law and order was exacerbated by the approach of the First World War. On July 22, 1916, a bomb exploded during a Preparedness Parade in San Francisco.[70] Thomas J. Mooney and Warren K. Billings were prosecuted for their alleged role in the crime. Mooney was sentenced to death, but the sentence was later commuted to life imprisonment, and in 1939 he was pardoned. Billings, sentenced to imprisonment, was released in 1939 and pardoned in 1961.

Stimulated by the San Francisco explosion, the state passed additional legislation to deal with the new forms of class and antigovernment warfare. California's Criminal Syndicalism Act was passed in 1919.[71] The statute defined *criminal syndicalism* as the "advocating, teaching or aiding and abetting the commission of crime, sabotage," including willful and malicious damage to physical property, or any other "unlawful acts of force and violence or unlawful methods of terrorism" for the purpose "of accomplishing a change in industrial ownership or control, or effecting any political change." The law made it a felony to organize or to knowingly become a member of any group or assemblage of people that taught or advocated the syndicalist doctrine.

The most noted conviction under the California law was that of Anita Whitney, a niece of United States Supreme Court Justice Stephen J. Field. Ms. Whitney was a member of the Oakland branch of the Socialist Party. In 1919 she attended a convention in Chicago that resulted in a split in the party, with the more militant faction forming the Communist Labor Party. The new party adopted a platform that rejected parliamentary methods and called for "a revolutionary class struggle." Joining the new party and participating in its meetings, Ms. Whitney nevertheless actively opposed the adoption of the call for revolutionary tactics. At her trial she testified that it

was not her intention to have the Communist Labor Party of California uti-
lize terrorism or violence. But her conviction was nevertheless upheld by the
United States Supreme Court on the ground that the state "may punish
those who abuse . . . [the freedom of speech] by utterances inimical to the
public welfare, tending to incite to crime, disturb the public peace, or
endanger the foundations of organized government and threaten its overthrow by unlawful means."[72]

The Court's decision reflected the anxieties of the era. But the resulting
suppression of radical speech and membership in prohibited organizations
augured a new age of government repression, the likes of which had not
been seen in America since the Sedition Act of 1798. This new era commenced with World War I and continued well through the administration of
President Eisenhower.

### FROM THE GREAT CRUSADE TO THE RED SCARE

In the summer of 1914, when World War I broke out in Europe, the
United States was without a standing army or a counterintelligence system.
The nation's Bureau of Investigation, established originally in 1909 (and later
renamed the F.B.I.), was still in its infancy and just concluding a two-year
campaign to suppress prostitution—known as the "white slave traffic."[73] As
late as the fall of 1916, the majority of the country appeared to favor staying
out of the war. Only six months later the United States was party to the
European conflict, and all at once the public and government alike became
extraordinarily concerned with pro-German, pacifist, socialist, and even
merely anti-British activities and propaganda.

Significantly, there were some 480,000 German and 350,000 Austro-
Hungarian, or "enemy," citizens in the United States at the time.[74] As early
as 1914 the Bureau of Investigation began preparing lists of dangerous enemy
aliens for possible internment. By March 1917, 1,768 suspect aliens had been
screened. A decision was reached to immediately detain 98 of this group
upon the country's entry into war. In the face of the substantial alien community, it is noteworthy that throughout the entire course of the First World
War, not more than 6,300 enemy aliens were arrested, and of these 4,000 were
released on bond. Thus, a group that could have supplied a great reservoir for
hostile political and military activity proved to be overwhelmingly neutral or
even loyal to the American cause.

The federal executive and Congress were not satisfied, however, that the
impending domestic dangers had been adequately guarded against. The government had at its disposal several criminal laws enacted during the Civil
War. These were aimed to prevent dissenters from seeking, through speech
or publication, to induce men to evade the draft. Existing laws also prohibit-

ed conspiracies, riots, and other means of disrupting recruitment and conscription. But the United States Department of Justice believed these statutes to be insufficient. There was no prohibition against persuading a person not to enlist voluntarily; neither were there provisions against individual efforts, rather than group conspiracies, to obstruct the draft.

Although existing laws would undoubtedly have sufficed to meet serious threats to the national interest, the demand for new legislation was widespread. Some recalled that the popular unrest and opposition during the Civil War had been handled through the imposition of martial law, and sought similar measures. One bill introduced in the Senate would have made the whole United States "a part of the zone of operations conducted by the enemy," and would have permitted the military trial, and upon conviction the execution, of any person charged with publishing anything that endangered the successful operation of the American forces.[75] A similar bill was prepared by Assistant Attorney General Charles Warren, who advocated the trial of subversive civilians by court martial.

President Wilson wished to head off such extreme legislation as both unnecessary and unwise. Yet he was aware of the growing fear of enemy sympathizers and the fact that even English and Canadian law found it necessary to guard against enemy propaganda. On June 15, 1917, an Espionage Act was enacted. Although the Act dealt primarily with such topics as espionage, the protection of military secrets, and the enforcement of neutrality, the opportunity was seized for the purpose of tightening controls against dissent and antiwar commentary generally. The Act made it a crime, punishable by twenty years' imprisonment, to (1) "willfully make or convey false reports or false statements with intent to interfere with the operation or success of the military"; (2) "willfully cause or attempt to cause insubordination . . . or refusal of duty in the military"; or (3) "willfully obstruct the recruiting or enlistment service of the United States."[76] The new law further authorized the issuing of search warrants for the seizure of property utilized for such unlawful purposes,[77] and made unmailable any materials coming within the new prohibitions.[78]

Woodrow Wilson approved the Espionage Act, asserting, however, "I shall not permit . . . any part of this law to apply to me . . . to be used as a shield against criticism."[79] Despite his view of himself as sympathetic to civil liberties and his declaration that he could not afford "to lose the benefit of patriotic and intelligent criticism," he nonetheless considered the Socialist Party as "almost treasonable" and urged the prosecution of war critics on the ground that "one conviction would probably scotch a great many snakes."[80]

Still, the new Espionage Law was not considered sufficiently stringent by others in authority. Attorney General Gregory pointed out that the original 1917 Act did not go far enough because it was only directed against deliberate or organized disloyal propaganda and failed to reach individual, casual, or impulsive utterances of disloyalty. Although Gregory was seeking only small modifications, the Senate Judiciary Committee came up, less than a year later, with a drastic amendment that was designed to stamp out all critical utterances. The amended Espionage Act, enacted on May 16, 1918,[81] is sometimes referred to as the Sedition Act. It added nine more offenses to the three previously defined. The law now also punished "saying or doing anything with intent to obstruct the sale of United States bonds, except by way of bona fide and not disloyal advice"; writing or saying anything "intended to cause contempt, scorn . . . or disrepute" toward the form of government of the United States, the Constitution, the flag, or the uniforms of the armed services; urging the curtailment of the production of any goods "necessary to the prosecution of the war"; and making statements "favoring the cause of any country at war with us . . . or opposing the cause of the United States therein." Violators were made subject to a maximum fine of $10,000 or imprisonment for twenty years.

There were nearly two thousand prosecutions under the Espionage Act but less than nine hundred convictions. Only ten arrests were made for sabotage, and a few others were made for causing insubordination or obstructing recruiting. Most prosecutions were for disloyal utterances—expressions of opinion about the merits of the war and its conduct. D. H. Wallace, an embittered veteran of the British Army was convicted and sentenced to twenty years' imprisonment for saying that "when a soldier went away he was a hero and when he came back . . . he was a bum." Robert Goldstein, who produced a motion picture titled *The Spirit of '76*, depicting the Revolutionary War, was sentenced to ten years in prison for his hostile portrayal of the British, now America's allies. In Windsor, Vermont, local minister Clarence H. Waldron was sentenced to fifteen years in prison for distributing to the parishioners a sheet explaining his opposition to the war: "Surely if Christians were forbidden to preserve the Person of their Lord and Master, they may not fight to preserve themselves."[82]

Under the new law it was criminal "to advocate heavier taxation instead of bond issues, to state that conscription was unconstitutional though the Supreme Court had not yet held it valid . . . to urge that a referendum should have preceded our declaration of War . . . [or to criticize] the Red Cross and the Y.M.C.A."[83] Courts and juries were caught in a patriotic fervor. They treated individual expression of opinion as statements of fact and condemned those uttering them for being false when they contradicted or differed from presidential or congressional proclamations. There was no need for any of these expressions of opinion to be directly addressed to soldiers or persons about to enlist. Judges held that any critical words that might conceivably reach the armed services were offensive, and consequently any critical public address before an audience containing draft-age men (between eighteen and forty-five) was punishable.

The harshest attitudes were displayed by the courts toward professed political radicals and revolutionaries, whether or not they voiced any support for the enemy. Socialist leader Rose Pastor Stokes was indicted for writing in a letter, "I am for the people and the government is for the profiteers." Judge Van Valkenburgh overlooked the distinction between factual misinformation and individual opinions and assured the jury that the objectionable words were false.[84] The judge also concluded that speaking against the war to an audience of women fell under the prohibition against inciting to mutiny, because the members of the female audience would in turn influence men of military age.

The trial of socialist leader Eugene V. Debs became the most celebrated case under the Espionage Act. The Socialist Party was opposed to the war, and the party platform, adopted in St. Louis shortly after America's entry into the conflict, stated, "We demand that the capitalist class, which is responsible for the war, pay its cost." The party further pledged itself to "active and public opposition to the war, through demonstrations, mass petitions and all other means within our power."[85] Debs himself insisted, however, "I have never advocated violence in any form. I always believed in education, in intelligence, in enlightenment, and I have always made my appeal to the reason and conscience of the people."[86]

It was for a speech made at the Socialist Party state convention in Canton, Ohio, that Debs was indicted and convicted. The speech took issue with former president Theodore Roosevelt, who had vociferously favored the war. Debs praised, instead, the "revolutionary forefathers" who were "opposed to the social system of their time" and, although they were "denounced," had "the moral courage to stand erect and defy all the storms. . . . That is why they are in history, and why the great respectable majority of their day sleep in forgotten graves."[87] In court, Debs, then sixty-two years old, proclaimed himself a socialist, a revolutionary, and an admirer of Soviet Bolshevism. He was sentenced to ten years' imprisonment, and the conviction was upheld by the Supreme Court in an opinion authored by Mr. Justice Holmes.[88]

The conviction of Eugene V. Debs was a final blow to the Socialist Party, whose national headquarters had been raided earlier in September of 1917. Most of its leaders were already in prison. At President Wilson's urging, leaders of the IWW were likewise prosecuted and given long sentences. Prosecutions under the Federal Espionage Act were only a partial measure of the battle against disloyalty. Both during the war and subsequently, when the Federal Espionage Act was no longer in force, other criminal prosecutions and sanctions—such as raids and deportations—were constantly directed against political radicals and dissenters.

Described as the era of the Red Scare, the war and the postwar period witnessed the widespread enactment of new antisedition laws throughout the various states. Similar to the 1902 New York criminal anarchy statute and the 1919 California criminal syndicalism law, these laws were enacted in two-thirds of the states during the period between 1917 and 1921. Specific prohibitions against the symbolic display of red flags were enacted, in addition, in thirty-three states.[89] A considerable number of persons were detained and tried under these state laws in the period immediately following the war.

In the postwar era, extensive use was made of the immigration laws as well. Amended in 1918, these laws permitted the exclusion and deportation of aliens affiliated with organizations that believed in, taught, or advocated the violent overthrow of the government. On November 7, 1919—the second anniversary of the Soviet revolution—and again, in January 1920, Attorney General A. Mitchell Palmer conducted nationwide raids on aliens belonging to various communist organizations. Although some four thousand aliens were detained without a warrant and had their documents and papers seized, only a few were finally deported. But the denial of the basic principles of due process, both in the raids and in the subsequent hearings before immigration officials, had serious and adverse effects upon the climate of political expression in the country.

Antiradicalism was manifested in other arenas, as well. In 1919 the United States House of Representatives refused to seat a Socialist Party leader, elected from Wisconsin, who had previously been indicted for conspiracy under the Espionage Act.[90] In 1920 the New York Assembly voted to expel five Socialist Party activists who already had been sworn in as members of the Assembly.[91] Legislative initiative was manifested also by the Overman Committee,[92] a subcommittee of the United States Senate Judiciary Committee, and the Lusk Committee in New York,[93] which investigated the evils of Bolshevism and the Red Menace. To further guard against subversive radicalism, many states instituted a security system requiring loyalty oaths from teachers. This practice became the precursor of the extensive loyalty programs for public employees that were to develop in America during and after the Second World War.[94]

"The suppression of Communists in 1919–20 was far more ruthless than that of pro-Germans in 1917–1918," wrote Nathaniel Weyl.[95] He attributed the difference to the fact that the Kaiser's allies in America had accepted, by and large, "the rules of the game." They accepted the sanctity of private property and believed in nationalism. The Marxists, by contrast, proposed a "transvaluation of all values," and advocated a world class dictatorship that would displace the national democratic system of Western society.

In response to the Marxist danger, Attorney General A. Mitchell Palmer warned the nation: "Like a prairie fire, the blaze of revolution is sweeping over every American institution of law and order . . . it is eating its way into the homes of American workmen; its sharp tongues of revolutionary heat are licking the altars of the churches, leaping into the belfry of the school bell, crawling into the sacred corners of American homes, seeking to replace marriage vows with libertine laws."[96] As a consequence of the vigorous and persistent campaigns launched against leftist radicalism in the late 1920s and early 1930s, communist organizations were driven underground.

CHAPTER FIVE

# People Power: Justice in a Pluralistic Society

The American Revolution . . . may teach mankind that revolutions are no trifles: that they ought never to be undertaken rashly; not without deliberate consideration and sober reflection; nor without a solid immutable, eternal foundation in justice and humanity; nor without a people possessed by intelligence, fortitude and integrity.

—John Adams, in Virginius Dabney, *The Patriots: The American Revolution—Generation of Genius*

Ordinary people [are] gaining power and control over the things that matter in our lives . . . when we combine non-violence [sic] with determination, when we treat them [police] as potential allies or intimates, we confuse them and open them to change.

—Abalone Alliance, Diablo Canyon encampment handout, 1980

## LIBERTY IN AN AGE OF TOTALITARIANISM

Franklin D. Roosevelt's New Deal was ushered in as the Red Scare was subsiding, and for the remainder of the 1930s there was a considerable relaxation of governmental and public concerns regarding radicalism and political dissent. Although the tensions of the waning Depression era were still extant, the political forces behind the New Deal were committed to a wider degree of governmental tolerance and a stricter observance of constitutional liberties. In addition, the National Labor Relations Act redirected much of the labor-related activism and dampened the influence of radical activists within the labor movement. Yet as the world and the United States moved toward the Second World War, anxieties began to manifest themselves anew. In addition to the old threat of communism, the new totalitarian regimes in Italy and Germany were demonstrating their capacity for aggression and expansionism, and the fear of Fascist and Nazi propaganda and suspected subversion in America were constantly mounting.

In 1938 the Dies Committee of the House of Representatives, the predecessor of the House Committee on Un-American Activities, began investigations into suspect political organizations and persons. About the same time, loyalty programs for government employees, unknown since World War I, returned to the public arena in new forms. Congress in 1939 passed the Hatch Act, which in part made it unlawful for any person employed by the federal government "to have membership in any political party or organization which advocates the overthrow of our constitutional form of government."[1] The Civil Service Commission interpreted the Act to require exclusion from government employment of members of "the Communist Party, the German Bund, or any other Communist, Nazi, or Fascist organization."[2] The ban was expanded in 1942 to require the removal of any employees whenever there was "reasonable doubt as to the loyalty of the persons involved to the Government of the United States."[3]

The strongest legislative response to the mounting tensions of the prewar era was the Alien Registration Act of 1940, which included the Smith Act, the first federal peacetime sedition law since the Alien and Sedition Acts of 1798. Named after its sponsor, Congressman Howard W. Smith of Virginia, the law was modeled after the New York Criminal Anarchy Act of 1902. The first section of the law punished, by ten years in prison or a $10,000 fine, any speech or publication causing or attempting to cause insubordination, disloyalty, or refusal of duty by members of the armed forces.[4] The major thrust of the Act was to prohibit any speech or publication advocating or teaching the "duty, necessity, desirability or propriety" of overthrowing national, state, or local governments "by force or violence."[5] The creation of or membership in any organization that taught or advocated such doctrine was similarly punishable by twenty years in prison or a fine not to exceed $20,000.

Eighteen members of the Socialist Workers Party were convicted in 1941 of conspiracy under the Smith Act. The convictions were sustained by the United States Court of Appeals.[6] Subsequently, in 1942, a group of twenty-eight alleged pro-Nazis was indicted in the District of Columbia for a conspiracy to violate the prohibitions against interference with the military effort. The trial, which was commenced in 1944 before Judge Eicher, was interrupted by the judge's death seven and a half months later. No retrial was held, and the indictment was later dismissed.[7]

These prosecutions remained rare despite the country's growing commitment to the defeat of German, Italian, and Japanese totalitarianism. Commenting on governmental attitudes toward political dissent and subversion during World War II, constitutional scholar Thomas I. Emerson concluded that this era saw "no repetition of the excesses of the [First] World War period. The nation remained relatively calm, and expression in opposition to the war was not suppressed."[8] One noted exception to the national calm was the expulsion of persons of Japanese ancestry from their homes on the West Coast and their detention in inland relocation centers.

American concern regarding disloyal populations goes back to old tensions with Native Americans, who were eventually restricted to secure reservations, and to the even earlier apprehension of Royalists (those remaining loyal to England's George III), who were confined or expelled during the Revolutionary War era. Substantial numbers of enemy aliens residing in America were later subjected to preventive detention during World War I, but those detained were noncitizens who were incarcerated only after careful scrutiny of their individual histories and records.

When on December 7, 1941, Japanese military aircraft staged an attack on Pearl Harbor, Hawaii, crippling the United States Pacific Fleet and leaving the West Coast vulnerable to further assault and possible invasion, war was quickly declared by Congress. In the further interest of national security, limitations were imposed on the movement of United States residents who were citizens of enemy nations. Initially, the F.B.I. worked systematically to intern, on an individual basis, enemy aliens believed to be dangerous. About two thousand Japanese residents were interned in this fashion, along with some sixteen hundred Germans and Italians.

But public pressure forced the abandonment of this slow, deliberate, due-process-of-law approach in favor of a sweeping military formula. After the fall of Singapore, Corregidor, and Wake Island, a new governmental policy divided America's Pacific Coast states into military zones and subjected local civilians of Japanese extraction to regulations issued by the War Department and the commanding general of the area.[9] Violators were subject to criminal penalties.[10]

About one hundred twelve thousand persons of Japanese extraction were thus evacuated collectively during the Second World War on the grounds of ancestry alone. Without prior hearing or trial, they were removed from their homes in the Pacific defense zone and interned outside the region. Of these, some seventy thousand were American citizens.

The new system of controls instituted what has been described as a "sordid campaign motivated by greed and bigotry."[11] Western and Southern Congressmen joined forces to demand "equal treatment" for all persons of Japanese extraction, regardless of citizenship or loyalty. Congressman John Rankin of Mississippi declared, "Once a Jap always a Jap! . . . You cannot regenerate a Jap, convert him, change him, and make him the same as a white man any more than you can reverse the laws of nature."[12] The fact that no acts of sabotage by Japanese Americans had been reported was taken by some "as conclusive evidence that . . . [the Japanese Americans] were holding back their strength in order to let loose a nationwide tornado of destruction."[13]

Under General John DeWitt, the West Coast Zone commander, three military orders imposed special restrictions upon persons of Japanese ancestry, whether American citizens or enemy aliens. All Japanese Americans in those zones were subjected to a curfew not applicable to other citizens or even to enemy aliens of other races.[14] Fearing further that this ethnic population, which had maintained strong overseas ties, might engage in espionage or sabotage or otherwise aid the Japanese cause, all western Japanese Americans—citizen and alien, old and young, male and female—were ordered to evacuate their homes on a few days notice.[15] Temporary quarters were set up for the evacuees, including the stables of the Fresno Race Track.[16]

When politicians from neighboring states expressed a fear of the mass influx of uprooted Japanese Americans, compulsory relocation camps were established in remote and barren areas. Those relocated were transported by train under military guard. They were permitted to carry with them only a few belongings and were installed in empty barracks, poorly insulated against the cold of winter and the heat of summer. The evacuees could not leave the relocation centers until they had been cleared by a loyalty investigation and until the War Relocation Agency had further found a place where they could be received without local hostility. Homes and businesses had to be sold or abandoned, educations were disrupted, careers discontinued, and a proud and obedient people, not one of whom was ever determined to be disloyal, were interned, dispossessed, and humiliated.[17]

In two world wars Americans of German, Italian, or other enemy descent were spared these measures. Even those continuing to maintain German or Italian citizenship remained free. Japanese Americans, it was argued, were different: they had kept to themselves, had not mingled with the general population, and had held firm to the customs and mores of their ancestral home. Having failed to dispel the impression that they had not fully embraced the social and political values of America, Japanese Americans were singled out for quasi-criminal penalties not for their commission of illegal deeds but because of their status as members of a politically or racially suspect population.

The nation's courts did little to alleviate the hardships that befell the internees. The legality of the evacuation program came up for review before the United States Supreme Court in the midst of the hostilities. In the first case, a Japanese American named Hirabayashi was convicted for violating the curfew orders issued by General DeWitt in California. In 1943 the court sustained Hirabayashi's conviction on the grounds of the military's belief in an impending Japanese invasion. Given the likelihood of support by local Japanese American sympathizers, the collective curfew order was held to be not an unreasonable exercise of military discretion.[18]

In December 1944, the Court had before it the much more difficult—and dubious—case of Korematsu, convicted for defying the military's evacuation program. Writing for the majority, Justice Black upheld the right of the military in wartime to exclude Japanese Americans from a domestic area designated as a defense zone.[19] He took care, however, to differentiate the situation before the Court from the unlikely case "involving the imprisonment of a loyal citizen in a concentration camp because of racial prejudice."[20]

That potentiality was presented by Mitsuye Endo, who, although acknowledged to be a loyal citizen, was refused permission to leave a relocation camp. The Supreme Court avoided the constitutional issue by holding that neither Congress nor the president's executive orders authorized the continued incarceration of Ms. Endo. She was freed, but the opinion contained less than a ringing endorsement of the dictum in the previous case. The Court left little doubt that if Congress had authorized it, the detention of Ms. Endo might well have been found to be constitutional.[21] Nonetheless, two years later, after the conclusion of the war, the Supreme Court, looking into the future, began to impose limitations upon the military's wartime power by declaring invalid the World War II court martial trials of civilians for common crimes committed in Hawaii.[22]

## THE WAGES OF THE "COLD WAR"

America's relative calm during World War II did not prevent the resurgence of the country's historical anxieties about subversion at the conclusion of the conflict. As the Nazi and Fascist threat receded, the pattern of the nation's Red Scare after World War I began to repeat itself. The postwar years "were dominated by the rise and the decline of the phenomenon known as 'McCarthyism' [after Red-baiting Senator Joe McCarthy]. As Cold War tensions mounted, restrictions on freedom of expression designed to promote national security steadily increased."[23]

This comprehensive assault on political dissent and alleged disloyalty occurred under the aegis of the earlier 1940 Smith Act. Though rarely utilized during the war, the Smith Act's prohibition against advocating the violent overthrow of the government of the United States became important in hunting communists after the war. The best known of the Smith Act prosecutions began with the July 1948 indictment of twelve members of the Communist Party of the United States' Central Committee, who were charged with a conspiracy to violate the Act's prohibitions. The Committee's chairman, William Z. Foster, did not go to trial, because of ill health, but the prosecution of the others commenced in March 1949 and continued until September 23. All defendants were found guilty, and the convictions were sustained in 1951 by the United States Supreme Court in *Dennis v. United States*.[24]

A total of twenty-three other prosecutions, involving one hundred twenty-nine defendants, were begun by the Department of Justice after the Supreme Court's affirmation of the *Dennis* convictions. Most of the prosecutions were on charges of conspiracy, and only eight were based on the Act's prohibitions of party membership. In one of the conspiracy cases, fourteen defendants were tried and convicted in Los Angeles both for advocating the overthrow of the government and for organizing the Communist Party.[25]

When the case *Yates v. United States* reached the United States Supreme Court in the spring of 1956, the Court produced one of the first judicial dampers on the government's campaign against communist activity. Five of the convicted persons were set free and new trials were ordered for the remaining nine. The Supreme Court held, in essence, that the trial court had failed to distinguish between the "advocacy of forcible overthrow as an abstract *doctrine* and advocacy of *action* to that end" (emphasis added). As a mere doctrine, the Court concluded, the advocacy of forcible overthrow is protected by the constitutional safeguards of freedom of speech. Advocacy of action, on the other hand, may be prosecuted for constituting "a clear and present danger" to organized government.

No further prosecutions under the Smith Act were instituted after the *Yates* decision. The indictment against the nine remaining *Yates* defendants, furthermore, was dismissed by the trial court. In all but one other pending cases the indictments were ultimately dropped. Only Scales, tried under the prohibition of Communist Party membership, was convicted and went to prison subsequent to the *Yates* decision.[26] Sustaining his conviction in 1961, Mr. Justice Harlan wrote the opinion of the Supreme Court in *Scales v. United States*. The law, he said, "does not make criminal all association" with an organization that has been shown to engage in illegal advocacy. There must be clear proof that a defendant "specifically intend[s] to accomplish [the aims of the organization] by resort to violence. . . . Thus the member for whom the organization is a vehicle for the advancement of legitimate aims and policies does not fall within the ban of the statute."[27] Scales's conviction was sustained only after the Court's finding that the evidence supported both the party's illegal "advocacy of action" and the accused's intent to resort to violence. Sentenced to six years in prison, Scales was granted clemency in December of 1962.

Throughout the war years various preexisting loyalty programs for federal employees remained uncoordinated and loosely enforced. But in March of 1947, President Truman, by executive order, proclaimed a new and comprehensive federal employee loyalty program.[28] The program required an investigation of every person entering civil employment in any department or agency of the executive branch of the federal government. Employment was to be denied, and employees could be removed, when "reasonable grounds exist for the belief that the person involved is disloyal to the Government of the United States." Among the activities and associations to be considered in determining disloyalty were the following: attempts at sabotage or espionage; knowingly associating with spies and saboteurs; engagement in, or advocacy of, treason or sedition; advocacy of violent revolution to alter the constitutional form of government; intentional and unauthorized disclosure of confidential documents; performance of one's duties so as to serve the interests of a foreign government; and, finally, membership or affiliation with any organization, foreign or domestic, designated as subversive by the attorney general of the United States.

The Truman program was superseded by yet a stricter system adopted early in President Eisenhower's administration.[29] The Eisenhower program instituted a more comprehensive loyalty/individual-security approach. The program inquired not only into political loyalty but also into personal conduct and stability, including associations that "tend to show that the individual is not reliable or trustworthy" and any criminal, dishonest, or "notoriously disgraceful conduct, habitual use of intoxicants to excess, drug addiction, or sexual perversion." Investigations were required not only for hiring but also for job retention. Some of the stringent requirements, however, were modified by the United States Supreme Court's holding that dismissal was authorized only in the interest of "national security" and that only those occupying "sensitive" positions were subject to these comprehensive standards.[30]

Eisenhower's executive order requiring loyalty-security investigations combined with several existing laws (including Public Law 733, passed in 1950,[31] and the Internal Security Act of 1950)[32] to impose a comprehensive system of clearances upon a yet larger segment of the military and civilian labor force. Professor Ralph Brown estimated that by 1958, nearly 13.5 million persons were covered by federal, state, and local loyalty tests. "Taking the total labor force at around 65,000,000, this means that at least one person out of five, as a condition of his current employment, has taken a test oath, or completed a loyalty statement, or achieved official security clearance."[33]

Another feature of the rigorous post–World War II campaign against disloyalty was the enactment of the Internal Security Act of 1950, popularly known as the McCarran Act. Passed over President Truman's veto shortly after the outbreak of the Korean hostilities, the new law was deemed necessary because of the Smith Act's perceived inadequacies. The McCarran Act distinguished between three categories of conspiratorial communist organizations—the "Communist-action" organizations, the "Communist-front" organizations, and, finally, the "Communist-infiltrated" organizations (depending on the degree of their penetration by subversive elements). The Act required the registration of all organizations falling within these categories with the attorney general, and called for information regarding organizational officers, financing, and memberships. Members of these organizations, furthermore, were prohibited from United States Government employment, were denied the right to hold office or employment with any labor union, and were prohibited from applying for or using a passport.

A Subversive Activities Control Board was also established with the power to determine whether given organizations fell within any of the designated categories, and to scrutinize individual membership in such suspect organizations. The McCarran Act provided further that in the event American territory was invaded or an insurrection in support of a foreign enemy occurred, or in case of a declaration of war by Congress, the president could proclaim the existence of an internal security emergency. The attorney general was authorized, upon such proclamation, to undertake the emergency detention of any person "as to whom there is reasonable ground to believe that . . . [he or she] probably will engage in . . . acts of espionage or of sabotage."

Because no communist-related organizations registered voluntarily under the McCarran Act, the government commenced action to compel registration by the Communist Party. Extensive and complicated proceedings followed, resulting in a review by the United States Supreme Court, which upheld the registration requirement.[34] The government then obtained indictments against the party, its officers, and its members for failing to register. Two of the members ordered to register appealed, and their case reached the United States Supreme Court. In 1965, in *Albertson v. Subversive Activities Control Board*,[35] the Court reversed the registration order of party members on the grounds that the order violated the privilege against self-incrimination. Said the Court, "the risks of incrimination which the petitioners take in registering are obvious. [The Registration] Form . . . requires an admission of membership in the Communist Party. Such an admission . . . may be used to prosecute the registrant under . . . the Smith Act . . . or under . . . the Subversive Activities Act . . . to mention only two federal criminal statutes."[36] Later, the indictment of the party itself was also overturned by the courts on the grounds that those who might register for the party would incriminate themselves individually in the process.[37]

The McCarran Internal Security Act's accomplishments in the war against subversion were limited. Although the Communist Party itself, as a "Communist-action organization," was ordered to register, its indictment for failing to do so was overturned, and no individual party members were compelled to expose themselves to the risks of registration. The Act's provision denying passports to communists was likewise held unconstitutional in 1964 on the grounds that it "too broadly and indiscriminately restricts the right to travel and thereby abridges the liberty guaranteed by the Fifth Amendment."[38] The prohibition of communists from activity in labor unions or from employment in defense facilities was also curtailed after review in the courts.

Robel, a shipyard worker, was indicted for being engaged in national defense work while a member of the Communist Party. His indictment was dismissed by the district court and appeal was taken to the United States Supreme Court, where the dismissal was upheld.[39] Finally, the authority of the government to carry out emergency detentions in the interest of national security, long under attack as an excessive and indiscriminate exercise of governmental power, was terminated in 1971 when the Internal Security Act was amended and the detention provisions were repealed.[40]

No history of the post–World War II measures against disloyalty and political radicalism would be complete without reference to the Communist Control Act of 1954.[41] Setting out to totally outlaw the Communist Party, the Act commenced by finding that "the Communist Party of the United States, although purportedly a political party, is in fact an instrumentality of a conspiracy to overthrow the Government of the United States." The Act declared further that the party constituted an authoritarian dictatorship within the republic, demanding for itself the rights and privileges accorded to political parties while denying to all others the liberties guaranteed by the Constitution. Based upon these findings, the Act withheld from the Communist Party and its affiliates all the rights and privileges accorded to lawful organizations.

The states of New Jersey, Connecticut, and New York moved to implement in practice this determination that the Communist Party was a "proscribed organization."[42] In 1954 a New Jersey candidate was denied the right to appear on a local election ballot on behalf of the Communist Party.[43] Ten years later the attorney general of Connecticut ruled that the Communist Party could not be on the ballot in the general elections in that state.[44]

In New York the state industrial commissioner in 1957 similarly denied the claim of a Communist Party member to unemployment insurance based upon his previous employment by the party. Moreover, the commissioner suspended the registration of both the United States and the New York Communist parties as "employers" under the New York unemployment compensation laws. The action of the commissioner with regard to the organizations was upheld by the state courts, while the decision concerning the individual claimant was reversed.[45] On appeal to the United States Supreme Court, the earlier decision suspending the Communist Party's registration under the employment laws was reversed. Bypassing many complex constitutional issues regarding the Communist Party's right to exist, the Court merely concluded that the Communist Control Act should not be construed to "require exclusion of the . . . [parties] . . . from New York's unemployment compensation system."[46] Much like the Smith and McCarran Acts, the Communist Control Act and its state clones had been largely emasculated by the impact of the United States Supreme Court's earlier rulings in *Yates* and *Scales*.

Writing in 1951, at the apex of America's Red Scare, Nathaniel Weyl summarized the country's historical record with regard to the struggle between authority and its political defiers:

> Throughout the 175 years of its national existence, the United States has been extraordinarily tolerant of both sedition and disloyalty. No modern state has ever defined the crime of treason so narrowly. No nation has ever surrounded the man accused of betraying his country with such a formidable barrier of constitutional protection or been so reluctant to punish conspiracies directed at its very existence. During most of America's wars, rebels and dissenters have been free to agitate against the military effort. . . .
>
> Yet in more recent periods of real or imaginary crisis, Americans have not hesitated to resort to vigorous suppression of disloyalty. . . . During World War I, although national security was not actually threatened by the pro-German, pacifist, and socialist minorities, an epidemic of prosecutions raged.
>
> After World War II, the United States government began to take increasingly stern measures against communism, designed to shatter both the underground apparatus of espionage and infiltration and the open party which propagandizes for revolution. The government conducted this offensive while aware of the fact that . . . major constitutional issues were at stake.[47]

## THE EXPLOSION OF PROTEST

The American government's intense campaign against communism and domestic subversion did not begin to ebb until the mid-1950s. Even following the decline of what has come to be described as the McCarthy era, the Cold War continued unabated, but its major manifestations were in the realms of America's military preparedness and foreign relations. The domestic concern over loyalty and political subversion was considerably eased. Yet many of the laws and security measures amassed during the disquiet of the post–World War II era, although no longer utilized, remained legally in effect or subject to ready recall. The potential of governmental oppression, asserted leading political and civil rights scholar Thomas I. Emerson, has thus continued to loom over the land.[48]

With attention averted from the internal communist threat, the nation began to witness a new rebellion against social restrictions and controlling laws—the black civil rights movement, leading to and receiving nourishment from the 1954 United States Supreme Court decision in *Brown v. Board of Education*. The movement, in its initial stages, resorted to little illegality or deliberate violence. Yet the activists' mere exercise of the constitutional rights of association and assembly, and their resort to marches, parades, and other visible forms of protest against racial inequality and abuse, frequently pitched them into conflict with oppressive laws and regulations enacted in the name of public order.

In the late 1950s and early 1960s, civil rights workers often encountered violent opposition from establishment forces all over the South. Segregationist mobs bombed and smashed Freedom Rider buses and severely beat riders when they stopped in terminals along the way. In some cases, state and local law enforcement officers aided the hostile mobs. In Birmingham and Selma, Alabama, police used cattle prods, attack dogs, and firehoses to disperse the nonviolent civil rights demonstrators—black and white. Sit-ins at segregated facilities more often than not did not lead to rapid changes in local segregation laws but rather to beatings, jail, fines, and even the confinement of protestors in state schools for delinquents.[49] America's domestic tranquility was shattered by a new challenge to authority.

By the early 1960s, nevertheless, the civil rights movement was achieving major successes throughout the South. Simultaneously, university students began campaigning for a greater voice in university affairs. The Free Speech Movement, as it was called, erupted on the Berkeley campus of the University of California. With the successful civil rights movement as a model, California students organized sit-down strikes and seized administration buildings. In 1964 the movement sprouted a national wave of campus unrest and uprisings. Designed to protest the lack of student influence in university administration, the absence of adequate African American student and faculty recruitment, and undue university involvement with military and business interests, the student revolts reached their zenith in a growing agitation for an end to the Vietnam War.

Significantly, neither the civil rights movement nor the student protests generated a high degree of physical violence against persons. "Generally, [the student] 'movement' . . . was limited to public acts of civil disobedience, strikes, occupation of buildings and demonstrations; at times it included symbolic imprisonment of university administrators or representatives of the military establishment and, occasionally, destruction of property," reported civil rights commentator Richard E. Rubenstein.[50]

Only with the 1965 riots in the Watts section of Los Angeles did African American resistance assume a decidedly violent mode. The violence spread to other cities the following summer. Earlier, before the Rochester, New York, riot of 1964, it was presumed that major disorders could occur only in the South and in the very large northern cities. After Rochester it became clear that no city in the nation was immune. As each year passed, more and more communities began to experience massive racially connected demonstrations and disorders.

Ironically, some programs of President Johnson's War on Poverty had already been implemented in Watts for a year before the riots occurred in August of 1965. Despite the expectation and even early manifestations of progress, one city after another in the urban North experienced revolts in their African American ghettos. The epidemic that commenced in August of 1965 continued through the spring of 1968. Some one hundred seventy-six cities recorded civil disturbances in 1967 alone. By the end of that summer, eight communities had experienced major disorders, characterized by multiple fires, extensive looting, and sniping.[51] The April 1968 assassination of Dr. Martin Luther King Jr. sparked further major riots in the few northern cities spared from earlier violence—Baltimore, Washington, and Pittsburgh—as well as in several other localities.

Generally, much of the 1960s urban unrest seems understandable in retrospect. But many particular manifestations of political protest and disorder are difficult to rationally explain or classify. In August 1965—following the arrest of a twenty-one-year-old black man for drinking, failing to stop at a red light, and inability to produce a driver's license—riots erupted in Watts, Los Angeles. Some ten thousand African Americans took to the streets as a consequence.[52]

This number represented about 10 percent of all African American men and women, between the ages of fourteen and forty-four, living in the South Los Angeles area. The violence was sustained for an extended period in the face of a major show of force by 1,000 police and eventually 13,000 National Guardsmen. Reviewing the Watts riots, after which several later riots were modeled, Anthony Oberschall described the nation's initial reaction as shock and fear.[53] There was strong belief that the riots were organized and led by a conspiracy of radical and disaffected groups in league with gangs and hoodlums, producing a black armed uprising against the police, the political authorities, and the whites in general.

Later analysis disclosed a totally different assessment. The riot, according to Oberschall,[54] was remarkable for the absence of leadership and organization and the lack of collective demands by either the rioters or the African American population. No spokesperson emerged from the ranks of the rioters. No barricades were set up and no effort was made to hold an area after the police were forced out. Although the initial riot against the police burst into a series of violent activities against other symbols of power and authority, no broader "insurrectionary or revolutionary pattern of action" developed.

The racial revolts of the 1960s, moreover, were inexplicable to many reform-minded Americans. Peter H. Rossi, Professor of Social Relations at Johns Hopkins University, observed:

> The significance of Watts was both its size and its timing. It was easy to understand why there were riots in Harlem; after all Harlem is widely thought to be the worst of urban ghettos. . . . But Los Angeles is the urban paradise to which so many Americans had migrated since World War II . . . the stucco bungalows of Watts hardly look like a slum. . . . Things were getting better, America felt, and a major rebellion was upsetting to a popular conception of continuing linear progress in the status of blacks in this country.[55]

Then, almost as unexpectedly, the racial explosion of the 1960s came to a hasty end. Although the cities nervously awaited the summer of 1969, only a score of minor incidents were reported.

To better understand the landscape and mood of political radicalism in the 1960s, one must not only look at the racial riots but also examine the student campus unrest, its interaction with the escalating national criticism of the Vietnam War, and the increasing youth opposition to compulsory military service. Campus activists, going back to the early 1960s, had called for the opening of university facilities for political debate, a greater student role in academic administration, more support for politically "persecuted" faculty members, the abolition of "racist" student and faculty recruitment, termination of the university involvement with the "military-industrial complex,"[56] and, finally, opposition to the system of academic draft exemptions as well as the military draft. Only rarely was the student unrest accompanied by calls for general, community-wide "open, fierce, and thoroughgoing rebellion"— as was done in a letter by a former student distributed on the University of California campus at Berkeley on September 10, 1964.[57]

The emergence of many campus disturbances frequently paralleled some of the banal chronology of the ghetto riots. At Berkeley much of the early agitation was triggered when the university administration advised student organizations that student-manned display tables would no longer be permitted on the university property at the Bancroft and Telegraph streets entrance, and that "advocative" literature and activities relating to off-campus political issues would be forbidden altogether.

On October 1, 1964, the police arrested Jack Weinberg, a nonstudent, for soliciting funds at a CORE (Congress on Racial Equality) table. He was carried into a police car, which was prevented from departing by large members of protesting students. That night, activists, demanding that all charges against suspended students be dropped, clashed with a few hundred antidemonstrators, allegedly fraternity men. The following day several hundred newly arrived policemen were posted around the demonstrators. The crowd of protesters and onlookers had swelled to more than seven thousand.

At this point, a temporary agreement between the administration, faculty, and students nearly defused the oncoming confrontation. The students were to desist from all means of illegal protest, no charges were to be pressed by the university against Jack Weinberg, and a tripartite committee was to be set up—consisting of students, faculty, and administrators—to discuss policies regarding on-campus political activity.

The next several months were marked by escalating disagreements, agitation, and protest rallies. On November 20, 1964, a mass rally attended by 3,000 participants was held on the steps of Berkeley's Sproul Hall with the participation of singer Joan Baez. The same day Mario Savio, a student previously charged with violating university rules, was placed on probation for the remainder of the semester, although the suspension of the other cited students was lifted. Eleven days later, the campus's Free Speech Movement issued an ultimatum demanding that all disciplinary actions against student leaders be lifted, that the administration refrain from imposing sanctions against students for political activity, and that standards for regulating speech on the campus be left to the courts, not to the campus administrators. The university failed to respond.

On December 2, a mass rally and sit-in by some one thousand participants was again held inside Sproul Hall. At 7:00 P.M. the police locked the doors, permitting no one else to enter. Early the following morning more than six hundred police officers assembled outside the building. Demonstrators were free to leave, but at 3:45 P.M. the officers began arresting those remaining. Seven hundred eighty-six demonstrators were arrested in a roundup that continued for more than twelve hours, but all were released from custody the following day. The Berkeley experience can be viewed as a prototype for hundreds of other expressions of protest throughout the nation.

The perspective of the thousands and thousands of African Americans, youths, and university students throughout the country who took part in the disobedience and direct-action campaigns of the 1960s is distilled in the diary of a seventeen-year-old Connecticut girl. Suzanne Williams was one of 150 people picketing the main gate of the Electric Boat Company in Groton, Connecticut, on July 21, 1966, to protest the launching of the forty-first Polaris submarine. Nine pickets, including Ms. Williams, attempted to enter the shipyard and later sat down at the gate blocking the path of spectators invited to the launching. The pickets were arrested, charged with trespassing, and arraigned. Ms. Williams later recited her version of the events:

> I've just gotten out of jail and I'm delighted to be free. It all happened this way. On July 21, along with others, I tried to get into the shipyard of Electric Boat in Groton, Connecticut to leaflet the launching of the Polaris submarine, *Will Rogers*. As I had anticipated, I was stopped by the EB security guard and the police, told I was trespassing and asked to leave. When I refused, I was dragged across the street into a waiting bus. We asked the officers if we were under arrest, but they wouldn't tell us.
>
> We then drove to New London and parked outside the courthouse. An officer came in and began booking us. . . . He told us all that if we did not cooperate in court we probably would get 30 days for contempt of court. At this point I had already decided not to cooperate, but his statement made me review the reasons for my decision.
>
> I had decided to talk to everyone in the interests of communication and

courtesy, but not to cooperate physically with the court. Primarily, I noncooperated for the same reason I had gone limp when taken into custody: I felt that my actions at Electric Boat were correct, that I should not assist others in interfering with these actions. Also, while I have great respect for justice, I have a number of objections to the present court system—for instance, that the court is the tool which our government uses to punish those who oppose immoral laws. . . .

When I declined to come forward to the bench, Judge George Kinmouth found me in contempt of court and sentenced me to 30 days. . . . Throughout the 30 days I cooperated with the jail in all respects, except that I fasted from Hiroshima Day to Nagasaki Day. I can give no real reason for cooperation with the jail in view of my noncooperation with the courts, as jails are certainly bad *per se*. . . .

On August 19 my 30 days were up and I went to Groton Circuit Court to appear before Judge Luke Stapleton on the original charges. I was again dragged into the court room, but this time was placed right in front of the bench, on the floor. The judge and I talked for several minutes. I told him why I could not, in good conscience, cooperate. He asked me questions concerning my education, employment, and various other matters. My impression was that he is a nice guy. However, when I continued to remain seated, he found me in contempt of court, and I was again sentenced, this time to 60 days. . . .

On Tuesday, September 27, Mr. Arnold Klau came to visit me. He is a lawyer of the American Civil Liberties Union and was interested in the facts that I had no counsel and [most of the time] no guardian . . . he understood my position in respect to the court, however, he suggested that I apply for modification of sentence, as he felt that the judge and I had the same respect for the concept of justice, and neither of us liked my imprisonment. My statement to Judge Stapleton was as follows: "I would like to apply for a reduction of my sentence to time served. My actions in court were taken for disrespect. They were not so intended."

The Judge then drove the considerable distance from Hartford to New London, opened court, and purged me of contempt. He then asked the prosecutor to *nolle* the other charges against me, as I had already served 68 days, and the prosecutor did so. Mr. Klau had seen me at 9:00 A.M. and I was released at around 4:00 P.M. on the same day. I was surprised to find that the judge was waiting outside the jail with Mr. Klau, and actually rode in the same car with us a good deal of the way to Hartford. He was very friendly. I am convinced there are good reasons for both noncooperation and cooperation with the court. This time I was moved to the former. I feel that my experience, as a whole, was a valuable one, although I now deplore jails and prisons more than ever.[58]

Suzanne Williams, a political protestor, disobedient, and offender, did not penetrate deeply into the criminal justice system. Her encounter with the police was superficial, her confrontation with the courts more pathetic than tragic, and she barely entered the corrections stage. She acquired, in the process of her political dissent, an arrest and jail record. Whether the imposition of these sanctions upon Suzanne Williams constituted a "just dessert" for her almost peevish misdeeds, or whether it helped either "deter" or "rehabilitate" her, remains uncertain. Moreover, whether her punishment helped or will help deter others from similar conduct is equally subject to speculation. In her mind Williams felt certain that she had to do what she did. The system of justice similarly proceeded to do what it was expected to do. But unlike the relatively banal history of Suzanne Williams, most other confrontations between political dissidents and the authorities tend to impose greater penalties upon the dissenters and heavier burdens upon the system of justice, seriously challenging the system's and the nation's notions of fairness, legality, and morality.

## INSURGENCY AND ALIENATED VIOLENCE

The tactics of protest, resistance, civil disobedience, and direct action have been marshaled in America against a wide range of targets: racial injustice, urban hopelessness, academic ivory tower isolation, and international military adventurism. For a time it seemed that any perceived wrong could be addressed by these methods as long as sufficient mass support could be mobilized. Generating such support, therefore, became the primary objective of the protest movements of the 1960s and early 1970s. As opposition to the Vietnam War grew, the lessons learned in Mississippi again became applicable to university campuses: at Berkeley (in 1969 during the governorship of Ronald Reagan), at Columbia, San Francisco, Cornell, Kent State, and Jackson State College. During the first weekend of May 1970, in response to President Nixon's decision to extend the Vietnam War into Cambodia, widespread protests were aired throughout the country. Meetings and demonstrations, "on an unprecedented scale," were held in colleges across the country.[59] At Kent State University, during what were described as predominantly peaceful protests, four students were killed by National Guard troops on May 4.

A newly appointed Commission on Campus Unrest, under the chairmanship of former Pennsylvania Governor William W. Scranton, was urged by President Nixon, in 1970, to identify the principal causes of what was perceived as a wave of campus violence. The Commission released its report on September 27, 1970, concluding that "the crisis on American campuses has no parallel in the history of the nation. This crisis has roots in divisions of American society as deep as any since the Civil War." The Commission further warned in its findings: "Too many Americans have begun to justify violence as a means of affecting [sic] change or safeguarding traditions."[60] Most disconcerting was the Commission's observation that while only a small number of students turned to violence, "an increasing number, not terrorists themselves, would not turn even arsonists and bombers over to law enforcement officials."

Almost concurrently with the report of the Commission on Campus Unrest, President Nixon asked Congress to authorize an additional 1,000 F.B.I. agents to concentrate primarily on campus disorders.[61] But the eventual conclusion of the Vietnam War acted to considerably relax the youthful and racial anxieties, which had reached explosive peaks. Still, even though the crisis was dissipated, in the preceding years the former turmoil had left deep wounds in the American psyche. A "loss of innocence" had occurred, a loss of faith and confidence in the goals and processes of the American dream.

The nation's history testifies that millions of disenfranchised Americans—Native Americans, African Americans, women, immigrants, laborers, leftists, rightists—had previously broken faith. But the 1960s were unique because mainstream middle-class America reached some of the same tragic conclusions. The middle-class youth of the country—and many of their elders—were no longer willing to endorse the assertions of the Commission on Campus Unrest that "the right to dissent is not the right to resort to violence" and that "crimes committed by one do not justify crimes committed by another."

On this widespread public loss of confidence in the lawful and orderly methods for effecting change, more extremist elements sought to build their strength. Earlier, the work of Dr. Martin Luther King Jr. had been directed toward integrating African Americans into the social, political, and economic life of America. Some of those who followed him concluded, however, that full African American emancipation could not be reached without the creation of autonomous African American political and economic institutions. It was this concept of separatism—including "an unmistakable anti-white animus, and a retreat from nonviolence"[62]—that was labeled "Black Power" by a Trinidad-born militant named Stokely Carmichael.

In his addresses Carmichael described the African American community in America as a "colony," proclaiming its need for "national liberation"(p.359). The writings of Cuba's Che Guevara, North Vietnam's Ho Chi Minh, and Franz Fanon, an African American physician who fought the French in Algeria, furnished the ideological basis for Carmichael's and the other African American activists' rhetoric. Many African American leaders began to accept Fanon's message that national liberation required violent revolution—not only to drive out the colonizers but to establish and solidify the identity of those seeking to be liberated.

Carmichael and his followers soon realized, however, that they lacked the manpower and resources to bring about a major rebellion. "We looked around and we didn't have but a handful of people," Carmichael confessed years later. In spite of this, the group continued its violent rhetoric, seeking from time to time to turn its words into deeds. A new Black Panther Party was organized in Oakland in 1966, with Carmichael as a founding member.

The Panthers, perceived by white radicals as the vanguard of a new American revolution, were courted by the militant Students for a Democratic Society and participated in the June 8, 1969, annual SDS convention in Chicago's Coliseum. When the SDS membership were derided by the Panthers as "armchair Marxists," for their failure to engage in actual struggles, the Weathermen faction stormed out of the convention to form its own independent revolutionary organization.

Deriving their name from a line in a Bob Dylan song—"You Don't Need a Weatherman to Know Which Way the Wind Blows"—the Weathermen symbolized a dramatic shift from political protest and resistance to nearly indiscriminate rage. Seeking to serve as a revolutionary vanguard, members of the new group, including leaders Bernadine Dohrn, Bill Ayers, and Mark Rudd, set out in the summer of 1969 to convert working-class youths to the revolution. At rock concerts, drive-ins, and college cafeterias, they sought to create disruptions in order to call attention to their causes, of which women's liberation became a central theme.

In October of 1969, a spectacular event was planned for Chicago—to commemorate the previous year's assault on the Democratic Convention and to correspond with the opening of the trial of the Chicago Eight, charged with causing the riot. Some twenty thousand participants were expected to descend on Chicago in the form of a guerrilla raid. But despite the natty appearance of Weathermen shock troops at Chicago's Lincoln Park on October 8—wearing helmets, combat boots, jeans, and padded clothing, carrying clubs and even gas masks—the events that followed resulted in an abysmal failure for the Weathermen. After a race through the streets, smashing the windows of shops and parked cars, the Weathermen were no match for the thousands of uniformed police and the hundreds of plainclothesmen who had been called out by Chicago's Mayor Daley. Despite the activists' broader revolutionary hopes, no working-class participants were in sight, and even the Black Panthers, who took part in a counterrally, criticized the Weathermen for being "anarchistic, opportunistic, adventuristic" (p.497).

Rejected by both the working-class and the black revolutionaries, Weathermen no longer talked about a mass movement and a people's war. Viewing themselves as the true remaining revolutionaries, they began discussing strategies of sabotage and terrorism—to jar the apathy and touch the conscience of society. In their growing isolation they were seeking relief and reinforcement in bizarre events and causes. At the Weathermen's final public meeting in Flint, Michigan, Bernadine Dohrn eulogized Charles

Manson, charged with the murder of Sharon Tate and her friends, for his attack on the "pigs"(p.502). Shortly thereafter the Weathermen organization went underground.

An estimated one hundred members of the leadership were living clandestinely by early 1970. "By whatever historic standard, the Weathermen were not very successful revolutionaries during the decade after they went underground," noted journalist and social historian Milton Viorst (p.503). "As fugitives," concluded Viorst, "the Weathermen were excellent, and the FBI failed dismally in its prolonged search for them."[63]

In the final decades of the twentieth century, other political dissenters and activists were to repeat the Weathermen's agenda of anarchistic, opportunistic, and indiscriminate violence. The adventures of the Symbionese Liberation Army, which included the involuntary recruitment of Patty Hearst, were elaborately described by the media. Other, sometimes violent, fringe groups that have failed to ignite popular mass response included the separatist New African Party, the Puerto Rican National Liberation Front, and racist organizations such as the paramilitary direct-action squads of the revived Ku Klux Klan, the White People's Political Association, the Order, and the Aryan Nation.

Unresolved historical political grievances often continued as sources of unrest during these turbulent years—giving rise to organizations such as the American Indian Movement (AIM). Spurred by the success of the civil rights and campus free speech movements, Native American activists manifested their efforts in the takeover of the Bureau of Indian Affairs headquarters in Washington, D.C., and the 1973 seizure of Wounded Knee, the site of the 1890 massacre of 300 defenseless Native Americans in the final Indian war.[64] Relentless federal prosecutions, however, brought the Indian protest movement to a premature end. But the nation's new mood toward the "Indian problem" was reflected by the fact that of the approximately twelve hundred arrested in connection with Wounded Knee, only one hundred eighty-five were brought to trial, and of these a mere eleven felony and four misdemeanor convictions were handed down by the court.

The 1970s and 1980s, in particular, saw the emergence of new causes and the growth of single-purpose political protest movements—dedicated to such diverse pursuits as environmental protection, animal rights, and the "right to life"—relying more on peaceful civil disobedience than on the type of violence used by the radical revolutionary activists of the 1960s. Somewhat earlier another small but vocal tax resistance movement emerged, complaining about the unfair taxation of American farmers and the disproportional allocation of tax monies for military expenditures. The economic hardships, especially in the farm belt, gave rise to such organizations as the Farmers Liberty Army, the National Freedom Movement, and the Posse Comitatus.

Several of these groups were committed to militant means. Yet despite noticeable exceptions, peaceful protest and disobedience again began to predominate as the American way of dissent. Typical of this return to nonviolent means, yet reflective of the continuing widespread popular discontent, were the nearly five hundred thousand youths who by the end of 1982 had failed to comply with the new 1980 military registration requirements introduced by President Jimmy Carter.

## AMERICAN JUSTICE *IN EXTREMIS*

Political dissent, disobedience, violence, and rebellion continued to manifest themselves in many arenas of American life as the nation entered the third century of its independence. These new interests and new challenges to authority centered around old issues: the rights of workers, the resurgence of racism, opposition to military service, and the status of women.

Some of these conflicts were clustered around relatively new controversies: the United States' use of nuclear power, the country's involvement in Central America's political turmoil, the unlawful sheltering of refugees from that war-torn region, the operation of abortion clinics, discrimination against HIV-positive individuals, the prohibition of school prayers, and discrimination based on sexual orientation. Small numbers of political activists accounted for some of these conflicts, while a few causes relied on mass participation. Some of the activists belonged to the radical left; others came from the orthodox right.

The responses of those in authority have been equally inconsistent. While some fourteen hundred protesters were arrested at New Hampshire's Seabrook nuclear power plant in April 1974 for militantly opposing nuclear weapons and power, no arrests were carried out in North Carolina a decade later when a school survey disclosed that, notwithstanding the Supreme Court's prohibitions, regular prayer recitation and Bible readings were being conducted in thirty-nine of the state's one hundred counties.

By the mid- and late 1980s a new cadre of American believers felt called upon to engage in forms of protest that, during the late 1970s, had seemed outdated and discarded. The new waves of protesters included not only the sons and daughters of the previous decades' leaders but also a new brand of much older and more seasoned activists, including prominent religious leaders and high elected officials—local, state, and federal. Among the new wave one could count former president Jimmy Carter's daughter, Amy, United States congressmen arrested for unlawfully protesting apartheid in front of South Africa's Washington embassy, fundamentalist ministers jailed in Nebraska for operating a "Christian School" without complying with state licensing requirements, and the Catholic and Protestant members of the Sanctuary Movement who continued to shelter victims of Central American political oppression.

Have the agencies of American justice responded fairly and effectively to these various manifestations of political dissent and violence? In the 1960s the initial impact of the mass demonstrations and violence was usually felt by the police. The sheer numbers of offenders often required major departures from standard police conduct. In Chicago in 1968 the police observed that because of the substantial numbers of troublemakers, they were unable to make "symbolic" arrests with "the expectation that cooler heads would prevail as a result." Police members recognized also that, until substantial National Guard and federal reinforcements arrived, strong measures on their part might intensify the disorder. Both spectators and looters were aware of the limitations imposed upon the police. One officer observed later that "most of the people knew that the police would not shoot . . . [unless deadly force was used by the rioters]. . . . Some of them would pass by you, and say sarcastically, 'We know you can't shoot, why do you carry the gun?' " [65]

The National Commission on Civil Disorders (the Kerner Commission)[66] set out in 1968 to take an inventory of criminal justice problems arising from the growing incidence of political unrest. The Commission concluded that mass arrests produced a breakdown in normal police evidence-gathering work. Relatively few successful prosecutions of offenders resulted, even though great overcrowding of jails and other detention facilities was reported.

The responses of the courts to those brought before them as a result of mass political disorder varied dramatically. No clear-cut policies regarding appropriate sanctions emerged. After the racially connected 1967 Detroit riots, Judge Crocket of the Detroit Recorder's Court commented:

> Black citizens . . . find it difficult to understand a system of criminal justice that charges 3,230 persons with felonies and then after imprisonment for days and the payment of thousands of dollars in attorneys fees, disposes of the first 1,630 of these felonies with 961 dismissals, 664 pleas to misdemeanors (trespass, petty larceny, and curfew violations) and only two convictions after trial on the original charge![67]

Assessing the performance of the courts, the National Commission on Civil Disorders concluded that the courts had set high and unindividualized bail to avoid the early release of those arrested, that the defendants involved were generally not accorded adequate legal representation, and that the sentences meted out in response to the disorders were unduly harsh. The Detroit courts, the Commission concluded, had dispensed mass, not individual, justice.

In Chicago, on the other hand, the penalties assessed were unusually light. More than 90 percent of those convicted of misdemeanors were fined rather than jailed. More than half of those so sentenced were fined less than

$15 each. What accounts for this leniency in the treatment of political activists by the criminal justice system? Tellingly, those brought to trial as a consequence of the violent civil disturbances in the nation's ghettos were for the most part young and politically inexperienced. Of those arrested in the 1967 Detroit riots, 21 percent were under 21 years of age, and 26 percent were between 21 and 25. Among those arrested in the 1968 Chicago riot, 51 percent were under 21 years, and another 19 percent between 21 and 25.

Other than causing a massive influx of cases, overwhelming police capabilities and jail capacities, those charged with urban riots and disorders posed no unique problems for the orderly conduct of American justice. Brought before the courts, they were generally inarticulate, subdued, polite, and cooperative. The only political activists posing special problems were students or those involved in the more ideological political demonstrations—the campus sit-ins, the Poor People's Campaign, and the anti–Vietnam War parades. The 1976 Task Force on Disorders and Terrorism recognized the different problems inherent in the trial of the more ideological political offenders: "Defendants wishing to employ the trial arena as a political forum, prosecutors wishing to bolster their cases, and a public more interested in the larger pattern in which an alleged crime . . . may figure than in the mundane details of the crime itself—all may contribute to the politicization of trials."[68]

In recent decades, it has become increasingly the function of America's courts to withstand overreaching legislatures as well as eager prosecutors in order to preserve tolerance toward dissenting words and conduct. Judges have nonetheless been reluctant to allow their courtrooms to become stages for political opposition and radicalism and have responded unfavorably to innovative defenses in the trials of political offenders. The *Berrigan* court rejected the argument that because the defendants were motivated by high moral concerns (their wish to stop America's alleged "international crimes" in Vietnam), they lacked the requisite *mens rea* for conviction. The "Nuremberg defense" was also advanced in several trials, to the effect that the doctrines derived from the post–World War II trial of the Nazi leadership made it incumbent upon individuals to resist governmental aggression, abuse of power, and criminality. By and large courts have declined to consider the defendants' moral values, the dictates of individual conscience, and the standards of international law in assessing the guilt or innocence of those brought before them on charges of political protest and resistance.[69]

## POLITICAL DISSIDENCE AND
## AMERICA'S QUEST FOR JUSTICE

One of the transcendent ironies of America's doctrinal unwillingness to consider or incorporate the concept of "political crime" in its legal framework is that this country's archives contain rich and unique examples with which to begin a thorough and scientific investigation of the phenomenon. America's history is replete with the richest ingredients of political protest, resistance, and rebellion, in terms of numbers of incidents; breadth and types of political, social, and economic causes pressed; diversity of actors; and the variety of governmental responses. Buried within this history are lessons of great value for proponents of change and defiers of authority, as well as for governments seeking to enforce authority and to control its opponents.

Above all, despite this country's failure to realize the New Jerusalem on its shores, despite its history of violent rebellion, and even despite its brutal and ignoble treatment of African Americans and native populations, American government and society have avoided some of the extremes other countries have been driven to in the suppression of political dissidence and crime. This nation has never experienced a reign of terror or (for most of the population) the long-term and irreversible oppressions and abuses of power that have occurred in less fortunate lands.

There is little doubt, moreover, that political criminality and rebellion, as much as more traditional and lawful forms of action, are responsible for many of the liberties and the social and cultural diversity for which the United States is most admired. In addition to its many outbursts of political violence, the United States has given rise to an even more important tradition of extralegal yet nonviolent means for inducing political change.

While one surveys four hundred years of political strife and reform in America, one hears, in the emerging nations of Asia and Africa, among the unstable regimes of Latin America, and even in the long-established countries of Europe, new battle cries and demands for national liberation, communal self-determination, and a greater measure of human rights. However, for these emerging nations, the American experience demonstrates that achieving independence does not end internal strife or domestic violence. Dissatisfied tribal, ethnic, regional, religious, linguistic, economic, and racial groups are not likely to forgo acts of dissent, subversion, insurrection, and rebellion to dramatize, protest, and rectify their civil, social, economic, and political grievances. There is, therefore, more than passing relevancy in the history of political dissidence in America, from colonial times to the present, despite this nation's present preeminence as a bastion of personal liberty and pluralistic justice.

One seeking a retrospective view of political criminality in America must, however, approach both epochs and their actors with skeptical caution. One is well advised to search behind ostensibly political claims and proclamations for meaningful and serious political motives and goals. It is not at all easy to clearly divine the phenomenon of political criminality at times when the rhetoric of "national liberation," "social justice," and "revolution" becomes fashionable and can be utilized to shield less noble purposes. One should also not be unmindful, in this connection, of the agitating role of the mass media, which has often seemed to provide a welcome mat for questionable "rebels," "reformers," and dispensers of various "countercultures."

Significantly, not all direct-action, civil-disobedience, and resistance movements have been based on the principle of nonviolence, a principle that traditionally has enhanced the moral authority of political dissenters. In many instances the discipline of nonviolence was breached either in word or deed, or both. When reformers relinquish in this way the moral high ground, the traditional enforcers of public order—police, prosecutors, and judges, as well as legislators—are provided with ostensible cause for zealous responses to what are at times minimal threats to the social and political order. One should be, likewise, as cautious of the appropriateness of some of the governmental responses to political disorder as to the authenticity of the assertions of political justification.

Reviewing America's historical record of governmental responses to individual and collective dissidence and resistance, one is compelled to conclude that many past measures of control have been crude and excessive. Much too big a segment of America's population, and much too large a portion of the country's liberties, have been sacrificed, from time to time, in the name of national security and public order.

The strong emphasis during the early days of the republic on a narrowly defined law of treason, in the interest of vigorous political debate and dissent, was misplaced in the nation's subsequent history. Vaguely phrased sedition laws, not requiring the commission of overt acts that pose an actual national threat, were increasingly utilized in the war against political dissent and disloyalty. Loyalty oaths, population displacements, the prohibition of membership in suspect political organizations, and massive domestic surveillance of political movements became the new tools for the protection of social order.

More recently, governmental response took the form of preventive action to infiltrate and neutralize, by disruption, intimidation, and burdensome prosecutions, those groups suspected of opposition to existing laws and policies. These measures tended, by and large, to adversely affect the innocent as well as the guilty and to interfere with the healthy process of social, economic, religious, and political criticism and opposition.

Having been cautioned to assume a skeptical stance vis-à-vis the claims of both would-be political offenders and the enforcers of public order, the reader nevertheless should not hasten to dismiss political criminality as an effective tool for accomplishing public policy changes. In recent decades, both the enhancement of civil rights in America and the conclusion of the Vietnam War have testified to the potency of political dissent and activism.

Nor should the reader overlook the serious domestic security problems created by political and pseudopolitical criminality as manifested in treason, espionage, and the detrimental release of vital secrets; in assassinations and attempted assassinations of public figures; in kidnappings, armed robberies, and bombings; in urban riots and looting of private property; and in the disruption of the workings of the armed services and public agencies.

One must note, finally, that four characteristics of American political dissidence and criminality unambiguously emerge from this country's history. First, the use of unorthodox and extralegal political means in America has been largely a manifestation of a reformist, rather than an insurrectionary, mission. Political disorder in this country has usually been directed toward modifying the use of power by government, not overthrowing it.

Second, the political diffusion and governmental decentralization inherent in American government, coupled with the common notion that it is not the structure and power of government but individual graspers and abusers that must be guarded against, have caused public dissatisfaction and political crimes to be directed not so much against "government" itself but against its subdivisions, its "agents," and particular groups viewed as representing one "establishment" or another.

Third, much of our nation's political violence and unrest, as pointed out by historian Richard Hofstadter, have "taken the form of actions by one group of citizens against another group rather than by citizens against the State."[70] Often, only when governmental authority is enlisted to advance one group's preeminence does the strife change from social, economic, or ethnic conflict to open antistate warfare.

Fourth, recent decades demonstrate the constant yet dramatic American shift from political rebellions, violent assemblies, and direct action to militant advocacy in the legislative halls and particularly in the courts. This may be described as America's progression from militant deeds to litigiousness. As long as America's extraordinary tools of legal reform do not lag far behind the needs and pressures for social, economic, and political reform, this more pacific trend might continue unabated in the country's constant striving for a pluralistic and just society.

*Part Three*

# PROTEST, REBELLION, AND SECESSION

## The Crisis of Legitimacy Worldwide

The highest duty is to respect authority.
  —Pope Leo XIII

Every great advance in . . . knowledge has involved the absolute rejection of authority.
  —Julian Huxley, *Lay Sermons*

All authority belongs to the people.
  —Thomas Jefferson

CHAPTER SIX

# Responses to Rebellion:
# The Quest for the "Honorable"
# Offender

When Charlotte Corday goes to Paris to murder Marat, she carries a copy of
Plutarch to fortify her determination, and as she is taken to the guillotine
the crowd murmurs, "She is greater than Brutus."
—David C. Rapoport, *Assassination and Terrorism*

## THE GRAVEST OF ALL OFFENSES:
## FROM ANTIQUITY TO THE MIDDLE AGES

The history of oppression, rebellion, bloodshed, dissent, civil disobedience, and actual warfare in the United States belies America's
continuing insistence upon a "myth of peaceful progress." The war against
authority has taken still other forms in other lands, which have been equally
shaped by the powerful forces of dissent and unrest. Throughout the world,
as in the United States, the challenge to the legitimacy of authority has taken
many forms through recorded history. The war against authority has resulted
in the reshaping of institutions in every corner of the globe and in every part
of society—from the family, to the church, and to the state. The war has
molded our languages, families, political philosophies, and constitutions. The
legitimating tools employed by authority throughout the ages have continu-
ally changed in an effort to meet, thwart, and repel those who have sought to
destabilize and overthrow authority. The quest for legitimacy has thus been
critical for all those in authority, whether their regime was characterized by
abusive excesses or recognized for fair and good governance.

Authority and its rules—the political criminal's raison d'être—are as old
as human society itself, and the existence of the political offender goes as far
back into history. Even in the murkiest depths of prehistory, tribal chiefs and
their customs and taboos set strict limits on social behavior. Anthropologist
Bronislaw Malinowski observed, even among the most primitive societies,

complex rules of conduct governing private life, economic cooperation, and public affairs.[1] Legal historian E. Sidney Hartland confirmed that "the savage is far from being the free and unfettered creature of Rousseau's imagination. On the contrary, he is hemmed in on every side by the customs of his people."[2]

In the societies Malinowski studied, the most hallowed of all customs were invariably those that prescribed the respective ranks, titles, tasks, and privileges of the members of the community. "From the sociological point of view," he asserted, "it would be possible to show that the whole structure of [society] is founded on the principle of *legal status*. By this I mean that the claims of chief over commoners, husband over wife, parent over child, and vice versa, are . . . exercised . . . according to definite rules, and arranged into well-balanced chains of reciprocal services."[3]

The rules and customs intended to preserve respect and obedience toward chiefs and other superiors (and entitling inferiors to corresponding rights) have indeed been deeply embedded in every human culture and society and have been documented among people as diverse in time and geography as the ancient Israelites, the Samoans of the Eastern Pacific, and the Ashanti of Africa's Gold Coast.[4] In different societies, these legitimizing tools were reinforced by mythology, religion, ritual, and law. The ancient Egyptians attributed godly parentage to their leaders, while the Greeks often endowed their rulers with supernatural qualities. When the Israelites' first king, Saul, ascended to the throne, the prophet Samuel "took a vial of oil, and poured it upon his [Saul's] head, and kissed him and said . . . the Lord hath anointed thee to be captain over his inheritance."[5]

Those of lesser rank were expected to treat with respect those who had been divinely selected for leadership. "Thou shalt not revile the gods, nor curse the ruler of thy people," commanded the Book of Exodus.[6] Offenders against those divinely privileged were cruelly and swiftly punished. When a common soldier, expecting a reward for his regicide, claimed to have slain King Saul, his rival David could not countenance this transgression against authority. The youthful David, the king to be, ordered the assassin's execution, exclaiming, "How wast thou not afraid to stretch forth thine hand to destroy the Lord's anointed?"[7]

Political scientist Gaetano Mosca observed that in most societies (and especially those encompassing more than a kinship group), the ruling classes rarely justify their political authority, or legitimacy, exclusively by their *de facto possession* of power.[8] Instead, they seek to advance a metaphysical or ideological formula (the "political formula") that portrays their possession of power as the logical and necessary consequence of the beliefs of the people over whom they rule. "Among ancient peoples the political formula not only rested upon religion but was wholly identified with it. Their god was preeminently a national god. He was the special protector of the territory and the people. He was the fulcrum of its political organization" (p. 74).

In Judeo-Christian societies, Mosca pointed out, the sovereign was said to reign because he was as God's anointed. So too in the Chinese polity, where the emperor ruled as the "Son of Heaven," and in Muslim societies, where political authority is traced through descent or delegation from the Prophet Mohammed (p.70). The ruler and the political formula under which he rules thus serve as the glue that binds the political community together.[9] Dissenters and rebels have therefore been viewed as a threat not only to the interests of the ruling elite but also to the very foundation of societal and governmental legitimacy: the political formula. Any potential erosion of legitimacy thus threatens "all persons who, from a diversity of backgrounds, have united under common beliefs, attitudes and customs of which the political formula is the keystone."

The treatment of offenses against the sovereign as a form of sacrilege was prevalent in the cultures of the eastern Mediterranean—Babylon, Egypt, Judea, Persia—as well as in the primitive African and Melanesian societies. However, the sanctity of rulers was not always viewed as absolute or universal. In ancient Greece and in republican Rome, experiences with tyrannical leaders led to a more qualified view of dissent and rebellion. Some of the most noted Greek and Roman philosophers, including Xenophon and Cicero, challenged the legitimacy of unjust rulers and governments.[10] Not only were the assassins of tyrants given the opportunity to flee into exile, to pay fines, or to otherwise expiate for their violence through confinement, but also they often were glorified for the killing of once-admired leaders.[11]

"The ancient Greeks and Romans had no word to correspond to [the] term assassination," writes political scientist David C. Rapoport.[12] "A killing was simply a means to an end; its moral significance depended entirely on the *nature* of the person killed. A man who struck a public personality down was either a murderer or a tyrannicide. And the word for tyrannicide was the same as that for 'liberator,' one who freed his country."[13]

In Rome, even those merely advocating or aspiring to tyranny were subject to severe public sanctions.[14] Roman history reports that Spurius Cassius, the author of a land reform bill, was assassinated by his own father, who suspected that the law was a step toward tyranny.[15] One regarded as a tyrant in early Rome was beyond the protection of the law. There was little judicial or other public inquiry into the justification for the assassin's deed.

Opposition to authority in classical Judea, Greece, and Rome was not always in response to abuses of political power. The Hebrews as well as the early Christians were persecuted as rebels largely because they would not submit to the semidivine status of the Caesars. Since the offering of sacrifice was the means by which subjects acknowledged the supremacy of the emperor, the refusal to do so was viewed as a rejection of temporal as well as divine authority. After Constantine embraced Christianity, the Church Fathers assumed a dramatically different posture toward political protest and resistance. Having submitted to the overlordship of Christianity, the emperor was held to be protected by heaven, and the Church enjoined its flock to obedience and loyalty to him.

Tyrannicide continued to be of intense academic and political interest throughout the Roman period. The educational texts of the declining Roman era and the early Middle Ages suggest that in the course of scholarly training students were frequently made to debate the legitimacy of this unorthodox political remedy.[16]

Despite these academic exercises, the later Middle Ages reserved the most barbarous of punishments for those who dared disrupt the feudal hierarchy by challenging the prevailing politico-religious, social, and economic order. During this time Christian Europe's responses to political assassination and rebellion were further affected by the development of new attitudes toward warfare. The Greeks and Romans, who practiced total war, believed that an enemy had no rights. The assassination of foreign rulers, much like tyrannicide, was therefore perceived as acceptable. But in medieval Christian society, a strict set of rules evolved to govern the conduct of warfare. Political historian David Rapoport noted that "a Christian knight like Galahad or Roland worried about the difference between fair and foul fighting; to an Achilles or a Ulysses the distinction would be incomprehensible."[17]

The increasing tendency in external warfare to distinguish between legitimate and illegitimate causes and means led to a parallel development in how medieval society perceived domestic challenges to the political order. There grew with regard to domestic warfare a pattern of distinguishing between legitimate and illegitimate means of producing political change, between acceptable and unacceptable forms of rebellion and insurgency.

These new codes were reflected in *Policraticus*, a twelfth-century text written by John of Salisbury, secretary to Thomas Becket. The author contended that although divine justice permitted tyrannicide, the killer could not be one who was bound to his victim through fealty (feudal ties), nor could he resort to dishonorable methods.[18] Those unwilling to conform to these stringent requirements were doomed to forever carry the stigma of unchivalry and dishonor, as well as ignominious, painful, and public death.

For the knight of the Middle Ages—who cherished honor and loyalty above all else—an assault against a superior was an offense against the fundamental order of feudal society and constituted a breach of his personal oath. Sir Thomas More's fictional island, Utopia, denied refuge within its boundaries, even to those who had killed a foreign ruler in the pursuit of the island's interests, "lest they contaminate virtuous citizens."[19] Foreigners alone were to be hired to carry out these questionable tasks, which in any case were permissible only to prevent war, and even then, since individual conscience could never justify assassination, only at the command of the government. This negative image of the assassin, claims Rapoport, resulted in a drastic decline in political killings during the medieval era.[20]

### FROM THE RENAISSANCE
### TO THE REVOLUTIONARY ERA

Reviewing European law from the Middle Ages to the modern era, historian Pitirim Sorokin confirmed that political offenders were, almost universally, subjected to the most extreme punishments the law could command.[21] Objects of both violent popular condemnation and intense hostility from those in authority, the dissident and rebel were generally portrayed as enemies of the ruler, the state, and its people. The citizen's resistance to or protest against those exercising the power of the state was viewed, accordingly, "as an act of hostility, identical to that of an enemy warrior who attacks the tribe, the city or the neighboring state in order to destroy it."[22]

This view of the political offender is reflected in the early and broad-ranging European laws prohibiting what is today called political crime, which originally was divided into two distinct categories: (1) alliances and intrigues with foreign powers (roughly the equivalent of today's "treason") and (2) domestic transgressions against the interests of the ruler. This distinction was first made by Roman law, which differentiated *proditio*, or "betrayal to an external enemy," from *crimen laesae majestatis*, or "internal offenses against the authority or person of the ruler."[23] The latter offense, derived from the Roman prohibition of *crimen majestatis populi romani imminutae*, or "the lessening of the dignity of the Roman people," was originally intended to bolster only the status and authority of Rome's plebeian magistrates, a function somewhat similar to the contempt powers exercised by modern courts. Later, this legal device was expanded to enhance and protect the status of all those exercising political authority.[24]

As the Roman power ebbed, the devices of *proditio* and *crimen laesae majestatis* became useful to a new set of rulers. The countries of continental Europe continued the Roman separation between "external" and "internal" political offenses. Both French and German law drew distinctions between political crimes involving aid to a foreign enemy (the French crime of *trahison* and the German *Verrat*) and domestic offenses concerning the citizen's relationship to his sovereign or government (the French *lèsé-majesté* and the German *Majestätsbeleidinung*). Early English legal commentators also resorted to *lèsé-majesté* to proscribe offenses against the sovereign's person and dignity.[25] With time, however, the distinction was dropped, and domestic violations were combined with foreign alliances under the English law of treason.

In France, as in other civil law countries, the *lèsé-majesté* crimes derived from Roman law were further divided into two categories: *lèsé-majesté humaine* and *lèsé-majesté divine*. The first comprised "every enterprise or offense committed against the person of the sovereign or against the interest of the state,"[26] while the second described crimes against the state religion, including heresy, schism, and sacrilege. Since the offense of *lèsé-majesté divine* was infrequently brought to prosecution[27] the law of *lèsé-majesté* served primarily to preserve the security and dignity of the monarchy rather than to enforce religious conformity.

To this end the French law of *lèsé-majesté* protected the king against acts of betrayal by foreign powers, against any challenges to or interferences with the exercise of the royal prerogatives, as well as against activities affecting his personal safety and dignity.[28] This emphasis on the personal protection of the ruler was typical of the European political order of the time. Throughout the Continent, "the picture . . . was one of power jealously guarded by a political ruler against the derogations and usurpations of powerful rivals, rather than one of an abstract entity, such as a 'state,' 'nation' or 'constitution' being protected against ideological assaults and mass revolutions seeking a change in the social and political order."[29]

French laws protecting the sovereign often ordained summary and harsh punishment for those accused of political resistance. Despite the procedural safeguards made available to conventional criminals, those struggling against established authority could be convicted on the basis of the flimsiest evidence: depositions by criminals, confessions induced by torture, or testimony coerced from children and spouses. Trials were frequently conducted in secret, by special tribunals, and without the right to counsel or the opportunity to defend oneself by calling witnesses. This disregard for procedure where political crime was concerned was articulated by Cardinal Richelieu: "There are some crimes which it is necessary to punish, then investigate. Among them, the crime of *lèsé-majesté* is so grave that one ought to punish the mere thought of it."[30] Accordingly, the penalties for political crimes in France were often gruesome. Execution by drawing and quartering (*l'ecartelment*) was common, accompanied by the confiscation of all the offender's property, the disinheritance of the offender's family, and the perpetual banishment of close relations from the realm.

The device of *lettres de cachet* provided an especially powerful weapon in prerevolutionary France's battle against disloyalty.[31] Issued on the order of the king and countersigned by one of his ministers, these documents allowed the preventive detention of political opponents without prior trial or an opportunity to refute the accusation. Confinement for an indeterminate period, usually without a right of appeal, could thus be authorized on the basis of vague charges or suspicions.

German laws governing the treatment of political offenders during the seventeenth and eighteenth centuries were hardly more lenient, based as they were on the same Roman law concepts that had animated the French system.[32] In Germany, as in France, all *crimen laesae majestatis*[33] were severely punished—usually by death or banishment. Often, the offender's property was confiscated. Again, the procedural protections available to the conventional criminal were denied the political offender. Thus, when Frederick the Great of Prussia, under the benevolent influence of Enlightenment philosophers, abolished the use of torture in criminal cases, the practice was retained with regard to political prisoners.[34]

In examining the treatment of political offenders in Germany, it is important to remember that until the 1871 unification, the country was a fragmented set of quarreling principalities, each with its own independent system of law and justice. This historic *kleinstaaterei* has been described as a "splintering of territories and dominions under a motley of little rulers."[35] After the Peace of Westphalia in 1648, Germany had been partitioned into more than eighteen hundred political subdivisions. Though the 1814 Congress of Vienna reduced the number of principalities to thirty-nine, each remained a separate and independent political unit.

The closest thing to a German central government at the time was the loosely structured Holy Roman Confederation, to which the individual German states owed little obedience and gave even less respect. German law therefore could not rely on the relatively abstract concept of the "state" in its definition of political crimes. Instead, as in the feudal tradition, political offenses were viewed primarily as a breach of faith with the ruler himself. It was this perspective of personal betrayal and loss of honor that turned political offenses into particularly shameful and dishonorable crimes in Germany.

With the coming of the Enlightenment, the campaigns to curtail judicial discretion and to enhance the role of legislative codification produced restrictions on the *laesae majestatis* crimes in Germany. Furthermore, the Roman distinction between offenses against the internal order of the state and those endangering its external security was reinforced, permitting a later differentiation between what were to be considered less serious and more serious political offenses.[36]

A more sophisticated approach to the classification of political offenses was introduced by the Prussian state law of 1794.[37] A distinction was made among high treason, or *Hochverrat* ("an act which tends by violence to change the constitution of the State or which is directed against the life or liberty of the head of state"); treason against the country, or *Landesverrat* ("crimes committed against the external security of the state"); and *Majestätsbeleidigung* ("offenses against the honor and authority of the sovereign, lesser princes, or other state officials in the discharge of their duties").[38] All three offenses were subsumed under the general heading of "crimes against the state," with specific penalties attached to each of the offenses. Although the procedural and substantive changes were substantial, the punishment of political offenders remained brutish. For the crimes of *Hochverrat* and *Landesverrat* the law prescribed humiliating forms of capital punishment, and imprisonment or banishment for the accused's family members. Those convicted of the lesser offenses could expect hard labor in irons.[39]

The English treatment of political crime during this time was markedly different from that of other European countries. Unlike Continental law, which had largely drawn upon the Roman legal tradition, English common law did not usually differentiate between external and internal political offenses, encompassing both types within the term *treason*. Furthermore, the scope of the crime of treason had been limited in the middle of the fourteenth century by legislation—the Statute of Treasons of Edward III.[40]

Despite this early attempt to circumscribe resort to the charge of "treason" against political opponents, the definition of the crime continued to steadily expand through judicial interpretation. The statute had originally limited the crime of treason to three narrow categories: (1) "compassing," or imagining, the death of the king, the queen, or their heir; (2) levying war against the king in his realm; and (3) being adherent to the king's enemies in his realm, giving them aid and comfort. Through liberal construction of the "compassing" and the "being adherent" provisions of the law, the scope of treason was stretched over the years, turning almost any resistance to government into "constructive treasons." The treason statute, at various times in English history, accordingly was used to encompass a wide range of political protests, including domestic rioting, fomenting rebellion in the colonies, the collection of information for the king's political opponents, as well as armed resistance to the agents or laws of the king.[41]

The expansion of "treason" to include forms of political dissent that did not directly threaten the king's life or person evidenced a profound underlying shift in the attitude of modern governments toward political offenders. No more was feudal loyalty the object of the law's protection. The emphasis had shifted to the maintenance of public order. English legal historian J. W. Cecil Turner noted that "the historical development of our nation tended steadily . . . to make . . . the stability of public order . . . the binding force of the body politic." Accordingly, judges became more active, "transforming the feudal conception of treason, as a breach of personal faith, into the modern one, which regards it as [the guardian against] 'armed resistance, made on political grounds, to the public order of the realm.' "[42] As the scope of the crime expanded in England, almost any resistance to the law could fall under the heading of treason. In 1710, for example, a riot intended to demolish nonconformist churches was held to constitute treason because it defied the newly enacted Toleration Act.[43]

The crime of sedition was another major tool available to English authorities for repressing political dissent. Considered a misdemeanor at common
law, the crime was punishable by imprisonment, fines, or pillory. Sedition
consisted of any communications designed or likely to bring about hatred,
contempt, or disaffection against the sovereign, the constitution, the government, or the administration.[44] Said Justice Allybone in 1688:

> No man can take upon him to write against the actual exercise of the govern-
> ment, unless he have leave from the government . . . be what he writes true
> or false. . . . It is the business of the government to manage matters relating to
> the government; it is the business of subjects to mind their own properties
> and interests.[45]

The crime of sedition grew to encompass all criticism of the king or his
government. Attempts to raise discontent among the populace, to press for
changes in existing law, to promote hostility between different classes of the
population, or to commit a disturbance of the peace were considered seditious.[46] Any censure of the king or his government for their errors, or
suggestions for fundamental changes in the state or church could constitute
sedition.[47] It was seditious to suggest that the sovereign had been misled or
mistaken in his policies, or to point out errors or defects in the law or government for the purpose of reforming them. "About the sole right English
judges . . . conceded to the subject was the right of humble and respectful
petition made to the Government in proper form," writes criminologist
Barton Ingraham in his extensive study of political crime in Europe.[48]

The movement for constitutionalism that followed the English revolution
of 1688 brought about the first major changes in the procedures applicable to
treason, culminating in the Trials for Treason Act of 1696.[49] Those accused of
treason were granted the right to a copy of the indictment at least five days
before trial, to secure a list of the jurors selected to try the case, to present
their own defense with the aid of witnesses called by them, and to obtain the
assistance of counsel assigned by the court, a right not extended to other
felony trials until 1837. Conviction required a voluntary confession in open
court or the testimony of two witnesses to overt treasonous acts. An additional enactment in 1708 required that the accused be presented a list of the
prosecution's witnesses at least ten days prior to trial.[50]

By the nineteenth century the English law of treason and sedition contained more elaborate safeguards than the laws of any other European
country. However, despite these reforms, the cruel treatment of those convicted of political crime persisted. By comparison to the barbaric punishments that continued to be imposed in England, "even the aggravated
forms of capital punishment prescribed by French and German law at the
time seem indulgent," claims Ingraham (p.673).

## THE OUTREACH OF THE FRENCH REVOLUTION

The decades preceding the French Revolution saw the increasing influence, throughout Europe, of the liberal writings of the French encyclopaedists and the other social and political thinkers of the era, including Montesquieu, Voltaire, and Beccaria. Equally indicative of the era's thinking were the reform-minded criminal codes instituted by such "enlightened monarchs" as Russia's Catherine the Great, Austria's Joseph II, and Prussia's Frederick the Great.[51]

France, picturesquely described as the "radiating center" of the new ideas, was also responsible for transforming some of these ideas into reality. The major ministers of Louis XVI were for the most part adherents of the new philosophies. The king himself was viewed as being "in the forefront of the movement for judicial reform."[52]

Indeed, political repression was not a major complaint during Louis' reign. When the Bastille—the major Paris prison for political and other offenders detained under *lettres de cachet*—fell to the Revolution on July 14, 1789, a mere seven prisoners emerged. It is likely, asserted André Maurois, that "Louis XVI was not overthrown for being despotic, but for being ineffectual—for being unable to use his powers to force the changes long overdue."[53]

The leaders of the French Revolution—a revolution endorsed by Charles James Fox, the leading English Whig of the time, as "the greatest event that has happened in the history of the world"[54]—initially advocated tolerance toward political dissent. The newly formed National Assembly, which had taken over the powers of the monarchy, nobility, and clergy, was dominated by followers of liberalism, with one-half of the Assembly's members being lawyers.

The first years after the Revolution produced significant reforms. Punishment was legally redefined, by a decree of January 21, 1790, as a solely personal sanction against the offender, thus eliminating attainder and other penalties against innocent members of a convicted person's family. An earlier decree (of October 9, 1789) had granted extensive procedural safeguards to all those accused of crimes, including the right to a copy of the accusation, to assistance of counsel, to confrontation of witnesses, to calling of witnesses for their own defense, and to a public trial.[55] *Lettres de cachet* were abolished in 1790, and the right to jury trials was extended to all felony cases, including treason. The reforms culminated in a new criminal code, adopted on October 8, 1791.[56] Political offenses were now classified as "crimes against the state" and were no longer viewed as injuries to the personal authority of the sovereign; thus the earlier concept of *lèse-majesté* was abandoned. Capital offenses were drastically reduced in number—from over one hundred crimes to thirty-two—though most of the offenses that continued to be punishable by death were political.

The 1791 code also drew a significant distinction between "crimes against the external security of the state" and "crimes against the internal security of the state." The first consisted of acts against France in her relations with foreign-nations, either in time of war or in time of peace. The second dealt with domestic plots against the sovereign, as well as acts or conspiracies designed to produce civil war and resistance to lawful authority.

Most crimes against the state remained subject to the death penalty. The code, however, created a lesser class of attempts against and challenges to the French Constitution—in an effort to protect the law and those charged with its execution against less serious infractions.[57] The relative liberality of the 1791 code was reflected in its elimination of offenses based solely on prohibited belief or speech. It was no longer a crime to hold membership in proscribed organizations. Nor was one prohibited from expounding doctrines and views unless they inflamed the public to immediate riot or rebellion against authority.

The postrevolutionary reforms were destined, however, to be cut short by continuing political turmoil. The new constitutional monarchy, with an infirm grasp upon the reins of power, had little chance to succeed, according to historian R. R. Palmer, "because it set up somewhat impractical institutions, because France went to war, because prices soared, because neither the King, nor the royalists, nor the churchmen, nor the working classes were satisfied with their new position."[58]

On August 10, 1792, Paris became the site of a mass uprising. The government yielded, calling for a national convention to draft a new constitution. Elections were conducted in the following weeks, and the new convention met on September 20, 1792. Two days later, actor-playwright Jean-Marie Collot d'Herbois moved that the monarchy be abolished. The convention so ordered, decreeing that September 22, 1792, be the first day of the new French Republic. The following January saw the execution of Louis XVI.

These events ushered in the infamous Reign of Terror, administered by the all-powerful Committee of Public Safety.[59] According to the graphic account of R. R. Palmer, anyone who had business with the Committee directed his or her steps to the Tuilleries, an old palace of the kings of France on the right bank of the Seine.[60] Inside, in a room with a large oval table covered with green cloth, matching the green paper on the walls, the Committee of Public Safety had its council meetings.

Twelve men made up the Committee. . . . The twelve never once sat at the green table at the same time. One presently ceased to sit at all, for he was put to death by the others. Some were habitually away. . . . But their presence was felt. . . . Of those who sat in the green room, though they had no chairman and recognized no one of themselves as chief, the best known outside its walls was [Maximilien de] Robespierre.[61]

Few members of the Committee had been prominent before the Revolution. Of the better-known leaders, George-Jacques Danton soon was out of favor, to be guillotined in 1794 by order of the Committee. Jean-Paul Marat, another Committee leader, was stabbed in 1793 by Charlotte Corday as he sat in a medicinal bath.

The new despotism swiftly created a battery of laws giving it sweeping new powers against alleged counterrevolutionaries. First among these was the Press Law of March 29–31, 1793, prescribing death for those who wrote or published materials advocating the dissolution of the state, the restoration of the monarchy, or the revival of any other authority that infringed on the new sovereign power of the people.[62]

The next step in the campaign of repression took place on March 10, 1793, when the Revolutionary Tribunal was set up.[63] Originally composed of twelve paid jurymen, five judges, and a public prosecutor, the Tribunal— during its seventeen months' existence—condemned 1,254 people (among them Marie-Antoinette) to execution by the guillotine. There was no appeal from this court, whose jurisdiction included "every counterrevolutionary enterprise or attack upon the liberty, equality, unity, or indivisibility of the republic . . . as well as all plots tending to . . . the establishment of any other authority hostile to the liberty, equality and sovereignty of the people"(p.221). The mission of this court and its procedures were summarized by a decree issued on October 10, 1793: "Revolutionary laws ought to be speedily executed"(p.265).

On September 17, 1793, the Law of Suspects was passed, providing that all "suspected persons" found at large be placed under detention (p.259). The definition of *suspected persons* was long and vague, including descriptions like "partisans of tyranny," "enemies of liberty," people who cannot account for their means of support, people who have not discharged their civic duties, those who had been denied certificates of good citizenship, "disloyal" ex-nobles and their families, and people who emigrated after the Revolution. The Law of Suspects also called for local "Committees of Surveillance" to compile lists of suspects for each district.

The "suspects" were to be placed in houses of detention or guarded in their own homes. Under the new law, the central Committee of Public Safety in Paris served as the central clearing house for information on arrests and seized evidence. Though some three hundred thousand persons were eventually declared "suspects," the number actually imprisoned never exceeded one hundred thousand. Many of those detained were never tried, and only a few were put to death. For the most part, detention was deemed sufficient as a preventive measure.

A particularly harsh decree of the Jacobins' Reign of Terror was the Law of June 10, 1794, designed to further expedite the processing of the hordes of suspects crowding the jails. The law broadened the jurisdiction of the Revolutionary Tribunal to include the old "enemies of the people"(p.299). The classification was to embrace all those who had worked for the royalist government or against the republican regime, compromised the war effort, reduced the nation's food supplies, spread false rumors or defeatist information, spoke ill of patriotism, undermined the liberty, unity, or security of the Republic, either in the conduct of their business or in the discharge of their public office.[64] The new decree further encouraged citizens to seek out and denounce these "enemies of the people."

Lawyer Georges Couthon, member of the Committee on Public Safety, introduced the proposed law at the Constitutional Convention. He argued that the revolutionary courts should abandon old-fashioned ideas about due process whenever political crime was concerned. The function of the courts was to protect society, not its enemies, he urged. Couthon suggested that the effective protection of society required the elimination of legal forms, which were ultimately no more than chicaneries invented by lawyers.[65]

To speed up adjudications, the prosecution no longer had to call witnesses to establish its case unless the existing documentary evidence was considered insufficient. Where witnesses were heard, the accused was no longer allowed to question them; thereby the opportunity to establish a defense was reduced markedly. The right to counsel was similarly done away with, and the Tribunal was limited to only two sentences: acquittal or death.

It was this last oppressive law that brought about the downfall of Robespierre on July 27, 1794. Despite the comprehensive terror and its repressive laws, historian R. R. Palmer noted wryly, the Committee on Public Safety had not "put to death enough of its enemies to establish its rule as a permanent regime"(p.362).

The successor regime eventually abolished the oppressive laws enacted during the Reign of Terror. A new constitution, "born in a horror of dictators," was adopted on August 22, 1795, setting up the rule of a five-man Directory, inspired by "revulsion against [the] Terror [that had] strengthened the original prejudice of the Revolution against strong central authority"(p.384). Before the new constitutional convention adjourned it also enacted, on October 25, 1795, a new code of criminal procedure, the *Code des Délits et des Peines*, which reinstituted most of the liberal principles of 1791.[66]

The turmoil, violence, and terror of France's immediate postrevolutionary period had major repercussions for the life and laws of the rest of Europe. France's victories over her neighbors spread panic—accompanied by waves of political repression—through the monarchical regimes of England and the Continent. Moreover, as France became the center of revolutionary zeal and propaganda, other European regimes hoped to immunize themselves against the spread of the contagious doctrines of republicanism and popular rule.

France did little to allay these fears. In an attempt to destabilize England, France sought alliances with the discontented peoples of Ireland. Although Anglo-Irish tensions had existed since the twelfth century, the English efforts to extend their influence to Ireland were largely ineffective until the seventeenth century. Ulster (long hostile to the southern counties of Ireland) was then colonized by Scottish Presbyterians, who through missionary efforts expanded the Protestant population in Catholic Ireland.[67] When Cromwell invaded Ireland and distributed 11 million acres of its best land to his soldiers, he pushed the indigenous Catholic population further west of the Shannon.[68] English laws, in addition, drastically limited the rights of the Irish people to vote and hold property.[69]

Even though some of these restrictions were lifted in the latter part of the eighteenth century, there remained a great deal of resentment against the English domination of Ireland. The discontent found vent in localized agrarian movements such as the Whiteboys, Rightboys, and Steelboys, who protested English penal laws, land laws, and rent rates. By the 1790s these movements had coalesced into Defenderism, which demanded land redistribution and lowered rents, and the United Irishmen, formed in the mostly Protestant North, which advocated democracy and a republican form of government. Becoming more and more radicalized and militant, these movements inspired a parallel republican movement in Great Britain.[70]

As a consequence, new controls against seditious writings and speech were instituted in England and Ireland. After the United Irish leaders were tried for sedition, the movement was suppressed, only to reemerge as a secret society taking part in a French plan to invade Ireland in 1796, an invasion stymied at the last minute by storms that scattered the French fleet.[71]

During this period English Prime Minister William Pitt was reported to be afflicted with visions of "thousands of bandits" sacking and burning the City of London.[72] Agitation by radical elements in England, combined with rising food prices, did indeed produce numerous riots in the country. At one London mass meeting in 1795, some 500,000 protestors were reported to have gathered—a number equal to one-quarter of the total population of Paris. As a consequence controls were instituted in England against imported revolutionaries and suspected seditionists. An alien registration law was passed in 1793 to safeguard England against dangerous French émigrés.[73] The panic continued unabated, and on May 23, 1794, legislation was passed suspending habeas corpus and authorizing the detention of suspected persons without trial.[74]

In 1795 England's Seditious Meetings Act prohibited any gatherings of more than fifty people to consider grievances or to address petitions to the king or Parliament, without prior notice to a local magistrate.[75] In 1797 Ireland's Insurrection Act conferred more sweeping powers upon the authorities and made oath-taking to prohibited societies a capital offense. In October of that year, habeas corpus in Ireland was partially suspended.[76] In February 1798 the English set out to "disarm" Ulster, the seat of United Irish activity. Large numbers of United Irish leaders were arrested and interned.[77]

In Dublin on May 23, 1798, a rebellion broke out and was quickly suppressed. But the revolt did spread south and west and was soon proclaiming the reformist agrarian platform of the Defender movement. When it was over, an estimated thirty thousand people had died on both sides as a result of the hostilities.[78]

The revolt was a major impetus for the 1801 Act of Union between Ireland and England. The all-Protestant Irish Parliament abolished itself and brought the island under direct rule from London, in whose government Protestants, but not Catholics, could serve.

The 1798 revolt did little to calm English anxieties about uprisings at home. In 1799 the Unlawful Societies Act declared various political groups to be "unlawful combinations" and provided for the punishment of members as well as of their aiders and abettors.[79] By 1800 Parliament had, in cases involving attempts on the king's life, eliminated even the ancient requirement that the testimony of two witnesses accompany any treason conviction.[80]

Neither the decline of the revolutionary threat from the Continent (upon the commencement of Napoleon's reign) nor the conclusion of the war with France brought tranquility to England. The return of some two hundred thousand retired wartime soldiers and sailors swelled the English labor market with unemployed and restless workers. Economic conditions were further aggravated by unemployment caused by improvements in manufacturing techniques and the shrinking of foreign markets. To many observers it seemed that the country was ready for social and political revolution. "The country at this time was in a state of great excitement," wrote legal historian Henry Cockburn. "I have never known a period at which the people's hatred of the Government was so general and so fierce."[81]

The governmental response to this unrest was further repression. New laws were passed, including the Unlawful Drilling Act of 1819, which prohibited attendance at meetings intended for training people in the use of arms.[82] Nevertheless, it appeared that the English policy of repression, much like those contemporaneously implemented in France and Germany, was achieving its goal. "Generally speaking," observed criminologist Ingraham, "this repression and slowly improving economic conditions must be credited with bringing the disturbances to an end."[83]

## A TALE OF TWO COUNTRIES: GREAT BRITAIN AND FRANCE TO THE MID-NINETEENTH CENTURY

The harsh treatment initially accorded political offenders by the European regimes in the post–French Revolution period was only the first swing of a pendulum that would continue to oscillate for the rest of the modern era. In most European countries, periods of conservatism and repression alternated with times of liberalism in which the political protester and rebel gained respect for his or her special motives and unique societal functions.

This was nowhere more true than in England, where Sir Robert Peel's assumption of the office of home secretary in 1822 marked the beginning of a new spirit of reform in the criminal justice system. During Peel's term, over one-half of the more than two hundred capital offenses were ascribed lesser penalties. Even before that, the legal effects of "attainder" (punishing an offender and his entire family without a trial) had been abolished.[84] The 1814 amendment of the Treason Act,[85] moreover, did away with the disemboweling of traitors while alive. It also provided that offenders dragged to their execution by horses could, upon the king's order, be afforded the benefit of a hurdle, and that beheading be replaced with hanging.

In 1823 England's mandatory death penalty for all felonies was mitigated, permitting judges to pronounce lesser penalties in all but murder cases. Treason, though not formally a "felony," seemed to be included in this reform by implication. In 1830 the Criminal Libel Act was also amended to abolish banishment, thus leaving fines and imprisonment as the only penalties for sedition.[86] Causes for political turmoil and uprising abounded but were adroitly turned aside by social and economic legislative reforms before outright rebellion by the people erupted.

The Elizabethan poor laws were reformed, and the long-festering disabilities heaped upon Roman Catholics since Elizabeth's reign were repealed by the Emancipation Act of 1829.[87] The franchise was expanded by the Reform Bill of 1832,[88] and restrictions on the importation of grains were repealed in 1846,[89] reducing the cost of basic foodstuffs. In addition, the dawning Victorian Age ushered in an unprecedented period of British prosperity and power. A signal of the effectiveness of the socioeconomic reforms and the newfound political-legal reforms was the fact that, except for the sanctions in Ireland, not a single execution for a political offense occurred in England between 1820 and Roger Casement's 1916 hanging for treason.[90]

Much of the political violence recorded in England prior to the mid-century stemmed from the Chartist movement. Unhappy that the Reform Bill of 1832 did not enfranchise the working class, a "People's Charter," advocating universal suffrage and other political reforms, gained widespread popular support in the years from 1838 to 1848. Chartist agitation led to general strikes and rioting in the industrialized cities. But when the Chartists turned from electoral reform to a socialist platform, they lost moderate supporters. The repeal of the Corn Laws and Victorian prosperity caused the Chartists to wither away.

The reformist approach to political turmoil in England was inspired in part by the earlier writings of Utilitarian philosopher Jeremy Bentham, who had pointed out that the punishment of political offenders was "superfluous," as well as "expensive."[91] Bentham argued that one who spreads "pernicious opinions or mischievous doctrines" should be allowed to speak out because "it will be to the interest of a thousand others to refute his theories, and so, it may well be to establish the truth more firmly than ever."[92] The evil of any penalty imposed, Bentham asserted further, was likely to be "greater than the evil of the offense." Severe penalties, he thought, might cause discontent among the offender's allies and supporters, as well as among foreign powers whose good will the authorities desired. Excessive punishment was also wasteful, according to Bentham, because it deprived the political offender's country of his potential contributions.[93]

The leniency prescribed by Bentham came to be a fixture of English practice, although no formal recognition or differentiation was granted to "political offenders" as a group. While severe penalties for crimes like sedition and high treason remained on the books, the harsh sentences mandated for those convicted were invariably mitigated by the agencies of justice or by the Crown.

Many convicted English "seditionists" were members of the educated and professional classes: journalists, publishers, and lawyers. Accordingly, prison authorities often allowed these offenders a special regime suitable to their means and station in life. The dramatic leniency toward those jailed for sedition was evidenced by the case of essayist and poet Leigh Hunt, who was convicted of seditious libel and sentenced to two years' imprisonment in 1812. While in prison, he was permitted to continue writing and editing his paper, the *Examiner*, and to receive friends and other visitors. Hunt's books, his piano, and fresh flowers were allowed into his cell to make his stay as comfortable as possible.[94] Nearly a century later the case of Arthur Alfred Lynch further typified this pattern. A member of Parliament, in 1903, Lynch was sentenced to death for aiding the enemy during the Boer War in South Africa. After serving three months in prison, Lynch's sentence was commuted, and he was released on parole. Reelected to Parliament in 1909, he was commissioned a colonel in the British Army in 1918.

Across the Channel, in France, the political climate was quite different. Threatened by plots and attempted coups, the Directory—the five-man executive council that had ruled France under the 1795 Constitution—had been increasingly forced to rely on the army for protection. And it was from the ranks of the army that Napoleon Bonaparte emerged at a time of "popular craving for order and [the] almost unbounded cynicism of former revolutionaries."[95] After dissolving the Directory, in 1800 Napoleon consolidated his power as First Consul through a set of new laws curtailing the publication and distribution of political journals, limiting the powers of juries, and deporting suspect persons. A special court was created to deal with brigandage and political offenses, while France's criminal system was altogether restructured through the introduction of the procedural *Code d'Instruction Criminelle* of 1808 and the substantive *Code Pénal* of 1810. These new Napoleonic laws provided for the execution, transportation, or banishment of political offenders.

Yet the drafters of the Napoleonic codes nonetheless acknowledged the special characteristics of political crime. Commenting upon the penalties of banishment and transportation they observed: "A man can in effect be a bad citizen of one country and not be one in another. . . . the presence of one guilty of a political offense ordinarily constitutes only a local danger which can be eliminated in the state to which he is banished."[96] The codes therefore excepted those condemned to transportation from the requirement of branding (*la flétrissuce*) on the grounds that since "political offenses . . . do not suppose the complete renunciation of all principles of honor and morality; [and] they do not have, as with other crimes, their necessary cause in the depravity of the heart," the hope remains of the transportee's "being restored to his rights of citizenship in the place of exile."[97] Recognizing, however, the inefficacy of traditional penalties as deterrents for the ideologically motivated, the drafters of the Napoleonic codes favored the confiscation of political offenders' property on the grounds that "legislation . . . ought to . . . seek to restrain the ambitious . . . for whom the fear of death holds no terrors, by the prospect of the poverty which, on his account, will pursue his family."[98]

Despite these early reforms, France's march toward the more liberal treatment of political offenders was interrupted by the reactionary outpouring from the survivors of the *ancien régime*. In 1815 when Napoleon's final military defeat sealed his fall from power, the French throne was assumed by Louis XVIII, brother of the executed Louis XVI. Upon their return to power, the aristocrats, embittered by the confiscation of their estates and by the executions of their family members during the Reign of Terror, were prepared to institute their own vengeful White Terror—named for the white Bourbon banner that had been supplanted by the "tricolor" of Republican and Napoleonic France. "If you have not lived through 1815, you do not know what hatred is," were the words used by André Maurois to describe the period.[99]

Recognizing his responsibility as a constitutional (rather than absolute) monarch, Louis XVIII nevertheless tried to bring the spirit of political compromise to his country. As pressures for a new round of repression grew, the king struggled with his own ultraroyalist legislature over the question of amnesty for the former officials of the Napoleonic regime. Although opponents of amnesty came up with a list of more than eleven hundred people to be excluded from the clemency grant, the king ultimately managed to limit the purge to nineteen leaders who had previously been turned over to the courts for trial, and to thirty-eight others sentenced to banishment. The amnesty law subsequently enacted[100] became a model followed by several successive nineteenth-century French regimes.

When Louis died in 1824, he was succeeded by the count of Artois, another brother of Louis XVI, who ruled as Charles X. A reactionary who had fled the Revolution, the new king attempted to restore the absolute monarchy of the *ancien régime*. In 1830 the Paris mob, led by discontented journalists, students, and workers, responded with three days of rioting. This developed into the July Revolution, during which Charles X fled to England, bringing to an end the elder Bourbon dynasty.

In his place the Duke of Orleans, member of a junior branch of the Bourbons, ascended to the throne as Louis-Philippe. Designated not king of France but king of the French, a "citizen king," who was devoted to the revolution, Louis-Philippe was responsible for the shift of political power from the old aristocracy to the new bourgeoisie. His regime brought a major liberalization in the legal treatment of political offenders. Criminologist Barton Ingraham attributes this dramatic development to the shaky and questionable legitimacy of the nineteenth-century French regimes:

> A government comes into power as a result of the unnatural death of its predecessor; its legitimacy is therefore under a cloud from the start; it attempts to heal the divisions within the society; it fails, encounters growing opposition and is forced to rely on legal repression to protect its existence; this may be successful for awhile, but, as soon as the unity of the ruling group dissolves and the government loses the support of its main prop (a loyal army), it is overthrown, usually by an uprising in Paris. The dreary repetitiveness of this pattern may have had a lot to do with the development of extremely relativistic attitudes toward political crime, particularly the 'internal' political crime of challenge to, or hindrance of, political authority.[101]

The growing French leniency toward political criminality was given a similar interpretation by Greek political scientist Pierre Papadatos. In times that witnessed much political, economic, and social torment and discord, with regimes shifting from conservatism to liberalism and back again, hedging one's bets appeared a pragmatic and wise policy. Papadatos suggested that the new liberal attitudes toward political offenders were a product of the revolutions in the first half of the nineteenth century. Since "the parties in power had found themselves alternately conquerors and vanquished,"

Papadatos wrote, "political offenders seemed unlucky players rather than criminals. [The conquerors] condemned them because they had been defeated in the struggle; happy, in their turn, were those who proclaimed themselves the legitimate government and who defended themselves in the name of the same moral laws formerly invoked against them."[102]

The new reign of Louis-Philippe brought into government the leaders of the liberal opposition to the former royalist regime, including Casimer Perier, Laffite, Guizot, and Lafayette. Dedicated to both constitutional monarchy and the control of the electoral process by the middle classes, these men were also committed to legal reforms intended to prevent the government's oppression of its political opponents.

Freedom of the press was unequivocally recognized upon the new monarchy's accession to power. The Constitutional Charter adopted on August 14, 1830, provided that "the French have the right to publish and print their opinions in conformity with the laws. Censorship may never be re-established."[103] The Charter called further for the enactment of laws guaranteeing trial by jury for press offenses and political crimes.[104]

The subsequent law of October 8, 1830,[105] repealed previous legislation prohibiting the publication of materials without prior government clearance. It provided that all political crimes (*délits politiques*) be tried by the assize court, sitting with a jury. The term *political crime*, now used explicitly for the first time in legal history, was to encompass the following: offenses against the internal and external security of the state, conspiracies and attempts against the king and his family, conduct encompassed under the term *civil war*, offenses of criticism and provocation against public authority through religious sermons and pastoral letters sent abroad, the display or distribution of seditious materials and signs, and any other offenses against the dignity of royal authority.[106]

The new and liberal attitude toward political offenses was further manifested in the 1832 revision of the 1810 Penal Code. The confiscation of property previously accompanying convictions for political crimes was abolished. Furthermore, three of the lesser political offenses were exempted from capital punishment: conspiracies (*complots*) as contrasted with attempts (*attentats*), the counterfeiting and passing of counterfeit monies, and the counterfeiting of the state seal.[107]

Under the 1832 revision of the Code, a mild form of confinement, labeled "detention," was made applicable to political offenders.[108] This contrasted with the older and more severe forms of imprisonment used against conventional criminals: forced labor (*travaux forcés*) and solitary confinement (*reclusion*). A sentence of detention was to be served "in one of the fortresses situated on the continental territory of the kingdom." The law further provided that the offender was permitted to "communicate with persons placed within the place of detention or with those outside," subject to regulations imposed by law.[109] An alternative sanction to detention, in the form of deportation or transportation to an overseas possession, was also introduced.[110]

For those detained in France, an 1833 regulation specified confinement in the central section of the Mont Saint-Michel fortress "entirely apart" from the buildings occupied by the other convicts.[111] Under the 1833 law political offenders were exempted from forced labor, but work was permitted "as a means of distraction and recreation for prisoners who demand it."[112] The law reflected a growing public perception that such offenders who differed from common offenders "as to education, social position and habits," although convicted of a crime, should not be subject to the regular penal regimen.[113]

Louis-Philippe and his ministers, intent on undoing the evils of the First Republic's Reign of Terror, hoped that these reforms and the moderate treatment of political offenders would produce the political tranquility France had so long sought. This was not to be, for there were no less than five attempts on Louis-Philippe's life in his first ten years in office. In time the new regime found itself "more exposed and disarmed than any of its antecedents had ever been."[114] Increasingly, those in authority felt forced to resort to traditional measures for controlling and disarming real and potential political opposition. New legislation criminalized the activities of public criers and bill posters engaged in political propaganda. Stricter controls were also imposed upon unauthorized associations, and seditious speech was again prohibited.

Once again, the pendulum had swung toward repression. By 1835 new laws allowed the assize court (where all "political crimes" were to be prosecuted) to be convened in prison, where unruly defendants could be better managed. Where the defendant refused to appear, or where he or she "disrupted the proceedings, the court was authorized to hear cases without his presence."[115] Since juries often tended to acquit in political trials, the laws were again amended, to allow a conviction by a simple majority rather than the traditional unanimous vote. Moreover, whenever the judges concluded that a jury verdict was wrong, they could recommit the case to a new jury.

## THE TREMBLING OF THE RULING CLASSES:
### 1848 TO WORLD WAR I

Louis-Philippe's regime, having started out with grand hopes for liberalization, finally came to a disappointing end in February 1848. An attempt to prevent a relatively minor political banquet in Paris ignited a mass revolution echoing the year-old phrases of Karl Marx and Friedrich Engels in *The Communist Manifesto*: "Let the ruling classes tremble at a Communist revolution. The proletarians have nothing to lose but their chains." Paris students and workers seized the city, proclaiming the arrival of the Second French Republic.[116] Once more, upon gaining power the former political agitators initiated their rule with considerable concessions to political freedom. Within days of the revolution, all violators of the press laws as well as all other political offenders were released and amnestied. On February 26, 1848, the death penalty was abolished for political offenses, and on November 4 the prohibition was incorporated in Article 5 of the new Constitution.[117]

The popular unrest, however, continued unabated, culminating in a second insurrection. The June uprising was finally put down through the intervention of the military, with thousands of workers dying at the barricades. Hopes for an end to the turmoil emerged toward the end of 1848, when Prince Louis Napoleon was elected president of the Republic. His presidency lasted three years and was brought to a conclusion by the president himself, in a December 1851 coup. Assuming power as Emperor Napoleon III, former president Louis Napoleon initiated a new era of political repression. Strict controls were imposed on the press, and all members of the national parliament, magistrates, and other officials were required to take an oath of allegiance.

The Second Empire instituted by Louis Napoleon alternated between conservatism and liberalism, bringing much economic prosperity but little freedom to the political life of the country. The regime was particularly weakened by a growing popular opposition to its authoritarian style. After France capitulated to German troops under the leadership of Wilhelm I and his chancellor, Otto von Bismarck, at Sedan in 1871, the revolutionary Paris Commune took over the French capital. In the resulting chaos, the nation's assembly met in Bordeaux and deposed Napoleon III, declaring him responsible for the "ruin, invasion, and dismemberment of France." After a "Bloody Week," in which some thirty thousand Parisians were killed at the barricades (exceeding the death toll of the 1783–84 Reign of Terror), the nation's Third Republic was ushered in.

France's Third Republic, continuing from 1871 until the First World War, witnessed at first a flourishing of economic and political liberalism. Only the persistent and indiscriminate violence of the anarchists threatened to reverse this trend. The rash of anarchist bombings, assassinations, and assassination attempts evoked little support or sympathy from either the regime or the masses. Between 1875 and 1910, assassinations (and attempted assassinations) were carried out against heads of state not only in France but also in Russia, Spain, Austria, Italy, the United States, Prussia, Belgium, and Japan.[118] In December of 1893 an anarchist bomb was thrown into the French Chamber of Deputies. In response to the anarchists' efforts to destroy all organized forms of government, special laws to deal with this unique threat were passed in France as elsewhere. Under these enactments, known as *lois scelerates* (villainous laws), the French tightened governmental controls over explosives, the press, and convicted offenders. Particularly significant was the extension of *rélégation*[119] (transportation to an overseas penal colony) to those charged with membership in the anarchist movement.[120]

Meanwhile, in Great Britain, the Victorian prosperity largely kept the specter of political unrest at bay. The reformist movement begun earlier continued, most notably in the expansions of the franchise first in 1867 and again in 1884–85.[121] Finally, in 1916, the vote was extended to virtually all men and women. Ireland, however, continued as a focal point of economic and political storms.

After Ireland's 1801 union with Great Britain, the English domination of that country continued. Not until the Catholic Emancipation of 1829 were Catholics permitted to sit in the British Parliament. Severe socioeconomic deprivations aggravated existing political grievances. The potato famine of 1846–47, causing the death of nearly one million Irish citizens,[122] inflamed popular hostility toward the English tenancy laws. There were wholesale evictions of tenants for failure to pay rents, producing social disruptions and large-scale emigration. Efforts to reform the land law failed, preserving the fundamental structure that kept the mostly Catholic Irish tenants in abject and unrelieved poverty.

In 1848 a group calling itself Young Ireland, prompted by the conviction of one of its leaders, John Mitchel, for sedition and convinced that direct action alone would relieve Irish suffering, attempted an attack on the police in Tipperary.[123] Of the three men tried for this first Irish military uprising in fifty years, the first, Charles Duffy, was acquitted of treason and later emigrated to Australia, where he became prime minister of the colony from 1871 to 1872 and was knighted for his services.[124] The second, William O'Brian, was convicted but was pardoned in 1856 and lived out his life alternating between Brussels and Ireland.[125] The third, Thomas Meagher, was convicted of treason and condemned to death. After his sentence was commuted to transportation, he escaped and made his way to New York, where he commanded the "Irish Brigade" of the Union Army in the American Civil War.[126] Ironically, John Mitchel, the man whose conviction sparked the rebellious attack, also escaped to the United States. There he enlisted his journalistic talents in the pro-slavery cause and served a short term of imprisonment for Confederate activities after the Civil War.[127]

While the English authorities became ever more watchful in Ireland, the massive emigration of Irish to the United States provided a safe haven for simmering free-Ireland activists. Back in Ireland, the secret Fenian Society, named for the circle of warriors of a third-century Irish hero-king, was founded shortly after the abortive Young Ireland uprising. In 1863 the Fenians founded a Dublin paper, *Irish People*, which the English closed in 1865, arresting its editor. In 1866 the writ of habeas corpus was suspended in Ireland, and many Fenians were confined.

The Fenians, officially constituted as the Irish Republican Brotherhood, made 1867 a busy year for the British authorities both at sea and on land, in Ireland as well as in England. They outfitted a ship, *Erin's Hope*, in the United States and sailed for Ireland with many Civil War veterans on board. After a short skirmish with the British, the ship and its crew were captured. Riots erupted in several Irish counties, and a raid was carried out on police barracks in Kerry. In Manchester, on the English mainland, the Fenians attacked a police wagon carrying two Irish Americans who had been arrested for agitation. A policeman was killed. Three attackers were captured and executed, thus becoming the "Manchester Martyrs," mourned by the Irish everywhere for years thereafter. Another Fenian was executed for the 1867 attempt to blow up the Clerkenwell Prison in London.[128]

The Fenian agitation generated new British interest in the plight of the suffering Irish tenants. The Reform Act of 1867 gave Ireland more representation in Parliament, disestablished the Church of Ireland (the Irish equivalent of the Church of England), and freed up land for purchase. In 1870 the first land reform act benefiting tenants was passed.[129]

All this was, however, a bit late, for 1870 saw the beginning of the Irish Home Rule Movement, advocating enlarged Irish autonomy.[130] The movement began slowly, but Charles S. Parnell's 1875 appearance in Britain's Parliament changed that. Parnell organized an "Irish Party" and was able to obstruct any parliamentary business until the Irish Party's agenda was attended to. He gained Fenian support in 1878 and became president of the Land League, which called tenants to boycott lands from which previous tenants had been evicted for failure to pay rent. The boycott resulted in agrarian unrest, violence, and incendiarism, which became known as the Land War of 1879–82.[131] Parliament responded with a double-edged program. It passed the Coercion Bill of 1881 to crush the agrarian revolt,[132] and also the Land Act of 1881 to give tenants "fair rent, fixity of tenancy, and freedom of sale."[133]

The Land Act did not address all of Ireland's problems. Parnell and the Irish partisans now sought more than land reform, turning to the home rule issue. In 1886 the first home rule bill failed, and agitation mounted.[134] The National League, an outgrowth of the outlawed Land League, was formed, and Parnell supported it, even though it was outlawed by the Perpetual Crimes Act of 1887.[135] The British attempted to placate the Irish with a series of new land reform measures,[136] but difficulties of administration and resistance by landlords kept the agrarian problems smoldering. When Parnell was disgraced in a divorce scandal, a new leadership did not emerge.[137]

While at the turn of the century it looked as if Ireland might be pacified, soon thereafter, Sinn Fein, Gaelic for "we ourselves," began a new quest for cultural, economic, and political independence. Sinn Fein's founder, journalist Arthur Griffith, advocated an Ireland in which Gaelic was spoken, Irish culture revived, and Irish political and economic autonomy prevailed.[138] For many, this ideal seemed impractical. It required the abandonment of English culture and customs adopted by the people, the transformation and diversification of the small-farmer and artisan economy, the defeat of opposition by the intransigent Ulstermen, and the acquiescence of a powerful neighbor—Great Britain.[139]

In 1914 a compromise Irish home rule measure was finally passed by Parliament,[140] but its implementation was delayed until the end of the Great War on the Continent. This delay resulted in the Easter Uprising of 1916, led by Patrick Pearse, of the Irish Volunteer Movement, and James Connolly, leader of a former Irish transport workers strike and founder of the Citizens' Army in Ireland. The revolt was poorly coordinated and easily suppressed. Connolly was wounded, captured, and shot; Pearse was tried by court-martial and similarly executed.[141]

The manner of the revolt's suppression, the executions, and Ireland's occupation by the British fueled popular sentiment for the rebels. Sinn Fein now became the primary vehicle for popular resistance to British rule. After the British parliamentary election that followed the World War I armistice, the seventy-three Sinn Fein members elected to the British Parliament met in Dublin in 1919 and declared an independent republic.[142] The British reacted by imprisoning every Sinn Fein sympathizer they could identify. On their part the independence-minded Irish, under the leadership of Michael Collins, recruited two small groups of gunmen as a means of undermining British rule by terrorism. Responding in kind, the British police deployed the hated Black and Tans against the rebels.[143]

As it became clear that the Irish people overwhelmingly supported Sinn Fein, negotiations opened that led to the establishment of the Irish Free State in 1922.[144] Eamon De Valera, the new leader of Sinn Fein, would not participate in the negotiations with the British and denounced any solution that would partition Ireland and leave Northern Ireland within Great Britain.[145] Arthur Griffith, vice-president of Sinn Fein, was elected the first president of the Irish Free State. Only ten years later, after the conclusion of a civil war between the Free Staters and the republican opposition,[146] did Griffith's sudden death in 1932 clear the way for the relenting De Valera to become the Free State's second elected president.

## THE LANDS OF THE DOUBLE-HEADED EAGLES:
## CENTRAL AND EASTERN EUROPE

### THE EMERGENCE OF GERMANY

Throughout this era, German responses to political offenses and offenders, much like those of the French and English, swung back and forth between conservatism and liberalism. The early German laws concerning political crime, like the French laws, were derived from the Roman principles of *crimen laesae majestatis*.[147] However, the more manifest feudal character of the Germanic culture produced a greater effort to preserve that society's hierarchical order. German codes thus included such offenses as *Lästerung* (insulting one's lord) and *Mord am Landesherrn* (murdering the lord), which were viewed as particularly grave threats to the social order and resulted in the offender's loss of status and honor.

With time, the severe penalties against political crime continued in effect and often were even increased. When Frederick the Great of Prussia prohibited the use of torture in criminal proceedings, as a concession to the liberal and enlightened thinking of the time, he nevertheless retained the practice in cases of political crime.[148] The Bavarian Penal Code of 1813,[149] one of the most influential penal codes of the century, prescribed death by decapitation as the punishment for high treason and required the public exhibition of the condemned person prior to execution, carrying a sign inscribed "Guilty of High Treason." The traitor's family was compelled to change its name, and a column of infamy was erected upon the offender's grave.

During the French Revolution and the Napoleonic aftermath, the German principalities witnessed waves of both liberalism and nationalism, as expectations of a freer—and a unified—Germany grew amongst the students and the intelligentsia. But the Congress of Vienna, at which Austria's Metternich predominated, reaffirmed the old structure of Germany, as a loose federation under Austrian hegemony. Metternich's fear of the emergence of German power resulted in the reactionary laws of 1819, designed to control the German universities and the press. Known as the Karlsbad Decrees, these laws allowed the administrative dismissal of teachers, without a hearing, for propagating "doctrines hostile to the public order and subversive of existing governmental institutions."[150] Prior press censorship was instituted, and a central investigating commission was created to inquire into "the origin and ramifications of the revolutionary plots and demagogical associations directed against the existing constitutions" of the German states. As a result of these and similar enactments it became high treason for persons to work toward German unification or to belong to societies committed to goals that would entail the loss of sovereignty by the disparate existing states. Pan-German patriotism thus became a capital offense.[151]

By the middle of the nineteenth century, however, attitudes toward political offenders were changing, both in the German scholarly literature and in legislative enactments. Because of the particularly influential role of legal scholars in the German system of justice, their views on political crime carried considerable weight. These scholars, however, were not all of the same view.

The conservatives called for increasingly severe penalties for political offenders. They pointed out that while common offenders merely violated legal requirements without denying their validity, political offenders denied the very legitimacy of the state and its laws. Because the political offender was presenting himself or herself as superior to the dictates of existing or "positive" law and was seeking to impose a private and subjective will upon the general will of society, he or she was deemed to be more dangerous and evil than the conventional offender.[152]

Many liberal or radical scholars, on the other hand, considered the moral compulsion and noble objectives motivating political offenders to be of utmost importance. Political crime, in their view, reflected defects in society and the state, rather than in the offender. Accordingly, combatting political crime often required reform of the state. Political offenders were therefore not to be viewed as criminals but as state critics and enemies. Accordingly, they were to be treated as prisoners of war. While these jurists were not willing to accord dissenters the right to oppose society by violent means, they nevertheless believed that the preventive measures required to restrain political dissidents should not be classified as criminal penalties.[153]

Even some of the more traditional writers recognized political crime as being less a violation of moral norms than a violation of the pragmatic and political order imposed by the needs of the state and of those in power. Given the special nature of political crime, these writers called for differential treatment of those charged with these offenses. The severe punishment of political criminals, some pointed out, indeed frustrated the state's ultimate objective of achieving national consensus. A more moderate approach to political opposition was thus recommended as a tool of future reconciliation.[154]

These considerations combined in time with Germany's older penal practices, which favored those of high status, to liberalize the system of sanctions applicable to political offenders. "Germany, being a status-oriented society, retained for at least fifty years beyond the French Revolution special lenient forms of punishment for high-status offenders," observed Ingraham.[155] Based on Roman law, which differentiated between *honestiores* (high-status persons) and *humiliores* (low-status offenders), the German system sought to continue in prison the distinctions existing in open society.

Detention in a fortress (*Festungsarrest*)—without the irons and the arduous labor forced upon common criminals—developed in eighteenth-century Germany as a special punishment for *honestiores*, the nobility and other high-status offenders. During the first half of the nineteenth century, this punishment was extended to other persons, particularly members of the educated classes, who with altruistic motives committed crimes not deemed dishonorable. Although these lenient laws did not specify the differential handling of political offenders as such, the traditions of the long-established system of *custodia honesta* began in time to accrue to their benefit.

The experiences of the German state of Württemberg well illustrate the progressive changes regarding the treatment of political offenders. While the 1810 laws concerning offenses against the state and king imposed severe penalties, they authorized the milder penalty of *Festungsarrest* for high-status offenders. In 1824 the law was changed to permit fortress penalties whenever the circumstances of the offender and the nature of the crime merited more lenient treatment. Attention thus began shifting from the offender's status to his or her motives and the character of the crime. The trend was carried even further in the 1849 law, which eliminated the factor of social status altogether from sentencing considerations.[156]

With the unification of Germany in 1871, the perception of political crime was drastically altered. Unification demonstrated that the previous regime's repression of Pan-German activism was both wrong and ineffective. The creation of the German Reich, representing a successful challenge to former laws against all-German patriotism, resulted in a new public awakening to the law's fallibility. Tolerance toward competing and conflicting ideas and programs gained support not only among radicals and liberals but also among the more conservative segments of the population as well.

An important change brought about by unification was the new German Penal Code. The federal Code reflected the period's strong interest in the issues of political activism and dissent. The debates on its adoption were lengthy and fierce, and the final Code was a product of political compromise. For many of the offenses against the state, and usually whenever extenuating circumstances were found to exist, detention in a fortress became an alternative penalty. The Code provided specifically that where a choice was allowed by law between detention in a fortress and confinement in a penitentiary, the latter sentence was not to be allowed "unless it is established that the offense has arisen as the result of a dishonorable state of mind."[157]

Prison sentences for political offenders were therefore now to be the exception rather than the rule. Only when the crime of high treason involved the murder (or the attempted murder) of the sovereign, when a serious act of treason was committed against the state (*Landesverrat*), or when serious rioting occurred against public officials was penitentiary confinement required.[158] Finally, the death penalty was to be imposed only for the murder, or attempted murder, of the kaiser or the reigning prince of the offender's native state or state of residence.[159]

Aware of the spread of radical economic and political doctrines, the German law prohibited, however, secret societies and incitement to class violence.[160] Seeking to build up German nationalism, Bismarck saw the international affiliations of both socialism and Catholicism as threats. New provisions of the Penal Code made it an offense for members of the clergy, in their preaching or writing, to make "affairs of the state the subject of comment or discussion in a manner dangerous to the public peace."[161] All Jesuits, furthermore, were banned from the territories of the Reich, and all religiously affiliated schools in Prussia were placed under the supervision of the state.

## RUSSIA: FROM CZARISM TO LENINISM

Despite Napoleon's failure to conquer Russia, Western influences continued to seep into Russian society.[162] Ideas challenging Russia's absolute monarchy and its encrusted aristocracy surfaced as Russian officers and men began to return from the pursuit of the retreating French. The country was now increasingly exposed to European liberal thoughts and socioeconomic developments. The new mood was reflected in the Russian literature of the period, exploding in the 1825 Decembrist Revolt by young aristocratic officers tired of the Romanov autocracy. Although the insurrection was ruthlessly suppressed by the newly enthroned Nicholas I, then commencing his thirty-year reign of oppression, the ancient autarchy could never fully recover.

A second breach in Russian despotism came with the Emancipation Edict of 1861, issued during the rule of reformist Czar Alexander II, who succeeded Nicholas I. Despite its potentially far-reaching effects, the Edict, purporting to liberate the serfs from their enslavement, had few immediate effects. The Edict's requirements for manumission were complex and steep. Although land was allotted to the serfs, for which they were to pay over a period of forty-nine years, it was conveyed to village communes (*miri*) rather than to individuals, and was to be redistributed every ten to twelve years in order to guarantee equality. Peasants, moreover, were permitted to buy only half the amount of the land they had cultivated as serfs. Since most serfs were unable to afford the annual redemption payments, they remained incapable of gaining economic independence.

Further concessions were granted to the people by the Zemstvo Statute of 1864, providing serfs a role in local government. Local government boards (*zemstva*)—on which nobility, townspeople, and peasants were equally represented—were authorized to levy taxes for such improvements as roads, bridges, schools, and hospitals. But after the 1864 attempted assassination of Czar Nicholas II by a student named Karakozof, many of these reforms were reduced to mere paper promises by the reactionary forces. The judicial reform efforts of 1864 were similarly curtailed after the 1878 acquittal of Vera Zasulich, assassin of the royal governor of St. Petersburg who had ordered the flogging of a student revolutionary.

The Decembrist Revolt and the Emancipation Edict produced only symbolic cracks in the iron wall of czarist autocracy. These attempts at revolution and reform did little to ameliorate the plight of the underprivileged. Disappointed by these failures, the Russian intelligentsia began to pursue the idea of awakening the *narod*, the total community, to the need for fundamental change. A segment of the Narodnik movement called Land and Freedom pursued a terrorist line, plotting to assassinate the czar in 1866, but in the summers of 1872–74 the majority of the Narodniks spread out into the countryside in an attempt to talk the peasantry into rebellion. The intelligentsia's pitiful failure to gain the trust of the peasants or even to engage them in a meaningful dialogue is dramatically recounted in Turgenev's *Virgin Soil*. Some peasants equated their self-appointed liberators with the Anti-Christ, and many Narodnik missionaries were turned in to the police.

After the frustrations of this experience, the major thrust of the movement, in the late 1870s and 1880s, became violence and terrorism. Under the aegis of *Narodnaya Volya* ("people's will"), the revolutionaries sought to coerce concessions from the government through the assassination of officials and other means of intimidation. In March 1881 *Narodnaya Volya*'s violence reached its high peak with the assassination of Czar Alexander II after a twenty-six-year reign. The czar's death, however, did not bring reforms but instead, a reinvigorated wave of repression and persecution.

From 1875 to 1895 the peasants suffered additionally due to a long agrarian depression. Government reforms in reducing the cost of land purchases and in resettling landless peasants did little to relieve the plight of the people. Peasants who had left for the cities during this period would return to their former villages to visit relatives and bring with them urban revolutionary doctrines. As urban revolutionary sentiment percolated out to the countryside, spontaneous peasant uprisings began to take place. In 1902, with yet another crop failure, the once-passive peasants banded together to seize available grain supplies.

The year 1902 also witnessed the formation of the Socialist Revolutionary Party. Reformers, henceforth, were to give growing attention to organizing the workers in Russia's emerging industrial establishments. Placated by concessions in the area of working conditions, gained through selective strikes in the late 1890s, the Social Democratic Labor Party emphasized immediate material gains for workers rather than pursuing the Marxist objective of restructuring the whole social order. Lenin denounced this "misguided" idea in *What Is to Be Done?*, but it was the czar's secret police rather than the

Marxist-Leninists who ultimately destroyed this counterweight to the revolutionary forces.

In the years between 1900 and 1904, the head of the political police, Zubatov, set out to penetrate the leadership of the burgeoning, but still illegal, trade union movement in order to protect it from revolutionary influences. Workers' associations flourished under the invisible hand of the political police, but the new organizations got beyond the control of the police. In 1903 Zubatov and his agents were exposed in Odessa. The exposure resulted in a bloody general strike. The manipulated labor societies were disbanded. However, in the process workers had been taught how to organize.

The year 1905 was a particularly eventful year in Russia. In February the massacre of hundreds of peaceful petitioners seeking to address Czar Nicholas II at the Winter Palace embittered the people. The peasants rose in February as well, and agrarian violence spread throughout the summer. The defeats of Russia's imperial armed forces at the hands of the Japanese in the Russo-Japanese War emboldened the rebels, and between July and August 1905 the Constitutional Assembly of the All-Russian Peasant's Union declared its program for abolishing all private property in land.

At one time or another, 1905 witnessed a strike by practically every segment of workers in Russia. While many of these were traditional strikes for such material benefits as the eight-hour day, political strikes were frequent, and labor joined with the revolutionary intelligentsia to demand an end to autocracy and the establishment of a democratic republic.

The government responded by offering concessions, including the promise of a representative parliamentary assembly, or Duma; universal suffrage; freedom of speech, conscience, and organization; the legalization of trade unions; and the cancellation of all "redemption" payments due from peasants for the land they occupied. After a winter lull in the growing conflict, fighting was renewed in the spring. By summer 1906, however, government authority was reasserted, and punitive military expeditions were sent forth to execute, flog, and otherwise punish agrarian rebels. A new effort was simultaneously made to keep the newly legalized, but still suspect, workers' unions under close police surveillance.

Czarist autocracy survived the 1905 revolution through a combination of concessions and repressions. The government did not, however, follow through in empowering the new institutions it created. Instead, it actively proceeded to undermine them, insensitive to the fact that in so doing it was also losing the support of the power centers that had stood with it in 1905— the army, the police, the bureaucracy, the gentry, business, and industry.

World War I exposed the impotence of government and the rot in its institutions. The costs in territory, material, and human lives were devastating. All the glue that had held the autocracy together was brittle. On March 8, 1917, a bread riot in Petrograd began the rapid collapse. When the soldiers in the garrison refused to fire on the crowds, the sinews snapped. On March 15, Czar Nicholas II abdicated. He was succeeded by a provisional government under Prince Georgi Evgenievich Levov and, shortly thereafter, by a republic under Aleksandr Kerenski, before the Bolsheviks under V. I. Lenin seized power on November 7, 1917. Thus the Romanov dynasty, founded in 1613, came to an abrupt end.

# CHAPTER SEVEN

# The Limits of Tolerance: Political Rebels at the End of the Millennium

> The policy of leniency of bourgeois governments towards their political enemies appears neither as an exercise of . . . charity nor as the achievement of a higher stage of civilization, but as one manifestation of a . . . "death wish" on the part of a class which had no desire to rule.
>
> —Barton L. Ingraham, *Political Crime in Europe*

## THE DECLINE OF LIBERALISM
## BETWEEN THE WORLD WARS

The basis for the nineteenth century's liberal flirtation with the political offender was succinctly articulated by Georges Vidal, a leading French legal scholar:

Whereas formerly the political criminal was treated as a public enemy, he is today considered as a friend of the public good, as a man of progress, desirous of bettering the political institutions of his country, having laudable intentions, hastening the onward march of humanity, his only fault being that he wishes to go too fast, and that he employs in attempting to realize the progress which he desires, means irregular, illegal and violent. If from this point of view, the political criminal is reprehensible and ought to be punished in the interest of the established order, his criminality cannot be compared with that of the ordinary malefactor, with the murderer, the thief, etc. The criminality [of the political offender] has not all the same immorality. It is only relative, dependent on time, place, circumstances, the institutions of the land, and it is often inspired by noble sentiments, by disinterested motives, by devotion to persons and principles, by love of one's country. In conclusion, the criminality is often only passing; the author of a political crime who is rather a vanquished, a conquered man, than a criminal, may become, as a result of a revolution favorable to his ideas, the conqueror of the morrow, who is called regularly and lawfully to direct and guide the state and the public administration of his country. The penal reaction exercised against him is not at all, then, like that against malefactors, who violate the ordinary law. . . . [Penal reaction against the political offender is not] a work of social defense against an attack upon immanent conditions of human existence, but is rather a . . . defense of caste, of political parties, against an attack upon an organization and upon a political regime historically transitory.[1]

With the approach of the First World War, this view was already in decline. The specter of a global "war to end all wars" intensified the spirit of nationalism, resurgent around the globe, and brought with it a wariness of critics and opponents of existing state authority. Those not recognizing the need to close ranks in the face of the impending foreign threat were perceived as subversives or even as enemy agents. In the United States, opposition to war was viewed and treated as seditious and treasonous. In France and elsewhere in Europe, the mobilization of national determination and resources likewise spurred a growing intolerance of political opponents by both the population and the government.[2]

Once the war had failed to reach an early resolution, this intolerance began to take a very serious toll on those who continued to engage in criticism of their government's military or political activities. In France, former interior minister Louis Malvy and political leader Joseph Caillaux—both active in the war-weary country's peace movement—were charged with treason, misfeasance in office, conspiracy to undermine external security, and furnishing damaging political and military information to the enemy.[3] On November 14, 1918, the expropriation of offenders' property as a penalty for violating France's external security laws was reinstituted.[4]

After the conclusion of World War I, in the era between the wars, the politics of intolerance continued to rise in France. French Fascist conspiracies in the 1930s, patterned after the successful exploits of the German Brownshirts, resulted in new counteractive measures by the government. After the army had to be called in to defend the legislature from an attack by a Fascist mob, major changes were instituted in the peacetime espionage law.[5] Not only was the definition of *espionage* expanded (to include "the disclosure of industrial and economic information") and the penalties increased (to permit once more the imposition of *rélégation*, or transportation), but also procedures were streamlined for the manifest purpose of dealing with these offenses "quickly and with the least fuss possible."[6]

A 1936 law granted the president of the republic and his council of ministers the power to dissolve all organizations that (1) assumed the form of combat groups or private militias, (2) provoked armed demonstrations, or (3) were committed to attacks on France's republican form of government or the integrity of the national territory.[7] Those participating in such organizations could be imprisoned for a period of from six months to two years. By decree, in November of the same year, the state council dissolved several Fascist organizations possessing such patriotic and colorful names as the National Popular Party and the Sons of the Fiery Crosses. The most drastic measures against political criminality were not instituted, however, until after Hitler's invasion of Czechoslovakia in March of 1939.

As war with Germany seemed inevitable, the French government moved to protect itself further against persons and activities likely to jeopardize the national security. Special emergency powers, available under the constitution, were assumed by the executive on March 19, 1939.[8] Penal Code provisions concerning crimes against the external security of the state were drastically expanded soon thereafter.[9] The new law reinstituted capital punishment for the more serious violations of the law of treason,[10] while the penalty of forced labor (previously applicable only to common crimes) was extended to offenses against the country's foreign security.[11] Most significant, all felonies and misdemeanors against the external security of the state— whether committed in time of war or peace—were now to be tried by military courts. The dramatic reversal of France's earlier lenient policies toward political opposition was made complete by Article 84 of the Penal Code, which provided that "for the purpose of imposing punishment, felonies and misdemeanors against the external security of the state shall be treated like ordinary felonies and misdemeanors."[12]

## THE ROAD TO TOTALITARIANISM

### THE RISE OF THE THIRD REICH

The trends taking place in the Western democracies were even more pronounced in Germany. The post–War World I Weimar Republic, established in 1919 after Germany's defeat, was unable to control the political unrest that followed the collapse of the country's military and industrial establishments. Throughout the country, the left wing organized soldiers' and workers' councils, plotting to take power in the country's industrial centers. Socialist regimes were established in the states of Bavaria, the Ruhr, Saxony, and Thuringia. Moreover, leftist elements of the Social Democratic Party (the Spartacus League) attempted to establish a national workers' government through a socioeconomic revolution in the Soviet style. During the ensuing unrest, Rosa Luxemburg and Karl Liebknecht, Spartacist leaders, were murdered in Berlin.

The Weimar government could not obtain support from the moderate or left-of-center elements in the country to control this chaos. Neither did the new government receive the backing of the more conservative or rightist parties, who with great contempt alleged that the Weimar centrists had "stabbed Germany in the back" during the World War.

Desperately seeking to protect itself against the political extremes of both the left and the right, the Weimar regime attempted to create its own set of political controls. Following the assassination of Walter Rathenau, the regime's Jewish foreign minister, a "Law to Protect the Republic" was passed.[13] A special High Court for the Protection of the Republic was also set up within the German federal judiciary to deal with the newly created offenses. Neither of these developments was to have much effect in controlling what had by then become an irresistible Nazi threat.

The Weimar government's problems in bringing these new political weapons to bear were aggravated by the limitations imposed by Germany's prevailing federal constitution. The police responsible for enforcing the new laws were controlled at the local rather than federal level. Because of this, the federal authorities had to rely on the cooperation of the separate German states to suppress increasingly bloody street battles between the Communists and Hitler's Brownshirts. The states, on the other hand, were likewise unable to coordinate their programs with those of the central government. It is reported, for example, that in the last election before Hitler took power,

> The Prussian Government, by a decree of July 30, 1930, barred all civil servants from supporting Nazi and Communist organizations. The wearing of Brown Shirts in Prussia was also forbidden, and so the SA [Hitler's "Brownshirts"] made do with white shirts. But the Central Government was not ready to take similar steps, and this duality largely canceled out the effects of regional measures.[14]

The federal-state jurisdictional divisions, which weakened the Weimar government, were aggravated by a rift within the governmental apparatus itself—between reformist liberals in the Reichstag and the conservatives who remained in control of the country's military, police, and judicial agencies. Kurt Tucholsky, a highly respected essayist of the era, accused the conservative-dominated judiciary of administering "political justice," in order to protect causes to which they were sympathetic:

> [Tucholsky] maintained that an observer could tell much of the character of a country from its legal procedure. . . . [He] constantly compared the treatment by the court of the left- and right-wing offenders. Liebknecht's [leftist] followers received [long] prison sentences. . . . "The Kappists [rightists] we let go free." Tucholsky reported that men who revealed the hiding places of secret arms were arrested while those in possession of the weapons went free. Reactionary students who trampled the [new] republican flag were left

untouched, while tramplers of the [discarded] imperial colors received three months. Tucholsky came to believe that the behavior of the courts toward the right was tantamount to giving it free reign to behave as it wanted no matter how criminal the action.[15]

Statistics compiled for the period of 1919–22 support Tucholsky's charges. They disclose a total of 354 reported murders by the right wing, and a mere 22 by the leftists. The average period of imprisonment imposed upon rightists convicted of murder was four months, compared to an average sentence of fifteen years in prison for leftists convicted of the same offense.[16] The executive branch showed similar sympathy toward violent right-wing organizations. When the federal government finally attempted to outlaw Hitler's Storm Troopers (the S.A., or *Sturmabteilung*) and the S.S. (*Schützstaffel*) in April of 1932, President Hindenburg promptly removed General William Groener, the minister who had announced the measure.[17]

Among the emergency laws enacted by the Weimar government, one specifically prohibited private citizens or groups from dispersing lawful meetings,[18] a tactic increasingly used by the National Socialist storm troopers to combat their political adversaries. It was this disruptive tactic that had brought Adolf Hitler and his followers into the Burgerbrau Cellar in Munich on November 8, 1923. Breaking into a meeting of Bavarian reactionary leaders, the Nazis forced those in attendance to support their march on Berlin. Once freed, the Bavarians withdrew their support, and Hitler's march the following day was dispersed by the police, ending the attempted Munich *putsch*. Its leader, Adolf Hitler, was sentenced to five years of fortress detention (*Festungshaft*), a term that was later reduced to less than one year.

It was not outright illegality, but rather conformity to the forms of the democratic process itself that ultimately brought the National Socialist Party to power. The middle class (pauperized by inflation), the youth (largely unemployed), and the veterans (disappointed because of neglect) swelled the Nazi ranks. The National Socialists went from 12 seats in the Reichstag, the national parliament, during 1928, to 107 seats in 1930, to 230 seats in 1932, and to 288 seats in 1933. They were the largest party in the Reichstag, though they never achieved a majority.

On January 30, 1933, Adolf Hitler was sworn in as chancellor of Germany by the ailing General Paul von Hindenburg, the country's president. At his disposal was not only the power to rule by emergency decrees, authorized by Article 48 of the Weimar Constitution, but also a host of other drastic laws enacted by Germany's desperate Weimar Republic in seeking to disarm its adversaries. It was with the aid of these and other newly enacted measures that he turned what appeared a lawful assumption of power into a *coup d'état*.[19]

The Nazis were not to be long troubled by the problems of German federalism. After their seizure of power, the former difficulty of lack of federal-state coordination was quickly solved by the decree of February 28, 1933, which stated that "if a state fails to take the necessary steps for the restoration of public safety and order, then the Central Government is empowered to take over the relevant powers of the highest state authority."[20]

The first important measure introduced by the new Hitlerian regime was modeled on the previously repealed Weimar "Law to Protect the Republic." The new "Emergency Decree to Protect the German People"[21] incorporated many of the provisions of the earlier law, and it was expanded through a new and ominous provision for taking into "protective custody" (*schützhaft*) anyone suspected of plotting to alter the constitution. This authorization of "protective custody" was to serve as the first step toward the establishment of the Third Reich's infamous concentration camps.[22]

After "protection" against the Reich's enemies had been established, the next step in the consolidation of Nazi power was the Reichstag fire of February 28, 1933. The event was utilized to trigger the "Emergency Decree of the Reich President for the Protection of the People and the State,"[23] under which capital punishment was extended to a large number of political offenses previously subject to lesser sanctions. The decree was quickly followed by the Enabling Act of March 23, 1933, in which the Reichstag essentially yielded its remaining legislative powers to what had finally become a dictatorship.[24]

The National Socialist Party was designated the only lawful political party in Germany on July 14, 1933.[25] Under the political theories propounded by the Nazis, Germany's "national community," and not the state, became the source of all law and the focus of all loyalties. The party was viewed as the sole expression of the "national community." Betrayal of either the party or the state constituted treason against the German national community. Since all social status under Naziism was theoretically derived from the community, the political offender—a rebel against the *Volk*, or people—was to be denied all dignity and humanity.

Under this view political offenders were subjected to more stringent police, court, and prison proceedings than were common criminals. Political offenders could be held in preventive detention for indeterminate periods. A People's Court of Justice (*Volksgerichthof*) was granted exclusive jurisdiction over the trial of treasonous offenses.[26] Consisting of three lay members and two legally trained judges, these courts used summary procedures, conducted their business in closed sessions, and had the power to exclude the accused's counsel.[27] For lesser political offenses, special two-man courts were constituted—with one representative each from the police and the S.S. (*Schützstaffel*).

Other laws aimed at controlling speech and dissent were soon passed.

The Law of December 20, 1934, "Against Malicious Attacks on the State and Party and for the Protection of the Party Uniform," ordained that "anyone may be prosecuted who purposely makes or circulates an untrue or coarsely distorted statement, purporting to be based on fact, which is intended to do grievous harm to the esteem in which the Reich is held, or to the welfare of the National Socialist German Workers' Party, or any of its organizations."[28]

The second paragraph of this law was known as the *Heimtueckegesetz*, strongly resembling the old English law of sedition. This measure called for the punishment of those who make "public statements which are spiteful or inflammatory, or express a low feeling or opinion of leading personages of the State or the National Socialist German Workers' Party, their decrees, or the arrangements instituted by them, which are intended to undermine the people's faith in their political leadership."[29] A contemporary observer reported that "eighty percent of all persons accused of any kind of political offense are condemned under it."[30]

With these measures directed to silence any dissent within the German citizenry, the next targets for the Nazi purge were the institutions of government and the structures of the party itself. The campaign of *Gleichschaltung*, or of unification and incorporation of all social institutions, began with the innocuous-sounding "Law for the Restoration of the Professional Civil Service" of April 7, 1933, which removed all Jews and "politically unreliable" employees from the government.[31] The phalanxes of lawyers who had participated in the liberal Weimar system were also purged, through a decree issued the same day, the "Law on the Admission to the Practice of Law."[32]

The party itself was eventually purged on the Night of the Long Knives, in which Ernst Röhm, the leader of the S.A., was executed by Theodor Eicke and Michael Lippert, the commandants of the Dachau concentration camp (p.239). Most of the victims of the purge went to their deaths believing that there had been some mistake, loudly proclaiming their allegiance to the Führer as they were hauled away in the dead of night. The purge was retroactively made "legal" by the law of July 3, 1934, proclaiming that "the measures taken on June 30 and on July 1 and 2 to strike down the treasonous attacks are justifiable acts of self-defense by the state"(p.240). The last remnants of legality had finally been cast aside.

Writing in 1979, criminologist Barton Ingraham, confounded by the Weimar regime's weakness in the face of what at first was merely a gang of street brawlers, concluded that liberal "bourgeois" regimes generally suffered from a self-defeating "strange chivalry" toward their internal political enemies—a sort of "death wish."[33] He argued that liberal "bourgeois" governments inherently lack the desire to rule and are more interested in trade and commerce than in political struggles for power. But this controversial explanation of the rise of German fascism is challenged by the factual context of the Nazi rise.

Though Hitler claimed that the German people were "tired of democracy," the truth is that the country had never wholeheartedly accepted it. The profoundly militaristic and hierarchical culture that had existed under the kaisers was uniquely adaptable to the emerging Fascist ideology and social structures. Revolving around concepts of duty, honor, and protection of the fatherland, this national heritage was warped by a worldwide depression, the terrible and wasting hyperinflation of the early 1930s, and the punitive "peace" imposed by the victorious Great Powers at Versailles. Weimar's relatively lenient treatment of its domestic political enemies was a reflection of political realities—of its enormous institutional weakness in the face of intolerable social, economic, and political conditions.

### DARKNESS AT NOON IN THE "WORKERS' PARADISE"

Many see the Nazi regime as the ultimate evil—as the greatest and most cruel attempt to extinguish humankind's ethnic, political, social, and religious pluralism. The Soviet Union's attempt to create a similar uniformity and a New Man was to end as an equal or even greater failure.

Since the founding of their state, and long before the Bolshevik Revolution, Russia's czars had their own methods for containing political crime and criminals. The Okhrana, or czarist political police, was extraordinarily effective, despite its eventual (and probably inevitable) failure to preserve the monarchy. So prevalent was the czarist penetration of suspect political organizations that "the farcical position was reached where, in 1908–09, four out of five members of the Bolshevik Party's St. Petersburg Committee were Okhrana agents." In fact, when *Pravda* was first published in 1912, its editor (Roman Malinovskii) and its treasurer (Miron Chernomazov) were also police agents.[34] The Bolsheviks merely refined the art of political control—and terror—to extraordinary levels.

Their system of repression began to take shape in the earliest days after the Revolution. The ensuing civil war against the remaining loyalists and alleged counterrevolutionaries provided the justification for the Bolsheviks to rule by decree—after dissolving the first and only constituent assembly. Vladimir I. Lenin's plain signature on brief communiqués could spell death for thousands who stood in the way of the state.

Under these decrees the regime began its first purges, rounding up political enemies and shooting them by the thousands. Among the first orders was Lenin's November 28, 1917, decree, "On the Arrest of the Leaders of the Civil War against the Revolution," which condemned the leadership and membership of the rival Kadet (Constitutional-Democratic) Party to death as "enemies of the people."[35] George Leggett, in his authoritative work on the period, notes that "the term 'enemies of the people,' used in the tradition of the French Revolution, literally put its victims outside the law, with every man's hand against them."[36]

An old Russian proverb suggests that one has "to break some eggs to make an omelet." The subsequent history of the Soviet regime, in its struggle to build the promised communist society, was to see the breaking of an inestimable number of eggs. On December 7, 1917, Lenin's new government established the CHEKA (the All-Russian Extraordinary Commission for Combating Counter Revolution, Speculation, Sabotage, and Misuse of Authority), and appointed as its chairman Feliks Dzerzhinsky. Through its subsequent incarnations as the "GPU," "OGPU," and later the "NKVD," this organization was ultimately to become the feared KGB, or "Committee for State Security."[37] The new CHEKA quickly began to fulfill its mandate "to suppress and liquidate all attempts and acts of counter-revolution [sic] and sabotage throughout Russia, from whatever quarter."[38]

As in other times and other places, external and internal threats to the new revolutionary government seemed to justify the institution of a new "reign of terror." The pressures of the civil war and the threats created by competing political forces were to prove a perfect complement to the Bolsheviks' ideas about the inevitability and desirability of a "dictatorship of the proletariat," making repression appear both ideologically legitimate and necessary. Leon Trotsky, commanding the Red Army throughout the civil war, referred admiringly to "that remarkable invention of the French Revolution which makes men shorter by a head," and spoke darkly of what was to come: "In not more than a month's time terror will assume very violent forms, after the example of the great French Revolution; the guillotine, and not merely the gaol, will be ready for our enemies."[39]

The "reign of terror" was at hand. Whites (noncommunists), Kulaks (small landowners), and other suspected and actual "counterrevolutionaries" would suffer under the wrath of the new regime. After an attempt on Lenin's life had failed, the remaining non-Bolsheviks—Kadets, Social Revolutionaries, and the other Mensheviks—were, for the most part, summarily shot, an action justified by Lenin's previous decrees declaring these unfortunates to be "outside the law."[40] Despite the hopes of the reformists and democratic socialists who had participated in the Revolution, the Red Terror had begun.

Lenin preferred to forget that Marx, even when advocating violent revolution, generally disapproved of the use of revolutionary terror, and strongly criticized its application by the Jacobins in the French Revolution, regarding such use as a sign of weakness and immaturity in the regime that practiced it. . . . . Lenin, recalling Marx's phrase of 1848 about the French Terror being simply the bourgeoisie's plebeian way of settling scores with feudal absolutism, proposed that, after the coming revolution in Russia, the Bolsheviks—"the Jacobins of contemporary Social-Democracy"—should, like the French Jacobins of 1793 . . . use terror to settle accounts with the autocracy.[41]

The rhetoric issuing from the party organs grew increasingly bloodthirsty as the Red Terror continued: "Let there be floods of blood of the bourgeois— more blood, as much as possible."[42] The Bolsheviks' deliberate choice to rule through terror became a fixture of the Soviet system, with even more bloody purges continuing after Lenin's death.

Recourse to terror had figured prominently in Russian history. Terror had raged in the savage cossack-peasant risings of Stenka Razin and Pugachev, and in their suppression by the iron hand of autocracy. . . . Now Lenin summoned the cruel atavistic terror of the Russians, harnessing it to his purpose.[43]

Lenin's terror had been only the prelude to the greater and more murderous regime of his successor, Joseph Stalin. Robert Conquest, in *The Great Terror*, estimates the number of Stalin's victims at over twenty million.[44] During his twenty-three years in power, Stalin further institutionalized totalitarian methods of controlling dissent. A huge system of prison camps was created, the GULAG. The lethal cold, starvation, and forced labor experienced by those sentenced to these institutions was well described by Aleksandr Solzhenitsyn in *The Gulag Archipelago*.[45]

The former czarist device of internal passports was reintroduced to control all movement within the socialist state.[46] This mandatory and comprehensive system of controls[47] classified one and all Soviet citizens into rigid categories, including *yevrey* ("Jew"), *tsigan* ("Gypsy"),[48] *rabochiy* ("worker"), *sluzhashchiy* ("civil servant"), *krestyanin* ("peasant"), or *uchashchisya* ("student").[49] The classifications, made by the security officer who filled out the form, evolved into a veritable caste system for an allegedly classless society.

The Soviet Union's attempt to exercise absolute control over the lives and minds of its citizens represented, much like the Nazi campaign, the ultimate striving for absolute power by those favoring authority over autonomy, those who valued conformity over freedom, stability over flourishing debate, uniformity over pluralism. As with other such attempts to extinguish the inexorable force of human rebellion, the Soviet experiment was destined to collapse.

## THE POST–WORLD WAR II ERA

After the Second World War had ended, one would have expected some movement toward leniency in the treatment of political offenders. But in 1944 in France, General Charles de Gaulle's Provisional Government set up mass trials of wartime collaborators, casting a new light on the often temporal meaning of "political crime." Post–World War II ordinances, clearly ex post facto in character, established the new offense of "national disgrace" to criminalize conduct that was ordained either legal or mandatory under the wartime Vichy government. These offenses included the following: active participation in the "governments or pseudogovernments" of France (between the German occupation of June 16, 1940, and the postwar liberation); adherence to or collaboration with Fascist organizations; and participation in artistic, literary, economic, and political activities that supported racism, totalitarianism, or the foreign enemy.[50]

Thousands who had served the occupying Germans or Marshal Petain's government were prosecuted. The underlying premise of these prosecutions was the utter illegality of the Vichy government and its consequent inability to issue legally binding rules and laws. The offenders, accordingly, remained bound by the French laws as they existed prior to the German occupation. This meant that French citizens could not claim, as a defense to charges of collaboration, that their actions had complied with the positive law under Vichy and the German occupation.

During the post–World War II period, France was preoccupied not only with the punishment of wartime collaborators but also with the more immediate dangers posed by a new set of political crises. Continuing emergencies in France's overseas possessions, combined with troublesome domestic unrest, ultimately resulted in an even harsher stance toward opponents of the regime. Though liberal attitudes lingered a short time for purely "domestic" political offenders, the line of demarcation gradually lost its meaning as manifestations of international movements and causes, such as communism and fascism, were experienced domestically, thus blurring the line between domestic and foreign security threats.[51]

Attempting to control the growing political unrest that threatened both metropolitan France and its North African possessions, the various governments of the Fourth Republic had imposed increasingly harsh emergency measures. In 1955 an "assignments to residence" law[52] was passed, allowing the removal of nationalist F.L.N. (National Liberation Front) sympathizers in Algeria to internment camps. Labeled a "preventive" police measure, and allegedly involving no guilt or punishment, the removal was exempt from the usual safeguards of the French criminal code. Later enactments during the de Gaulle regime extended the internment law to France itself.[53]

Increasingly, the government resorted to the "special powers" available to it in emergencies under the Constitution.[54] By 1958 military tribunals had assumed jurisdiction over offenses related to the Algerian violence.[55] Suspects could be detained in police stations for an extended time without access to their families or lawyers and without formal criminal charges.[56] Finally, the conditions under which persons could be deprived of French citizenship were broadened in 1961.[57]

The most extreme legal development during the Algerian unrest was the ordinance of June 4, 1960, drastically revising the French Penal Code and the Code of Criminal Procedure.[58] The revisions abandoned the traditional division of crimes into those threatening external security and those threatening internal security. They also required that in time of war all offenses against state security, whether felonies or misdemeanors, were to be tried by military authorities.[59] In time of peace, however, these offenses, according to a 1963 revision, were to be handled by a special "Court for the Security of the State."[60] The earlier right to a jury trial was abandoned. Only a shadow now remained of the nineteenth-century policies that had given political offenders preferential treatment—both in terms of substantive provisions and procedurally—over ordinary criminals.

The unrest culminated in the end of France's Fourth Republic. In May of 1958, to face a possible F.L.N. insurrection—including a threatened invasion of the French mainland by the disgruntled French armed forces stationed in Algeria—General de Gaulle was called back to office. Initially appearing to support French control of Algeria, de Gaulle worked instead toward a compromise settlement, which culminated in Algerian independence in 1962.

The United Kingdom faced less of a domestic threat than France, but it too has had particular "blind spots" regarding those fighting for independence from British rule. Political offenders in British possessions and dependencies such as India, Pakistan, Ghana, Nigeria, Jordan, and Palestine were uniformly subjected to different and harsher controls than were common offenders. In many of these territories, emergency regulations, patterned after Britain's experience in Northern Ireland, permitted long-term confinement or so-called administrative detention of suspected political offenders without apprisal of charges, trial, or conviction.[61] These administrative detentions were used to devastating effect in Northern Ireland, where at one point as many as fifteen thousand political suspects were held in administrative detention at a time. Other special provisions of law to deal with Irish unrest continued to be enacted.[62]

If there had been a death wish on the part of the liberal forces in Germany after World War I, as claimed by Barton L. Ingraham, it had evaporated by the end of the Second World War. When the Federal Republic of West Germany came into being after the Allied occupation, the pre-Nazi-era liberal treatment of political offenders was not reintroduced. Mindful of the past weaknesses of the Weimar Republic in the face of enemies from both the left and the right, the new leaders sought to safeguard Germany's democratic regime against those who would seek to subvert it.

In its Basic Law (*Grundgesetz*) of 1949, Germany guaranteed to its citizens the basic rights of life, liberty, freedom of religion, conscience, speech, press, and association.[63] The law, however, specifically exempted from its protections "associations, the objects or activities of which conflict with the criminal laws or which are directed against the constitutional order or the concept of international understanding."[64] The Basic Law further specified that "whoever abuses the freedom of expression . . . in order to attack the free, democratic basic order, shall forfeit these basic rights,"[65] and also that "parties which . . . seek to impair or abolish the free and democratic basic order or to jeopardize the existence of the Federal Republic of Germany, shall be unconstitutional."[66]

Commenting on West Germany's new policies regarding political offenders, Ingraham admits that "the Founding Fathers of the Bonn constitution had resolved to defer no more to the principle of the absolute neutrality of the democratic state in the face of political parties, regardless of their nature and objectives."[67] In decreeing the dissolution of groups like the neo-Nazi Socialist Reich Party and the German Communist Party, the Federal Constitutional Court reaffirmed that Germany was to be a "valiant democracy."[68]

In its pursuit of internal security and social control, the U.S.S.R. differed dramatically from other countries that have struggled with the question of political protest and resistance. Traditional Western jurisprudence had long faced the argument that political, as distinguished from common, crimes have special characteristics and demand differential treatment. But in a totalitarian society where the state owns all property and controls all institutions, no transgression can be characterized as nonpolitical. Any offense against persons, property, or ideology is necessarily perceived as an offense against the state and hence a political crime. No leniency can be extended to an offender, therefore, on the grounds that the offense was politically motivated.

Soviet criminal law, indeed, had labeled some crimes as particularly "political" and therefore meriting the harshest of penalties. Though President Gorbachev proposed substantial revisions in the criminal codes, several "Especially Dangerous Crimes against the State," as well as a number of lesser political offenses, remained in the R.S.F.S.R. Code. Article 64[69] included under *treason* such acts as failing to return from a foreign country[70] (an offense punishable by death). *Espionage*, defined by Article 65, applied to the transfer of economic as well as military secrets. *Terrorist acts*, defined by Article 66,[71] consisted of gravely injuring a public official "for the purpose of undermining or weakening Soviet authority."[72]

"Anti-Soviet propaganda" was dealt with by Article 70,[73] which outlawed "agitation or propaganda carried on for the purpose of subverting or weakening the Soviet power . . . or the circulation [of] slanderous fabrications which defame the Soviet state and social system."[74] Possession of "anti-Soviet" literature had been prosecuted under this prohibition. Economic crimes were also seen as political in the U.S.S.R. *Sabotage*, in Article 68, was defined as attempts to engineer mass destruction, while *subversion*, set forth in Article 69, covered acts or omissions against economic entities "intended to obstruct their normal work."[75]

Moreover, Article 72, describing "organizational activity directed towards commission of especially dangerous crimes against the State," was often used to prevent the formation of competing political parties. Article 190 further prevented group activities that "are associated with obvious insubordination to the demands of representatives of authority."

The Soviet psychiatric system served as yet another potent weapon in the government's suppression of political protest and dissidence. The law established several procedures by which the authorities could rid themselves of troublesome dissent. Article 59 governed "commitment to a psychiatric hospital"; Article 60, the "assigning, changing, and terminating the application of compulsory measures of a medical character to mentally ill persons"; and Article 63, the "application of compulsory measures of medical character to alcoholics and drug addicts."

The roots of Soviet psychiatric terror in fact predate the Bolshevik Revolution. The first recorded case of Russian suppression of dissent by means of psychiatry goes back to one Pyotr Chaadayev (1793–1856), a philosopher and critic of the regime. In 1836 Czar Nicholas I claimed Chaadayev to be suffering from "derangement and insanity." By assuming an ostensibly benevolent stance toward the well-being of his subject, the czar "had in one neat stroke punished Chaadayev for publishing . . . a critical [article] of his regime, and at the same time discredited the ideas expressed therein by declaring that they were those of a sick mind."[76]

Upon these early beginnings, the postrevolutionary Soviet regime was able to build an elaborate system for the psychiatric punishment and control of political opponents. A study of some five hundred well-documented cases, in the period from 1962 to 1977, disclosed that psychiatric sanctions had been utilized against a wide range of deviants from the political and social conventions firmly laid down by the state. Most patients indeed consisted of (1) advocates of human rights or democratization, (2) nationalist activists, (3) would-be emigrants, and (4) religious believers.[77]

Born in idealistic fervor, the Soviet Revolution sought to create a politically and economically new man, *homo sovieticus*. This revolutionary promise, quickly extinguished by Lenin's Red Terror, ultimately led to Stalin's campaign to destroy the very soul of political man—to eliminate all thought not planted by authority, to crush even the possibility of dissent. In the case of the Soviet Union, this development led not only to repressions at home but also to the crushing of the 1953 East German uprising, the 1956 Hungarian revolt, and the Prague Spring of 1968. This tale of unfulfilled revolutionary promises turning into oppressive nightmares has recurred throughout the modern era as governments have continued to grapple with their own legitimacy as well as that of their political opponents.

Other totalitarian governments under Soviet influence resorted, in their war against dissidence and rebellion, to both traditional and innovative systems of oppression, control, and punishment. Vaguely defined offenses against "national security," as well as the flourishing of crimes such as "slandering socialist reality" and "economic crimes" were crafted to encompass even the mildest deeds or expressions challenging the totalitarian state, its ideology, or its leadership. The charge of "terrorism" was likewise misappropriated to encompass such conduct as efforts to escape from Marxist oppression in East Germany.[78]

Under totalitarian, authoritarian, or other one-party regimes, efforts to create competing political, social, and economic organizations have been deemed offenses against state security. Writing, publishing, or distribution of either fiction or nonfiction portraying or criticizing public and private conditions has often been viewed as sedition or as slander of the state. Even membership in primarily nonpolitical organizations—such as Solidarity, the independent labor union in Poland—was defined as a criminal offense. Placing posters, announcements, or signs in any public place other than those specifically designated by the authorities became a misdemeanor.[79] Accordingly, three persons were fined for laying wreaths bearing the legend "Solidarity" at the foot of a monument to the 1944 Warsaw uprising.[80]

Despite the Soviet Union's unusually harsh treatment of its political opponents, the communist "bloc" of nations was never as monolithic as it may have appeared to Western observers. The Soviet Union was not able to impose absolute uniformity upon its satellites. Emigration restrictions, a fixture in the Worker's Paradise, varied considerably in countries like Rumania and Cuba. The Rumanian government permitted, and at times actively encouraged, the emigration of selected populations—including ethnic Germans, Hungarians, and Jews. Cuban policy under Fidel Castro likewise placed few barriers in the path of those choosing to depart for political or economic reasons. With the contemporary disarray of the Soviet Union's former empire, this diversity has not only increased but has become the order of the day.

### THE DECLINE OF "POLITICALS" IN THE AGE OF TERROR

Generally, the belief that political offenders should be treated leniently—and should be exempted from extradition to the regimes against which they offended—gained acceptance from the international community throughout the nineteenth century. At the same time, however, nations were also coming to agree that some classes of actors and some acts of political dissidence should be excluded from the protections accorded to the "politicals." This negative reaction was the outcome of the growing fears of the threat of public disorder and possible anarchy posed by widespread and indiscriminate resort to political violence and terrorism.

The *clause d'attentat*, first formulated by Belgium in response to the attempted assassination of France's Napoleon III in 1856, set out to modify the international extradition treaties by denying the favored political offender status to assassins and assailants of heads of state or of their immediate families.[81] The *clause* served to define the limits of tolerance toward those challenging authority. Under the *clause*, which other nations quickly adopted, protection from extradition was no longer available to those who had perpetrated violence against kings, presidents, and other heads of states or their families.[82]

Criticizing the *clause*, I. A. Shearer insisted:

> It may be questioned whether there are not times in the history of some countries when assassination is the only practical means whereby the rule of a tyrant may be ended. On the other hand, if assassination should always be regarded as an excessive measure, not deserving of protection under extradition law, it may be questioned why the operation of the clause is restricted to heads of State and their immediate families [and does not] include . . . all government ministers and perhaps other officials as well.[83]

But despite this and other objections, the *clause d'attentat* became enshrined in the international law of extradition. Political activists were thus put on notice that no government repression, abuse of power, or even state terror can ever justify violence against the very individuals who serve as the symbols of state power.

The emergence of militant anarchism in the late nineteenth century spurred the creation of another class of political offenders that was not accorded protection from extradition. The globe-trotting and deliberately violent anarchists, who repudiated all governments and social organizations, were seen as qualitatively different from other political dissidents. Even the then distant United States was not spared their menacing presence—witness the 1901 assassination of America's president William McKinley by Leon Czolgosz, an expatriated anarchist. Viewing anarchists with profound abhorrence, representatives of a broad spectrum of political persuasions—from monarchists to republicans, from conservatives to liberals—agreed that they had to be stamped out.

In 1894 the English courts ruled on whether anarchist activity could qualify for the political crime exception. *In re Meunier*[84] involved an anarchist who escaped from France to England after exploding bombs in a crowded café and in an army barracks. The English court refused to recognize Meunier's crime as political. Judge Cave wrote:

> In order to constitute an offense of a political character, there must be two or more parties in the State, each seeking to impose the Government of their own choice on the other. . . . In the present case there are not [such two parties] . . . for the party with whom the accused is identified . . . by his own voluntary statement . . . is the enemy of all government. Their efforts are directed primarily against the general body of citizens.[85]

The decision reflected the prevailing view that anarchism was not a political movement or rebellion but rather a general threat to all nations. In 1902 the Pan American Convention lent further support to the *Meunier* decision, explicitly excluding anarchistic acts from consideration as political offenses.[86]

The anarchists' fate constituted the writing on the wall for those political activists whose conduct was to fall outside the specified and internationally acceptable boundaries of political conflict. In the early decades of the twentieth century, the political offender continued to be treated with leniency and with special consideration, but the social, economic, and political turmoil in the era before, between, and after the two world wars was also giving rise to a new global search for political stability. Governments dependent for survival upon fragile coalitions of divergent parties were no longer willing to tolerate the heavy domestic costs of a militant political opposition. The political offender suddenly seemed less an agent of needed political reform and more a destroyer of public order.

The twentieth century thus saw growing international restrictions on the activities of the political offender and a constriction of the political offense exception to extradition. As global diplomacy, travel, and business flourished, crimes against these institutions were increasingly seen as threats to the well-being of a newly interdependent world. Increasingly, the notion of international outlawry, a concept dating back to the ancient crime of piracy,[87] became institutionalized as a fixture of international law. Multinational conventions expanded the earlier doctrine of piracy as constituting a "crime against all nations" to encompass new offenses affecting the international community: counterfeiting,[88] white slavery,[89] and narcotics traffic.[90] These crimes not only were universally condemned but also were subjected to universal enforcement and extradition. The continuing movement to restrict the political offense exception and to assist in the international surrender of offenders charged with heinous crimes was further hastened by domestic laws such as the French Extradition Law of 1927, which provided that the political exception was not to apply to "acts of odious barbarism and vandalism prohibited by the laws of war."[91]

The world community's growing resolve to fight odious classes of political protest, resistance, and rebellion was greatly strengthened by the assassination of Yugoslavia's King Alexander during his 1937 visit to France. Especially troubling to the forces of law and order was France's inability to obtain the extradition of the suspected "political" offenders from Italy. One of the League of Nations' final acts, in 1938, was therefore to propose an international convention against terrorism, barring all resort to violent political means as well as any inducement, encouragement, or assistance for such actions.[92] The convention's objective was to establish that violent and nonparliamentary politics deserved no respect or tolerance from the international community of civilized nations.

But the League's hopes for an international system that would condemn, as well as prevent, political violence were ultimately destroyed in the conflagration of World War II. The war further demonstrated the futility of the League's dream of reducing political violence. At the war's conclusion, the underground resistance movements that had fought against Nazi, Fascist, and Japanese occupations were replaced by the new militant forces fighting for national liberation. As tribes, ethnic communities, regions, and entire nations sought to define their own destinies and territories, the remaining far-flung empires of Europe were shattered by rebellions and upheaval. The anticolonial struggles, from India's relatively peaceful campaign of civil disobedience to more violent outbursts in other parts of Asia and Africa, accounted for a dramatic growth in the number of independent countries—from the 65 members of the League of Nations to the United Nations' current roster of over 180 members.

The campaign against colonialism and for national self-determination combined with a new body of internationally proclaimed human rights to reinvigorate, in many ways, the nineteenth century's image of the political offender as a "noble" actor. At the same time, however, increased global interdependence (social, economic, and political) produced a steady and dramatic expansion in the scope of the international law, thereby restricting the weapons and means available to political offenders in their wars against authority and against other real or imagined enemies. As the international community developed new laws and procedures for apprehending and punishing those who transgress against the existing global order, the emerging body of "international crimes" acted to reduce and diminish the older safeguards that were introduced for the protection of political offenders.

The creation of an expanded class of universally condemned international crimes was hastened by the Nuremberg judgment at the conclusion of World War II. Building on the existing law of war, the Nuremberg tribunal first affirmed "war crimes" (as defined by the 1907 Hague Convention and the 1949 Geneva Conventions, "offenses against foreign nations, their nationals, and prisoners of war") as international offenses. The tribunal also affirmed "crimes against peace" as international offenses. Finally, it defined and recognized "crimes against humanity," making it possible for the first time in world history to punish a nation's abusive acts against its own citizens.

As enemies of all mankind (like the anarchists before them), those engaged in acts of international criminality could expect sanctuary from no nation. Stripped of the political offense exception, these enemies of all nations could expect prosecution wherever they sought to hide. Reinforcing these principles, the 1951 Convention Relating to the Status of Refugees specifically denied refugee status and protection to those who had "committed a crime against peace, a war crime, or a crime against humanity."[93]

Nearly a quarter of a century after the Nuremberg trials, the General Assembly of the United Nations followed this previous pattern by designating the South African institution of apartheid as "a crime against humanity."[94] Through resort to principles developed in the international war against piracy and slavery and further articulated by the Nuremberg tribunal and subsequent conventions, the international community can place an entire category of political activists and militants (claiming to be politically motivated) outside the traditional protections afforded to political offenders under extradition treaties as well as to lawful belligerents by the laws of war.[95]

The standing of the political offender was further curtailed by the 1948 Genocide Convention,[96] which set out to safeguard national, ethnic, racial, and religious communities. Making it an international crime to take the life of members of such communities, cause them serious bodily or mental harm, or deliberately inflict upon them conditions calculated to bring about their destruction, the Convention specifically proscribed genocide and related crimes from qualifying as political offenses. Moreover, it obligated all nations to grant extradition requests for those charged with genocide offenses.[97] On

November 25, 1988, after nearly four decades of American reticence, the United States ratified the Convention on the Prevention and Punishment of the Crime of Genocide.[98]

The campaign against war crimes, crimes against peace, crimes against humanity, and genocide thus crafted a category of international outlaws, echoing the ancient classes of brigands and pirates, whose members are to be shunned by all by being summarily placed outside the bounds of civilized society. But seeking to address other abuses of political power, beyond those manifested in warfare and in genocide, the community of nations faced great difficulties in reaching agreement about the international response to "terrorism."[99] As early as 1930, the Swiss Federal Tribunal ruled that terrorist offenses fell outside the political offense exception. Granting extradition in the case of one charged with terrorist activities, the court noted that "acts which are not . . . directed to the realization of a particular political object . . . but which serve merely terroristic ends  . . . cannot give rise to asylum."[100] The Supreme Court of Argentina took a similarly firm stance, declaring in 1968 that "extradition will not be denied where we are dealing with cruel or immoral acts which clearly shock the conscience of civilized peoples."[101]

Expanding on the nineteenth-century *attentat* exception, several contemporary treaties excluded all assassinations from protection as political offenses.[102] An example is the extradition agreement of the Council of the League of Arab States, approved on September 14, 1952, of which Egypt, Iraq, Jordan, Saudi Arabia, and Syria were signatories.[103] Though the agreement specifies that political offenders are not to be extradited between the member nations, it stipulates that the assassination of heads of state or their families, attempts on the lives of heirs to the throne, premeditated murder, or other acts of terrorism are not to be recognized as political offenses.[104]

In its continuing war against terrorism, the community of nations has chosen not so much to concentrate on a clarification of this ill-defined phenomena as on outlawing specific examples of terroristic conduct. By so doing the world community has demonstrated a remarkable readiness to condemn and punish as terroristic specified classes of politically related offenses, including those that are disruptive of essential international institutions (e.g., offenses against aircrafts)[105] or endanger international agents or other internationally protected persons (e.g., diplomats).[106] The designation of these selected classes of political criminality as being internationally proscribed imposes a duty on all cooperating nations not only to apprehend those charged with such conduct but also to subject them to either extradition or prosecution—a duty summarized by the maxim *aut dedere aut punire* ("extradite or punish").

There is ample evidence of a growing international desire to protect the world community against common enemies, a commitment that goes back to ancient efforts to suppress piracy. Emmerich de Vattel, writing in the mid-nineteenth century, concluded that persons who commit offenses against the human race "may be exterminated whenever they are seized." Vattel elaborated:

> Although the justice of each nation ought in general to be confined to the punishment of crimes committed in its own territories, we ought to except from this rule those villains, who, by the nature and habitual frequency of their crimes, violate all public security and declare themselves the enemies of the human race. [The latter] attack and injure all nations by trampling under foot the foundations of their common safety. [107]

Pursuing Vattel's mandate, in the concluding decades of the twentieth century the world community has made a decided movement toward defining an increasing number of internationally significant offenses as "universal." This movement testifies to the willingness of nations to forgo their political differences and to join in condemning, punishing, and denying "political" status to offenses against the indispensable institutions of the world community: diplomatic personnel, the freedom of the high seas, and the security of civil aviation.[108]

Advocates of political militancy have argued that the new international willingness, under the banner of a war against terrorism, to curb the privileged status previously extended to political offenders has gone overboard. They suggest that the lines between political offender, freedom fighter, insurgent, and terrorist have become blurred—intentionally confused by the ideological and rhetorical excesses of the forces of law and order. This confusion, they argue, makes all claims to political purpose and motive, however valid, seem inherently suspect. But while some political activists fear that allowing such confusion to continue may threaten the basic moral instincts of this nation and of similar liberty-striving democracies, others point to the urgent need to clearly differentiate between such noble rebels as George Washington and the terrorist madmen who sent a Pan-American planeload of 259 innocent passengers plummeting to earth at Lockerbie.

### POLITICAL DISSIDENCE, RESISTANCE, AND INSURGENCY AT THE END OF THE TWENTIETH CENTURY

The modern record of the political resister and rebel's treatment by the governments of Europe clearly demonstrates a continuing vacillation between extended eras of conservative repression and shorter periods of liberal permissiveness. While for more than a hundred years the liberal democracies of the West have been inclined toward leniency, this century's Bolshevik, Fascist, Nazi, and other totalitarian regimes have viewed and treated the political dissenter as their deadliest enemy. Furthermore, during the second half of this century, no predominant pattern of response to political unrest and rebellion has emerged within the world community of nations. Instead a great diversity of responses has been developed to deal with the increasingly troublesome phenomena of political rebellion, protest, resistance, and criminality—a diversity correlated with geographic regions, ideological camps, prevailing political systems, and specific time periods. Nevertheless, four major contemporary patterns or models of response to political opposition and resistance may be identified.

### THE TOTALITARIAN MODEL

The most drastically punitive responses to political dissidence have been offered by the modern totalitarian states. The records of Nazi Germany and the pre-1991 Soviet Union starkly illuminate the inevitability and tragic outcome of "abuse of power" wherever an absolutist and millennial ideology combines with an absolutist and pathological leadership.[109] Although Nazi- and Soviet-style absolutism appear to be rapidly falling out of favor around the world, any optimism must remain guarded during an era that has witnessed the sacrifice of over twenty million human lives on the altar of Leninism-Stalinism (excluding millions of others who were uprooted and forcibly resettled)[110] and the brutalization, enslavement, annihilation, and outright extermination of twenty-five million "undesirable" humans in the twelve brief years of the promised thousand-year Hitlerian Reich.

Within a relatively short span of time, this century's totalitarian extremes (Naziism-Fascism and Stalinism-Maoism) turned the elimination of political opponents into a brutal science. Racial, ethnic, religious, ideological, economic or other groups (e.g., non-Aryans, Jews, gypsies, Crimean Tartars, Jehovah's Witnesses, socialists, Kulaks, and homosexuals) were irrevocably assigned to the status of "state enemies." By such mere classification, the state's hunt for real and imagined opponents shifted from an emphasis on individual deeds and guilt to a system of unrelenting collective sanctions arbitrarily imposed upon designated classes and communities.

Still, unexpected changes in the status of the political offender have taken place during the past five years in the hitherto totalitarian states of Eastern Europe. The highly successful "Velvet Revolution" (so denominated by Vaclav Havel, the former president of Czechoslovakia) swept through the former six nations of the Eastern bloc (Bulgaria, Czechoslovakia, East Germany, Hungary, Rumania, and Poland), liberating the three formerly

Soviet-ruled Baltic states (Estonia, Latvia, and Lithuania), and turning the formerly centralized government of the remaining states of the former Soviet Union into a weak contemporary version of the old Holy Roman confederation—all with barely a gunshot. As oppressive political structures precipitously withered away, the cadres of the former Stalinist-Marxist party, police, and military stood relatively still in the face of the virtual dismantling of their old institutions of power. The transition from the old, communist authority to new, allegedly democratic institutions was also carried out with minimal changes in personnel and without the banishment or imposition of penal sanctions upon the former abusers of power.

One is reminded, in this connection, of Ingraham's portrayal of the nineteenth- and twentieth-century liberal leniency toward political oppositions and offenders as evidencing a tired bourgeoisie's death wish. Could the new and inexplicable "chivalry," exhibited by Eastern Europe's totalitarian regimes in their final days, likewise be attributed to a contemporary death wish on the part of an exhausted Marxism-Leninism-Stalinism?

As political liberty and diversity seem to be gradually replacing the stifling uniformity of totalitarianism throughout the world, an enthusiastic observer might be tempted to proclaim the arrival of the prophetic millennium. Indeed, although military and one-party regimes still prevail in much of Africa, Asia, and Latin America, only China, North Korea, and Cuba remain as reminders of the almost extinct monolithic communist state. Yet despite the prevailing view that we are now witnessing Western-style democracy's final triumph over totalitarianism (a victory begun with democracy's World War II defeat of Nazi Germany and militarist Japan), we must not become overconfident that the eternal war against abuse of power has been permanently won. It may be that we are seeing, in the lands of the former communist camp and elsewhere, only a transitional stage of readjustment and restructuring, masquerading as a turn to democracy. Opportunistic leaders may be merely proclaiming the slogans and symbols of democracy and legitimacy to woo Western and other political and financial support. While it seems certain that the socioeconomic institutions of Marxism-Leninism are being buried, it is by no means clear that the tools of political repression will be interred alongside the corpse. Already there are suggestions that old repressive methods may again be advanced and instituted by those in power, who will rationalize these methods by alleging new emergencies and the need to curtail growing ethnic, social, and economic unrest.

## THE DEMOCRATIC MODEL

The leniency exhibited by the democratic governments of the West toward political protesters and rebels stands in stark contrast to the harsh treatment meted out to dissidents by totalitarian regimes. Democracies have generally adopted a tolerant approach to the burgeoning ranks of political dissenters, a tolerance reflected particularly in the constant expansion of political and civil liberties through both legislative and judicial reform. This expansion of political rights has greatly depleted the power of the state over political activism. While a great number of traditional political offenses (particularly those involving acts of violence) continue to be treated as severe crimes, other prohibited forms of dissent and protest have been transformed into lawful conduct.

Although many of the regimes flying the banner of democracy have drastically narrowed the spectrum of political criminality through the decriminalization of most earlier speech, press, association, and status offenses, there has been little evidence of a general liberalization of attitudes toward political offenders as a group. The demands for leniency made by political offenders, claiming to constitute a class of altruistic and nonvenal actors, have thus remained unheeded.

Admittedly, the growing recognition of the right to speak critically and provocatively of authority has meant, in the United States and in other democracies, that such historical offenses as sedition and political conspiracy have withered away. The recognition of the right to belong to unorthodox political organizations has eviscerated former "unlawful membership" offenses. Other forms of political conduct once perceived as criminal now come within the safeguards offered under civil and political rights. Labor has won the right to organize and to engage in collective action. Women have obtained the right to political franchise. And demands for social and political justice by people of color, immigrants, homosexuals, and other minorities are being received with increased understanding and sympathy.

Yet against the background of this growing liberalization, questionable exceptions continue to persist. Throughout the democratic world lawmakers and the judiciary continue to turn a deaf ear toward pleas for leniency from selectively disfavored political dissenters. Some Western European nations (not yet fully recovered from their Nazi or Fascist experiences) consider the renewed advocacy of totalitarian doctrines unacceptable. The West German Constitution, seeking to redeem the nation from its past, specifically outlawed Naziism as an ideology and as a political party.[111] Similarly, the Communist Party, as well as its members and sympathizers, were singled out for persistent persecution in the United States for nearly seven decades, and particularly during the McCarthy period—although throughout the same era other democracies, including France and the United Kingdom, continued to tolerate domestic Communist parties and activities.[112] Similar selectivity with regard to political liberty has been applied toward adherents of the Palestine Liberation Organization in Israel, as well as toward members of fundamentalist Muslim organizations in many westernized Arab countries. The Provisional Irish Republican Army continues to be outlawed in Great Britain, and for a long time organizations agitating for racial justice in South Africa were viewed as terroristic, and members were subjected to particularly harsh and extraordinary penalties.[113]

Other than in these exceptional cases, the relative political stability that has characterized the domestic affairs of the democratic nations during the last third of the twentieth century acts to enhance these countries' lenient attitudes toward political dissenters and activists. The relative political calm has been responsible not only for the expansion of political and civil rights, and thus a constant narrowing of the types and classes of prohibited political activity, but also for a leniency in sentencing practices and a willingness to offer amnesties to convicted political offenders.

## THE AUTHORITARIAN MODEL

Between the two hitherto described extremes—the cruel repression in the totalitarian camp, on one hand, and the leniency of the liberal West, on the other—lie the zealous, intolerant, and frequently inconsistent policies carried out by the Third World *authoritarian* regimes toward their real and imagined political opponents. Although these regimes (unlike their *totalitarian* cousins in the Fascist and Marxist camps) have not sought total control over all facets of their nations' political, economic, and social life, they are, nevertheless, set apart from the democracies of the West due to their non-elective and often military-based forms of governance.[114]

This *authoritarian* group of countries offers yet another perspective on the contemporary treatment of political protesters and rebels. Inherently unstable, these regimes must feel compelled to resist the divisive, centrifugal forces emanating from clan rivalries, interregional hostilities, and colonially perpetuated class structures. The leaders of these nations often emerge from tribal or proletarian origins. They tend to come to power through extralegal means—having little interest or faith in legitimizing their authority through electoral politics. After dealing harshly with their own predecessors, many of these leaders and ruling cliques severely restrict access to power for all but their own hand-picked successors.

Many of the authoritarian regimes—in Africa, Latin America, and Asia—have managed to combine the worst features of Stalinist Marxism (apathy, crushing bureaucracy, and institutionalized terror) with the flaws of capitalism (socioeconomic injustice, corporate corruption, and personal greed). Political conflict and constant unrest become inevitable when these Third World regimes attempt to solve their many problems through a single absolutist doctrine, such as religious fundamentalism, Marxism, or Maoism; a centralized "command" economy; one-party rule; favoritism for certain tribes, clans, or ruling classes; or, finally, a personality cult, such as Peronism, Aminism, Duvalierism, Marcosism, Kaddafism, or Saddamism.

Some commentators have suggested that the authoritarian regimes of Latin America and of postcolonial Africa and Asia—despite their resort to death squads, kidnappings, disappearances, secret tribunals,[115] and other methods for the brutal liquidation of political opponents—have retained some nineteenth-century chivalry toward political opponents. Although authoritarian governments have often resorted to inappropriately declared "states of emergency,"[116] "states of siege," and "martial law"[117] to tighten their grip over unruly or restless populations, they have on occasion shown inexplicable gallantry toward their opponents. At the conclusion of successful coups d'état in such places as the Dominican Republic, Uganda, or Ethiopia, deposed heads of state have often been allowed to discreetly depart in peace. In other places they have been ceremoniously delivered to the nation's airport—with one-way travel arrangements. Former political luminaries in countries such as Syria, Yemen, or Haiti, finding themselves out of favor with their ruling allies, have often been extended appointments to their country's diplomatic posts in distant capitals. Even commanders of failed military rebellions have occasionally been allowed to depart in peace. Evidently, newly established regimes may prefer their challengers' departure overseas to an unexplained death or a politically sensitive prosecution at home.

### THE HUMANITARIAN LAW MODEL

A fourth contemporary approach to political offenses and their perpetrators revolves not around the nature of the responding government (whether democratic, totalitarian, or authoritarian) but around the magnitude of political disturbances or rebellion. Many countries, regardless of ideological stripes, have afforded special treatment to participants in civil wars or mass protests, particularly where those rebelling against the government command the support of a large segment of the population. Countries as geographically and ideologically diverse as Afghanistan, Ethiopia, Nicaragua, and Israel have chosen in recent years to respond to their political opponents (particularly when they constituted a large and quasi-military community, such as the Mujaheddin, Contras, or Intifada activists) not as criminals but as quasi-warriors. By treating armed opponents as if they were de facto belligerents, governments have in fact accorded domestic insurgents some of the same protections available under international law to enemy soldiers.

Rebels are not thereby granted protection from the hazards of death or injury, which are inherent in any conflict or war. But granting injured or surrendered rebels the equivalent of prisoner-of-war status is an admission of the honor and legitimacy long withheld from domestic rebels.

This growing, though unheralded, injection of the rules and practices of international war into domestic conflicts has been vigorously supported, in recent years, by the International Committee of the Red Cross. But the practice is not a modern innovation. As previously noted, the British, despite their determined effort to subdue the American rebellion, adhered to a similar practice, and no American patriot was tried and executed for treason during the War of Independence. The Union Army in America's Civil War also followed the same practice. No Southern rebel was tried and executed for the offense of treason either during or after the War between the States.[118]

Many contemporary contests between those in authority and those proclaiming autonomy (confrontations that historically might have been considered totally domestic) are being increasingly perceived as quasi-international conflicts in which the international law of warfare is expected to play a role. Where domestic laws and practices regarding political offenders once went totally unchallenged by the community of nations, the impact of international standards of warfare are now being felt. The countries of the post–World War II world have grown to view the national treatment of political rebels as bearing on the world community's well-being. How a given country or regime sanctions its political offenders is no longer viewed as a totally domestic matter. Increasingly, domestic political activists are of interest not only to world media and public opinion but also to the United Nations and other international agencies and to practitioners of international law.

As the twentieth century draws to an end, one must recognize the rich diversity of the prevailing worldwide responses to the threats posed by political dissidents. These "rebels" inevitably bring forth unique responses from the regimes they set out to sensitize, reform, or overthrow. While totalitarian regimes have indiscriminately expanded the reaches of political criminality in an effort to stifle even the least-threatening expressions of popular opposition, the Western democracies have traveled an opposite road, liberalizing and decriminalizing political activity. The third approach, exemplified by unstable Third World regimes, combines brutal suppression of dissent with occasional displays of generosity—however self-serving—toward defeated opponents. The fourth formula (followed in most instances when mass rebellion or insurgency becomes too large a problem for domestic criminal law enforcement) de-emphasizes the political rebel's criminality and advances his or her belligerency status. An implicit admission by the ruling authority that its power is being seriously contested, this approach also reflects the hope for reciprocal treatment if things go badly for those newly assuming the reins of power.

## Part Four

# FROM THE CRISIS OF AUTHORITY TO THE RESTORATION OF LEGITIMACY

The voice of the people is the voice of God . . . [but] the voice of the mob is near akin to madness.

—Alcuin, "Letter to Charlemagne," *Works*

# CHAPTER EIGHT

# Legitimacy in a Pluralistic World

The verdict of the World is conclusive.

—Saint Augustine

All political societies are composed of other, smaller groups of different types, each of which has its interests and maxims. . . . The will of these smaller groups always must be examined from two distinct perspectives: for the members of the small group, it is a general will; for the large society, it is a private will, which is very often found to be upright with regard to the smaller group and vicious with regard to the larger society.

—Rousseau, *Political Economy*

## THE CRISIS OF LEGITIMACY
## AND THE FUTURE OF PUBLIC ORDER

For nearly a century and a half, a number of prominent philosophers, political scientists, and sociologists (beginning with Karl Marx and Friedrich Nietzsche) have been voicing their concern over the growing challenges facing political legitimacy in the age of modernity.[1] To place these warnings in proper perspective, the reader is invited to turn back to the Prologue, in which we stressed the significance of legitimacy as a central component in the stability of political life and governance. We pointed out there, moreover, that even among the most ancient and primitive of clans, tribes, and other human congregations, those in control had sought to fortify themselves by something both more transcendental and more binding than the mere possession and exercise of naked or de facto power. This striving for a more enduring justification of the right to govern can be described as a quest for "legitimacy."

Legitimacy, pointed out Italian political philosopher Gaetano Mosca in

1896,[2] is sought by the ruling class through the advancing and acceptance of a "political formula"—a metaphysical or ideological formula that justifies the existing exercise or proposed possession of power by rulers as the logical and necessary consequence of the beliefs of the people over whom the power is exercised. Most recently, the United States Supreme Court, in a similar vein, noted that "the Court's power lies in its legitimacy, a product of substance and perception that shows itself in the people's acceptance of the judiciary as fit to determine what the Nation's law means and to declare its demands."[3]

A rich variety of doctrines—mythical, transcendental, and rational—some proclaiming the "divine rights" of princes and kings or the entitlements of patrimony or seniority, others professing the duties due elders and parents or the obligations imposed by "nationalism," the "social contract," and "majoritarianism"—have long supplied the requisite political formulas to legitimate authority, east and west, north and south. Attempting to classify former and existing legitimating doctrines, German sociologist Max Weber emphasized three categories: the "patrimonial," the "rational-bureaucratic," and the "charismatic."[4] In the first, authority seeks to legitimate itself through resort to what Weber describes as the "eternal yesterday"—the ancient and traditional customs and habits that endow the patriarch or patrimonial prince with the right of domination. In the second category, legitimation is derived from a resort to legal, rational, and bureaucratic means. Here domination is justified by virtue of the belief in the validity and binding effect of existing laws and political institutions. The charismatic category, according to Weber, describes a process of legitimation founded on the extraordinary and personal gifts of grace possessed by the leader, and on the people's devotion and confidence in the leader's "revelation, heroism, or other qualities of individual leadership."[5]

History has seen the emergence, decline, and return of the various legitimation categories enumerated by Weber. History has also given rise to other formulas of legitimation. But regardless of the specific categories or formulas advanced or accepted by various nations and states in the modern era, a growing number of political philosophers have been arguing that the overall legitimacy of the state's authority has been declining.[6] The forecasting of the decline of the modern state's legitimacy goes back to Karl Marx and Friedrich Nietzsche. Marx, writing in 1844, attributed legitimacy's decline to the particular structure and defects of modern capitalism, which alienate man from society and authority.[7] Nietzsche, speaking in 1888, saw legitimacy's major problem as the "advent of nihilism."[8]

Later political analysts and social critics, including Seymour Martin Lipset, John H. Schaar, Jürgen Habermas, and Michel Foucault, have attributed the crisis of the modern state's legitimacy to such diverse causes as over-bureaucratization and the proliferation of rules (that in the end foster a spirit

of evasion), the erosion of traditionalism, the decline of general public morality and civil culture, and the expansion of the cult of individualism. Lipset
urges that "if at any time the status of the major conservative groups is threatened, or if access to politics is denied to emerging groups at crucial periods,
the system's legitimacy will . . . [be put] in question."[9] He points out also
that the legitimacy, and therefore the stability, of government depends
on economic development as well as on the effectiveness of the political system (p.88).

Inadequately answered by these forecasters, however, is the question of
whether the contemporary decline of legitimacy is unique or a recurring
phenomenon in world history. Lipset, who attributed the emergence of the
crises of legitimacy to the drastic social, economic, and political changes
brought about by the age of modernity, claimed nearly two decades ago that
the crises are a "recent historical phenomenon" (pp.88–89). Adding to Marx's
and Nietzsche's warnings concerning alienation and the advent of nihilism,
Lipset suggested that crises of legitimacy are in great part the outcome of
growing and "sharp cleavages among groups which are able, because of mass
communication, to organize around different values [and structures] than
those previously considered to be the only acceptable ones" (p.88). Other
recent commentators have expanded the list or have merely reiterated the
effects of the demise of mythology and traditionalism and of the unprecedented emphasis on individualism and its primacy—all of which combined
to undercut support for more communal agendas and institutions.

It is also interesting that the prophets of the "crisis of legitimacy" have
centered their attention, by and large, on the status and affairs of the modern state. It is to the declining efficacy of the political formulas of old, and
to the ever more precarious stability of the modern stare, that they have
addressed themselves. Little attention has been directed by them to similarly pressing questions of legitimacy in such other human settings and
institutions as the church, the family, the school, or the workplace.

Without a doubt, the Protestant Reformation's challenge to the alleged
"revolting pride" of the Roman Catholic Church, and Martin Luther's
Ninety-five Theses, nailed to the door of the Wittenberg church on October
31, 1517, produced a monumental crisis of authority in the then Christian
world. Luther's extremely lucid language reverberates with surprisingly
modern terms: "I say, then, neither pope, nor bishop, nor any man whatever
has the right of making one syllable binding on a Christian man, unless it be
done with his own consent. Whatever is done otherwise is done in the spirit of tyranny."[10]

Yet with the passage of time, issues of legitimacy in Christianity (as well
as in Judaism, Islam, and most other religious denominations) have failed to
receive due public and secondary attention. The Christian church has con-

tinually found itself unable to keep up with rapidly shifting material and spiritual situations and with the changing values and expectations of its flock, despite its numerous attempts to restore scriptural legitimacy, which produced hundreds of splinter groups (Lutheran, Pentecostal, Baptist, Quaker, and others too numerous to detail) that wrote their own scriptures and, in many cases, splintered even further. Today one can see further challenges to the authority and legitimacy of widely fragmented Christian, Jewish, Moslem, and other churches. In America and throughout the world, within Christianity and outside, a battle is being waged between religious and secular legitimacy, between fundamentalism and reformism. Abortion, the role of women in religious practice, social justice, liberation theology—all create new challenges to authority. But comprehensive assessments or solutions are nowhere in sight.

Much of the same neglect has long befallen the crises of legitimacy in the family, school, and workplace. With more than half of all marriages in the United States ending in divorce and with 30 percent of the nation's children being born out of wedlock,[11] the evidence of the American family's social and legal pathology is overwhelming. That schools suffer from a similar malaise regarding the validity of their authority and the credibility of their educational mission is testified to not only by rampant schoolroom violence but also by the declining confidence of parents as well as employers in the quality of the finished educational products. The workplace, too, is not immune to problems of legitimacy. While some attempts have been made to legitimize the authority of the workplace, notably the union movement, management's right to rule tends to be enforced in an old-fashioned way through the carrot of paychecks and the stick of termination.

But the main thrust of this volume cannot be diverted, at this late time, toward critically needed assessments of legitimacy in the family, school, workplace, or other traditional institutions of society. Our task calls for a return to the crisis of legitimacy within the so-called modern nation-state.

For a long time concerns about the declining legitimacy of the state appeared to be mostly theoretical, as there were few symptoms of malaise. But this is no longer the case. The recent and unprecedented growth of political turmoil and disorder worldwide, coupled with familial, religious, and other institutional declines, compels us to face the continuously haunting questions: Is the current global unraveling of authority indeed a manifestation of the chronic and long-predicted crisis of legitimacy, or is it the product of passing (seasonal or periodic) factors? In either case, what, if anything, can be done to help restore the legitimacy of authority and begin the reconstruction of public order?

Any further endeavor to refine the etiology of the crisis of authority and to project the prospects for worldwide public order in the decades to come must go much beyond the reiteration of the Preface's claim that "as the twentieth century draws to a close, undeclared yet unceasing civil and communal wars rage around the globe." The forecasting of the future of domestic tranquility requires first that we distill firmer data and more detailed conclusions from the historical accounts of the American and global struggles between authority and autonomy (contained in Chapters Three, Four, Five, Six, and Seven). We must further reconsider, in light of that history, the continuing validity of the analytical formulations and the prospective strength of the dialectical forces originally introduced in the Prologue.

The former chapters aptly demonstrate that despite the expansion and growth of the social, psychological, and political sciences, little has been attained in curtailing the incidence of domestic political discontent, resistance, and conflict during the final decades of the twentieth century. What more are we expected to have learned (from this book's sweeping historical and contemporary panoramas of political protest and rebellion) that might affect the prospects for intranational public order in both the near and distant future? What evidence can be derived from sources other than those previously discussed, whether scholarly or otherwise, to help further elucidate potentials for a future community of countries and peoples free of domestic conflicts and violence? What conclusions, finally, can we reach regarding the historical utility of the eternal struggle between authority and autonomy—and how are we to balance its sometimes beneficial and sometimes corrosive effects on governance, society, and individuals?

As the twentieth century draws to a close, grave challenges are posed by the current war against authority not only to the trappings but also to the very foundations of authority. From violence-ridden schoolrooms to abortion clinic bombings, from recurring abuses of power in Haiti and civil disobedience by public officials in the United States to the mindless killings of innocent Catholics and Protestants in Northern Ireland,[12] from the Los Angeles riots to the ethnic wars in the former Soviet Union, Yugoslavia, and Africa, the devastating effects of the war against authority are widely felt. As Senator Patrick Moynihan vividly notes in his recent book, *Pandaemonium*, the war against authority, unchecked and lacking guiding philosophical, moral, or legal principles, has reached a disastrous stage.[13]

What is currently needed, therefore, in the marketplace of ideas and in the public awareness, is not a further foretelling of the doom to be brought about by racial and ethnic conflict, tribalism, fundamentalism, or other challenges to authority. This warning task has already been performed by many authors and writings.[14] What is lacking in the recent literature and discussions regarding the ongoing worldwide unraveling of authority is a deeper historical and analytical examination of the roots of the problem and the direction of necessary remedies.

Some commentators, among them Robert Kaplan, have attributed the escalating worldwide chaos to a variety of material causes, including population explosion, environmental abuse, and nationalistic aberrations.[15] Samuel Huntington, on the other hand, claims that material or economic causes are not the fundamental sources of the existing and the widely expected future strife.[16] He insists further that the source of conflict in the New World will not be primarily ideological, but emphasizes instead the importance of "culture" and "civilization" in the etiology of conflict. Huntington, however, fails to recognize the sociopsychological force of legitimacy (which includes what was previously identified by Mosca as the "political formula")[17] and the important role it plays in the dynamics of the eternal conflict between authority and autonomy. While culture and civilization do play a part in both international and domestic conflicts, it may be that their manifestation as catalysts of strife assumes critical importance only after an initial erosion or delegitimization of existing authority.

In making civilizational differences the primary culprits of future strife, Huntington fails to explain, however, why differing civilizations are bound to find themselves in increasing conflict situations. Huntington possibly wants us to deduce from his skeletal thesis that it is inherent in the nature of all civilizations to seek to convert all others by whatever means possible, whether pacific or militant. If that indeed is the Huntingtonian premise, then we must once more address ourselves to the substantial rather than merely superficial or "cosmetic" issues which divide and pitch civilizations against each other. These issues, one might suggest, possibly revolve around the primary question of how legitimacy of authority is conceived and how crises of legitimacy are to be overcome in diverse cultures. Possibly the most critical cultural or civilizational conflicts of modernity could be distilled to the choice between a return to and a greater reliance upon eternal, "natural," or "scriptural" sources of legitimacy, and an opposite effort to search for and implement a restructured, "democratic," consensual, and ever-changing social contract.

The mission of this book is to advance the discussion regarding the roots of chaos and its cures: not to offer a talisman or panacea, but to urgently seek understanding as well as approaches to remedial ways and means. In its search for remedies, this book has earlier undertaken a detailed examination of past and present wars against authority to reveal their protagonists, their nourishing roots, their rhetoric and doctrinal underpinnings, their processes and their attainments, as well as their failings. Following this examination, we will now undertake to explore the restructuring or possible creation of philosophical and jurisprudential principles and guidelines that might give rise to more just, as well as more effective, responses to the ongoing and future wars against authority. In approaching this task, it becomes increasingly evident that the empty rhetoric accompanying former President Bush's proclamation of a "New World Order" after the perceived end of the Cold War has not sufficed to stem the tide of the newly emerging strife. Much more than a mere slogan is needed to supply the world community with both new legitimizing principles of authority and stabilizing institutions of governance.

This century's profusion of international, regional, and local wars; the drastic relocation of traditional labor, capital, production, and trade centers; and the unrelenting pressures of urbanization and of racial, ethnic, social, economic, and gender mobility have all dramatically affected the power structures of countries, communities, and families. Unprecedented global migrations, growing interracial, interethnic, intergender, and interreligious competition (only sometimes modified by a spirit of cooperation), have caused the breakdown of many traditional social, economic, and political norms and relationships.

Since it is no longer possible to rely on the continued segregation of diverse peoples or on the static maintenance of the status quo between majorities and minorities, the rich and the poor, men and women, young and old, pluralistic coexistence, peaceful or otherwise, is the order of the future. The new era's principles of politics and governance can therefore no longer rely on traditional, archaic, and exclusive notions of legitimacy. Pluralistic societies must foster and rely upon pluralistic doctrines of legitimacy. Yet while such old doctrines as divine rights, state sovereignty, the nation-state, familial duty, and even the social compact and majoritarianism have been challenged, few new principles of social organization, cohesion, and legitimacy have been introduced to take their place. The path toward a new, constantly changing, pluralistic yet cooperative world order is evidently a difficult one. But it is one for which the United States might be able to provide foundation stones, as well as building experience. The lessons learned from America's pursuit of life, liberty, and happiness, from the eighteenth to the twentieth century, as well as from its own violent history and successful reconciliations, might well qualify for the preparation of an instructional manual to prevent here and elsewhere the repetition of similar or even worse bloodshed in the century to come.

## LOOKING FOR THE LODESTAR
## WHILE GROPING IN THE DARK

Pitirim Sorokin's classic study of peace and war on the European Continent and throughout the European empires, spanning the fifth century B.C. to the twentieth century A.D., concluded that during the twenty-five hundred years in question, the purportedly civilized European community enjoyed an average of not more than four peaceful years for each year of violent conflict.[18] Ted Robert Gurr's survey of more contemporary history disclosed an equally troubling record. During the past two centuries, ten of the thirteen most deadly world conflicts—including the American Civil War, as well as the Soviet, Chinese, Spanish, and Nigerian civil wars—were not international but domestic wars and rebellions. Violent internal conflicts were reported in 114 out of the 121 countries surveyed by Gurr in the period between 1961 and 1968.[19] "Since 1945," Gurr noted in 1970, "violent attempts to overthrow governments have been more common than national elections."[20]

Although the concluding decade of the twentieth century has seen the generally unexpected demise of communist totalitarianism—a monumental event contributing to a worldwide shift toward more democratic governance[21]—the historical patterns of international and domestic conflict and warfare have not abated. The conclusion of the Cold War, as already seen, not only has created new power and legitimacy vacuums but also has failed to do away with or modify other domestic and international rivalries and dissatisfactions. Speaking of the future, Robert S. McNamara, former United States secretary of defense and World Bank president, warned:

> I'm not so naïve as to believe this post-cold-war world would be without conflict. There have been 125 wars leading to 40 million deaths, largely in the third world, after World War II and before the Gulf War. These were not a function of ideological differences between East and West. They were a function of the age-old causes of war—boundary disputes, economic conflicts, ethnic tensions.[22]

Ignoring such compelling testimony, America's government and community of scholars have, by and large, stubbornly and erroneously continued to deny that political unrest and resistance remain serious domestic problems, thus tending also to overlook the growing crisis abroad. They have persisted in their unwillingness to direct attention to political dissidence and rebellion as a distinct and potentially expanding category of criminality and disorder, and in their insistence that the United States' future is unlikely to be substantially affected by this malaise. Yet the vulnerability of the United States not only to its own old stock of militants but also to a growing number of newly arrived immigrants and illegal aliens, transporting to these shores Old World hostilities, was clearly demonstrated by the 1993 assassinations near the CIA's headquarters in greater Washington,[23] as well as by the bombing of the World Trade Center in New York City.[24] Both events have been attributed simply to men with relatively recent ties to America.

America's continuing refusal to scrutinize its own domestic "Pandora's box" of political dissidence and crime has prevented the collection of relevant statistical and other data from which one could begin to consider the future prospects for politically connected domestic violence. The gap in information is startling, given the glut of general criminal materials that have been collected and published in the United States in recent decades.

Crime and punishment are admittedly of grave concern, as well as being big business and major employers in America. In 1993 nearly 800,000 police officers derived their livelihood from combating crime. The total number of inmates in state and federal prisons and jails in June of 1994 exceeded 1,012,000, up from 315,947 in 1980; and the number of prison guards, correctional officers, and others engaged in the supervision of convicted offenders exceeded 555,000.[25] Some 224,000 persons were serving as judges or as lesser functionaries of the judicial branch. Another 117,000 were engaged in prosecutorial functions, some 15,000 in public defense work, and more than 7,000 in miscellaneous criminal justice assignments.[26] An unspecified percentage of the 744,000 members of the private legal profession devoted some portion of their practice to the defense of criminal cases.[27] The more than 14 million offenses reported to police in 1993 provided the fuel that stoked this elaborate machinery.[28]

In 1969, at what seemed the height of the country's post–World War II domestic political unrest, United States Senator John McClellan warned the nation against a terrorist "war against the police" and a "wave of guerrilla warfare" slashing America.[29] Yet no government agency, nor any private organization, had set out systematically to analyze the kinds or frequency of political dissidence and crime that emerged thereafter in America—violent or nonviolent, individual or collective. Because of this lack of recordkeeping, the extent of political unrest and strife in the United States remains impossible to measure.

How much political resistance and criminality have taken place in America during the past several decades? What segment of the country's disorder and disharmony are attributable to politically related dissidence and rebellion? What do we know about periodic fluctuations, growth, and decline in this area? One seeking a response to these fundamental questions finds few answers in the existing literature or in the traditional research approaches. Both private reports and official records relating to political unrest and crime are deficient and unrevealing.

Unlike other categories of public disorder and criminality, where law enforcement reports, victim complaints, and victimization surveys are used to measure the extent of the problem, offenses against authority are not identified or tabulated. The *1978 Statistical Abstract of the United States* listed only one class of crimes that it defined as "political"—political assaults and assassinations. The compiled data was supposed to include all attacks "on persons holding political office or upon any individuals or groups for political reasons." Without a reservation, the *Abstract* reported an incredible total of merely eighty-one political assaults and assassinations in the United States between 1835 and 1968.[30] To reach this outcome, both the Civil War and the Reconstruction era violence had to be totally overlooked. Not surprisingly, no follow-up tabulation of political criminality has been attempted.

More recently, however, the U.S. Justice Department's *Sourcebook on Criminal Justice Statistics* began in 1984 to focus on the specific phenomenon of international terrorism as it affected American citizens or property, domestically and overseas.[31] Included in this data have been incidents of kidnapping, hostage taking, bombing, armed attacks, hijacking, assassination, sniping, threats, hoaxes, and other forms of terror. The compilations reflected a significant worldwide growth in terrorism from a total of 224 incidents in 1973 to 401 in 1982. Yet in 1982 only 14 incidents of international terrorism were reported in all of North America, including 4 bombings, 4 hijackings, 2 snipings, and 4 hoaxes. In 1991 a total of 23 American citizens were reported as casualties of international terrorism.[32] The same year, the total number of international terrorist incidents reported worldwide reached 557, with half of them occurring during the two months of Operation Desert Storm.[33] These United States government reports, while belying Senator McClellan's 1969 forecast of a wave of guerrilla warfare in America and providing pathetically little support for the often-repeated calls for a total American war against "terrorism," do not serve as appropriate indicators of the general erosion of public confidence in and support for governmental authority.

One will seek in vain, among different official sources, for other information about political legitimacy and its defiance in contemporary America. The *1985 Sourcebook of Criminal Justice Statistics* did supply some data on various categories of crime likely to attract politically motivated perpetrators. Under the classification of "skyjacking," a total of 270 occurrences was reported in the United States for the period between 1968 and 1984.[34] Yet in the period from 1985 to 1990, the number of these occurrences dropped to 20.[35]

Bombing incidents may also carry strong political undertones. Of a total of 2,074 successful as well as attempted bombings reported in the United States in 1975, 76 targeted law enforcement buildings and vehicles, 62 involved other government property, and 11 involved international establishments. The selection of these public targets may suggest political motives, but official records fail to document such connections or to explain the sudden drop in reported bombings to 687 in 1983,[36] or the subsequent rise to 1,528 occurrences in 1990.[37] It is noteworthy also that out of nearly 85,000 arson incidents reported in 1990, over 4,000 were directed against public structures, once more suggesting possibilities of political grievances.[38] Similarly, some 1,112 assaults on state and local law enforcement officers in 1990 reportedly resulted from civil disorders and riots.[39]

Despite these fragments of governmental data, no clear picture of the current status of the growing challenge to legitimacy emerges. No existing public records compile such political crimes as treason, sedition, or political conspiracies, which are inextricably connected to opposition to authority. Neither do official statistics tabulate such offenses as civil disobedience, draft evasion, and desertion, or politically motivated tax evasion.

But even if appropriate statistical categories were established for politically motivated offenses, there would still probably continue to be gross deficiencies in the data. In many instances, political violations are directed against governmental institutions rather than against individuals, and therefore do not result in widely circulated victim complaints. Since the government, its agencies, and its authority are the ones primarily affected by treason, sedition, espionage, prohibited foreign travel, or membership in outlawed political parties, information on violations might be deliberately suppressed out of fear of public embarrassment or in the interest of continued surveillance.

Most political offenses, testifying to an underlying loss of confidence in the legitimacy of authority, do not readily come to police and public attention until they reach a state of open confrontation. Many political offenses are carried out in a clandestine and furtive manner. Behind every known dissenter, rioter, and bomber there may be therefore hundreds of those who remain quietly disgruntled and constitute potential conspirators. For every open confrontation there may be scores of aborted conspiracies.

Unlike ordinary criminals, political offenders, finally, are often possessed by an urge to tell the world of their exploits, even claiming credit for the offenses of others. In their struggle against authority, political activists have learned therefore to conduct their campaigns not only on the battle fronts but also on bulletin boards, newspaper pages, and, most important, on the television screen. In so seeking to demoralize their enemies, political activists are often given to grave exaggerations of their numbers and their attainments.

The measurement of political dissatisfaction as well as the forecasting of potential disquiet continue to be greatly hampered by absent and questionable data. Only once in United States history has a comprehensive survey of political crime been undertaken. A 1969 report by the National Commission on the Causes and Prevention of Violence concluded that during the preceding five years more than two million Americans had participated in collective demonstrations, riots, and terrorism to further various political agendas. "No more than a fifth of them took part in activities proscribed by law, but their actions reportedly resulted in more than 9,000 casualties, including some 200 deaths, and more than 70,000 arrests," noted the report.[40]

The National Commission also reported that in the mid-1960s the United States experienced more civil and political agitation than most other nations.[41] Although America was ranked twenty-fourth in the severity of civil disturbances compared with other nations, the total number of reported incidents exceeded the world average. About 11 of every 1,000 Americans took part in civil or political strife, compared with an average of 7 per 1,000 of the population in other countries.

The most illuminating comparison, however, comes from contrasting America with the seventeen other democratic nations on the European Continent and with the United Kingdom. The United States experienced more overall disturbances than any of the European countries, even though the strife tended to be less intense. Regarding America's worldwide ranking, the Violence Commission Staff Report observed that "with few exceptions, the countries more strife-torn than the United States [had actually] experienced internal wars, like Venezuela, Algeria and Indonesia."[42] How the United States ranks at this time we cannot tell. No follow-up assessment was undertaken, and, consequently, no reliable tracing of American political strife trends can be made.

Seeking historical perspectives, the National Commission also undertook in 1969 to examine the earlier record of political violence in the United States. A review of newspaper reports, spanning the years 1819 to 1968, culled reported cases of political violence during that 150-year period. Included in the categories studied were events involving "an attack on an official or group of officials for any reason or an attack on an individual or group of individuals for political or social reasons."[43] Labor violence was included, as were other incidents rising out of economic, racial, religious, or political conflicts. The events of the Civil War were excluded, and these alone involved a total of nearly two million rebel combatants in the South, or nearly one-tenth of the combined populations of both the Union and the Confederacy.

The 150-year evidence accumulated by the commission demonstrated, once more, that the problem of political violence in America is not new. "By its very persistence," asserted the commission staff, "it is a serious . . . problem for our society . . . for its roots run very deep."[44] Even so, these conclusions are based on partial evidence only. Charged with investigating public violence only, the National Violence Commission addressed only collective and openly conducted strife, excluding less visible types and varieties of unlawful activity carried out for political reasons. Particularly neglected was individual as well as group conduct short of violence—including strikes, draft and tax evasion, and other illegal actions—in the pursuit of political protest, reform, and rebellion. The statistical and analytical record of political dissatisfaction and strife in America has thus remained literally unknown to scholars and policymakers alike.

## A REBELLIOUS NATION NO MORE?
## THE VULNERABILITIES OF AMERICA

Many in America continue to believe, or at least to assert, that their country is substantially unique, that its major trials ended with the Revolutionary and Civil Wars (or with the civil rights reforms of the mid-twentieth century) and that their land will stand henceforth aloof from the strife that engulfs other people. The citizens of other countries often hold similar beliefs. Occurrences such as the French Revolution, the signing of England's Magna Carta, the launching of the Glorious Revolution, the Khomeini Revolution in Iran, or more recently Eastern Europe's "Velvet Revolution" are sometimes viewed as mythological, epochal dividing lines between a turbulent past and an everlasting tranquil future. But history has demonstrated that neither the divine commandments of antiquity, the democratically based social compacts of the Enlightenment, the absolutist utopias of the recent past, nor even the technological advances and socioeconomic reforms of the present have brought humanity closer to the "millennium."

In 1848 Reverend Theodore Parker spoke harsh words when he summed up the history of the United States and its people: "We are a rebellious nation; our whole history is treason; our blood was tainted before we were born."[45] Some believe his to have been an accurate assessment. Yet despite the pivotal role played by protest, resistance, and rebellion in American history, political dissidence and disobedience have rarely given rise to mindless rage and destruction in the United States. American rebellion has been aimed predominantly not at an outright overthrow of the government but toward changes in particular policies or the restructuring of specific political, social, or economic institutions.

"An arresting fact about American violence, and one of the keys to an understanding of its history," observes historian Richard Hofstadter, "is that very little of it has been insurrectionary. Most of our violence has taken the form of action by one group of citizens against another group, rather than by citizens against the state."[46] Political strife in America therefore can be summarized as an internal conflict between subnational clusters and communities—sometimes vying for dominance but most often merely seeking a greater portion of the country's ideological, political, social, or economic pie.

The reformist mold of America's political struggles and the absence of insurrectionary strands in the nation's political struggles may be attributed to historical factors that worked against the creation of one permanent ruling class, or of enduring and restless masses of subjugated classes or communities. At one time or another in the history of this country, almost each community making up the contemporary political, economic, or social power-base felt itself to be deprived and unacknowledged. Hardly any faction or group in American society has totally refrained, therefore, from resort to extralegal means during its ascendance to or, occasionally, descendance from power.

Hofstadter further attributes the distinctive quality of political unrest in America to a combination of the people's political pragmatism and the nation's unique socioeconomic makeup. It has been, moreover, the wide diffusion and constant modification of political power in America that has greatly reduced the incidence and duration of mass or nationwide outbreaks of political disorder. Elsewhere in the world, when more centralized and less pluralistic regimes (founded on decreed ideologies, imposing command economies, and led by a single political cadre or figure) prevail, popular dissatisfaction tends, predictably, to be directed toward the ruling core that controls both public and private life. Antistate and contra-authority instincts and agitation—fixtures of political life in the modern, media-amplified era—are likely, on the other hand, to be less massive and more readily diffusible in highly decentralized and pluralistically organized societies. America's decentralized political, social, and economic powers (distributed among federal, state, and local organs, as well as between the public and private sectors) have therefore been greatly responsible for the distinct character of this country's struggles against authority. Only the Revolution and the Civil War produced a direct and countrywide confrontation between the populace and central political authority.

Ever since Alexander Hamilton and James Madison articulated their concerns about the potential conflict between "factions" in democracy,[47] American history has indeed reflected the continuity of intergroup discords—conflicts between immigrants and indigenous people, between white plantation owners and black slaves, between established, old-line Atlantic Coast craftsmen and new working-class immigrants, between North European Protestants and ethnic Catholics, between agrarian Southerners and Northern entrepreneurs, between industrial workers and capital managers, between Northern white urban labor and migrating Southern blacks, between college students and autocratic university administrations, between liberated women and traditional male institutions, between ghetto dwellers and their racial and economic adversaries, between those favoring social and sexual orthodoxy and those following nonorthodox orientations, and, more recently, between "right to life" proponents and "pro-choice" advocates, and between a growing elderly population and an emerging generation of younger Americans no longer confident about the inexhaustible fortunes of the American Dream.

Given growing centrifugal developments and stresses, domestic strife may indeed intensify. While reason suggests that internecine struggles are likely to continue unless political stages are created for the new "voices," these voices often result in further discord rather than harmony. "The glory of America [lies] in its assimilationist era," wrote Thomas L. Hughes of the Carnegie Endowment recently. Hughes then proceeded to warn that "today what was centripetal is becoming centrifugal. Pluralism is pushing us more and more in the direction of *pluribus*, away from *unum*."[48]

In undertaking to assess the prospects for public tranquility in America by exploring the future balance between traditional assimilation, on the one hand, and militant pluralistic separatism on the other, particular attention must be given to the question of race and racial politics. Historically, as we have seen, the public order of the modern Western world and particularly of America has relied in great part upon the perceived "social contract"—the consent of the populace. This consent was derived from the people's acceptance of governmental legitimacy. Writing nearly two hundred years ago, Alexis de Tocqueville noted that "the republican government exists in America, without contention or opposition, without proofs or arguments, by a tacit agreement, a sort of *consensus universalis*."[49]

But as Hannah Arendt wisely noted in 1969, de Tocqueville also "predicted almost a hundred and fifty years ago that 'the most formidable of all ills that threaten the future of the Union arises,' not from slavery, whose abolition he foresaw, but 'from the presence of a black population upon its territory.'"[50] Arendt pointed out that the reason for de Tocqueville's concern with the future role of America's African Americans, and to a lesser extent the role of Native Americans, "lies in the simple and frightening fact that these people had never been included in the *consensus universalis* of the American republic."[51] The obvious conclusion, therefore, is that until this inclusion is satisfactorily undertaken, the legitimacy of American governance and the maintenance of public order cannot be assured. "Consent [of the governed], in the American understanding of the term, relies on the horizontal version of the social contract, and not on majority decisions," Arendt urged in her exceptionally insightful commentary on the meaning of and the future prospects for this nation's social compact.[52]

America's racial and ethnic demographics, moreover, are changing dramatically—driven by massive waves of immigration from Latin America, the Near East, and the Far East. Although new immigrants have historically fueled the American Dream with their vitality and competitive spirit, the new populations have often also been the victims of suspicion and resentment by communities who imagine their own privileges and jobs threatened. The backlash from establishment groups often takes the form of political, economic, and physical abuse and oppression, and in turn provokes violent responses on the part of the victims.

An equally troubling development might be the discernable change in the American public's mind-set—a loss of faith in the "myth of peaceful progress" that has sustained the majority of this nation for so long. The traditional American confidence in unending political and economic "progress" has been shattered by governmental as well as private-sector inefficacy, bureaucratization, greed, corruption, and outright criminality. Moreover, the stability historically derived from the country's more settled rural traditions has been replaced by the restlessness, homelessness, and other ills produced by urban and suburban sprawl. The virtual closing of the country's territorial frontier, the economy's sluggishness in the face of competitive challenges from abroad, the lessened expectations of economic and social betterment, the emergence of the "new poor" and "new homeless," and the increased militancy of the underprivileged, alienated, or otherwise disgruntled segments of the population—all these can be counted to produce a climate less resistant to social, economic, and political unrest and disorder.

Two decades ago, the United States governmental Task Force on Disorders and Terrorism pointed out that a community's changeover from indifference or hostility toward dissidence or subversive activity to a more sympathetic stance or even to active support for the forces of rebellion is insidious and nourished by the cumulative effect of a host of minor social, economic, and political dissatisfactions, rather than by a single massive factor.[53] The task force observed also that substantial segments of the American community were not merely politically apathetic but also surprisingly naive in their beliefs and in their reactions to political manipulations. "This segment is easy prey for extremists and is materially influenced by the apparent success of radical action," the task force warned.[54]

To combat extremist appeal and to reduce the risks of widespread public disaffection, the task force urged "the creation of social conditions which promote the general well-being of communities." The task force recommended further that the government strive actively to promote general "social satisfaction" so that anything disruptive of a sense of overall well-being "is perceived by the substantial majority as inimical [to the common good] and [is therefore] to be repudiated."

Yet the pursuit and promotion of general "social satisfaction" has become, of late, more difficult than ever before. Unemployment continues, and among the African American population it has reached catastrophic dimensions. Family stability is in decline. Unmarried teenage pregnancies are corrupting the welfare and parenting systems. The spread of sexually transmitted diseases, which is occurring across the racial and social spectrum, is proving to be one of humanity's worst epidemics.

In the economic realm, business and corporate stability have been adversely and possibly irreparably affected by reckless financing, junk bonds, greedy buy-outs, and takeovers. The costs of America's economic aid and military policing abroad have outstripped the cost of rebuilding the nation's ghettos and policing its delinquents, criminals, and homeless. Attention to international security and welfare have for too long outpaced the commitments to domestic security and welfare. No wonder that the Pepsi generation and "Generation X" are not as satisfied and joyous as they were supposed to be.[55] America's socioeconomic pathology is certainly on the rise, with no clear indication of relief in sight.[56]

Any attempt to forecast either stability or disorder in America (in the realms of ideology, politics, race, economics, ethnicity, and other social issues) is likely to suffer, moreover, from the traditional but undue reliance that most forecasters place on assumptions of individual and public rationality. Most scholars and government officials gloss over the role of chance and banal situational factors in the kindling and feeding of political unrest. They often fail to take into account nonacute but real and long-festering grievances (economic, social, ethnic, or gender-based). They further tend to overlook the destabilizing roles played in the annals of history by psychopathic or inherently bored, restless, and identity-seeking lower-, middle-, and upper-class activists.

Reflecting upon the dynamics of unrest and rebellion, social historian Eric Hobsbawm tellingly noted:

> Most of the great revolutions which have occurred and succeeded, have begun as 'happenings' rather than as planned productions. Sometimes they have grown out of what looked like ordinary mass demonstrations, sometimes out of resistance to the acts of their enemies, sometimes in other ways—but rarely if ever did they take the form expected by organized revolutionary movements, even when these have predicted the imminent occurrence of a revolution. That is why the test of greatness in revolutionaries has always been their capacity to discover the new and expected characteristics of revolutionary situations and to adapt their tactics to them. Like the surfer, the revolutionary does not create the waves on which he rides, but balances on them.[57]

### PROMISES AND UNSATISFIED EXPECTATIONS

The dramatic growth of inexpensive and virtually undaunted global print and electronic media, the increasingly activist and sometimes provocative role played by mass communications in the shaping of public consciousness, the unrelenting stimulation produced by instant audio-visual sounds and images, and the profusion of convenient and speedy means of travel, have made contagion an increasingly important factor in the worldwide spread of political strife. Disorder in one family, workplace, precinct, community, town, state, country, or federation can quickly spread to others. This was readily demonstrated by the contagious 1960s and 1970s student and racial unrest, originating on the Continent and spreading across the Atlantic and then through America. It was similarly attested by Eastern Europe's political and economic revolutions of the 1980s, and Africa's tribal and ethnic turmoil and violence a decade later. Those who continue to believe in America's or any other country's insular existence ignore the fact that the global winds of popular unrest and rebellion no longer honor national boundaries.

Still, America currently appears as an island of tranquility in the midst of a stormy global sea. The activism of America's abortion warriors, environmental extremists, racist militants, religious zealots, and other self-proclaimed messiahs of one stripe or another, seems minuscule alongside such traumas as the dismantling of the former Soviet empire, the internecine wars between and within the successor states, the less-than-cordial breakup of modern multinational countries such as Czechoslovakia and Yugoslavia, and the political blood baths that have taken place in Cambodia, El Salvador, Guatemala, Haiti, Liberia, Rwanda, Somalia, and other, new as well as older, countries of Asia, Latin America, the Caribbean, and Africa.

The current demands of nations, peoples, groups, and individuals around the world for the substance as well as the trappings of authority (including the safeguarding of "self-rule," "identity," "security," "nondiscrimination," and "prosperity") are not materially different, it should be noted, from the claims for greater justice made in America's midst by Native Americans, African Americans, the gay community, feminists, pro-lifers, pro-choice proponents, the aged, the homeless, children, and others. Often, the claims in what German philosopher G. F. W. Hegel has described as the "struggle for recognition" abroad differ only in the degree or the intensity of the claimants' hopes or desperations.[58] A thorough analysis as well as a challenging update of this universal struggle for recognition, including its symbiotic relation to legitimacy and its current crisis, were recently provided by Francis Fukuyama, in *The End of History and the Last Man*.

Many of the lesser-developed as well as developing nations of the world have indeed yet to pass through some of the birth pangs of freedom and justice experienced earlier by the countries of the Western world. Some of the emerging nations are likely today and tomorrow to be repeating England's seventeenth- and eighteenth-century civil and political rebellions, the French Revolution's upheavals, the American Revolution's turmoil, and the especially agonizing struggle of brother against brother that America had to endure on its way toward greater national unity, political liberty, and socioeconomic progress. The news accounts emanating from the countries of Central America, Africa, and Southeast Asia harken back to earlier histories of the European and North American continents— replete with tribal, caste, ethnic, and economic conflicts, a seemingly endless series of coups, assassinations, civil wars, and even less fathomable outbursts of hate and violence.

Throughout the world, the Age of Revolution is not yet over. "Liberty," the foremost of America's and France's triple revolutionary goals, still remains greatly unattained by many countries, peoples, races, castes, minorities, and other communities. The right to "property," articulated in the United States Constitution, has only recently been permitted to emerge in the former socialist camp. The goals of "equality" and "fraternity" (both part of revolutionary France's socioeconomic objectives) have not even been generally defined, much less implemented, in most contemporary states. Not until the post–Civil War adoption of the Fourteenth Amendment did America articulate a right to equality, and both the French and Soviet revolutionary experiences regarding the implementation of equality and fraternity have been grim at best. Only now, in the aftermath of Leninism-Marxism's recent demise, might new explorations of less totalitarian formulations of socioeconomic justice be undertaken in a world increasingly proclaiming democracy. Still awaiting definition and reasonable limitation is the American Declaration of Independence's guarantee of the "pursuit of happiness."

Moreover, despite modern nationalism's assertion of self-rule as a central doctrine, it is significant that this principle was not implemented except in a few European and other select nations until the end of the nineteenth century.[59] Most peoples had to wait for the end of the First, and more commonly the Second, World War before the call for independence was sounded for them.

At the conclusion of the First World War it seemed, indeed, that a new era had dawned on humanity. The victorious Allies, responding to America's President Woodrow Wilson's Fourteen Points,[60] had agreed on the new right to self-determination, and consequently the world map was to be redrawn in an effort to realize this promise. New countries were created in the process: Austria, Czechoslovakia, Egypt, Estonia, Iraq, Hungary, Latvia, Lithuania, Poland, and Yugoslavia. The League of Nations, idealistically forged out of the horrors of war, was to prepare other colonial peoples in Asia, Africa, and elsewhere for eventual self-rule through a preparatory "mandate" system.[61]

Places such as Lebanon, Palestine, and Syria; Cameroon, Ruanda-Urundi, Southwest Africa, Tanganyika, and Togo; and New Guinea and Samoa were to be readied for future autonomy.

The League's dreams of implementing peace and world order through the promotion of self-determination and international cooperation were, however, never to be realized. In the era between World Wars, the Great Powers continued to build up their military might, guard their spheres of political influence, squabble over colonial possessions, hoard resources, engage in economic exploitation, and expand markets. Pan-German nationalism and military expansionism in central Europe, Italy's colonial aggression in Ethiopia, Spain's Civil War (which turned the country into the world's testing ground for new weapons and military tactics), and the Soviet Union's unremedied insecurity coupled with expansionism (on the Baltic and in Poland) eventually led to the eruption of the Second World War.

The post–World War I promises of self-determination made by the victorious Allied nations were vigorously reiterated after the surrender of the German, Italian, and Japanese Axis at the end of World War II. In its Charter, the new United Nations asserted a commitment to "the principle of equal rights and self-determination of peoples."[62] This objective was reaffirmed in the *Declaration on the Granting of Independence to Colonial Countries and Peoples,* which recognizes that "all peoples have the right to self-determination; by virtue of that right they freely determine their political status and freely pursue their economic, social, and cultural development."[63] Similar phrases were echoed in many subsequent international declarations and agreements: the *Declaration on the Inadmissibility of Intervention into the Domestic Affairs of States;*[64] the United Nations *Declaration on Principles of International Law concerning Friendly Relations among States in accordance with the Charter of the United Nations;*[65] the *International Covenant on Economic, Social, and Cultural Rights;* and the *International Covenant on Civil and Political Rights.*[66] Principle VIII of the later Helsinki Accord of 1975 was most explicit:

> By virtue of the principle of equal rights and self-determination of peoples, all peoples have the right, in full freedom, to determine when and as they wish, their internal and external political status, without external interference, and to pursue as they wish their political, social, and economic development.[67]

This post–World War II surge toward the self-determination of all peoples was expected to satisfy the yearnings of the remaining millions of non-self-governing colonial populations. The global map was to be redrawn once more—this time, to some extent, by the colonized and indigenous peoples themselves. However, the global struggle for political liberty and social justice was not about to subside.

New political unrest and rebellion emerged as grievances produced by *domestic* oppressions and injustice (contrasting with the former complaints against foreign abuses of power) were aired within the new nations of Africa, Asia, and Latin America. Internal struggles, in quest of political hegemony, for greater power-sharing, and particularly for socioeconomic justice, continued to be fought within the very same countries that not too long ago had won their independence from their colonial masters.

Across the globe, domestic conflicts—ideological, political, ethnic, religious, social, and economic—account for most of the bloodshed since the end of the Second World War. In these intranational conflicts, the Katangans were defeated in their bid for secession from the Congo, and the Biafrans lost a bloody war against Nigeria. The people of Bangladesh, on the other hand, won their war for independence from Pakistan. The Slovaks attained their separation from the former Czechoslovak Republic through relatively peaceful means, but Yugoslavia's Slovenes, Croats, Bosnians, and Macedonians have found their separations more difficult and at times particularly violent.

Elsewhere the Catalans and Basques have not fully satisfied their claims for political autonomy from Spain; rebels motivated by socioeconomic claims persist in Colombia and Peru; indigenous populations press for their rights in Myanmar and Indonesia; and militant Catholics and Protestants continue in their campaigns against each other and against the governments of Ireland, Northern Ireland, and Great Britain. In India, Kashmiris and Sikhs, as well as Hindus and Muslims, have been waging a desperate political and religious war; the Tamils press on with their struggle against Sri Lanka's Sinhalese majority; and the Francophone Quebeçois threaten secession from their English-speaking partners in the Canadian union.

Independence, as has been noted, was regained in Estonia, Latvia, and Lithuania, nations forcibly incorporated into Stalin's Soviet empire more than half a century earlier. Similarly reclaimed has been the autonomy of the Ukrainians, Moldavans, Armenians, Georgians, Tajikis, Kyrgyzsis, Uzbekis, and a score of other peoples previously colonized by czarist and later by Leninist-Stalinist imperialism. But the Corsicans in France, the Palestinians in the West Bank, and the Eritreans in Ethiopia continue pressing their still unsatisfied causes. Other groups that have been denied the opportunity to cultivate their identities or to exercise their religious and cultural heritage— the Bahai in Iran, the Shiites in Iraq, the Copts in Egypt, and the Muslims in Bulgaria—have sought world support for their causes. Yet other endangered minorities elsewhere require adequate forms of protection and justice: the Tutsi in Rwanda, the Hutu in Burundi, the Koreans in Japan, the Kurds in Iraq and Turkey, and the Native Americans in the New World. Still more ethnic or linguistic groups argue for greater autonomy—Germans in

Northern Italy, Hungarians in Rumania, Flemings in Belgium, Macedonians in Greece, Bretons in France, and Scots in the United Kingdom.

To the surprise of others, three-quarters of the Scots recently questioned told public opinion pollsters that they wanted either greater autonomy or total independence from England.[68] "Whoever in the past would have dreamed of Breton nationalism or a Scottish national party?" responded Sir Isaiah Berlin. He then proceeded to point out with alarm the prospect of "many small nations filled with national pride and hatred and jealousies, egged on by demagogues, marching against each other as they did in the Balkans around 1912."[69]

Historian John Lukacs likewise raised the melancholy prospects of a proliferation of small states or statelets, perhaps "a bubbling new Levantine world, a subcivilization ruled by brigands and traders—another reversion to something that existed before the Modern Age."[70] Joining in the lamentations was Thomas L. Hughes, Chairman of the Carnegie Endowment for International Peace: "[S]ubnational tensions are reviving, sometimes in primitive forms. . . . There is something primordial about all this worldwide provincialism, chauvinism, separatism, ethnicism, and fundamentalism."[71]

A similar concern about the pitfalls of political fragmentation was voiced nearly a century and a half ago by British historian Lord Acton. Responding to the then militant advocacy and spread of nationalism in Europe, Lord Acton, a prominent leader of the era of imperialism, spoke of the benefits of multiethnic and multinational governance as contrasted with the hazards of the homogeneous nation-state. A state composed of a single people, Acton feared, "overrules the rights and wishes of the inhabitants, absorbing their divergent interests in a fictitious unity; sacrifices their several inclinations and duties to the higher claim of nationality, and crushes all natural rights and all established liberties for the purpose of vindicating itself."[72] On the contrary, Acton noted in 1862, the combination of different nations and communities under the same sovereignty "provides against the servility which flourishes under the shadow of a single authority, by balancing interests, multiplying associations, and giving to the subject the restraint and support of a combined opinion. . . . Liberty provokes diversity, and diversity preserves liberty."[73]

There is little doubt that the current worldwide dissatisfaction with such dated and tired political formulas and legitimation doctrines as the "nation-state," "national sovereignty," "social compact," and "majoritarian rule" is what in part fuels the ongoing challenge to authority and accounts for much of the political turmoil and strife spreading like a dreaded ancient epidemic through Africa, the Balkans, Central Europe, the Far East, and the Americas. In places like Czechoslovakia, Somalia, and Yugoslavia, the disingenuousness of the doctrines of "nation-state" and "national sovereignty" is what is currently tearing the countries apart. In other parts of the world, even an approximation of a nation-state is impossible. With hundreds of tribes and a multiplicity of castes, how many countries in Africa or Asia could pass the requisite tests for "peoplehood" or "nationhood"?

References to a binding "social compact" have become, similarly, mere subterfuges for abuse of power and reigns of terror by elected as well as by self-appointed rulers and regimes. The social compact apologists claim simply that because those in authority managed at one time to piece together a "state," invoked some "political formula," and succeeded in proclaiming a constitution, all people under their power are bound to accept their rule and are required to play by the laws (the "positive law") imposed upon them. Such a notion of a social contract (whose origins are often attributed to a nation's "forefathers" and whose dictates are said to be binding upon their descendants forever, regardless of changing realities and aspirations) has increasingly been found wanting. Similarly challenged is the related doctrine of majoritarianism, insisting that majority vote and majority rule are the appropriate and just means for determining, interpreting, and implementing the social compact for a whole nation or state.[74]

There is no magical cure for the inherent inconsistencies that riddle the ailing notions of the "nation-state," "sovereignty," "social compact," and "majoritarian rule." Moreover, in the new and intensively interdependent world, the allegedly "sovereign" state finds itself less and less immune to challenges either from within or without. Contemporary states may be too large to accommodate the diverse internal interests of the disparate communities of which they are comprised. At the same time they may be too small to withstand the external pressures—for greater justice for all those within it—coming from the community of nations and from the world media.[75] The continued functioning of simplistic articulations of doctrines of "nation-state" and the "social compact" as legitimating formulas for political authority cannot be assured. These formulas and their accompanying principles require theoretical and practical rehabilitation in order to shore up their credibility in a world that insists on new foundations of legitimacy for institutions that for very long were accepted on faith.

## THE QUEST FOR NEW LEGITIMACY

It is more and more evident that the much-heralded end of the Cold War, the reduction of superpower rivalry, and the proclamation of democracy's "total victory" have provided no respite to the old conflicts between the "they" and "we," between majorities and minorities, between those exercising power and those striving for greater autonomy, between those asserting the legitimacy of their authority and those challenging it. The shredding of the Iron Curtain, rather than portending the "end of history" and proclaiming democracy's final triumph over totalitarianism,[76] simply yielded center stage to a new struggle in which old, as well as newly empowered, nations, peoples, tribes, castes, classes, and other political or socioeconomic groups confront each other and the world around them—all competing for more power and authority and, firstly, for attention.

Some commentators attribute this growing and perilous communal quest for greater identity, security, prosperity, and autonomy to the unreasonable expectations introduced into the world community by the misguided idealism of America's World War I president, Woodrow Wilson. *New York Times* writer David Binder reports that at the height of that war, when President Wilson urged that "self-determination for Europe's myriad ethnic minorities . . . would provide stability in the post-war environment," his secretary of state, Robert Lansing, "expressed his grave concern [and belief] that the idea might make the world more dangerous." Lansing reportedly argued that self-determination would breed discontent, disorder, and rebellion. "The phrase is simply loaded with dynamite. It will raise hopes which can never be realized. It will, I fear, cost thousands of lives. What a calamity that the phrase was ever uttered! What misery it will cause!" Lansing claimed.[77]

Other observers point out that it is the very vagueness of such concepts as "peoples," "nationhood," "minorities," "autonomy," and "self-determination" that adds to the present calamity. In the legal formulations developed by the United Nations, it is only a "people" or a "nation" that is recognized as being entitled to total self-determination (or to sovereign independence).[78] Less coherent communities—ethnic, religious, or cultural—come under the designation of "minorities,"[79] a status that may protect them against such abusive practices as genocide and extreme discrimination but does not guarantee them any precise forms of self-rule. Yet who is to determine whether a community constitutes a people or a nation or a mere minority? And by what criteria is one to judge? And if a community falls short of peoplehood or nationhood, to what form of self-rule, and to what safeguards, should it be entitled?

Scholars as well as practitioners of the arts of politics and law have sought to answer these questions for the past century and a half. John Stuart Mill made an initial effort to define nationhood by concentrating on two requirements: (1) a community's or people's wish to be governed together, and (2) the common links or a "common sympathy" created by shared language, history, and beliefs. It has recently been argued in the *Economist* of London that "ignoring one half or the other of this definition has caused grief among nations since."[80] Some nationalists, mostly on the wings and religious nationalists, the *Economist* points out, emphasized the "common links" and thus "put too much weight on the less voluntary side" of this definitional formula. The Nazis went to the other extreme by identifying nationhood with "blood" or "race." To Americans, on the other hand, land, language, and political commitments seem to matter most. Still others, preaching internationalism, have downplayed ancestry, as well as cultural and religious loyalties, in favor of newly emerging regional as well as global affiliations.

What is critically evident, however, is that no consensual definition regarding the makeup of either peoples or minorities has developed within the world community in recent years. Who, therefore, is to tell the Bosnians, Palestinians, Kurds, Druze, Scots, Basques, Quebeçois, and Bretons that they are not a people, and consequently, are not entitled to self-determination? And if that is indeed the case, what lesser forms of autonomy should be made available to minorities and subnational communities, who very much like "peoples" have a "wish to be governed together"?

Objective and universal standards for defining peoplehood and minorityhood, of self-determination and autonomy, cannot be expected to be crafted soon objectively and universally. Moreover, the worldwide expectations and demands for self-determination and autonomy, or for other formulas of self-rule, cannot be turned back to the pre-Wilsonian era. The contemporary challenge to authority and the ongoing quest for the legitimacy of power must, therefore, be acknowledged as existing and ever-expanding forces. The ongoing conflicts, indeed, cannot be attributed primarily to the Wilsonian promise of self-determination nearly eighty years ago. It is not Woodrow Wilson who single-handedly opened this Pandora's box. It is the broader and worldwide development of individual and communal consciousness that accounts for the growing shift away from archaic, inflexible, and authoritarian doctrines of power and authority to new, more flexible, and democratically oriented doctrines—a trend evident not only in the arenas of national politics but also applicable to the governance of the family, schools, churches, workplaces, and other communities and congregations.

Regardless of specific causations, the unrest created by the unfilled promises, aspirations, and demands—just or unjust, reasonable and otherwise—of the world's peoples (including indigenous populations, minorities, and other subnational communities) is growing more and more intense. Throughout the world individuals as well as groups seek to protect and enhance their claims for identity, security, prosperity, and autonomy. Countries that fail to deal with past deprivations and present expectations decisively, courageously, effectively, and justly will become embroiled in unrest, internal strife, and wars of secession. Governments and states that are unsuccessful in accommodating or resolving their people's growing demands for greater autonomy and justice will be swept away. It is the fear of this eventuality that has led such a well-seasoned historian as John Lukacs to warn against the prospects of "new feudalism" and "new barbaric chieftains."[81]

Successful countries will inevitably be the ones capable of transforming themselves into more representative and flexible pluralistic composites.[82] Unless they carry out this transformation, China and India, the world's last extant great multi-ethnic empires (and to a lesser degree also the new Russian Federation), might go the way of the earlier Soviet conglomerate.[83]

Innovative principles and processes of governance—that recognize the globe's growing pluralistic realities and are based on greater tolerance for diversity, incorporate new forms of federalism and consociationalism, and enhance local autonomy and communal empowerment—are essential if states are to avoid the divisiveness and turmoil that are increasingly manifested today. Dramatic changes are required not only in the principles but also in the procedures employed by governments and their bureaucracies. The future requires the replacement of monolithic political and socioeconomic dogmas (and their accompanying centralized systems of governance) with a maximization of locally determined and pluralistic priorities and institutions.[84] The future demands, further, resort to governmental decision-making processes and procedures that maximize the people's perceptions of empowerment and participation in authority. An emphasis on what has recently been described as "procedural justice" merits considerable attention.[85]

It is in this light that we must view and assess the growing worldwide confrontation between the forces of religious-political fundamentalism and the forces of pluralistic democracy. The first camp (in places like the Vatican, Iran, Algeria, or Israel's Mea Shearim) admittedly proclaims and adheres to the absolute primacy of some never-changing scriptural or ideological truth, be it Catholic, Islamic, or Jewish law. The second camp (however diverse and disparate) places its reliance on a democratically derived and constantly modifiable social compact. The deepening conflict between these two dramatically opposite approaches to the formulation and structuring of political legitimacy is now threatening to replace the earlier Cold War as a major axis of global conflict. Because of this troublesome potential, it is doubly urgent that the concept of political legitimacy and its diverse and often conflicting formulations (first introduced in the Prologue and again reviewed at the beginning of this Epilogue) be reexamined.

German sociologist Max Weber, we noted earlier, discerned three fundamental types of legitimacy: the "traditional," the "legal," and the "charismatic."[86] Within the first of these categories (the "traditional") one can readily find a fitting niche for the divine right of kings, the rights of tribal chiefs, and the authority of parents. Legitimacy based upon scriptural fundamentalism (whether biblical, Koranic, or otherwise) or upon other absolutist formulations (such as "scientific Marxism" or "nationalism") is closely affiliated with the "traditional" formula. In the "legal" category one might include theories of authority derived from the social contract and its related majoritarian principle. Democratic formulations of legitimacy can thus be generally viewed as falling within the "legal" category. "Charismatic" legitimacy might be perceived as an independent and exclusive form of authority, but it often manifests itself in collaboration with either the "legal" or more frequently the "traditional" category of authority.

The history of twentieth-century totalitarian governance well illustrates the fatal outcome of a merger between "absolutist-fundamentalist" and "charismatic" claims to legitimacy, as in the cases of Hitlerism and Stalinism. Insane tyranny and mass murder often become the final steps in that process. In contrast, many authoritarian (as distinguished from totalitarian) regimes in Africa, Asia, and Latin America have initially relied not on ideological claims of legitimacy but on a combination of naked power and "charisma," degenerating in time into economic corruption and political despotism.

As one scrutinizes the growth of the contemporary conflict between the forces proclaiming the "social contract" and "democracy" and those claiming adherence to "scriptural" or other "absolutist legitimacy," one should first seek to apply the lessons learned from historical experience. The bloody records of such absolutist-charismatic leaders as Lenin, Stalin, Hitler, Mussolini, Idi Amin, and Castro should admittedly suffice to foster in any sound-minded person a preference for more humane forms of legitimacy and governance. But politics and the affairs of the world are not always governed by lessons of history or by the forces of sanity. What might be more relevant, as well as reassuring, for the future, in the face of the escalating mortal conflict between democratic and absolutist legitimacy, are the new realities created by pluralistic development worldwide. In an evolving pluralistic world where social, economic, media, and technological forces overwhelm the separatism of old, and where isolation and segregation are no longer tolerated, it is a foregone conclusion that fundamentalist or scriptural legitimacy cannot long prevail as effective formulas for the governance of countries or other large and complex communities.

# Epilogue:
# Toward a New Social Contract

Our desires and pleasures spring from society; we measure them, therefore, by society and not by the objects which serve for their satisfaction. Because they are of a social nature, they are of a relative nature.

—Karl Marx and Friedrich Engels, *Wage Labor and Capital*

There is but one law for all, namely . . . the law of humanity, justice, equity—the law of nature, and of nations.

—Edmund Burke, *Impeachment of Warren Hastings*

The future, one might confidently conclude, belongs to the democratic-"social compact" camp. But that camp, too, requires a restructuring and revitalization of its formulations of the concepts of legitimacy. Fortunately, the United States is in a unique position, due to its history, system of governance, political institutions, and public attitudes, to foster the sort of change needed to bring about more polyvocal, pluralistic, and decentralized governance. Throughout its history this country has demonstrated a particular capacity to adjust and readjust to changing social, economic, and political needs. One primary question regarding the future, however, is whether America will further concur in, or indeed lead with, newly required reforms, or whether it, like so many other nations and societies in the recent past, will struggle in vain against the needs of an emerging pluralistic world order.

In seeking to develop the required new pluralistic agendas, institutions, and processes, the world community, as well as the United States, may benefit from the counsel offered to the newly established American republic by its Founding Fathers. James Madison recognized that a pluralistic society must seek ways to energize the various components of its populace to assume an active and responsible role in public affairs. He believed in particular in the importance of "factions," functioning within the greater community and serving as agents of change.[1] As one of the authors of the Federalist Papers, he appeared to share Lord Acton's conviction that pluralism does not require splintered governance but, instead, that "diversity preserves liberty."[2] Thomas Jefferson similarly feared that "the abstract political system of democracy lacked concrete organs."[3] He called therefore for the implementation of "elementary" or "small" republics—envisioning the subdivision of the country into smaller self-governing units such as townships and wards. Jefferson urged that in "these little republics would be the main strength of the great one"[4] and that through them "every man in the state" would become "an acting member of the common government."[5] Jefferson's most cherished political dream (somewhat reminiscent of Jethro's advice to the biblical Moses to relinquish central power and to appoint judges who would mete out local justice)[6] was therefore "to divide [government] among the many, distributing to every one exactly the functions he [was] competent to."[7]

So committed was Jefferson to the idea of decentralization that he summed it up once as follows: "As Cato concluded every speech with the words, *Carthago delenda est*, so do I every opinion, with the injunction 'divide the counties into wards.'"[8] The basic assumption behind the Jeffersonian premise, Hannah Arendt insightfully points out, is "that no one could be called happy without his share in public happiness, that no one could be called free without his experience of public freedom, and no one could be called either happy or free without participating, and having a share, in public power."[9]

From the classical principles of authority and governance aspired to by America's Founding Fathers one can readily glide over the span of nearly two hundred years to take notice of newer and particularly relevant contemporary articulations of the requisites for legitimacy in the age of modernity. The recognition that the walls of separation (dividing the people of the world into distinct countries, nations, ethnic and religious communities, tribes, clans, and families) are crumbling requires doctrinal as well as pragmatic responses. A doctrinal response was contained in the writings of the Continental and British political theorists of the first quarter of the twentieth century, advocating the principles of pluralism. Challenging the orthodox and monistic theory of exclusive state sovereignty—which ignores or downplays the rights, interest, and capabilities of the smaller and more specialized subnational groups—pluralism was vigorously supported by such political and economic leaders as F. W. Maitland, G. D. H. Cole, Leon Duguit, Harold Laski, and Ernest Barker as supplying an appropriate doctrine for the governance of complex political institutions. Describing the orthodox conception of state sovereignty as "arid" and "unfruitful," the uncompromising pluralists called for greater recognition and public roles for such organizations as trade unions and churches, as well as for other voluntary associations serving vocational, economic, religious, and political needs.[10] Professing the belief that the state "ought to make room for varieties of social customs, religious and moral beliefs, and habits of associations," the advocates of pluralism pleaded for the distribution of political power through several distinct institutions "which can limit one another's action."[11]

Through the advocacy of a limited and decentralized government, pluralism, as a political theory, serves well the needs of modern pluralistic communities and states that face the aspirations and demands of ever disparate and diversified conglomerates of humanity. Pluralism can thus serve as a modern starting point for addressing the current need for the revitalization of democracy's somewhat frayed legitimating doctrine.

At their apex, both the Roman and Ottoman empires practiced such political and applied pluralism. During the early Roman Empire, for example, Augustus (29 B.C.–14 A.D.) ordered that the governors of conquered provinces were to respect local customs and were to give their populations extensive rights of self-government. The town and tribal councils (*consilia* or *koina*) gained the freedom of assembly and the right to bring their grievances before the emperor or the senate.[12] At a later time, Hadrian (117–38 A.D.), in his military reforms, removed the distinctions between the auxiliary units (*auxilia*), generally manned by soldiers from the provinces, and the legions, generally manned by Romans. While the provinces were expected to contribute men for the defense of the Empire, they were allowed to maintain a social separateness. Provincial soldiers were formed into separate units, which allowed them to exercise their distinct military expertise. Numidian cavalrymen, Parthian archers, Celtic slingers, and other minority specialist units contributed greatly to the defense of the Empire.[13]

The Ottoman Empire, much maligned throughout modern history, had also demonstrated some of the positive attainments from combining pluralistic reality with pluralistic institutions of governance. The autonomy granted to the diverse religious communities that made up the empire, in matters of family and personal law; the high degree of self government available to distinct ethnic groups; the decentralization of much of the Empire's core power—all these contributed to a nearly unique and sometimes happy merger between authority and autonomy. "From the moment of his accession," writes Lord Kinross, "Mehmed II (1450–81 A.D.) has seen himself as the heir to the classical Roman Empire and its [Byzantine] Christian successor. Now his conquest of Constantinople confirmed him as such. . . . In these terms Mehmed required that, side by side with the ulema, the Islamic authority, there should reside within the walls of Istanbul the Greek Orthodox Patriarch, the Armenian Patriarch, and the Jewish Chief Rabbi."[14] That this combined creative perception and exercise of pluralistic reality, coexistence, and authority did not effectively continue throughout the five centuries of the Ottomans is one of the primary reasons why the Turkish conglomerate turned from a spectacular "Zenith of Empire" into the "Sick Man of Europe."

Learning from these and many other lessons of history, one may safely argue that the wide-ranging and diverse dynamic that produces in modern society a potpourri of values, beliefs, and ideas can best be accommodated and given affirmation and empowerment through the recognition of pluralistic realities and the advancement of pluralistic institutions and practices. Pluralism accepts, celebrates, and thrives on diversity, while recognizing, most importantly, *e pluribus unum*—the requisites of the common weal.

Equally significant for the structuring of pluralistic governance and justice is another and yet even more contemporary political doctrine, again developed on the Continent and in the United Kingdom during the final quarter of the current century. Denominated *subsidiarity* and described as "the ghastly Euro-word," the doctrine promises to supply one of the supporting pillars for the building of legitimacy amidst diverse and potentially conflicting populations and interests. Having emerged in conjunction with the planning for a unified Europe (a continent to be united by an overriding parliament, executive, and judiciary), subsidiarity was advanced as a counterforce by the national groups fearing domination and oppression from above. The principle of *subsidiarity* "means that the smallest unit of society which can properly perform a given function, should be allowed to do so. A larger organization should not take over a task which can be adequately accomplished at a lower level. Thus, the State should not interfere unless individuals and private groups are unable to perform their work for the general welfare."[15]

With its origins attributed to earlier Calvinist sources, subsidiarity has been given new life by proponents of the European Union and its president, Jacques Delors, specifically, in their attempt to forge a workable governmental framework, or political formula, for a new federalized Europe composed of diverse nation-states.[16] Responding to national and local concerns over undue centralization and bureaucratization, the founding treaty of the European Economic Community reiterated that "the Community shall act within the limits of the powers conferred upon it by this treaty. . . . In areas which do not fall within its exclusive competence, the community shall take action, in accordance with the principle of subsidiarity, only if and in so far as the objectives of the proposed action cannot be sufficiently achieved by the member states and can therefore, by reason of the scale or effects of the proposed action, be better achieved by the Community. Any action by the Community shall not go beyond what is necessary to achieve the objectives of this treaty."[17] Although subsidiarity has fallen somewhat out of favor recently owing to growing economic and political uncertainty in Europe, the principle can nevertheless contribute significantly to an effective and coherent pluralistic political doctrine. The principle embodies the growing desire of individuals and groups to vest power and authority in localized or decentralized political mechanisms, capable of responding to grass-roots needs and better able to effectively carry out particularized policies and programs. Properly implemented subsidiarism should enable individuals and communities to retain closer political contact and involvement with governing bodies and thereby avoid excessive bureaucratization.

Not only innovative principles and institutions are required for the successful implementation of pluralistic governance. Greater emphasis upon governmental resort to "procedural justice"—consisting of processes and procedures that provide high control of the process for disputants and other interested parties and that are socially and psychologically perceived by the populace as standing for fairness and equity[18]—is equally necessary. The emerging discipline of procedural justice, which "views people as more interested in issues of process and issues of outcome, and . . . addresses the way in which . . . [people's] evaluations of experiences and relationships are influenced by the form of social interactions,"[19] offers great potentials for the structuring of a better and longer-lasting balance between authority and autonomy.

The building of legitimacy or a consensus in a complex organization, community, nation, or federation is admittedly a difficult task (as has been evident in recent years in the case of the united East and West Germanies).[20] But the principles of pluralism and subsidiarity seek to reform traditional majoritarian rule and lessen its potential tyranny by modifying and diversifying it through the introduction of decentralizing and consensus-based elements.

No formula, however, other than the total insistence upon absolute consensus in all institutions and decisions of governance can fully do away with the fear of the tyranny of the majority. The inevitable question remains: What would happen if one of the smaller groups advocated or practiced something intolerable to the others—human sacrifice or patricide, for example? The answer is that on some fundamental issues, the majority, however decentralized or curtailed its power, would prevail. No pluralistic society can ever fully escape occasional majoritarian intervention. But modification of political theorist George H. Sabine's formulation perhaps best summarizes our conclusion: "For my own part, then, I must reserve the right to be a pluralist when I can and a monist when I must."[21]

Political commentator William Safire recently counseled, somewhat similarly, that "as unstable states convulse in tribal realignment, we should remind the reshufflers: The political system that delivers the most freedom is the one that cherishes diversity within national unity."[22] A new domestic and world order requires that a constant readjustment in power-sharing become the rule rather than the exception. The most recent scramble of America's Republicans and Democrats to offer updated contracts and covenants to the nation's populace is an indication of this new direction.

The new American and world order further requires a drastic about-face from the old ideal of a melting pot to the more colorful and diverse image of a peoples potpourri.

As previously oppressed, troubled, and restless people are allowed to reap the political, social, economic, and spiritual benefits of liberty and justice, we may be able to forge new, more multi-ethnic, multireligious, multiracial, and multicultural—as well as more resilient and longer-lasting—human linkages and entities (international, regional, federal, national, local, and familial) to better serve the needs and hopes of mankind. Seven decades ago, Italian political scientist Roberto Michels of the University of Perugia, suggested that "perhaps history is nothing but the struggle between different concepts of authority or between different groups personifying different kinds and degrees of authority."[23] Perhaps this remains the best summary of history to date.

# *Notes*

In citing works in the notes, short titles have generally been used. Works cited in more than one chapter have been identified by the following abbreviations.

Ingraham, *Political Crime*  Barton L. Ingraham, *Political Crime in Europe: A Comparative Study of France, Germany, and England* (Berkeley: University of California Press, 1979).

Kittrie and Wedlock, *Tree of Liberty*  Nicholas N. Kittrie and Eldon D. Wedlock, Jr., eds., *The Tree of Liberty: A Documentary History of Rebellion and Political Crime in America* (Baltimore: Johns Hopkins University Press, 1986).

Schafer, *The Political Criminal*  Stephen Schafer, *The Political Criminal: The Problem of Morality and Crime* (New York: Free Press, 1974).

Weyl, *Treason*  Nathaniel Weyl, *Treason: The Story of Disloyalty and Betrayal in American History* (Washington, D.C.: Public Affairs Press, 1950).

## PROLOGUE

1. For a recent count, see James Adams, *Secret Wars* (London: Hutchinson, 1987), 1; "Carnage Unseen," Editorial, *New York Times*, April 12, 1993, E12.
2. *The Oxford Dictionary of Quotations* (London: Oxford University Press, 1955), 303.
3. Stephen Rosenfeld, "Sovereignty and Suffering," *Washington Post*, Oct. 2, 1992, A29, col. 1.
4. Pranay Gupte, "Why the Center May Not Hold," *Newsweek*, June 29, 1987, 3.

5. T. L. Friedman, "Today's Threat to Peace Is the Guy Down the Street," *New York Times*, June 2, 1991, E3.

6. "Goodbye to the Nation-State?" *Economist*, June 23, 1990, 11. See also Edwin M. Yoder Jr., "Strange New World: The Rise of the Modern Micro-State," *Washington Post*, June 24, 1990, C2.

7. Gaetano Mosca, *The Ruling Class* (New York: McGraw-Hill, 1939), 70.

8. Ibid.

9. Ethiopia Const. (revised) art. II, in Graham Hancock, *The Sign and the Seal: The Quest for the Lost Ark of the Covenant* (New York: Crown Publishers, 1992), 92.

10. See generally Edwin S. Corwin, *National Supremacy* (New York: Henry Holt & Co., 1913).

11. Hans Kohn, *Nationalism: Its Meaning and History* (New York: D. Van Nostrand Co., 1955), 14.

12. See Harold J. Laski, "Social Contract," in vol. 14 of *Encyclopedia of the Social Sciences* (New York: Macmillan, 1949), 127. See also John F. Fenton, *The Theory of the Social Compact and Its Influence upon the American Revolution* (New York, 1891).

13. Kittrie and Wedlock, *Tree of Liberty*.

14. John Locke, *On Civil Government*, ch. 8, in *Introduction to Contemporary Civilization in the West: A Source Book*, 3d ed. (New York: Columbia University Press, 1960), 1030.

15. Uri Ra'anan et al., *State and Nation in Multi-Ethnic Societies: The Breakup of Multinational States* (Manchester: Manchester University Press, 1991).

16. Bob Black and Adam Parfrey, *Rants and Incendiary Tracts: Voices of Desperate Illumination, 1558 to Present* (New York: Amok Press, 1989), 53–54.

17. Michel Foucault, "Two Lectures," in *Legitimacy and the State*, ed. William Connolly (New York: New York University Press, 1984), 201–21.

18. Hannah Arendt, *Crisis of the Republic* (New York: Harcourt, Brace & World, 1969), 307.

19. Matthias N. Forney, *Political Reform by the Representation of Minorities* (New York: By the Author, 1894), 29.

20. Simon Sterne, *Representative Government and Personal Representation* (Philadelphia: J. B. Lippincott & Co., 1871), quoted in Forney, *Political Reform*, 35–36.

21. Leonard Courtnay, *Nineteenth Century* (July 1879), quoted in Forney, *Political Reform*, 33–34.

22. Hugh D. Graham and Ted Robert Gurr, eds., "A Comparative Study of Civil Strife," in vol. 1 of *Violence in America: Historical and Comparative Perspectives* (New York: Praeger, 1969), 3.

23. Anatol Rapoport, *The Origins of Violence: Approaches to the Study of Conflict* (New York: Paragon House, 1989); cf. Francis Fukuyama, *The End of History and the Lost Man* (New York: Avon Books, 1992).

24. Nathan Gardels, "Two Concepts of Nationalism: An Interview with Isaiah Berlin," *New York Times Review of Books*, Nov. 21, 1991, 19.

25. Ibid., 20.

26. James Boyle, ed., *Critical Legal Studies* (Aldershot, England: Dartmouth, 1992), xli–xliii.

27. See generally "Symposium: A Critique of Rights," *Texas Law Review* 62 (1984): 1363; Tom Campbell, *The Left and Rights: A Conceptual Analysis of the Idea of Socialist Rights* (London: Routledge & Kegan Paul, 1983).

28. William Safire, "The Great Reshuffle," *New York Times*, Feb. 1, 1993, A19, col. 1.

29. Adda B. Bozeman, *The Future of Law in a Multicultural World* (Princeton: Princeton University Press, 1971), 165–66.

30. Thomas L. Friedman, "Today's Threat to Peace Is the Guy Down the Street," *New York Times*, June 2, 1991, sec. E.

31. Ibid.

32. Ibid.

33. Gardels, "Two Concepts of Nationalism," 15.

## CHAPTER 1   FIREBRANDS: CONTENDERS FOR CHANGE

1. Num. 16:1–13.

2. Rollo May, *Power and Innocence: A Search for the Sources of Violence* (New York: W. W. Norton & Co., 1972), 223; subsequent citations appear within parentheses in text.

3. Dante Alighieri, *The Divine Comedy*, trans. John Ciardi (New York: W. W. Norton & Co., 1954); *Inferno* 34, 177.

4. Schafer, *The Political Criminal*, 156.

5. May, *Power and Innocence*, 220.

6. Gaetano Mosca, *The Ruling Class* (New York: McGraw-Hill, 1939).

7. Michel Foucault, *The Order of Things* (London: Tavistock Publications, 1970), 328.

8. Richard B. Morris, *Seven Who Shaped Our Destiny: The Founding Fathers as Revolutionaries* (New York: Harper & Row, 1973), 2.

9. Ibid., 259–65.

10. William A. Bonger, *Criminality and Economic Conditions* (New York: Agathon Press, 1967).

11. Ibid., 684.

12. See Schafer, *The Political Criminal*, 124–25 (reviewing Bonger).

13. Bonger, *Criminality*, 649.

14. Zeev Ivianski, vol. 2 of "Individual Terror: Revolutionary Violence in the Late Nineteenth and the Beginning of the Twentieth Centuries" (Ph.D. diss., Hebrew University, 1973), 57. n.30. Ivianski's data is based on B. S. Itenbert, *Dvizhenie Revoliutsiyanovo Narodnichestva* (Moscow: izd. Nauka, 1965).

15. Ibid., 58.

16. Martin Malia, *Alexander Herzen and the Birth of Russian Socialism: 1812–1855* (Cambridge: Harvard University Press, 1961), 5.

17. Senate Committee on the Judiciary, *Report on Domestic and International Terrorism*, 97th Cong., 1st sess., 1981, 26.

18. C. A. Krause, "Colombian Guerrillas: Alienated and Threatened," *Washington Post*, March 2, 1980, sec. A.

19. Karl M. Schmidt and Carl Lieden, eds., *The Politics of Violence: Revolution in the Modern World* (Englewood Cliffs, N.J.: Prentice-Hall, 1968), 86–88.

20. Matthew Ross Lippman, *Through Their Eyes: A Glance at the Personality of the Political Offender in America* (Washington, D.C.: American University Law Library, 1976), 2. Lippman is due credit for many of the portrayals of American offenders cited in this chapter.

21. J. Kirkpatrick Sale, "Ted Gold: Education for Violence," *Nation*, April 13, 1970, 424.

22. Thomas Powers, *Diana: The Making of a Terrorist* (Boston: Houghton Mifflin Co., 1971), 76.

23. Marshall B. Clinnard and Richard Quinney, *Criminal Behavior Systems: A Typology* (New York: Holt, Rinehart & Winston, 1967), 180.

24. Bayard Rustin, "Towards Integration as a Goal," reprinted in *AFL-CIO American Federationist*, Jan. 1969, 6.

25. Senate Committee, *Report on Terrorism*, 28–29.

26. James F. Kirkham, Sheldon G. Levy, and William J. Crotty, *Assassination and Political Violence: A Report to the National Commission on the Causes and Prevention of Violence* (Washington, D.C.: U.S. Government Printing Office, 1969), 62–67.

27. See also the subsequent discussion of the pseudopolitical offender, 51.

28. David G. Hubbard, *The Skyjacker: His Flights of Fantasy* (New York: Collier Books, 1971).

29. David G. Hubbard, "A Glimmer of Hope: A Psychiatric Perspective," in *International Terrorism and Political Crime*, ed. M. Cherif Bassiouni (Springfield, Ill.: Charles C. Thomas, 1975), 31.

30. Hubbard, *Skyjacker*, 178–79.

31. U.S. Department of Justice, *Sourcebook of Criminal Justice Statistics—1980* (Washington, D.C.: U.S. Government Printing Office, 1981), 328.

32. Sidney Monas, *The Third Section: Police and Society in Russia under Nicholas I* (Cambridge: Harvard University Press, 1961).

33. Ivianski, "Individual Terror," 254.

34. Ibid., citing *Die Welt* (Vienna), June 12, 1903.

35. Antoly Scharansky, *Fear No Evil* (New York: Random House, 1988).

36. Judg. 4:1–21.

37. *Apocrypha: Book of Judith* (New York: Nelson, 1957).

38. Sergei Nachaeyeff, "Revolutionary Catechism," in *Assassination and Terrorism*, ed. David C. Rapoport (Toronto: Canadian Broadcasting Corp., 1971), 29–84.

39. Ibid., 83.

40. Freda Adler, *Sisters in Crime: The Rise of the New Female Criminal* (New York: McGraw-Hill, 1975), 101.

41. H. H. A. Cooper, "Woman as Terrorist," in *The Criminology of Deviant Women*, ed. Freda Adler and R. J. Simon (Boston: Houghton Mifflin Co., 1979), 151.

42. Senate Committee, *Report on Terrorism*, 19.

43. Alice Cook and Gwyn Kirk, *Greenham Women Everywhere: Dreams, Ideas, and Actions from the Women's Peace Movement* (London: Pluto Press, 1983), 50–54.

44. See, e.g., *United States v. Aguilar*, 883 F.2d 662 (9th Cir. 1989).

45. Schafer, *The Political Criminal*, 134.

46. Gina Lombroso-Ferrero, *Criminal Man According to the Classification of Cesare Lombroso* (Montclair, N.J.: Patterson Smith, 1972). See also Cesare Lombroso, *L'Uomo Delinquente* (Milan: Editoriale Scientifica 1876); Cesare Lombroso, *Crime: Its Causes and Remedies*, trans. Henry P. Horton (Boston: Little, Brown & Co., 1918).

47. Lombroso-Ferrero, *Criminal Man*, 102.

48. Ibid., 119.

49. Ibid., 294–98, citing Lombroso-Ferrero and R. Laschi, *Il Delitto Politico e le Rivoluzioni* (Turin: Bocca, 1890).

50. Ibid., 305–7, citing *Gli Anarchici* (Turin: Bocca, 1894); quote at 305.

51. Robert K. Merton, "Social Problems and Sociological Theory," in *Contemporary Social Problems* (New York: Harcourt, Brace & World, 1966), 775–822.

52. Ibid., 810.

53. See Robert K. Merton, *Social Theory and Social Structure* (New York: Free Press, 1968), 194–97.

54. J. Anthony Lukas, *Don't Shoot—We Are Your Children!* (New York: Random House, 1971), 123.

55. Powers, *Diana*, 13.

56. Lippman, *Through Their Eyes*, 5, citing *Washington Star*, June 6, 1968, 3.

57. Jerrold M. Post, "Fundamentalism and the Justification of Terrorist Violence," in *Terrorism* 11, no. 5 (1988): 370.

58. R. J. Maley, "Potential for Terrorism in the Soviet Union," *Terrorism* 13, no. 1 (1990): 60.

59. David Dellinger, *Revolutionary Non-Violence* (Indianapolis: Bobbs-Merrill Co., 1970), 14.

60. "Conspiracy of Compassion," *Sojourners*, March 1985, 17.

61. J. Guadelupe Carney, *To Be Revolutionary: An Autobiography* (San Francisco: Harper & Row, 1985), 429.

62. Lippman, *Through Their Eyes*, 14, citing Rowland, "Against the System," in Alice Lynd Collector, *We Won't Go* (Boston: Beacon Press, 1968), 45–46.

63. Ibid., 14, citing *The Diary of Che Guevara.*
64. Dietrich Bonhoeffer, *Letters and Papers from Prison* (New York: Macmillan, 1953), 19.
65. Lippman, *Through Their Eyes*, 7, citing Daniel Ellsberg, "Servants of the State," interview by Studs Terkel.
66. Ibid., 3.
67. Lukas, *Don't Shoot*, 323.
68. Kenneth Keniston, *Young Radicals: Notes on Committed Youth* (New York: Harcourt, Brace & World, 1968), 123.
69. J. Cohen, citing Samual Melville, introduction to *Letters from Attica* (New York: Morrow, 1972), 77–78.
70. Daniel Berrigan, *No Bars to Manhood* (New York: Doubleday & Co., 1970), 26.
71. Powers, *Diana*, 38.
72. Jessica Mitford, *The Trial of Dr. Spock* (New York: Vintage Books, 1970), 11.
73. Henry Schipper, "A Trapped Generation on Trial," *The Progressive*, Jan. 1974, 48.
74. Cook and Kirk, *Greenham Women*, 27–28 (statement of Susan Labb).
75. Berrigan, *No Bars*, 49.
76. Dave Foreman, "No Compromise in Defense of Mother Earth," *Mother Earth News*, Winter 1985, 17–18.
77. Jane Alpert, "I Bombed the Federal Building," *Rolling Stone*, July 23, 1981, 21.
78. Kirkham, Levy, and Crotty, *Assassination*, 64, 69.
79. Bill Wylie-Keillerman, "A Subversive Calendar of the Heart," *Sojourners*, Jan. 1985, 32.
80. Tim Wallis, "A Pledge of Resistance: A Contingency Plan," *Sojourners*, Aug. 1984, 10.
81. "Civil Disobedience Pledge," reprinted in *Sojourners*, Jan. 1985, 8.
82. Phillip Finch, "Renegade Justice," *New Republic*, April 25, 1983, 10.
83. Francie du Plessix Gray, "Profiles," *New Yorker*, March 14, 1970, 115.
84. Clinnard and Quinney, *Criminal Behavior Systems*, 182.
85. *Washington Post*, June 26, 1976, C8.
86. Eugene L. Meyer, "Slayer Did It with Honor," *Washington Post*, Oct. 26, 1975, A1, A24.
87. Maurice Parmalee, *Criminology* (New York: Macmillan, 1918), 462.
88. Ibid., 462–65.
89. Kirkham, Levy, and Crotty, *Assassination*, 62.
90. Ibid., 1–2 (emphasis supplied).
91. Schafer, *The Political Criminal*, 137.
92. Brian McConnell, *The History of Assassination* (Nashville: Aurora, 1970), 79.
93. Kirkham, Levy, and Crotty, *Assassination*, 60.

94. Nicholas N. Kittrie, *The Right to Be Different: Deviance and Enforced Therapy* (Baltimore: Johns Hopkins Press, 1971).

95. *Manchester Guardian Weekly*, April 3, 1971.

96. *Le Monde*, no. 143, Jan. 15, 1972.

97. See S. P. de Boer, Es Dreisser, and H. L. Verhear, eds., *Biographical Dictionary of Dissidents in the Soviet Union, 1956–1973* (Boston: Martinus Nijhoff Publishers, 1982), 450.

98. George Orwell, *The Road to Wigan Pier* (London: Victor Gollancz, 1937), 64.

99. James Calhoun, *Community Conflict* (New York: Free Press, 1957), 24.

100. See Richard Hofstadter and Michael Wallace, *American Violence: A Documentary History* (New York: Alfred A. Knopf, 1970), 180–81.

101. R. F. Farnen, "Terrorism and the Mass Media," *Terrorism* 13, no. 2 (1990): 112, quoted in Anzovin, *Terrorism*, 97.

102. Fred Ferretti, "What Do You Do with a Man Who Says He Has the Right to Steal," *Washington Post Book World*, Feb. 27, 1972, 8.

103. Eldridge Cleaver, *Soul on Ice* (New York: Dell, 1968), 26.

104. Philip Berrigan, *Prison Journals of a Priest Revolutionary* (New York: Holt, Rinehart & Winston, 1970), 35.

105. Vincent Bugliosi and Curt Gentry, *Helter Skelter: The True Story of the Manson Murders* (New York: W. W. Norton & Co., 1974), 245–50, 297, 312, 389.

106. Ibid., 220–21.

107. The following account is largely based upon Les Payne, Tim Findley, and Carolyn Craven, *The Life and Death of the SLA* (New York: Ballantine Books, 1976), 332–54; see also Kittrie and Wedlock, *Tree of Liberty*, 562–64.

108. Robert B. Kaiser, *R.F.K. Must Die! A History of the Robert Kennedy Assassination and Its Aftermath* (New York: E. P. Dutton & Co., 1970), 270.

109. Ibid., 273, 276.

110. Schafer, *The Political Criminal*, 156.

111. Ibid., 138–40.

112. Lawrence Kohlberg and Elliot Turiel, "Moral Development and Moral Education," in *Psychology and Educational Practice*, ed. Gerald S. Lesser (Glenview, Ill.: Scott, Foresman, 1971).

113. Ronald Duska and Mariellen Whelan, *Moral Development: A Guide to Piaget and Kohlberg* (New York: Paulist Press, 1975), 79.

114. Lawrence Kohlberg, "Stages of Moral Development as a Basis for Moral Education," in *Moral Education: Interdisciplinary Approaches*, ed. C. M. Beck, B. S. Crittendon, and E. V. Sullivan (Toronto: University of Toronto Press, 1971), 86–88.

115. Parmalee, *Criminology*, 101–2 and accompanying notes.

116. Ibid., 465.

117. Kittrie, *Right to Be Different*; and Kittrie and Wedlock, *Tree of Liberty*, 634.

## CHAPTER 2   ABUSE OF POWER

1. Exod. 5–11.

2. Elaine Pagels, *The Gnostic Gospels* (New York: Vintage Books, 1989), 76–81.

3. William Connolly, "The Dilemma of Legitimacy," in *Legitimacy and the State,* ed. William Connolly (New York: New York University Press, 1984), 238–39.

4. Roberto Michels, "Authority," in *Encyclopedia of the Social Sciences,* vol. 2, ed. Edwin R. A. Seligman (New York: Macmillan, 1930), 319.

5. *Oxford Dictionary of Quotations,* 2d ed. (Oxford: Oxford University Press, 1955), 1.

6. Paul Span, "Civil Liberties Attorney Embraced the Constitution," *Washington Post,* Jan. 28, 1991, A9.

7. 1 Sam. 8:11–17.

8. Aristotle, *Politics* 5, in Walter Laqueur and Yonah Alexander, eds., *The Terrorism Reader: A Historical Reader* (New York: Meridian Books, NAL Penguin, 1987), 10.

9. George W. F. Hallgarten, *Why Dictators?* (New York: Macmillan, 1954); George W. F. Hallgarten, *Devils or Saviours: A History of Dictatorship since 600 B.C.* (London: Oswald Wolff Publishers, 1960).

10. Hallgarten, *Devils or Saviours,* 7–17; and P. N. Ure, *The Origin of Tyranny* (Cambridge: Cambridge University Press, 1922).

11. Ibid., 61.

12. See, e.g., Hannah Arendt, *The Origins of Totalitarianism* (New York: Meridian Books, 1958).

13. Hallgarten, *Devils or Saviours,* 1–3.

14. Henry Morgenthau, *Secrets of the Bosphorus* (London: Hutchinson & Co., 1918), 198–214; James Ring Adams, "Facing Up to an Armenian Genocide," *Wall Street Journal,* Aug. 12, 1983, 25.

15. Justin McCarthy, *Muslims and Minorities* (New York: New York University Press, 1983), 121.

16. Karl Dietrich Bracher, *The German Dictatorship: The Origins, Structure, and Effects of National Socialism* (New York: Praeger, 1970).

17. Ibid., 420.

18. Robert H. McNeal, *Stalin: Man and Ruler* (New York: New York University Press, 1988); *New York Times,* Feb. 4, 1989, A1.

19. Ibid., 182–83.

20. David Hawk, "The Killing of Cambodia," *New Republic,* Nov. 15, 1982, 21.

21. Craig W. Nelson and Kenneth I. Taylor, *Witness to Genocide: The Present Situation of Indians in Guatemala* (London: Survival International, 1983), 12.

22. Ibid., 12.

23. Ibid., 23.

24. W. George Lovell, "Maya Survival in Ixil Country, Guatemala," *Cultural Survival Quarterly,* Nov. 4, 1990, 10–11.

25. Siyamend Othman, "Kurdish Nationalism: Instigators and Historical Influences," *Armenian Review*, Spring 1989, 54–56.

26. Andrew Whitley, "The Kurds: Pressures and Prospects," *Round Table*, July 1980, 251.

27. Clyde Haberman, "The Kurds in Flight Once Again," *New York Times Magazine*, May 5, 1991, 52.

28. Ibid., 54.

29. David Hawk, "The Killing of Cambodia," *New Republic*, Nov. 15, 1982, 17.

30. Ben Kierman, "The Genocide in Cambodia, 1975–79," *Bulletin of Concerned Asian Scholars*, Spring 1990, 35.

31. Ibid., 39.

32. Ibid., 18.

33. Hawk, "Killing of Cambodia," 18.

34. Ibid.

35. *Washington Post*, Feb. 4, 1989, A24.

36. Robert O'Harrow Jr., "Bearing the Wounds of Country's War," *Washington Post*, Dec. 15, 1992, sec. A.

37. Otto Kircheimer, *Political Justice: The Use of Legal Procedure for Political Ends* (Princeton: Princeton University Press, 1961).

38. Patricia Hewett, *The Abuse of Power: Civil Liberties in the United Kingdom* (Oxford: Martin Robertson & Co., 1982), and *State Crimes: Punishment or Pardon* (Queenstown, Md.: Aspen Institute, 1989).

39. E.g., Amnesty International, *Torture in the Eighties* (London: Amnesty International Publications, 1975) and *"Disappearances": A Workbook* (London: Amnesty International Publications, 1981).

40. Jethro K. Leiberman, *How the Government Breaks the Law* (New York: Stein & Day, 1972).

41. U.N. General Assembly, *Declaration of Basic Principles of Justice for Victims of Crime and Abuse of Power*, 40/34; *Guide for Practitioners on the Basic Principles of Justice for Victims of Crime and Abuse of Power*, A/Conf. 144/20; *Measures for Implementation of the Declaration of Basic Principles of Justice for Victims of Crime and Abuse of Power*, E/AC 57/1988/NGO/1.

42. Anatol Rapoport, *The Origins of Violence: Approaches to the Study of Conflict* (New York: Paragon House, 1989), xiv.

43. James A. Schellenberg, "On Human Dominance Systems," in *Dominance, Aggression, and War*, ed. Diane McGuinness (New York: Paragon House, 1987), 298.

44. Brian Crozier, *The Rebels* (London: Chatto & Windus, 1960), 15.

45. Ibid., 19.

46. Ibid., 105–7.

47. John Locke, *Two Treaties of Government*, ed. Thomas I. Cook (New York: Hafner Publishing Co., 1947), 233.

48. Crozier, *The Rebels*, 242.

49. Sheldon S. Wolin, "Foreword," in Chalmers Johnson, *Revolutionary Change* (Boston: Little, Brown & Co., 1966), viii.

50. T. H. Wintringham, *Mutiny* (London: Stanley Nott, 1936), 10.

51. Crane Brinton, *Anatomy of Revolution* (Englewood Cliffs, N.J.: Prentice-Hall, 1938).

52. James M. Rosenau, "Internal War as International Event," in *International Aspects of Civil Strife*, ed. Rosenau (Princeton: Princeton University Press, 1964).

53. Harry Ekstein, ed., *Internal War: Problems and Approaches* (New York: Free Press of Glencoe, 1964), 23.

54. Harry Ekstein, "On the Etiology of Internal War," in *Revolution*, ed. Bruce Mazlish, Arthur D. Kaledin, and David B. Ralston (New York: Macmillan, 1971), 18.

55. Ibid., 24–27.

56. James C. Davies, ed., *When Men Revolt and Why* (New York: Free Press, 1971), 85–86.

57. Pirke Avot, *Ethics of the Fathers* (New York: Judaica Press, 1979), 157.

58. Alexis de Tocqueville, *The Old Regime and the French Revolution* (New York: Doubleday, 1955), 180–82.

59. Eric Hoffer, *The Ordeal of Change* (New York: Harper Colophon Books, 1964), 4–5.

60. Karl Marx and Friedrich Engels, *The Manifesto of the Communist Party* (New York: International Publishers Co., 1968), 9.

61. Ibid., 9–21.

62. Karl Marx and Friedrich Engels, *Wage Labor and Capital* (Chicago: Charles H. Kerr, 1986).

63. James C. Davies, "Toward a Theory of Revolution," *American Socialist Review* 6 (1962): 5–19.

64. Davies, *When Men Revolt*, 214, quoting de Tocqueville, *The Old Regime*, 214.

65. Ibid., 133.

66. Ibid., 135.

67. Ted Robert Gurr, *Why Men Rebel* (Princeton: Princeton University Press, 1970).

68. Ibid., 5.

69. Ibid., 9.

70. Ibid., 26, 70. In advancing these classes of needs Gurr builds upon the hierarchy of needs elucidated in the earlier work of A. H. Maslow, "A Theory of Human Motivation," *Psychological Review* 50 (1943): 370, as well as the work of Harold Lasswell and Abraham Kaplan, *Power and Society* (New Haven, Conn.: Yale University Press, 1950), 55–56, and W. G. Runciman, *Relative Deprivation and Social Justice* (Berkeley: University of California Press, 1966), 9.

71. James C. Coleman, *Community Conflict* (New York: Free Press, 1957).

72. Gurr, *Why Men Rebel*, 168–69.

73. Lyford P. Edwards, *The Natural History of Revolution* (Chicago: University of Chicago Press, 1927), 99.

74. Gurr, *Why Men Rebel*, 182.

75. Ibid., 186.
76. Hannah Arendt, *On Revolution* (New York: Viking Press, 1963), 153.
77. William A. Gamson, *Power and Discontent* (Homewood, Ill.: Dorsey Press, 1968), 9.
78. Gurr, *Why Men Rebel*, 232.
79. Roy Pearson, "The Dilemma of Force," *Saturday Review*, Feb. 10, 1968, 24.
80. H. D. Lasswell and A. Kaplan, *Power and Society: A Framework for Political Inquiry* (New Haven, Conn.: Yale University Press, 1950).
81. Gurr, *Why Men Rebel*, 317.
82. Ibid., 358.
83. Sigmund Freud, *Civilization and Its Discontents* (New York: W. W. Norton & Co., 1961), 47.
84. Harold D. Lasswell, *Psychopathology and Politics* (New York: Viking Compass Books, 1960), 180–81.
85. Freud, *Civilization*, 79.
86. Ibid., 43.
87. Neil J. Smelser, *Theory of Collective Behavior* (New York: Free Press, 1963), 16.
88. See notes 31–34 and accompanying text.
89. Gamson, *Power and Discontent*, 45.
90. William C. Mitchell, *The American Polity* (New York: The Free Press, 1962), 142.
91. See generally Anatol Rapoport, *The Origins of Violence: Approaches to the Study of Conflict* (New York: Paragon House, 1989), 3–94.

## CHAPTER 3    SEEDS OF DISCONTENT

1. Richard B. Morris, *Seven Who Shaped Our Destiny: The Founding Fathers as Revolutionaries* (New York: Harper & Row, 1973).
2. Kenneth Keniston, *Young Radicals: Notes on Committed Youth* (New York: Harcourt, Brace & World, 1968).
3. Weyl, *Treason*.
4. James Willard Hurst, *The Law of Treason in the United States: Collected Essays* (Westport, Conn.: Greenwood Publishing Corp., 1971).
5. Shakespeare, *Hamlet*, 4.4.
6. Walter G. Simon, "The Evolution of Treason," *Tulane Law Review* 35 (1961): 667, 673.
7. Weyl, *Treason*, 13.
8. "The Trial of Peter Messenger [et al.], at the Old Bailey for High Treason, in Tumultously assembling themselves in Moorfields, and Other Places, Under Colour of Pulling Down Bawdy Houses" (1668), in Thomas B. Howell, ed., VI *State Trials* (London: T. C. Hansard, 1812), 879.
9. Jonathon Elliot, vol. 2 of *The Debates in the Several State Conventions on the Adoption*

*of the Federal Constitution Recommended by the General Convention of Philadelphia in 1787* (Philadelphia: J. B. Lippincott & Co., 1896), 487.

10. Statute of Purveyors (1350), 25 Edw. III, Stat. 5, ch. 2, V *State Trials* 975–76.

11. Virginius Dabney, *Virginia: The New Dominion* (Garden City, N.Y.: Doubleday, 1971), 1–68.

12. See *Cramer v. United States*, 325 U.S. 1, 13, 14 (1945).

13. James Willard Hurst, "Treason in the United States," *Harvard Law Review* 58 (1944–45): 226.

14. "Culpeper's Report on Virginia in 1683," *Virginia Magazine of History and Biography* 3 (1896): 225–27. See also "Note—Sir Henry Chicely," *Virginia Magazine of History and Biography* 17 (1909): 145–46.

15. An Act for the Better Preservation of the Peace of Virginia, and Preventing Unlawful and Treasonable Associations, *Virginia Statutes at Large, 1682–1710*, ed. W. Hening (Charlottesville: University Press of Virginia, 1969), 9–12.

16. The Trial of Colonel Nicholas Bayard, in the Province of New-York for High-Treason, XIV *State Trials* 471.

17. Charles J. Hoadly, *Records of the Colony or Jurisdiction of New Haven, from May 1653, to the Union. Together with the New Haven Code of 1656* (Hartford, Conn.: Case, Lockwood & Co., 1858).

18. An Act For Treasons, Assembly of Feb. 25–March 19, 1638, Thomas Bacon, *The Laws of Maryland at Large (1637–1763)* (Annapolis: Jonas Green, 1765).

19. An Act to Prevent all Traiterous Correspondence With Her Majesty's Enemies (Aug. 31, 1706), *The Acts and Resolves, Public and Private, of the Province of Massachusetts Bay (1637–1763)* 1 (Boston: Wright & Potter, 1869), 595.

20. Weyl, *Treason*, 14. In fact, a wife's murder of her husband was full-fledged treason under English statutory law. See Statute of Purveyors (1350), 25 Edw. III, Stat. 5, ch. 2., V *State Trials* 975.

21. An Act concerning Negroes and other Slaves, Proceedings and Acts of the General Assembly of Maryland, Sept. 1664, *Civil Rights and the American Negro: A Documentary History*, ed. Albert P. Blaustein and Robert L. Zangrando (New York: Trident Press, 1968), 9.

22. 4 Mass. Ct. Rec., part 1:419 (1660); E. Powers, *Crime and Punishment in Early Massachusetts (1620–1692)* (Boston: Beacon Press, 1966), 343.

23. Kittrie and Wedlock, *Tree of Liberty*, 13, 28–31. See also James Alexander, *A Brief Narrative of the Case and Trial of John Peter Zenger* (Cambridge: Harvard University Press, 1963), 58–69.

24. Samuel E. Morison, Henry S. Commager, and William E. Leuchtenberg, *A Concise History of the American Republic*, 2d ed. (New York: Oxford University Press, 1983), 37.

25. Simon, "Evolution of Treason," 673.

26. Dryden, "The Hind and the Panther," in *The Best of Dryden*, ed. Louis I. Bredvold (New York: Ronald Press, 1933).

27. Sir John Harrington, *The Letters and Epigrams of Sir John Harrington* (Philadelphia: University of Pennsylvania Press, 1930).

28. See Weyl, *Treason*, 24.

29. Bradley Chapin, *The American Law of Treason* (Seattle: University of Washington Press, 1964), 10. Much of the subsequent historical discussion in this section is based on this source. Other texts that have been regularly consulted include: John R. Alden, *Rise of the American Republic* (New York: Harper & Row, 1963); John M. Blum, *The National Experience: A History of the United States* (New York: Harcourt Brace Jovanovich, 1977); Dexter Perkins and Glyndon Van Deusen, *The American Democracy: Its Rise to Power* (New York: Macmillan, 1964).

30. Chapin, *American Law of Treason*, 28.

31. Richard Hofstadter, William Miller, and Daniel Aaron, *The American Republic* (Englewood Cliffs, N.J.: Prentice-Hall, 1959), 104, 158 n.2.

32. Clarence E. Carter, *The Correspondence of General Thomas Gage with the Secretaries of State: 1763–1775* 1 (New Haven, Conn.: Yale University Press, 1931), 68.

33. Wallace Brown, *The King's Friends: The Composition and Motives of the American Loyalist Claimants* (Providence: Brown University Press, 1965), 7.

34. Chapin, *American Law of Treason*, 19.

35. Robert Middlekauff, *The Glorious Cause: The American Revolution (1763–1789)* (New York: Oxford University Press, 1982), 181.

36. 35 Henry VIII, ch. 2., *Great Britain Session Laws* (London: Thomas Bartlett, 1543), 30–35.

37. George Bancroft, *History of the United States* (New York: D. Appleton & Co., 1891–92), vi, 230, 233–34.

38. See Kittrie and Wedlock, *Tree of Liberty*.

39. Tea Act of 1773, reprinted in Middlekauff, *The Glorious Cause*, 219.

40. Hofstadter, Miller, and Aaron, *The American Republic*, 164–65.

41. There were four Intolerable Acts: the Boston Port Act, March 31, 1774; Massachusetts Government Act, May 20, 1774; Administration of Justice Act, May 20, 1774; and the Quebec Act, June 22, 1774. See *Documents of American History*, ed. Henry S. Commager (New York: Appleton-Century-Crofts, 1949), 71–74.

42. Hofstadter, Miller, and Aaron, *The American Republic*, 165–66.

43. Chapin, *American Law of Treason*, 19, citing *Acts of the Privy Council of England (1613–1783), Colonial Series*, V, 391–92.

44. Middlekauff, *The Glorious Cause*, 246. The Suffolk Resolves were authored by Dr. Joseph Warren and adopted by Suffolk County on September 9, 1774.

45. Alden, *Rise of the American Republic*, 233–44.

46. Chapin, *American Law of Treason*, 22–23.

47. John R. Alden, *General Gage in America, Being Principally a History of His Role in the American Revolution* (New York: Greenwood Press, 1948), 233–44. The proclamation was issued only after getting the support of the House of Commons.

48. See generally Ethan Allen, *A Narrative of Colonel Ethan Allen's Captivity, from the Time of his Being Taken by the British, Near Montreal, on the 25th Day of September, in the Year 1775, to the Time of his Exchange, on the 6th Day of May, 1778* (Philadelphia: Printed for the Author, 1799).

49. See An Act to impower His Majesty to secure and detain Persons charged with, or suspected of, the Crime of High Treason committed in any of His Majesty's Colonies or Plantations in America, or on the High Seas, or the Crime of Piracy, 17 Geo. III, ch. 9, I *Acts George III 3 Regis Decimo-Septimo* (London: Charles Eyre & William Strahn, 1777), 311.

50. Chapin, *American Law of Treason*, 72.

51. Carl van Doren, *Secret History of the American Revolution* (New York: Viking Press, 1951), 22.

52. Worthington C. Ford and Gaillard Hunt, eds., *Journals of the Continental Congress (1774–1789)* (Washington, D.C.: U.S. Government Printing Office, 1904), 3:331.

53. Ibid., 195 n.1, citing *Pennsylvania Gazette*, March 13, 1776.

54. Van Doren, *Secret History*, 13–15.

55. Ford and Hunt, *Journals of the Continental Congress (June 5–Oct. 8, 1776)*, 5:475.

56. Chapin, *American Law of Treason*, 38.

57. Ibid., 38–39.

58. The constitutions of New Jersey, New York, and Delaware, for example, explicitly included English common and statutory law. See DEL. CONST. (1776) art. XXIV; N.J. CONST. (1776) art. XXII; N.Y. CONST. (1776) § 3, all reprinted in William Spindler, *Sources and Documents of the United States Constitution* (Dobbs Ferry, N.Y.: Oceana Publications, 1973), 203, 372, 452.

59. An Act to Prevent the Erecting Any New and Independent State within the Limits of this Commonwealth, Dec. 3, 1782, XI *The Statutes at Large of Pennsylvania from 1682 to 1801,* ed. James T. Mitchell and Henry Flanders (Harrisburg, Pa.: Harrisburg Publishing Co., 1906), 14.

60. An Act More Effectually to Punish adherence to the king of Great Britain within this State (Mar. 30, 1781) (4th Sess.) ch. 48, I *Laws of the State of New-York: Being the First Seven Sessions* (Albany: Weed Parsons & Co., 1886), 189.

61. Hurst, *Law of Treason*, 260–61. See also An Act to Punish Certain Crimes and Misdemeanors, and Prevent the Growth of Torryism, 1777–1780, *Maryland Laws* ch. 20 (Annapolis: Frederick Green).

62. An Act for the Punishment of Certain Offenses, (Mon. Oct. 7 Assembly) ch. 5, IX *The Statutes at Large, Being A Collection of all the Laws of Virginia from the First Session of the Legislature in the Year 1619,* ed. William W. Hening (Richmond, Va.: J. & G. Cochran, 1821), 171.

63. Chapin, *American Law of Treason*, 41.

64. Hurst, *Law of Treason*, 245.

65. Chapin, *American Law of Treason*, 64.

66. Ibid., 42–43.

67. See IX *Penn. Stat.* 45–47; Wilson, *Acts of the New Jersey Council and General Assembly*, 4–5; Hening, IX *Statutes of Virginia*, 168; 1777 *Laws of Maryland* ch. 20, sec. 29; I *Laws of the State of New York*, 173–84; *Perpetual Laws of the Commonwealth of Massachusetts*, 357–62.

68. For an interesting study of the loyalists who suffered under these measures, see Brown, *The King's Friends.*

69. Chapin, *American Law of Treason*, 70–71.

70. Ibid.

71. An Act for the Attainder of Divers Traitors if they Render Not Themselves by a Certain Day, and For Vesting Their Estates in a Commonwealth, and for More Effectually Discovering the Same and for Ascertaining the Lawful Debts and Claims Thereupon, IX *Penn. Stat.* 201–15.

72. *Respublica v. Malin*, 1 U.S. (1 Dall.) 33 (1778); *Respublica v. Carlisle*, 1 U.S. (1 Dall.) 35, 36 (1778); *Respublica v. Roberts*, 1 U.S. (1 Dall.) 39 (1778).

73. Letter of June 16, 1782, to (British) General Haldimand, in Henry Hall, *Ethan Allen: The Robin Hood of Vermont* (New York: D. Appleton & Co., 1892), 175–79.

74. Letter of March 9, 1781, to Samuel Huntington, President of Congress, ibid., 177.

75. James T. Adams, *History of New England* (Boston: Little, Brown & Co., 1921); and Thomas Hutchinson, *The History of Massachusetts, from the first settlement thereof in 1628, until the year 1750* (Salem, Mass.: T. C. Cushing, 1795).

76. Ibid., 303.

77. "General Courts' Declaration, that horrid and unnatural rebellion exists within this commonwealth" (1786), in *Acts and Resolves of the Commonwealth of Massachusetts* (Boston, Mass.: Wright & Potter, 1893), 424–26. See also "Resolve approving General Lincoln's conduct in his overtures of recommending certain descriptions of insurgents" (1786), ibid., 423–24 ("than opposition to the legal authority of the State, with force of arms, is treason and rebellion"); "An Act Describing the Disqualifications to which persons shall be subjected, who have been, or may be guilty of treason or giving aid and support to the present rebellion, and to whom a pardon may be extended" (1786), ibid., 176–80.

78. Catherine D. Bowen, *Miracle Philadelphia: The Story of the Constitutional Convention* (Boston: Little, Brown & Co., 1966).

79. Ibid., 4.

80. Morison, Commager, and Leuchtenberg, *A Concise History*, 305.

81. Bowen, *Miracle*, 4.

82. Max Farrand, *The Records of the Federal Convention of 1787* 2 (New Haven, Conn.: Yale University Press, 1911), 168, 182. The two page cites are to two successive versions of the Constitution's treason clause: the first (the resolution of July 23), allows the legislature to define the crime of treason. The next version (issued by the Committee of Detail, Monday, Aug. 6, 1787), was the first to include a specific (and limited) definition of the crime.

83. James Madison, *The Federalist* No. 43 (Ontario: Mentor, 1961), 273.

84. Hurst, *Law of Treason*, 399.

85. Bowen, *Miracle,* 222.
86. See *The Federalist* No. 84 (Ontario: Mentor, 1961), 511.
87. Bowen, *Miracle,* 222.
88. "Instructions for the Deputies Appointed to Meet in General Congress on the Part of this Colony," in *The Writings of Thomas Jefferson* (Washington, D.C.: Thomas Jefferson Memorial Society of the United States, 1903), 211, 215.
89. Ibid.
90. See generally Thomas P. Slaughter, *The Whiskey Rebellion: Frontier Epilogue to the American Revolution* (New York: Oxford University Press, 1986).
91. Weyl, *Treason,* 83–85. Judge Paterson based his conclusions on the English common law, citing Blackstone as authority. According to Blackstone, "levying war against the King" included "pulling down all enclosures, meeting houses, prisons or brothels."
92. Ibid.
93. Ibid.
94. Ibid., 28.
95. An Act concerning Aliens, 1 Stat. 570 (1798), reprinted in Kittrie and Wedlock, *Tree of Liberty,* 85–86.
96. An Act for the Punishment of Certain Crimes against the United States, 1 Stat. 596 (1798), reprinted in Kittrie and Wedlock, *Tree of Liberty,* 86–87.
97. Thomas I. Emerson, David Haber, and Norman Dorsen, *Political and Civil Rights in the United States* 1, 3d ed. (Boston: Little, Brown & Co., 1967), 38.
98. Weyl, *Treason,* 92.
99. Nathaniel Weyl, *The Battle against Disloyalty* (New York: Thomas Y. Crowell, 1951), 40.
100. Weyl, *Treason,* 87.

### CHAPTER 4   BENEFITS OF THE PROMISED LAND

1. *Reports of the Proceedings and Debates of the Convention of 1821,* ed. H. Carter, W. Stone, and M. Gould (New York: Da Capo Press, 1970), § 219.
2. Gerald R. Baydo, *A Topical History of the United States* (New York: Forum Press, 1974), 299.
3. Ibid., 1–15.
4. Nat Turner, *The Confession, Trial, and Execution of Nat Turner, the Negro Insurrectionist* (New York: AMS Press, 1975), 1–15.
5. See, e.g., Black Code, 1856 LA. ACTS §§ 1–105.
6. See *Elkison v. Deliesseline,* 8 F. Cas. 493 (C.C.D.S.C. 1823) (No. 4,366).
7. An Act concerning Negroes and other slaves, reprinted in *Civil Rights and the American Negro: A Documentary History,* ed. Albert P. Blaustein and Robert L. Zangrando (New York: Trident Press, 1968).

8. The Trial of Mrs. Margaret Douglass for teaching colored children to read, 7 *Am. State Trials* 45, ed. John Lawson (1853).

9. N.Y. Const. (1846) art. III, § 1.

10. *Roberts v. City of Boston*, 59 Mass. (5 Cush.) 198 (1850).

11. 7 Stat. 18 (Nov. 28, 1785).

12. 7 Stat. 13 (Sept. 17, 1778), reprinted in *Indian Affairs, Laws, and Treaties*, 2d ed., ed. Charles J. Kappler (Washington, D.C.: U.S. Government Printing Office, 1903), 5.

13. 30 U.S. (5 Pet.) 1, 17 (1831).

14. *Worcester v. Georgia*, 31 U.S. (7 Pet.) 515 (1832).

15. 7 Stat. 478 (Dec. 29, 1835).

16. Baydo, *Topical History*, 158–59.

17. Kittrie and Wedlock, *Tree of Liberty*, 135.

18. See *People v. Faulkner, A Documentary History of American Industrial Society*, ed. J. R. Commons and E. Gillmore (New York: Russell & Russell, 1958), 4:315–33.

19. Elizabeth C. Stanton, Susan B. Anthony, and Matilda Gage, eds., *History of Woman Suffrage* 1 (New York: Fowler & Wells, 1881), 70–73.

20. *United States v. Anthony*, 24 F. Cas. 829 (C.C.D. N.Y. 1873) (No. 14,459).

21. For an account of the suffragettes' protest and imprisonment this time, see Doris Stevens, *Jailed for Freedom* (New York: Schoken Books, 1976).

22. "Texas Declaration of Independence," in Benjamin P. Poore, ed., *The Federal and State Constitutions, Colonial Charters, and Other Organic Laws of the United States* (Washington, D.C.: U.S. Government Printing Office, 1877), 1752.

23. Baydo, *Topical History*, 86.

24. Weyl, *Treason*, 212.

25. Thomas I. Emerson, David Haber, and Norman Dorson, *Political and Civil Rights in the United States* 1 (Boston: Little, Brown & Co., 1967), 41 n.1.

26. Russel B. Nye, *Fettered Freedom: Civil Liberties and the Slavery Controversy (1830–1860)* (East Lansing: Michigan State College Press, 1949), 175–76.

27. Rollin G. Osterweis, "The Idea of Southern Nationalism," in *The Causes of the American Civil War*, ed. Edwin C. Rozwenc (Boston: D. C. Heath & Co., 1961), 134; and Charles A. Beard and Mary R. Beard, *A Basic History of the United States* (New York: New Home Library, 1944), 269.

28. Frank L. Owsley, *Plain Folk of the Old South* (Chicago: Quadrangle Books, 1965).

29. Ray A. Billington, *American History before 1877* (Totowa, N.J.: Littlefield, Adam & Co., 1965), 193.

30. Ibid., 209 n.1.

31. James D. Richardson, *A Compilation of the Messages and Papers of the Presidents (1789–1897)* (Washington, D.C.: U.S. Government Printing Office, 1896), 3304.

32. Weyl, *Treason*, 275.

33. Ibid., 279.

34. U.S. CONST. art. I, § 9.

35. *Ex parte Merryman*, 17 F. Cas. 144 (C.C.D. Md. 1861) (No. 9487).

36. "Message to Congress in Special Session," July 4, 1861, in *Complete Works of Abraham Lincoln* 2, ed. John G. Nicolay and John Hay (New York: Francis D. Tandy Co., 1894), 55.

37. 71 U.S. 2, 127 (1866).

38. Weyl, *Treason*, 264.

39. 18 U.S.C. §§ 371–3, 2384 (specifying a fine not more than $20,000 or imprisonment not exceeding twenty years) (originally enacted as Act of July 31, 1861, ch. 33, 12 Stat. 284).

40. *United States v. Greathouse*, 26 F. Cas. 21 (C.C.N.D. Ca. 1863) (No. 15,254).

41. Confiscation Act, 50 U.S.C. § 212 (1982) (originally enacted as an Act of Aug. 6, 1861, ch. 60, 12 Stat. 319).

42. See particularly Article 153, Instructions for the Government of Armies of the United States in the Field (April 25, 1863), 192.

43. Weyl, *Treason*, 269–71.

44. *Cummings v. Missouri*, 71 U.S. (4 Wall.) 356 (1867).

45. 71 U.S. (4 Wall.) 366 (1867).

46. See generally Harold M. Hyman, *Era of the Oath: Northern Loyalty Tests during the Civil War and Reconstruction* (Philadelphia: University of Pennsylvania Press, 1954).

47. J. Beard and M. Beard, *The Rise of American Civilization* (New York: Macmillan, 1930), 291.

48. Richard E. Rubenstein, *Rebels in Eden: Mass Political Violence in the United States* (Boston: Little, Brown & Co., 1970), 36. An 1871 statute, 17 Stat. 13–15, created emergency powers for dealing with this post-Reconstruction crisis. It permitted the suspension of habeas corpus in cases of rebellion.

49. *Slaughterhouse Cases*, 83 U.S. (16 Wall.) 36 (1873).

50. *Plessy v. Ferguson*, 163 U.S. 537 (1896).

51. H.R. Doc. No. 1, 42d Cong., 3d Sess. 391 (1872), reprinted in *Documents of United States Indian Policy*, ed. Francis P. Prucha (Lincoln: University of Nebraska Press, 1975), 137–41.

52. "The First Annual Message of President Chester A. Arthur, Dec. 6, 1881," reprinted in James D. Richardson, *A Compilation of the Messages and Papers of the Presidents (1789–1897)* 8 (Washington, D.C.: U.S. Government Printing Office, 1896), 54.

53. E. M. Coleman, *Laws of the Colonial and State Governments Relating to Indians and Indian Affairs, 1663–1831* (Washington, D.C.: Thompson & Romans, 1832), 42–43.

54. *United States v. Kagama*, 118 U.S. 375 (1886).

55. See generally Ray A. Billington, *The Protestant Crusade (1800–1860): A Study of the Origins of American Nativism* (New York: Rinehart, 1938).

56. Donald L. Kinzer, *An Episode in Anti-Catholicism: The American Protective Asssociation* (Seattle: University of Washington Press, 1964).

57. 22 Stat. 58, ch. 126.

58. Richard M. Brown, "Historical Patterns of Violence in America," in *Violence in America: Historical and Comparative Perspectives* 1, ed. Hugh D. Graham and Ted R. Gurr (New York: Praeger, 1969), 40.

59. See generally Robert F. Hoxie, *Trade Unionism in the United States* (New York: Russell & Russell, 1966); and Robert J. Hunter, *Violence and the Labor Movement* (New York: Macmillan, 1914).

60. See Harold Relyea, for U.S. Senate, Special Committee on National Emergencies, *A Brief History of Emergency Powers in the United States* (Washington, D.C.: U.S. Government Printing Office, 1974), 32.

61. Baydo, *Topical History*, 380.

62. *In re Debs*, 158 U.S. 564, 598–99 (1894).

63. S. B. Garland, "Labor and the Democrats: With Friends like These . . . ," *Business Week*, July 15, 1991, 41.

64. Brown, "Historical Patterns," 54.

65. E.g., 10 U.S.C. § 331 (federal aid to state governments); 10 U.S.C. § 332 (the use of the militia and armed forces to enforce federal authority); and 10 U.S.C. § 333 (president's authority to use the armed forces or the national guard to suppress "domestic violence" or any conspiracy to hinder the execution of state or federal laws of constitutional dimension).

66. The convictions were affirmed by the Illinois Supreme Court in *Spies v. People*, 122 Ill. 1 (1887). A petition to the United States Supreme Court for a writ of error, on the ground that the Illinois aiding and abetting statute violated the accused's rights under the Fourteenth Amendment, was dismissed. See *Spies v. Illinois*, 123 U.S. 131 (1887).

67. "Speech of the Condemned," reprinted in *Rants and Incendiary Tracts*, ed. Bob Black and Adam Panfrey (New York: Amok Press, 1989).

68. N.Y. PENAL LAW §§ 160, 161. This law was upheld by the United States Supreme Court in *Gitlow v. New York*, 268 U.S. 652 (1925).

69. Emerson, Haber, and Dorson, *Political and Civil Rights*, 50 n.1.

70. Ibid., 51.

71. 1919 Cal. Stat. 281.

72. *Whitney v. California*, 274 U.S. 357, 371 (1926).

73. Nathaniel Weyl, *The Battle against Disloyalty* (New York: Thomas Y. Crowell, 1951), 87.

74. Ibid., 90.

75. Thomas E. Carroll, "Freedom of Speech and the Press in War Time: The Espionage Act," *Michigan Law Review* 17 (1919): 621, 663 n.110.

76. Espionage Act, 40 Stat. §§ 217, 218, 219 (1917), 50 U.S.C.A. § 33 (1926).

77. 18 U.S.C.A. §§ 611–633.

78. 18 U.S.C.A. §§ 343–344.

79. Ray S. Baker, *Woodrow Wilson: Life and Letters* 6 (New York: Charles Scribner's Sons, 1937), 36.

80. Ibid., 283.

81. Espionage Act of May 16, 1918, 40 Stat. § 553, repealed by 41 Stat. §§ 1359–1360 (1941).

82. Weyl, *Treason,* 92–93.

83. Emerson, Haber, and Dorson, *Political and Civil Rights,* 55 n.1.

84. Weyl, *Treason,* 93 n.3.

85. *St. Louis Declaration of the American Socialist Party* (1917).

86. McAlister Coleman, *Eugene V. Debs: A Man Unafraid* (New York: Greenberg Publishers, 1930), 292.

87. Max Eastman, *Heroes I Have Known* (New York: Simon & Schuster, 1942), 62.

88. *Debs v. United States,* 249 U.S. 211, 217 (1919).

89. Emerson, Haber, and Dorson, *Political and Civil Rights,* 58 n.1.

90. Zechariah Chaffee, *Free Speech in the United States* (Cambridge: Harvard University Press, 1941), 247–69.

91. Ibid., 269–82. See also Lawrence H. Chamberlain, *Loyalty and Legislative Action: A Survey of Activity by the New York State Legislature, 1919–1949* (Ithaca, N.Y.: Cornell University Press, 1951), 48–51.

92. Senate Judiciary Committee, *Bolshevik Propaganda: Hearings before a Subcommittee, pursuant to S. Res. 439 & 469,* 65th Cong., 2d and 3d sess., 1919, 3–5, 23–24.

93. Chamberlain, *Loyalty and Legislative Action,* 9–52.

94. Emerson, Haber, and Dorson, *Political and Civil Rights,* 327 n.1.

95. Weyl, *Treason,* 123 n.3.

96. Irving Stone, *Clarence Darrow for the Defense* (Garden City, N.Y.: Doubleday, Doran & Co., 1941), 368.

## CHAPTER 5  PEOPLE POWER

1. 153 Stat. 1147, 1148 (1939), 5 U.S.C. § 118(j).

2. Civil Service Circular No. 222, June 20, 1940, reprinted in Eleanor Bontecou, *The Federal Loyalty-Security Program* (Ithaca, N.Y.: Cornell University Press, 1953), 285–87.

3. Civil Service War Regulations, § 18.2(c)(7), 7 Fed. Reg. 7723 (1942).

4. 454 Stat. 670, § 1, 18 U.S.C.A. § 2387.

5. 554 Stat. 670, §§ 2 & 3, 18 U.S.C.A. § 2385.

6. *Dunne v. United States,* 138 F.2d 137 (8th Cir. 1943), *cert. denied,* 320 U.S. 790 (1943).

7. *United States v. McWilliams,* 54 F. Supp. 791 (D.D.C. 1944), 163 F.2d 695 (D.C. Cir. 1947).

8. Thomas Emerson, David Haber, and Norman Dorson, *Political and Civil Rights in the United States* 1 (Boston: Little, Brown, & Co., 1967), 61.

9. Executive Order No. 9066, 7 Fed. Reg. 1407 (Feb. 19, 1942).

10. Act to Provide a Penalty for Violation of Restrictions, 56 Stat. 173 (1942).

11. Nathaniel Weyl, *The Battle against Disloyalty* (New York: Thomas Y. Crowell, 1951), 336 n.54.

12. Morton Grodzins, *America Betrayed: Politics and the Japanese Evacuation* (Chicago: University of Chicago Press, 1949), 86.

13. U.S. House, 77th Cong., 2d Sess., 1944, H. Rept. 2124, 247–52.

14. See *Hirabayashi v. United States*, 320 U.S. 81, 63 S. Ct. 1375, 87 L. Ed. 1774 (1943).

15. See *Korematsu v. United States*, 323 U.S. 214 (1944).

16. *Hearings on S. 1647 before the Senate Committee on Government Affairs*, 96th Cong., 2d Sess., March 18, 1980, 245–51 (statement of Hiroho Komehawa Omato).

17. Ibid., 18–22 (statement of Jerry J. Enomato); ibid., 23–40 (statement of Japanese-American Citizen's League advocating passage of S. 1647 to the Committee on Governmental Affairs, March 18, 1980).

18. *Hirabayashi v. United States*, 320 U.S. 81, 635 S. Ct. 1375, 87 L. Ed. 1774 (1943).

19. *Korematsu v. United States*, 323 U.S. 214, 65 S. Ct. 193, 89 L. Ed. 194 (1944).

20. Ibid., 214.

21. *Ex parte Endo*, 283 U.S. 383 (1944).

22. *Duncan v. Kahanamoku*, 327 U.S. 304, 66 S. Ct. 606, 90 L. Ed. 688 (1946).

23. Emerson, Haber, and Dorson, *Political and Civil Rights*, 62.

24. 341 U.S. 494, 71 S. Ct. 857, 95 L. Ed. 1137 (1951).

25. *Yates v. United States*, 106 F. Supp. 891; 107 F. Supp. 408; 225 F.2d 146 (9th Cir. 1955).

26. *Scales v. United States*, 367 U.S. 203, 81 S. Ct. 1469, 6 L. Ed. 782 (1961).

27. *Scales v. United States*, 367 U.S. 222.

28. Executive Order No. 9835, 12 Fed. Reg. 1935 (March 21, 1947).

29. Executive Order No. 10450, 18 Fed. Reg. 2489, 3 C.F.R. 1953 Supp. 72, 5 U.S.C. § 631 (April 1953).

30. *Cole v. Young*, 351 U.S. 536, 76 S. Ct. 861, 100 L. Ed. 1396 (1956).

31. Pub. Law 733, 81st Cong., 2d Sess., 64 Stat. 476 (1950), 5 U.S.C. §§ 21–1 to 22–3.

32. 3364 Stat. 987 (1950), 50 U.S.C. §§ 781–794, 811–826.

33. Ralph S. Brown Jr., *Loyalty and Security: Employment Tests in the United States* (New Haven, Conn.: Yale University Press, 1958), 181.

34. *Communist Party v. Subversive Activities Control Board*, 367 U.S. 1, 81 S. Ct. 1357, 6 L. Ed. 2d 625 (1961).

35. 383 U.S. 70, 86 S. Ct. 194, 15 L. Ed. 2d 165 (1965).

36. Ibid., 77.

37. *Communist Party v. United States*, 384 F.2d 957 (D.C. Cir. 1967).

38. *Aptheker v. Secretary of State*, 378 U.S. 500, 84 S. Ct. 1659, 12 L. Ed. 2d 992 (1964).

39. *United States v. Robel*, 254 F. Supp. 291 (W.D. Wash. 1965); 389 U.S. 258 (1967).

40. 85 Stat. 347.

41. Communist Control Act of 1954, 68 Stat. 775 (1954), 50 U.S.C. §§ 841–844.

42. Ibid., § 3.

43. *Salwen v. Rees*, 16 N.J. 216, 108 A.2d 265 (1954); 50 U.S.C. §§ 841–844.

44. See *New Haven Journal Courier*, Jan. 22, 1964.

45. *In the Matter of the Claim of Albertson, In re the Matter of the Claim of Communist Party*, 8 N.Y.2d 77, 202 N.Y.S.2d 5, 168 N.E.2d 242 (1960).

46. *Communist Party v. Catherwood*, 367 U.S. 389, 81 S. Ct. 1465, 6 L. Ed. 2d 919 (1961).

47. Weyl, *Treason*, 303.

48. Emerson, Haber, and Dorson, *Political and Civil Rights*, 63.

49. Kittrie and Wedlock, *Tree of Liberty*, 484 (citing *Mississippi Violence v. Human Rights* [Atlanta: Committee for the Distribution of the Mississippi Story, 1963], 434–41).

50. Richard E. Rubenstein, *Rebels in Eden: Mass Political Violence in the United States* (Boston: Little, Brown & Co., 1970), 32.

51. Report of the National Advisory Commission of Civil Disorders (Washington, D.C.: U.S. Government Printing Office, 1968), 66.

52. Governor's Commission on the Los Angeles Riots, *Violence in the City—An End of or Beginning*, Dec. 2, 1965, popularly known as the McCone Report.

53. Anthony Oberschall, "The Los Angeles Riot of August, 1965," in *Cities under Siege: An Anatomy of the Ghetto Riots, 1964–1968*, ed. David Boesel and Peter H. Rossi (New York: Basic Books, 1971), 84.

54. Ibid.

55. Ibid., 409.

56. A term, coined by President Eisenhower in his farewell address, referring to the close relationship between the armed forces and the nation's industrial capability.

57. Jack C. Douglas, *Youth in Turmoil* (Chevy Chase, Md.: National Institute for Mental Health, 1970), 215.

58. "My 67 Days in Prison," WIN, *Peace and Freedom through Nonviolent Action*, Oct. 20, 1966, 2–4.

59. Anthony Platt, *The Politics of Riot Commissions, 1917–1970* (New York: Macmillan, 1971), 473; *New York Times*, Oct. 3, 1970, 35.

60. Ibid., 476.

61. *New York Times*, Sept. 27, 1970, Education sec.; and Platt, *Politics of Riot Commissions*, 525.

62. Milton Viorst, *Fire in the Streets: America in the 1960s* (New York: Simon & Schuster, 1979), 347.

63. Kittrie and Wedlock, *Tree of Liberty*, 561.

64. Rex Wyler, *Blood of the Land* (New York: Vintage Books, 1982); and Deloria Vine Jr., *God is Red* (New York: Dell, 1973).

65. "Criminal Justice in Extremis, Administration of Justice during the April, 1968, Chicago Disorder," *University Chicago Law Review* 36 (1969): 455, 477.

66. *Report of the National Advisory Commission of Civil Disorders* (Washington, D.C.: U.S. Government Printing Office, 1968), ch. 13.

67. Crocket, "Recorder's Court and the 1967 Civil Disturbance," *Journal of Urban Law* 45 (1968): 841.

68. National Advisory Committee on Criminal Justice Standards and Goals, *Report of the Task Force on Disorders and Terrorism* (Washington, D.C.: U.S. Government Printing Office, 1976), 277.

69. See also *United States v. Kroncke*, 459 F.2d 697 (8th Cir. 1972); *United States v. Simpson*, 460 F.2d (9th Cir. 1972). See generally Patterson, "The Principles of Nuremberg as a Defense to Civil Disobedience," *Missouri Law Review* 37 (1972): 33.

70. Richard Hofstadter, *American Violence: A Documentary History* (New York: Alfred A. Knopf, 1970).

### CHAPTER 6   QUEST FOR THE "HONORABLE" OFFENDER

1. Bronislaw Malinowski, *Crime and Custom in Savage Society* (London: Routledge & Kegan Paul, 1926).

2. Sidney Hartland, *Primitive Law* (New York: Kennikat Press, 1970), 138.

3. Malinowski, *Crime and Custom*, 46.

4. Adamson Hoebel, *Law of Primitive Man* (Cambridge: Harvard University Press, 1961), 196–97, 240, 319.

5. 1 Sam. 10:1.

6. Exod. 22:28.

7. 2 Sam. 1:14.

8. Gaetano Mosca, *The Ruling Class* (New York: McGraw-Hill, 1939), 70.

9. Ingraham, *Political Crime*, 136; quote at 145.

10. David C. Rapoport, ed., *Assassination and Terrorism* (Toronto: Canadian Broadcasting Corp., 1971), 7.

11. Pierre A. Papadatos, *Le Délit politique: Contribution á l'étude des crimes contre l'ét* (Theses No. 507) (Geneva: Librarie E. Droz, 1954), 8, 10, 12.

12. Rapoport, *Assassination and Terrorism*, 7.

13. Ibid.

14. Cicero, "No Fellowship with Tyrants," cited in Walter Laqueur and Yonah Alexander, eds., *The Terrorism Reader: A Historical Reader* (New York: Meridian Books, NAL Penguin, 1987), 16.

15. Ibid.

16. Rapoport, *Assassination and Terrorism*, 8.
17. Ibid., 10.
18. John of Salisbury, "On Slaying of Public Tyrants," in Laqueur and Alexander, *Terrorism Reader,* 12–24.
19. Rapoport, *Assassination and Terrorism*, 10.
20. Ibid., 5.
21. Pitirim Sorokin, *Social and Cultural Dynamics* 2 (New York: American Book Co., 1937), 530–33.
22. Papadatos, *Le Délit,* 1.
23. Ibid., 11.
24. Ibid.
25. *Black's Law Dictionary,* 6th ed., 1990 at 902.
26. Daniel Jousse, *Traite de la Justice Criminelle de France* (Paris: Deburer père, 1771), 674.
27. Ibid.
28. Theodore Momsen, *Le Droit Penal Romain,* trans. J. Duquesne (Paris: A. Fontemoing, 1907), 232.
29. Ingraham, *Political Crime,* 44–45.
30. Papadatos, *Le Délit.*
31. Ingraham, *Political Crime,* 46 n.13.
32. Christian Baltzer, *Die geschichtlichen Grundlagen der privilegierten Behandlung politischer Straftäter im Reichsstrafgesetzbuch von 1871* (Bonn: Ludwig Rohrscheid Verlag, 1966), 34–36.
33. Ibid., 35.
34. Ibid.
35. *The Tower and the Abyss: An Inquiry into the Transformation of the Individual* (New York: George Braziler, 1957), 52.
36. Ingraham, *Political Crime,* 424.
37. Ibid., 49.
38. Papadatos, *Le Délit,* 36.
39. Baltzer, *Die geschichtlichen,* 36–37, 55–64, 148.
40. First Treason Act, 25 Edward III, Stat. 5, ch. 2 (1352).
41. Ingraham, *Political Crime,* 50.
42. J. W. Cecil Turner, *Kenny's Outlines of Criminal Law,* 18th ed. (Cambridge: Cambridge University Press, 1962), 388–89.
43. *King v. Dammaree,* 9 Anne (No. 443), 15 *State Trials* 521, 611–612 (1710).
44. Ingraham, *Political Crime,* 53–55.
45. *Case of the Seven Bishops,* 4 James II, 12 *State Trials* 183 (1688).
46. Sir James F. Stephen, *Digest of Criminal Law* (London: Macmillan, 1877), art. 93, at 56.

47. Sir James F. Stephen, *A History of the Criminal Law of England* 2 (London: Macmillan, 1883), 348.

48. Ingraham, *Political Crime,* 659.

49. Papadatos, *Le Délit.*

50. Ingraham, *Political Crime,* 56.

51. Ibid.

52. Ibid.

53. André Maurois, *A History of France* (New York: Farrar, Straus & Cudahy, 1956), 257–87.

54. David H. Willson, *A History of England* (New York: Holt, Rinehart & Winston, 1967), 604.

55. Adhemar Esmein, *Historie de la Procedure Criminelle en France* (Paris: L. Larose et Forcel, 1882), 410–69.

56. Jean Batiste Sirey, I Lois Annotées 4 (1789). See also Ingraham, *Political Crime.*

57. I Lois Ann., 4 (1789).

58. R. R. Palmer, *Twelve Who Ruled: The Year of the Terror in the French Revolution* (Princeton: Princeton University Press, 1971), 20.

59. Ibid., 21.

60. Ibid., 3–4.

61. Ibid.

62. I Lois Ann., 227 (1793).

63. Ibid., 221–22, 248, 271 (1793).

64. Ibid.

65. Palmer, *Twelve Who Ruled,* 365.

66. Code des Délits et des Peines, I Lois Ann., 362 (1795).

67. Robert J. Foster, *Oxford Illustrated History of Ireland* (New York: Oxford University Press, 1989).

68. Ibid., 109 (map).

69. 1 Wm. & Mary, 2d sess., ch. 9. These laws were modeled on the English Penal Laws with which Elizabeth I sought to combat Roman Catholic sentiments and pretensions to the crown. See the Supremacy Act, 1 Eliz., ch. 1, and its successors, 5 Eliz. ch.1; 13 Eliz. ch. 2; 23 Eliz. ch. 1; 27 Eliz. ch. 12; and 35 Eliz. ch. 1.

70. Foster, *Oxford Illustrated History,* 274.

71. Ibid., 277–78.

72. Willson, *History of England,* 606.

73. Aliens Act, 33 Geo. III ch. 4 (1793).

74. Habeus Corpus Act, 34 Geo. III ch. 54 (1794).

75. Seditious Assemblies Act, 36 Geo. III ch. 8 (1795).

76. Foster, *Oxford Illustrated History,* 276.

77. Ibid., 278–79.

78. Ibid., 280.
79. Unlawful Societies Act, 39 Geo. III ch. 79 (1799). An "unlawful society" was defined as one that required members to take an unlawful oath or that kept details of its organization or membership secret from the general body of members. Ibid.
80. Treason Act, 39 & 40 Geo. III ch. 93 (1800).
81. Henry Cockburn, *Examination of Trials for Sedition in Scotland* 2 (Edinburgh: David Douglas, 1888), 204.
82. Unlawful Drilling Act, 60 Geo. III & I Geo. IV ch. 1 (1819).
83. Ingraham, *Political Crime,* 706.
84. The Attainder of Treason and Felony Act, 54 Geo. III ch. 145 (1814).
85. Treason Act, 54 Geo. III ch. 146 (1814).
86. Amendment of Criminal Libel Act, 11 Geo. IV & I Wm. IV ch. 73 (1830).
87. 10 Geo. IV & I Wm. IV ch. 73 (1829).
88. 2 & 3 Wm. IV ch. 64 (1832).
89. 9 & 10 Vict. ch. 22 (1846).
90. Ingraham, *Political Crime,* 713.
91. Jeremy Bentham, *Treatise on Legislation* 2, trans. Charles M. Atkinson (London: Oxford University Press, 1914).
92. Ibid., 123–24.
93. Ibid., 124–25.
94. *Dictionary of National Biography* 10 (London: Oxford University Press, 1921–22), 268.
95. See Ingraham, *Political Crime,* 245. See also E. J. Hobsbawm, *The Age of Revolution* (New York: Mentor Books, 1962), 96.
96. I & II Code Pénal de 1810, reprinted in Ingraham, *Political Crime,* 68–70.
97. Ingraham, *Political Crime,* 23–24.
98. Ibid., 27.
99. Maurois, *History of France,* 375.
100. Amnesty Law, I Lois Ann. 933 (1816).
101. Ingraham, *Political Crime,* 259–60.
102. Papadatos, *Le Délit,* 44.
103. Const. Charter art. 7, I Lois Ann. 1235 (1830).
104. Const. Charter art. 69, ¶ 1, I Lois Ann. 1237 (1830).
105. I Lois Ann., 1242 (1830).
106. This last provision was held over from Article 10 of the Law of March 25, 1822. I Lois Ann., 1073 (1822).
107. II Lois Ann., 125 (1832).
108. Ibid., art. 7, ¶ 5.
109. Ibid., art. 20.

110. Ibid., art. 17.
111. II Lois Ann., 179 (1833).
112. Ibid.
113. Ibid.
114. Francois Guisot, *Memoirs* 3, trans J. W. Cole (London: Gently, 1869), 180.
115. II Lois Ann. 277, 280 (1835).
116. Maurois, *History of France*, 396–98.
117. III Lois Ann. 8, 11 (1848).
118. Ernest A. Visetelly, *The Anarchists* (London: John Lane, 1911), 3–20.
119. IX Lois Ann., 201 (1885).
120. XI Lois Ann., 809 (1894).
121. 48 Vict. ch. 10 (1886); 48 & 49 Vict. ch. 23 (1886).
122. Foster, *Oxford Illustrated History*, 324.
123. Ibid., 310–17.
124. Ibid., 311 n.xx.
125. Ibid., 314 n.xxii.
126. Ibid., 312 n.xxi.
127. *The Columbia Encyclopedia* (New York: Columbia University Press, 1946), 615.
128. Ibid.
129. Foster, *Oxford Illustrated History*, 396–97.
130. Ibid., 398–99.
131. Ibid., 406.
132. 44 & 45 Vict. ch. 3 (1881).
133. 44 & 45 Vict. ch. 49 (1881).
134. Foster, *Oxford Illustrated History*, 423.
135. 50 & 51 Vict. ch. 20 (1887).
136. E.g., 50 & 51 Vict. ch. 23 (1887).
137. Foster, *Oxford Illustrated History*, 424.
138. Ibid., 456–57, 456 n.xli.
139. See ibid., 459.
140. 4 & 5 Geo. V ch. 90 (1914).
141. Foster, *Oxford Illustrated History*, 477–84.
142. *The Columbia Encyclopedia* (New York: Columbia University Press, 1946), 1635–36.
143. Foster, *Oxford Illustrated History*, 494–502.
144. 12 & 13 Geo. V ch. 4 (1949).
145. Foster, *Oxford Illustrated History*, 502–11.
146. See ibid., 511.
147. Baltzer, *Die geschichtlichen*, 34–36.

148. Ibid., 35–36.

149. Ibid.

150. Ingraham, *Political Crime*, 92, 93–95.

151. Ibid., 141.

152. J. F. H. Abegg, *Lehrbuch der Strafrechts-Wissenschaft* (Neustadt a.d.: Orla, 1836).

153. See, e.g., Georges Vidal, *Cours de Droit Criminel et de Science Penitentiaire*, 5th ed. (Paris: Rousseau, 1916), 111–12, quoted in Ferrari, "Political Crime," *Columbia Law Review* 20 (1920): 308.

154. Baltzer, *Die geschichtlichen*, 78–121.

155. Ingraham, *Political Crime*, 90–91.

156. Ibid., 142.

157. Penal Code of 1871, 1871 Reichsgesetzblatt 127, art. 20. For translation, see *The Imperial German Code*, trans. R. H. Gage and A. J. Waters (Johannesburg: W. G. Horton & Co., 1917).

158. 1871 RGBI 127, arts. 31–37.

159. Ibid., art. 80.

160. Ibid., arts. 128–30.

161. Ibid., art. 130a.

162. The following account is based on Merle Fainsod, *How Russia Is Ruled* (Cambridge, Mass.: Harvard University Press, 1963), 5–62.

## CHAPTER 7   THE LIMITS OF TOLERANCE

1. Georges Vidal, *Cours de Droit Criminel et de Science Penitentiaire*, 5th ed. (Paris: Rousseau, 1916), 111–12, quoted in R. Ferrari, "Political Crime," *Columbia Law Review* 20 (1920): 308.

2. Patrick Moynihan, *Pandaemonium* (New York: Oxford University Press, 1993), 140.

3. Otto Kirchheimer, *Political Justice: The Use of Legal Procedure for Political Ends* (Princeton: Princeton University Press, 1961), 62–76.

4. V (n.s.) Lois Ann. 289 (1918).

5. VI (n.s.) Lois Ann. 1179 (1934).

6. Ibid., 1180.

7. V. A. D. Dalloz, IV *Recueil Périodique et Critique* 169 (1936).

8. VIII (n.s.) Lois Ann. 1153 (1939).

9. Ibid., sec. 1, ch. 1, title I.

10. VIII (n.s.) Lois Ann. 1395, arts. 75–77 (1939).

11. Ibid., art. 83.

12. Ibid., art. 84, sec. 4.

13. I Reichsgesetzblatt 585 (1922).

14. Karl D. Bracher, *The German Dictatorship: The Origin, Structure, and Effect of National Socialism* (New York: Praeger, 1970), 185.

15. Harold L. Poor, *Kurt Tucholsky and the Order of Germany (1914–1935)* (New York: Charles Scribner's Sons, 1968).

16. Ibid., 247.

17. Bracher, *German Dictatorship*, 173–74.

18. I RGBI 296 (1923).

19. William W. Fearnside, "National Socialist Ideology in German Criminal Law" (Ph.D. diss., University of California, Berkeley, 1949), 224.

20. Bracher, *German Dictatorship*, 205.

21. I RGBI 35 (1933).

22. Hannah Arendt, *The Origins of Totalitarianism* (New York: Harcourt, Brace & World, 1966), 423–25.

23. I RGBI 83 (1933).

24. Bracher, *German Dictatorship*, 197.

25. Opposition Political Parties, I RGBI 479 (1933).

26. I RGBI 341 (1934).

27. Ibid.

28. Reprinted in Edith Roper and Clara Leiser, *Skeleton of Justice* (New York: E. P. Dutton & Co., 1941), 93.

29. Ibid.

30. Ibid., 94.

31. Bracher, *German Dictatorship*, 213.

32. Ibid.

33. Ingraham, *Political Crime*, 248–56.

34. George Leggett, *The Cheka: Lenin's Political Police* (Oxford: Clarendon Press, 1981), xxiv. See generally Peter Stansfield Squire, *The Third Department: The Political Police under Nicholas I* (Cambridge: Harvard University Press, 1968).

35. Ivo Lapenna, *Soviet Penal Policy* (Westport, Conn.: Greenwood Press, 1980); Leggett, *The Cheka*, 13.

36. Leggett, *The Cheka*, 14.

37. Ibid., 44.

38. This proclamation is from the minutes of the Sovnarkom meeting which authorized the Cheka's formation. See ibid., 17.

39. Ibid., xxxv.

40. Ibid., 59, mentions the May 23, 1918, resolution condemning the Kadets and a June 14, 1918, resolution expelling other political factions.

41. Ibid., xxxiv.

42. *Krasnaya Gazeta*, Sept. 1, 1918, cited in Leggett, *The Cheka*, 109.

43. Leggett, *The Cheka*, 55.

44. Robert Conquest, *The Great Terror: A Reassessment* (New York: Oxford University Press, 1990), 486.

45. Aleksandr I. Solzhenitsyn, *The Gulag Archipelago, 1918–1956: An Experiment in*

*Literary Investigation* 1 & 2, trans. Thomas P. Whitney (New York: Harper & Row, 1973).

46. See Decree of the Central Executive Committee of the Council of People's Commissars, Dec. 27, 1932, from *Izvestiia*, no. 358, Dec. 28, 1932, translated in *Slavonic* 1 (and *East European*) *Review* 11, no. 3, 695, reprinted in Mervyn Matthews, *Party, State, and Citizen in the Soviet Union: A Collection of Documents* (London: M. E. Sharpe, 1989), 164–66.

47. The passport system is governed by Articles 1, 7, 12, 13, 14, 15, 22, 25, 37, and 38 of the Grazhdanskii Kodeks R.S.F.S.R. (Civil Code). See Thomas B. Smith, *The Other Establishment* (Chicago: Regnery Gateway, 1984), 48–49.

48. Ibid., 30–34.

49. Ibid.

50. VIII Lois Ann. 1629 (1944).

51. Marc Ancel, "Le Crime politique et le droit pénal du XXe siecle," *Revue d'Historie Politique et Constitutionelle* 2 (Jan.–March 1938): 103.

52. V. A. D. Dalloz, XXXVIII *Le Bulletin Législatif* 366 (1955).

53. XL Dalloz BL 452 (1957); XLI Dalloz BL 673 (1958).

54. Article 38 of France's 1958 Constitution granted the government special powers for a one-year period subject to legislative ratifications. These powers may be exercised for the "maintenance of order" and the "safekeeping of the state." CONST. (1958), art. 38.

55. XLI Dalloz BL 676 (1958).

56. Ibid.

57. XLIV Dalloz BL 148 (1961).

58. Code de procédure pénale, XLIII Dalloz BL 432 (1960).

59. C. Pr. Pén., art 697.

60. C. Pr. Pén., art. 698.

61. Civil Authority [Special Powers] Act [Northern Ireland] of 1922. See, e.g., 2 & 3 Geo. VI ch. 50 (1939).

62. See, e.g., 21 & 22 Eliz. II ch. 53 (1973); 22 & 23 Eliz. II ch. 56 (1974); 24 & 25 Eliz. II ch. 8 (1976); 32 & 33 Eliz II ch. 8 (1984).

63. Grundgesetz (1949), in U.S. Department of State Publication 3526, *The Basic Law for the Federal Republic of Germany* (Washington, D.C.: U.S. Government Printing Office, 1949).

64. GG, art. IX.

65. GG, art. XVII.

66. GG, art. XXI.

67. Ingraham, *Political Crime*, 610.

68. V *Entscheidungen des Bundesverfassungsgerichts* 85, 139 (1959).

69. Leggett, *The Cheka*, 81.

70. Zigmas A. Butkus, "Major Crimes against the Soviet State" (Thesis, Washington, D.C., Law Library, Library of Congress, 1985), 4.

71. Ibid., 24, citing *Sovetskoe Ugolovnoe Pravo, Osobennaia Chast'* [Special Part of the Soviet Criminal Law] (Moscow: Izdatel'stvo Moskovskovo Universiteta, 1975), 42.

72. Matthews, *Party, State, and Citizen*, 87.

73. See Butkus, "Major Crimes," 12.

74. Ibid., 26.

75. Ibid., 34.

76. Sidney Block and Peter Reddaway, *Soviet Psychiatric Abuse: The Shadow over World Psychiatry* (Boulder, Colo.: Westview Press, 1985), 16. See also Sidney Block and Peter Reddaway, *Psychiatric Terror* (New York: Basic Books, 1977).

77. Ibid., 30.

78. In 1976, an East Berlin court sentenced a West Berliner to fifteen years in prison for having helped ninety-six East Germans to flee to the West. The East Berlin City Court found him guilty of "organized human trafficking, sabotage, espionage and terrorism." *New York Times*, Jan. 27, 1976, 2.

79. Law of Misdemeanors (Poland), art. 63(a) (July 28, 1983).

80. Lawyer's Committee for International Human Rights, *Poland: Three Years After* (New York: Lawyer's Committee for International Human Rights, 1984), 86.

81. Ivan A. Shearer, *Extradition in International Law* (Manchester: Manchester University Press, 1971), 185.

82. Ibid.

83. Ibid.

84. 782 W.B. 415 (1894).

85. Ibid., 419.

86. 1902 Pan American Convention, art. 2.

87. For more recent materials on piracy, see Convention on the High Seas, April 29, 1958, 450 U.N.T.S. 82, T.I.A.S. No. 6465.

88. International Convention for the Suppression of Counterfeiting Currency, April 20, 1929, 112 L.N.T.S. 371, T.I.A.S. No. 2623.

89. Convention for the Suppression of the White Slave Traffic, CIII BRITISH AND FOREIGN STATE PAPERS 245 (1914).

90. Convention of 1936 for the Suppression of the Illicit Traffic in Dangerous Drugs, June 26, 1936, 198 L.N.T.S. 299, T.I.A.S. No. 4648.

91. Extradition Law of March 10, 1927 (France, unofficial trans.), in American Society of International Law, *Research in International Law* (Concord, N.H.: Rumford Press, 1935).

92. Manley O. Hudson, ed., *International Legislation* (Washington, D.C.: Carnegie Endowment for International Peace, 1941), 7:862–78.

93. Convention relating to the Status of Refugees, Final Act of the United Nations Conference of Plenipotentiaries on the Status of Refugees and Stateless Persons, April 22, 1954, 606 U.N.T.S. 267, 19 U.S.T. 6223, T.I.A.S. No. 6577.

94. G.A. Res. 2923, 27 U.N. GAOR Supp. No. 30, 25, U.N. Doc. A/8730 (1972).

95. Manuel R. Garcia-Mora, *International Law and Asylum as a Human Right* (Washington, D.C.: Public Affairs Press, 1956), 33, 91.

96. Convention on the Prevention and Punishment of the Crime of Genocide, Dec. 9, 1948, 78 U.N.T.S. 277, T.I.A.S. No. 1021.

97. Ibid.

98. On this date the instrument of ratification of the treaty by the United States was deposited with the Secretary General of the United Nations.

99. Jerold M. Post, "Current Understanding of Terrorist Motivation and Psychology: Implications for a Differentiated Antiterrorist Policy," *Terrorism* 13, no. 1 (1990): 65–67.

100. *In re Kaphengst*, Oct. 7, 1930, cited in *In re Ockert*, 1933–34 Ann. Dig. 369–70 (1940).

101. *Re Bohme* (Supreme Court of Argentina), 62 A.J.I.L. 784–85 (1968).

102. M. Cherif Bassiouni, *International Extradition and World Public Order* (Dobbs Ferry, N.Y.: Oceana Publications, 1974), 410.

103. 159 BRITISH FOREIGN STATE PAPERS 606.

104. Ibid., 4.

105. See 1971 Montreal Convention, T.I.A.S. No. 7570 (outlawing the sabotage of aircraft); 1970 Hague Convention, T.I.A.S. No. 7192 (proscribing hijacking); 1963 Tokyo Convention, T.I.A.S. No. 6768 (addressing offenses committed on board aircraft).

106. Convention to Prevent and Punish the Acts of Terrorism taking the Form of Crimes against Persons and Related Extortion that are of International Significance, OAS/Off.Rec./Ser.P/English, Third Special Session, General Assembly, AG Doc. 88 rev. 1 corr. 1, Feb. 2, 1971. See also Convention on the Prevention and Punishment of Crimes against Internationally Protected Persons, including Diplomatic Agents, G.A. Res. A/3166 (XXVIII) (1974).

107. Emmerich de Vattel, *Les Droit des Gens*, trans J. Chitty (Philadephia: T. & J. W. Johnson & Co., 1863), book 1, ch. 19, p. 233.

108. Convention on the Prevention and Punishment of Crimes Against Internationally Protected Persons, including Diplomatic Agents, G.A. Res. A/3166 (XXVIII) (1974); Convention on Offenses and Certain Other Acts Committed on board Aircraft, 704 U.N.T.S. 219, 20 U.S.T. 2941, T.I.A.S. No. 6768 (Sept. 14, 1963); Convention on the High Seas, April 29, 1958, 450 U.N.T.S. 82, 13 U.S.T. 2312, T.I.A.S. No. 6465.

109. Jerrold M. Post and Robert S. Robins, *When Illness Strikes the Leader* (New Haven, Conn.: Yale University Press, 1993).

110. *Washington Times*, Feb. 6, 1989, A11.

111. Ingraham, *Political Crime*, 267.

112. See the Internal Security Act of 1950 (the McCarran Act), 64 Stat. 987 (1950); the Communist Control Act of 1954, 68 Stat. 775 (1954). See also Kittrie and Wedlock, *Tree of Liberty*, 393–480.

113. Similarly, South Africa's apartheid laws provided that persons writing letters to Africans likely "to encourage feelings of hostility between the white and other inhabitants will be presumed to have done so with intent to endanger the maintenance of law and order." Convicted as terrorists, such letter writers were subject to the death penalty. Terrorism Act, No. 83 of 1967, § 2. L. Rubin, *Apartheid in Practice*, U.N. Publication OPI/533 (1976), 40.

114. Jeanne Kirkpatrick, *Dictatorships and Double Standards* (New York: Simon & Schuster, 1982).

115. In Liberia, for example, a supreme military tribunal consisting of five army officers, sitting in camera, was given exclusive power over the trying of treason cases. Bill Berkeley, *Liberia, A Promise Betrayed: A Report on Human Rights* (New York: Lawyers Committee for Human Rights, 1986), 15.

116. International Commission of Jurists, *States of Emergency: Their Impact on Human Rights* (Geneva: International Commission of Jurists, 1983). Under Poland's Constitution, a state of emergency permitted the prohibition of strikes and public protests, the establishment of internment camps for political suspects, restrictions on the freedom of travel, the institution of wiretapping, and state interception of correspondence.

117. Despite the absence of explicit martial law provisions in Polish law (Art. 33 of the Constitution authorized the imposition of a "state of war" only in instances of external threat to the state security), Poland's communist government on December 13, 1981, declared a state of war, thereby imposing martial law in response to Solidarity's domestic threat. Lawyers Committee, *Poland*, 13.

Chile's military government, on the other hand, had established two legal stages in its martial law scheme: states of emergency and states of siege, with the first requiring reinstatement every ninety days.

118. Instructions for the Government of the Armies of the United States in the Field (April 24, 1863), in Kittrie and Wedlock, *Tree of Liberty*, 192–93.

## CHAPTER 8   LEGITIMACY IN A PLURALISTIC WORLD

1. Westel W. Willoughby, *The Ethical Basis of Political Authority* (New York: Macmillan, 1930); William Connolly, ed., *Legitimacy and the State* (New York: New York University Press, 1984).

2. Gaetano Mosca, *The Ruling Class* (New York: McGraw-Hill, 1939), 10.

3. *Planned Parenthood v. Casey*, 112 S. Ct. 2791, 2814 (1992).

4. Max Weber, "Legitimacy, Politics, and the State," in *Legitimacy and the State*, ed. William Connolly (New York: New York University Press, 1984), 33–34.

5. Ibid., 34.

6. John H. Schaar, "Legitimacy in the Modern State," in *Legitimacy and the State*, ed. William Connolly (New York: New York University Press, 1984), 104.

7. Karl Marx, "Critical . . . Notes on . . . Social Reform," in *Legitimacy and the State*, ed. William Connolly (New York: New York University Press, 1984), 20.

8. William Connolly, "Legitimacy and Modernity," in *Legitimacy and the State*, ed. William Connolly (New York: New York University Press, 1984), 1.

9. Seymour Martin Lipset, "Social Conflict, Legitimacy, and Democracy," in *Legitimacy and the State*, ed. William Connolly (New York: New York University Press, 1984), 88..

10. David Noss, *A History of World Religions* (New York: Macmillan, 1990), 503.

11. U.S. Department of Commerce, *Statistical Abstract of the United States, 1994* (Washington, D.C.: U.S. Government Printing Office, 1994), 73, 90. Data represents 1991 figures.

12. See, for example, press accounts of Rev. Jesse Jackson and Mayor Sharon Pratt Kelly (disrupting traffic in protest against the denial of self-rule for the District of Columbia), e.g., "Jackson Arrested in Statehood Protest," *Washington Times*, July 2, 1993, B3.

13. Patrick Moynihan, *Pandaemonium* (New York: Oxford University Press, 1993), 98.

14. Ibid., 173–74. See also Thomas L. Hughes, "Pluralism and the Politics of Peace," *Cosmos: A Journal of Emerging Issues* 1, no. 1 (1991): 4–5; John Lukacs, *The End of the Twentieth Century and the End of the Modern Age* (New York: Ticknor & Fields, 1993).

15. Robert Kaplan, "The Coming Anarchy," *Atlantic Monthly*, Feb. 2, 1994, 44–76.

16. Samuel Huntington, "The Clash of Civilizations?" *Foreign Affairs* 72 (Summer 1993): 3.

17. Gaetano Mosca, *The Ruling Class* (New York: McGraw-Hill, 1939), 70.

18. Pitirim Sorokin, *Social and Cultural Dynamics: Fluctuations of Social Relationships and Revolutions* 3 (New York: American Book Co., 1937), 409–75.

19. Ted Robert Gurr, "A Comparative Study of Civil Strife," in *Violence in America: Historical and Comparative Perspectives* 1, ed. Hugh D. Graham and Ted R. Gurr (New York: Praeger, 1969), 13.

20. Ibid.

21. Joshua Muravchik, *Exporting Democracy: Fulfilling America's Destiny* (Washington, D.C.: AEI Press, 1990).

22. Felicity Barringer, "After the Thaw: The Residual Role for the Military," *New York Times*, Feb. 3, 1992, A8.

23. Maria Koklanaris, "CIA Suspect's Home Country to Assist Police," *Washington Times*, Feb. 11, 1993, p. 1, col. 1.

24. Ralph Blumental, "F.B.I. Inquiry Failed to Detect Any Sign of Attack," *New York Times*, March 6, 1993, p. 1, col. 3.

25. U.S. Department of Justice, *Sourcebook of Criminal Justice Statistics: 1991* (Washington, D.C.: U.S. Government Printing Office, 1991), 22.

26. Ibid., 22.

27. U.S. Department of Commerce, *Statistical Abstract of the United States, 1990* (Washington, D.C.: U.S. Government Printing Office, 1990), 182.

28. *1991 Justice Sourcebook,* 256.

29. W. Hinckle, "An Editorial Preface," *Scanlan's,* Jan. 1971, 11–12.

30. U.S. Bureau of the Census, *Statistical Abstract of the United States: 1978,* 99th ed. (Washington, D.C.: U.S. Government Printing Office, 1978), 183.

31. U.S. Department of Justice, *Sourcebook of Criminal Justice Statistics: 1984* (Washington, D.C.: U.S. Government Printing Office, 1985), 443.

32. *1991 Justice Sourcebook,* 428.

33. U.S. Department of State, *Patterns of Global Terrorism: 1991* (Washington, D.C.: Department of State, 1992), 1. Following the war the number of incidents fell precipitously and the postwar level was actually below 1990 levels of 456 incidents. Ibid.

34. Ibid., 405.

35. *1991 Justice Sourcebook,* 428.

36. Significantly, 69 deaths and 326 personal injuries were caused by these explosions. Ibid. For the 582 bombing attacks on private residences and the 585 assaults on commercial operations, no breakdown of motives was given. Ibid. Political or not, bombing declined sharply after 1975. In 1983, a total of 687 incidents occurred, yet in 1984 the figures rose again to 803. Ibid.

37. *1991 Justice Sourcebook,* 425.

38. Ibid., 427.

39. These 1,112 incidents were part of a total of 71,794 assaults on state and local law enforcement officers in 1990. Ibid., 418.

40. Gurr, "Comparative Study of Civil Strife," 445.

41. Ibid.

42. Ibid., 448.

43. Sheldon G. Levy, "A 150-Year Study of Political Violence in the United States," in *Violence in America: Historical and Comparative Perspectives* 1, ed. Hugh D. Graham and Ted R. Gurr (New York: Praeger, 1969), 66.

44. Ibid., 77.

45. Weyl, *Treason,* 204.

46. Richard Hofstadter and Michael Wallace, eds., *American Violence: A Documentary History* (New York: Alfred A. Knopf, 1970), 10.

47. Theodore J. Lowi, *The Politics of Disorder* (New York: W. W. Norton & Co., 1971), 31–35.

48. Thomas L. Hughes, *Pluralism and the Politics of Peace* (Washington, D.C.: Cosmos Club, 1991), 4–6.

49. Alexis de Tocqueville, *Democracy in America* (New York: Random House, 1945), vol. 1, p. 419.

50. Hannah Arendt, *Crises of the Republic* (New York: Harcourt, Brace & World, 1969), 89–90.

51. Ibid., 90.

52. Ibid.

53. National Advisory Committee on Criminal Justice Standards and Goals, *Report of the Task Force on Disorders and Terrorism* (Washington, D.C.: U.S. Government Printing Office, 1976), 41.

54. Ibid.

55. Douglas Coupland, *Generation X* (New York: St. Martin's Press, 1991); Jeff Giles, "The Myth of Generation X," *Newsweek,* June 6, 1994, 62.

56. Despite the proliferation of press and other media reports on such topics as American family breakdowns, illegitimate births, unemployment, alcoholism, and other substance abuse, no comprehensive compilation and analysis of the country's socio-economic pathology, similar to the United Kingdom's portrayal in Barbara Wootton's *Social Science and Social Pathology* (London: Allen & Unwin, 1959), has ever been undertaken here.

57. Eric J. Hobsbawm, *Revolutionaries* (New York: Pantheon Books, 1973), 89.

58. Francis Fukuyama, *The End of History and the Last Man* (New York: Avon Books, 1992).

59. Gregory A. Fossedal, *The Democratic Imperative: Exporting the American Revolution* (New York: Basic Books, 1989), 242–46.

60. James Trager, *The People's Chronology* (New York: Holt, Rinehart & Winston, 1979), 784.

61. See generally Nicholas N. Kittrie, *International Responsibility for the Colonial People* (Lawrence: University Library, 1951).

62. U.N. Charter art. 1, ¶ 2. See also Articles 55 and 56.

63. *Declaration on the Granting of Independence to Colonial Countries and Peoples,* G.A. Res. 1514 (XV), U.N. GAOR, 15th Sess., Supp. No. 16, 66, U.N. Doc. A/4684 (1960).

64. *Declaration on the Inadmissibility of Intervention into the Domestic Affairs of States,* G.A. Res. 2131 (XX), U.N. GAOR, 20th Sess., Supp. No. 14, 11, U.N. Doc. A/6014 (1965).

65. *Declaration on Principles of International Law concerning Friendly Relations and Co-operation among States in accordance with the Charter of the United Nations,* G.A. Res. 2625 (XXV), U.N. GAOR, 25th Sess., Supp. No. 28, 121, U.N. Doc. A/8028 (1970).

66. *International Covenant on Economic, Social, and Cultural Rights,* G.A. Res. 2200 (XXI), U.N. GAOR, 21st Sess., Supp. No. 16, 49, U.N. Doc. A/6316 (1967) (entered into force Jan. 3, 1976); *International Covenant on Civil and Political Rights,* G.A. Res. 2200 (XXI), U.N. GAOR, 21st Sess., Supp. No. 16, 52, U.N. Doc. A/6316 (1967) (entered into force Mar. 23, 1976). See Article 1 of both documents.

67. *Conference on Security and Co-operation in Europe, Final Act,* Dep't St. Bull., Aug. 1975, 8826, 14 I.L.M. 1292 (1975).

68. "Scotland; For Auld Lang's Syne," *Economist,* March 6, 1993, p. 59, col. 1.

69. Nathan Gardels, "Two Concepts of Nationalism: An Interview with Isaiah Berlin," *New York Review of Books,* Nov. 21, 1991, 20–21.

70. John Lukacs, *The End of the Twentieth Century and the End of the Modern Age* (New York: Ticknor & Fields, 1993).

71. Thomas L. Hughes, "Pluralism and the Politics of Peace," *Cosmos: A Journal of Emerging Issues* 1, no. 1 (1991): 4–5.

72. Lord Acton, "Nationality," in *Nationalism: Its Meaning and History*, ed. Hans Kohn (Malabar, Fla.: Robert E. Krieger, 1955), 124.

73. Ibid.

74. Willoughby, *Ethical Basis*, 219–35.

75. Paul Kennedy, *Preparing for the Twenty-first Century* (New York: Random House, 1993), 122–34.

76. Fukuyama, *End of History*.

77. David Binder, "As Ethnic Wars Multiply, U.S. Strives for a Policy," *New York Times*, Feb. 7, 1993, p. 1, col. 3.

78. U.N. Charter art. 1, ¶ 2.

79. U.N. Charter art. 1, ¶ 3.

80. "Une Certaine Idee de la France," *Economist*, March 6, 1993, 89–90.

81. Lukacs, *End of the Twentieth Century*.

82. Adda B. Bozeman, *The Future of Law in a Multicultural World* (Princeton: Princeton University Press, 1971); Robert A. Dahl, *Dilemmas of Pluralistic Democracy: Autonomy v. Control* (New Haven, Conn.: Yale University Press, 1982).

83. Nicholas D. Kristof, "China, the Conglomerate, Seeks a New Unifying Principle," *New York Times*, Feb. 21, 1993, E5, col. 1; Edward A. Gargan, "In India, Nationhood Rips Along Old Seams," *New York Times*, Feb. 24, 1993, E3, col. 1; "Russia: Things Fall Apart," *Economist*, Jan. 30, 1993, 47.

84. Seymour Martin Lipset, "Social Conflict, Legitimacy, and Democracy," in *Legitimacy and the State*, ed. William Connolly (New York: New York University Press, 1984), 88–103.

85. John Thibaut and Laurens Walker, *Procedural Justice: A Psychological Analysis* (Hillsdale, N.J.: Lawrence Erlbaum Associates, 1975); E. Allan Lind and Tom R. Tyler, *The Social Psychology of Procedural Justice* (New York: Plenum Press, 1988).

86. Weber, "Legitimacy, Politics, and the State," 32–34.

## EPILOGUE

1. Lowi, *Politics of Disorder*, 32–35.

2. Lord Acton, "Nationality," in *Nationalism: Its Meaning and History*, ed. Hans Kohn (Malabar, Fla.: Robert E. Krieger, 1955), 124.

3. Quoted in Hannah Arendt, *On Revolution* (New York: Viking, 1965), 238.

4. Ibid., 257.

5. Ibid.

6. Exod. 18:17–23.

7. Arendt, *On Revolution*, 257.

8. In his letter to John Cartwright, June 5, 1824 (quoted in Arendt, *On Revolution*, 252).

9. Arendt, *On Revolution*, 258–59.

10. "Pluralism," in *Encyclopedia of Social Sciences*, ed. Edwin Robert Seligman (New York: Macmillan, 1930), 170.

11. "Pluralism," in *A Dictionary of Political Thought*, ed. Roger Scruton (New York: Harper & Row, 1982), 357.

12. Fritz Heichelheim, *A History of the Roman People* (Englewood Cliffs, N.J.: Prentice-Hall, 1984), 291–98.

13. Ibid., 360.

14. J. Lord Kinross, *The Ottoman Centuries: The Rise and Fall of the Turkish Empire* (New York: Morrow Quill, 1977), 110, 113.

15. "Subsidiarity," in *Dictionary of Political Science*, ed. Joseph Dunner (New York: Philosophical Library, 1964), 504.

16. "A Milder, Mellower Jacques Delors," *Economist*, June 27, 1992, 56.

17. Treaty of the European Economic Community, Art. 3b.

18. G. S. Leventhal articulated six principles for procedural justice: consistency, bias suppression, accuracy of information, correctability, representativeness ("voice"), ethicality. G. S. Leventhal, "What Should Be Done with Equity Theory? New Approaches to the Study of Fairness in Social Relationships," in *Social Exchange: Advances in Theory and Research*, ed. K. Gergen, M. Greenberg, and R. Willis (New York: Plenum Press, 1980), 27–55; G. S. Leventhal, J. Karuza, and W. R. Fry, "Beyond Fairness: A Theory of Allocation Preferences," in *Justice and Social Interaction*, ed. G. Makula (New York: Springer-Verlag, 1980), 167–218.

19. Lind and Tyler, *Social Psychology*, 1. Lind and Tyler thus note: "Procedural justice enhances commitment and loyalty to groups and institutions." Ibid., 209.

20. "Germany: Half-Hidden Agenda," *Economist*, May 21, 1994, 3–34.

21. George H. Sabine, "Pluralism: A Point of View," *American Political Science Review* 27 (Feb. 1923): 34, cited in Willoughby, *Ethical Basis*, 449.

22. William Safire, "The Great Reshuffle," *New York Times*, Feb. 1, 1993, A19.

23. Roberto Michels, "Authority," in *Encyclopedia of the Social Sciences*, ed. Edwin Robert Siligman (New York: Macmillan, 1930), 320–21.

# Index

Library of Congress Cataloging-in-Publication Data

Kittrie, Nicholas N., 1928–
The war against authority : from the crisis of legitimacy to a new
social contract / Nicholas N. Kittrie.
p.   cm.
Includes bibliographical references and index.
ISBN 0-8018-5050-9 (acid-free paper)
1. Authority.   2. Legitimacy of governments.   3. Social contract.
I. Title.
HM271.K58   1995
303.3′6—dc20   94-47530